SCHOOLS AND SOCIETIES

SOCIOLOGY FOR A NEW CENTURY

A PINE FORGE PRESS SERIES

Edited by Charles Ragin, Wendy Griswold, and Larry Griffin

Sociology for a New Century brings the best current scholarship to today's students in a series of short texts authored by leaders of a new generation of social scientists. Each book addresses its subject from a comparative, historical, and global perspective, and in doing so, connects social science to the wider concerns of students seeking to make sense of our dramatically changing world.

- *An Invitation to Environmental Sociology*   Michael M. Bell
- *Global Inequalities*   York Bradshaw and Michael Wallace
- *Schools and Societies*   Steven Brint
- *How Societies Change*   Daniel Chirot
- *Ethnicity and Race: Making Identities in a Changing World*
  Stephen Cornell and Douglas Hartmann
- *The Sociology of Childhood*   William Corsaro
- *Cultures and Societies in a Changing World*   Wendy Griswold
- *Crime and Disrepute*   John Hagan
- *Gods in the Global Village: The World's Religions in Sociological Perspective*   Lester R. Kurtz
- *Waves of Democracy: Social Movements and Political Change*
  John Markoff
- *Development and Social Change: A Global Perspective*
  Philip McMichael
- *Aging and Inequality*   Fred C. Pampel
- *Constructing Social Research*   Charles C. Ragin
- *Women and Men at Work*   Barbara Reskin and Irene Padavic
- *Cities in a World Economy*   Saskia Sassen

Forthcoming:

- *Families and Public Policy*   Diane Lye

SCHOOLS AND SOCIETIES

STEVEN BRINT

University of California, Riverside

PINE FORGE PRESS

Thousand Oaks ◆ London ◆ New Delhi

For information:

Pine Forge Press
A Sage Publications Company
2455 Teller Road
Thousand Oaks, California 91320
(805) 499-4224
Internet: sdr@pfp.sagepub.com

Sage Publications Ltd.
6 Bonhill Street
London EC2A 4PU
United Kingdom

Sage Publications India Pvt. Ltd.
M-32 Market
Greater Kailash I
New Delhi 110 048 India

Production Editor: Sanford Robinson
Editorial Assistant: Windy Just
Production Assistant: Karen Wiley
Designer: Lisa S. Mirski
Typesetter: Rebecca Evans
Cover: Ravi Balasuriya
Print Buyer: Anna Chin

Printed in the United States of America

02 03 10 9 8 7 6 5 4 3 2

Library of Congress Cataloging-in-Publication Data

Brint, Steven G.
   Schools and societies / by Steven Brint.
     p. cm. — (Sociology for a new century)
   Includes bibliographical references and index.
   ISBN 0-8039-9059-6 (pbk.: acid-free paper)
   1. Educational sociology—United States. 2. Schools—United
States—Sociological aspects. I. Title. II. Series.
LC191.4.B75 1997
306.43—dc2197-33953

 This book is printed on acid-free paper that meets Environmental Protection Agency standards for recycled paper.

BRIEF CONTENTS

Detailed Contents

About the Author

Steven Brint is Professor of Sociology at the University of California, Riverside. He is the coauthor of an award-winning study of two-year colleges, *The Diverted Dream* (with Jerome Karabel), and author of *In an Age of Experts: The Changing Role of Professionals in Politics and Public Life*. He is currently at work on a study of American colleges and universities.

About the Publisher

Pine Forge Press is a new educational publisher, dedicated to publishing innovative books and software throughout the social sciences. On this and any other of our publications, we welcome your comments and suggestions.

Please call or write to us at:

Pine Forge Press
A Sage Publications Company
2455 Teller Road
Thousand Oaks, CA 91320
(805) 499-4224
E-mail: sales@pfp.sagepub.com

Visit our new World Wide Web site, your direct link to a multitude of online resources: http://www.sagepub.com/pineforge

Sociology for a New Century offers the best of current sociological thinking to today's students. The goal of the series is to prepare students, and in the long run, the informed public, for a world that has changed dramatically in the last three decades, and one that continues to astonish.

This goal reflects important changes that have taken place in sociology. The discipline has become broader in orientation, with an ever growing interest in research that is comparative, historical, or transnational in orientation. Sociologists are less focused on "American" society as the pinnacle of human achievement and more sensitive to global processes and trends. They also have become less insulated from surrounding social forces. In the 1970s and 1980s sociologists were so obsessed with constructing a science of society that they saw impenetrability as a sign of success. Today, there is a greater effort to connect sociology to the ongoing concerns and experiences of the informed public.

Each book in this series offers in some way a comparative, historical, transnational, or global perspective to help broaden students' vision. Students need to comprehend the diversity in today's world and to understand the sources of diversity. This knowledge can challenge the limitations of conventional ways of thinking about social life. At the same time, students need to understand that issues that may seem specifically "American" (for example, the women's movement, an aging population bringing a strained social security and health care system, racial conflict, national chauvinism, and so on) are shared by many other countries. Awareness of commonalities undercuts the tendency to view social issues and questions in narrowly American terms and encourages students to seek out the experiences of others for the lessons they offer. Finally, students need to grasp phenomena that transcend national boundaries—trends and processes that are supranational (for example, environmental degradation). Recognition of global processes stimulates student awareness of causal forces that eclipse national boundaries, economies, and politics.

Schooling occurs at a number of sociological intersections between family and public, between individual and organization, between present and future. More than any other major institution, schooling and schools are political, and virtually everyone has opinions to voice and interests to promote. Steven Brint musters a wealth of comparative material to show how schooling around the world is shaped by social forces even as it tries to shape the societies of the future. Students, parents, and policymakers will all have a better understanding of the schools they attend, support, and fight about after reading this book.

The daily papers in the United States are full of stories about national testing, multicultural curricula, bilingual education, vouchers, values teaching, the virtues and vices of "conceptual math," teacher qualifications, and a host of other school-related issues. The intensity of debate about these issues suggests that Americans are unusally preoccupied with their schools. Hovering over these debates is an abiding concern about whether children are learning the things they will need to know to succeed in an information-rich, global economy.

What many people do not appreciate is how often school issues are at the center of public passions in other countries as well. A government in Canada decides to lower teacher qualifications to bring more teachers into the schools and a full-fledged national crisis ensues. A political party in France calls for stricter controls on subsidies to Catholic schools and dormant, but centuries-old divisions in French society spring to life again. A report on bullying in Japanese primary schools becomes a national cause celèbre. Other social institutions may be as important as schools, but often it is schooling that people around the world really seem to care about.

The power of schooling to excite public passions is not as surprising as it first seems. Most days of the year, hundreds of millions of parents turn over temporary custody of their children to these public houses of instruction. Parents naturally hope this will be time well spent. In particular, the hopes parents entertain for their children's later life success are caught up in the power of schools to equip children with skills and attitudes that will help them. Collectively, too, citizens hold high expectations of schooling. Perhaps outside of the legal system, no other social institution is as thoroughly implicated in collective concerns about national identity, intergroup relations, and future progress.

This book is based on a new approach to understanding schools as social institutions. It moves away from the now rather tired debates between functionalists and conflict theorists over whether schools serve the whole of society or primarily the interests of elites. The forms of schooling we have today originated in particular social class contexts, and they have been significantly advanced by the nation-building purposes of state elites. However, as these forms developed they began to serve purposes that were legitimated at least in societal terms. These purposes include transmitting school knowledge, helping to socialize the young, and selecting motivated and able people to move ahead in the educational and occupational structure.

The book is intended to do more than summarize the existing sociological literature on schooling. It is intended to bring that literature into a more coherent focus than has been available so far.

The book also offers new ways of thinking about key issues. Here are just a few examples: It classifies the systems of schooling in the industrialized world in a way that reveals how different systems influence the life chances and outlooks of the students who participate in them. It provides the first comprehensive treatment of schooling in the developing world. It offers a new way of thinking about social stratification and educational outcomes. And it provides the first overview of how the school reform measures proposed over the past 20 years have worked out in practice.

Schools and Societies is designed for use in both sociology departments and schools of education. It can serve as the main text in upper-division undergraduate courses in the sociology of education or in graduate-level courses in the sociology of education or the social foundations of education. It can be used also as a supplementary text in courses on social institutions, socialization, and social stratification. Instructors who use the book as a primary text will find that they have ample room to supplement the book with readings of their own choosing, either to enrich and highlight materials covered in the book or to provide alternative interpretations of school processes and outcomes discussed in the book.

We are living at a time when the first signs of a global culture are emerging. The next generation of adults will be in closer touch with people in many countries around the world. Studies of schooling have not, by and large, caught up to the emergence of global society. I have written this book in the hope that it will encourage the upcoming generation of educators, social scientists, and engaged citizens to think about schooling from a perspective more appropriate to the world that is emerging. I hope that the book also conveys the intellectual excitement of using the tools of sociology to look at schools from this global comparative perspective.

ACKNOWLEDGMENTS

When Wendy Griswold asked if I would be interested in working on this book, I had just finished a major study of the professions. I thought this book would make a good transitional project and would not take long to write. I was mistaken in this second assumption. The gaps in my understanding quickly ended my plans for fast work of this book.

Fortunately, the finished work seems to me to have been worth the extra time and effort it required. My first thanks, therefore, go to Wendy Griswold for that fateful telephone call—and for her encouragement and collegiality throughout. My second thanks go to Steve Rutter. Because of his attentiveness and good spirits, he has helped to make writing the book a pleasurable experience in unexpected ways.

Several scholars have commented on chapter drafts or sections of chapters. They have helped me to sharpen the arguments and saved me from more than a few errors. I would like to thank Jutta Allmendinger, Burton Clark, Doug McDowell, Susan Eckstein, Bruce Fuller, Maurice Garnier, David Grusky, Mark Hanson, Barbara Heyns, Michael Hout, Dan Lortie, Christine Musselin, Caroline Persell, Rob Read, Lennart Svensson, David Tyack, Roger Voothroyd, and Pamela Barnhouse Walters for comments that helped to improve the quality of the book. Fred Muskal read the entire manuscript in draft form and provided particularly helpful comments. I would also like to thank Clifton Adelman, David Cohen, Adam Gamoran, Elizabeth Hansot, Michael Hout, Jerome Karabel, Paul Kingston, Thomas Mortenson, John Meyer, Gary Natriello, Lois Peak, George Psacharopoulos, Joan Slepian, Alex Star, Lennart Svensson, and David Swartz for sending along data or bibliographic information that helped.

Several graduate students (and one undergraduate) from Yale University worked with me on a project examining urban school reform, the results of which found their way into Chapter 9. I would like to thank Louise Deng,

Joyce Lee, Ephraim Radner, Eve Weinbaum, and Renee White for their work on that project. I am also grateful to the Iscol Family Foundation, and particularly to Jill Iscol, for supporting that research.

David Boyns worked as my research assistant during most of the period in which I drafted the manuscript. In addition to tracking down source material, he provided useful comments on chapter drafts and a good, critical mind on which to try out ideas. Becky Smith edited the manuscript with an eye to improving its clarity and accessibility. The book is much better for her efforts. Last, and most important, my wife, Michele Salzman, helped with compositional problems on many occasions and provided sustaining encouragement on all occasions.

Although I make some criticisms of schooling in this book, I am a great believer in the humanistic and scientific education for which it is a preparation. I would like, therefore, to dedicate this book to my children, Juliana and Ben, who are now at the beginning of their schooling, in the hope that they will continue to become well-educated people: knowledgeable, open to the world, principled, wise, and active.

Steven Brint

CHAPTER 1

Schools as Social Institutions

The words *education* and *schooling* are sometimes used interchangeably, but they are not the same. Education, learning about the particular ways of a group, occurs willy-nilly throughout life—at home, in peer play, at religious ceremonies, at work. These informal processes of learning occur in every distinct social group. Young Ponapean Islanders in the South Pacific, for example, learn from parents or neighbors that "the quietness of a man is like the fierceness of a barracuda," and they also learn how to shape bark to make a watertight canoe. American children also learn most of the things that equip them to survive in their society—from how to act if approached by a stranger to how to operate kitchen appliances—from the people around them, in the course of daily life. The same is true of important parts of education in every group and every society: Much of what individuals find it necessary to learn for survival and acceptance is taught outside of schools.

As the title *Schools and Societies* suggests, this book is not about education. Instead, it is about schooling, which is the more organized form of education that takes place in schools, and about the consequences of this organized form of education for individuals and for societies. Although schooling is in some ways more limited than education, it has great influence on the members of society. We are on strong ground to limit our scope to the study of schooling, because so much organized social effort goes into the formal education found in schools. It is also much easier to compare what happens in schools in different countries than it is to discuss the truly inexhaustible subject of what happens in educational processes generally, a topic that is more or less synonymous with the study of culture.

A related distinction is the one between two academic disciplines: the philosophy of education and the sociology of schooling. The philosophy of education concerns itself primarily with how education ought to be organized and the ends that it ought to serve. Sociology concerns itself with what schools are actually like, with why schools are the way they are, and with the consequences of what happens in schools.

This distinction is not intended as a criticism of philosophy. Even from a sociological standpoint, asking good questions about what "ought to be" often makes the "is" more visible and clear. For example, the philosopher's idea that education ought to provide a way of experiencing universal themes such as consciousness through humanities study provides a good vantage point for sociological investigations of how changing national interests and cultural traditions help to shape humanities curricula. Both the study of what ought to be and the study of what actually exists have a legitimate place in the universe of thought, but sociology is primarily concerned with what actually exists and how it came to be.

• • • • • • • • • • • • •

MARK TWAIN'S EDUCATION ON THE MISSISSIPPI

In *Life on the Mississippi,* the American writer Mark Twain provides a memorable reminiscence of his apprenticeship as a Mississippi riverboat captain. Twain's portrait reminds us of the difficulty of learning hard subjects and about what is gained and lost in the educational process. It also raises important questions: Why are so few teachers as effective as Mr. Bixby? And why have schools displaced on-the-job apprenticeships in so many fields?

Like many adventurous boys in the 1830s, young Sam Clemens (Twain's original name) longed to pilot one of the magnificent steamboats that carried the vast assembly of humanity—from roustabouts to fine ladies—and their cargo up and down the great Mississippi. Clemens managed to apprentice himself to a veteran pilot, a Mr. Bixby, in return for $500 to be paid out of his first wages as a pilot. Twain recalls the "easy confidence" with which he began his ordeal of learning the river. "I supposed that all a pilot had to do was keep his boat in the river, and I did not consider that could be much of a trick, since it was so wide."

This easy confidence did not last the morning. Bixby began his lessons by pointing out some landmarks on the river where the water changed depth.

> Presently he turned on me and said:
> "What's the name of the first point above New Orleans?"
> I was gratified to be able to answer promptly, and I did. I said I didn't know.
> "Don't *know*? . . . Well, you're a smart one!" said Mr. Bixby. "What's the name of the *next* point?"

Once more I didn't know.

"Well, this beats anything. Tell me the name of *any* point or place I told you."

I studied for a while and decided that I couldn't.

" . . . You—you—don't know?" mimicking my drawling manner of speech. "What *do* you know?"

"I—I—nothing for certain."

"By the great Caesar's ghost, I believe you! You're the stupidest dunderhead I ever saw or ever heard of, so help me Moses! The idea of *you* being a pilot—*you*! Why, you don't know enough to pilot a cow down the lane."

Thus begins the education of the young Mark Twain on the Mississippi River. Soon Clemens's notebook "fairly bristles" with the names of towns, "points," bars, islands, bends, and reaches on the river, for the only way to get to be a pilot is to "get the entire river by heart." When he has finally completed his apprenticeship on the river, Twain reflects on what he has gained—and lost—in the effort:

Now when I had mastered the language of this water, and had come to know every trifling feature that bordered the great river as familiarly as I knew the letters of the alphabet, I had made a valuable acquisition. But I had lost something too. All the grace, the beauty, the poetry, had gone out of the majestic river! . . . A day came when I began to cease from noting the glories and the charms which the moon and the sun and the twilight wrought on the river's face; another day came when I ceased altogether to note them. . . . All the value any feature of it had for me now was the amount of usefulness it could furnish toward compassing the safe piloting of a steamboat. (Twain [1896] 1972:31, 48-9)

· ·

THE SOCIETAL IMPORTANCE OF SCHOOLING

Although schooling is only a subset of education, it is very highly valued. One indicator is that schooling takes up a large amount of young people's time. If we assume that the average young person spends six hours in school five days a week and nine months a year for at least 12 years, the total number of hours in school between the ages of 6 and 18 is almost 13,000. For the increasing number of people who complete a college degree, that figure climbs to over 17,000 hours of schooling. People who graduate from college will have spent, on average, one out of six of their waking hours in school from their 6th through their 21st year—and that's not counting homework! As Figure 1.1

shows, children spend more time in school than they do watching television and playing with friends during the course of an average week. Moreover, school hours are more important as socializing agents for most children, given the amount of attention school requires and the highly involving competitions and group interactions that occur there. Judging simply in terms of the amount of time they take up, schools are also substantially more important than other community socializing agents, such as churches and recreational activities (see Figure 1.1). Even those who attend religious services every week, for example, spend only approximately one-tenth the time in their churches, synagogues, or mosques between the ages of 6 and 18 that they do in their schools.

Another indicator of the importance that modern societies place on schooling is the amount of money they are willing to spend on it. Indeed, the most fundamental thing to be said about schooling in the contemporary world is that it involves substantial expenditure. Citizens devote relatively large amounts of their hard-earned money to build schools, to maintain school grounds, to purchase equipment and materials, to pay the salaries of teachers and staffs, and so on.

Compared with other industries, the contemporary education "industry" is impressively large. In the United States, expenditures on schooling from kindergarten to college account for approximately 7 percent of the gross domestic product (GDP). More than $400 billion is spent on education each year in the United States (Organization for Economic Cooperation and Development [OECD] 1994:66). This amount is less than half as much as Americans spend on health care, but nearly twice as much as the construction industry's share of the GDP, four times the share of either the food products or industrial machinery industries, and 10 times the share of the auto industry (U.S. Bureau of the Census 1994b:447).

Another good measure of a society's commitment to schooling is the number of people working in schools. Schoolteachers are by far the largest occupation classified as "professional" by the U.S. Bureau of the Census, numbering nearly 4.4 million in 1993. College instructors and professors accounted for another three-quarters of a million, pushing the total number of teachers in the United States well past 5 million. Another 635,000 people worked in educational administration (U.S. Bureau of the Census 1994b:407). The United States now has three teachers for every engineer, three for every nurse, eight teachers for every lawyer, and nine teachers for every doctor.

Expenditures on schooling are similarly high throughout the developed world. As Table 1.1 indicates, in the richer industrial societies spending on education at all levels typically accounts for between 5 and 8 percent of the

FIGURE 1.1

Approximate Total Number of Hours Spent on Various Activities
for an Average American Child, Ages 6-18

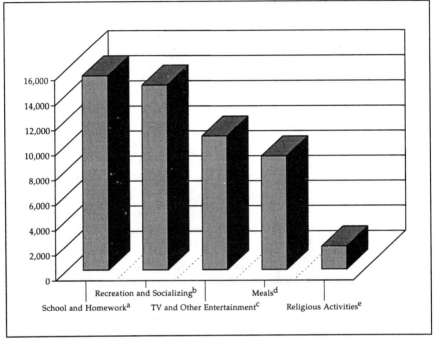

a. School and homework: Calculated as 6 hours of school and 1 hour of homework per school day.

b. Recreation and socializing: Calculated as 2.5 hours per day during the school year and 6.5 hours per day during summer vacation.

c. TV and other entertainment: Calculated as 2.5 hours per day.

d. Meals: Calculated as 2 hours per day.

e. Religious activities: Calculated as 2 hours per week (churchgoers only).

GDP (OECD 1995:73). The United States is on the high side (along with Canada and several Scandinavian countries); Germany and Japan are on the low side. People in developing countries may place even more faith in schooling as a road to economic and social progress, but they have fewer resources to devote to it. In developing countries, expenditures on schooling typically average between 2 and 3 percent of GDP. But they sometimes reach up to one-quarter of the government's total budget (United Nations Educational, Scientific, and Cultural Organization 1993, Table 4.1).

TABLE 1.1

Educational Expenditures as a Percentage of GDP,[a] Selected Countries, 1992

Country	Educational spending as a percentage of GDP
Finland	7.9
Canada	7.4
Hungary	7.3
United States	7.0
Switzerland	6.8
Denmark	6.7
France	5.9
Ireland	5.7
Australia	5.5
Spain	5.2
Netherlands	5.0
Germany	4.9
Japan	4.8

Source: Organization for Economic Cooperation and Development (1995:73).
a. GDP = gross domestic product

Why does virtually every country on the planet want to invest such large amounts of money in schooling? The answer is complex. Schooling was at one time limited to a small elite—no more than the top 2 or 3 percent of the population—and it was run by private academies or by church officials. In Europe, the shift to schooling for the masses began in the late 1700s led by kings who wanted to build a stronger loyalty to the state among poorer populations, particularly those living in the hinterlands (Bendix 1968:243-8). In the United States, the shift to mass schooling began a short time later, in the early 1800s, and was linked to an evangelical enthusiasm for building civic virtue in the new democracy. Later, it became linked to the effort of the Protestant mainstream to Americanize new immigrants. In a heterogeneous society, composed of many ethnic and religious groups, schools were "the closest approximation to an American established church. They provided . . . values later identified as 'the American way of life' " (Berthoft 1971:438).

Today, schooling is often thought of as a kind of all-purpose panacea. Most people think that school attendance is an important route to a better life. Governments and employers think it makes people better citizens and better, more productive workers. Indeed, in the developing world, schooling is associated with economic progress to such a degree that governments have often spent more on schools than is economically prudent. More and better education is also very often thought to be the best solution to the common problems that ail most societies. Epidemics of drug use? poverty? teen-age pregnancy? abusive parents? The first solution that many people think of is to try to change attitudes and behaviors through "more education" in public schools (Graham 1993).

Most important, schooling has become strongly associated with interests of the nation-state in the development of a trained workforce and well-disciplined citizenry. Elementary and secondary schooling is primarily an activity of the state. It is supported by taxes and provided free of charge to children. Some number of years of attendance is usually compulsory. This amount may vary from 5 or 6 years in many developing countries to 10 or 11 years in most of the industrialized world. Indeed, although they were often confronted by religious and ethnic opposition, nation-building states were able in the end to control the provision of primary and secondary schooling in every country but the Netherlands, where religious divisions prevailed. Today, primary and secondary schooling is primarily a publicly financed activity in every country but the Netherlands, although the private share may be as high as 25 percent as is the case in Australia and Spain (OECD 1995:136-58). Higher education is a different matter. Here a rich mixture of public and private alternatives very often coexist. The United States, Japan, and Great Britain have quite large private higher education sectors. Germany and most Scandinavian societies provide higher education almost exclusively through public institutions (OECD 1994:66, 74-5). Table 1.2 shows the mix of public and private funding at all school levels for 11 developed countries.

Given the preponderance of governmental control of schooling today and the nearly universal attendance of young people through age 14, it is remarkable to think that education in Western Europe and the United States before the late eighteenth century was almost entirely private or church run. It is even more remarkable that formal schooling even in the elementary and early secondary school years was limited to only a small upper crust instead of covering 100 percent of the population.

ORGANIZATIONAL CHARACTERISTICS OF SCHOOLS

As befits the social expenditure devoted to it, schooling is a much-thought-about and highly organized activity. In this respect, it contrasts sharply with the willy-nilly character of most other kinds of education. However, the organization of schools has also been criticized for serving the needs of society (or society's elites) to the detriment of individuals.

TABLE 1.2

Percentage Public Enrollment by Level, Selected Countries, 1991-2

Country	Primary school	Secondary school	Higher education
Sweden	99	99	99
Hungary	99	99	99
Japan	99	82	21
Germany	98	93	NA
United Kingdom	95	93	17[a]
Canada	94	94	93
United States	90	91	76
France	85	76	87
Spain	65	69	91
Netherlands	31	20	45

Source: Organization for Economic Cooperation and Development (1995:136, 158).
a. Data are for 1992.

Neither the level of care nor the criticisms are surprising once we appreciate that schools are powerful institutions. They are society's major means of shaping its young and of sorting them for future roles.

The Logic of School Organization

Organizationally, schools have many clearly positive features as compared to less formal processes of education in everyday life. These positive features have to do with schools' selectivity and sequencing of curricular materials and their efforts to maintain strong boundaries between what they do and do not allow into the classroom.

Selectivity. Schools are highly selective about what they teach. Overt commercialism, popular fashions, popular music, street language, and racial and ethnic prejudices are among the things usually selected out. Language and literature, math and science, history, social studies, and a few other subjects are nearly always selected in. To some degree, communities choose what they want to allow into the purified environment of the schools, but these decisions must be made on the grounds of intellectual merit. Sometimes these choices become part of political conflict in communities. Should sex education be taught? Should world history take a truly global perspective or a Western perspective? Because schools emphasize intellectual merit, however, these conflicts only very rarely permit purely popular elements to infiltrate the classroom environment.

Sequencing. The curriculum of the classroom, as compared to the curriculum of everyday life, is sequenced for efficient learning. It is organized in a progressive way. Features that are fairly fundamental and accessible to the young must be mastered first. Later lessons build on earlier learning. Building on prior knowledge makes lessons more easily comprehensible and allows teachers to monitor student progress in learning elementary tasks before more complex tasks are attempted.

Boundaries. Schools make efforts to maintain strong boundaries in relation to the outside world. Undesirable features of the ordinary environment are ruled out of order by teachers and administrators who maintain these boundaries. In school, for example, older children don't learn how to creatively torment younger children, although they may learn this "skill" in their neighborhood gangs. They do not learn how to swear or give free rein to prejudice. Instead, they learn how to read, write, and calculate. High- and low-status identities that exist outside of the school are in principle, if not always in fact, treated with indifference within its confines. It doesn't matter whether a student is rich or poor, Protestant or Catholic, male or female. The controlling identity is supposed to be academic. What happens in the purified environment of the school is all that is meant to count.

Through these three features, the organization of schools is intended to provide individuals with an opportunity to escape from the limitations of nature and of the social groups into which they are born. Most education that occurs outside of schools simply reproduces the skills, worldviews, and customs of a particular group. In contrast, schools provide a kind of "magic carpet" that can allow students to escape from the confines of their own particular group and make contact with a broader environment.

The Underside of School Organization

Not everyone sees the basic principles of school organization in such an idealistic light. Among social critics, schools are often described as threatening and dispiriting places, where the young are subjected to a regime based on equal parts fear and mind-numbing boredom. Needless to say, theirs is a picture of schooling that compares most unfavorably with the free-flowing, creative, and nonthreatening character of more informal educational processes.[1] Here is what one critic, John Holt (1964), had to say about American schools:

To a very great degree, school is a place where children learn to be stupid. . . . Infants are not stupid. Children of one, two, or even three throw the whole of themselves into everything they do. They embrace life, and devour it; it is why they learn so fast, and are such good company. Listlessness, boredom, apathy—these all come later. Children come to school curious; within a few years most of that curiosity is dead, or at least silent. Open a first grade or third grade to questions and you will be deluged; fifth graders say nothing. (P. 157)

If schools are purified and elevated environments, they are quite clearly also hierarchical, rule-bound, strictly disciplined, relatively impersonal, and continuously graded environments. Schools are, in these respects, the first performance-based bureaucracies that most people encounter. A clear chain of command descends from school board to superintendent to principals to teachers with students at the bottom of the chain. The rights and obligations of students, teachers, and administrators are strictly regulated by formal administrative rules and by informal rules of decorum, whose violation elicits sharp censures. The personal characteristics of students, who may be considered little more than "immature workers," are typically of less interest to teachers than their success at mastering their lessons and conforming to classroom rules. Testing is a continuous vexation felt in many a brow, palm, and bladder.

Moreover, in most schools, relatively little about classroom life is spontaneous or charged with emotion. John Goodlad (1984), whose research group studied 1,000 American classrooms in the late 1970s and early 1980s, summed up the results of his investigation:

The physical environments of most of the classrooms [was] devoid of amenities likely to provide comfort, unattractive or at least aesthetically bland, and cramped for space. They lacked . . . decoration in the form of wall hangings, prints of good paintings, contrasting colors on walls, doors, and cupboards. . . . The picture is of increasing drabness as one moves upward through the grades. . . . [The] relationship between teachers and classes of students was almost completely devoid of outward evidences of affect. Shared laughter, overt enthusiasm, or angry outbursts were rarely observed. . . . I wonder about the impact of the flat, neutral emotional ambience of most of the classes we studied. Boredom is a disease of epidemic proportions. (Pp. 226-7, 229-30, 242).

Holt's (1964) judgment, shared by generations of critics, was that schools "make children stupid" by making them fearful of their performance and bored by the ways in which they are expected to learn. However, those who are more sympathetic to the practices of the schools see the same characteristics deplored by Holt—discipline, rules, and tests—as precisely the characteristics that allow "immature workers" to learn difficult lessons with some measure of efficiency and success.

The evidence is mixed on this point, which is perhaps why the argument has persisted for 250 years. Most students adapt relatively easily to a structured environment and do not find school particularly alienating. This is mostly true for students whose home life has a consistent level of order and whose parents are supportive of the educational mission of the schools (Clark 1983). Indeed, for many students, schools provide a relatively engaging and supportive refuge from the vicissitudes of an unstable home life, where fostering, nurturing, and cultivation are less in evidence than they are in schools.

Moreover, both teacher morale and student learning appear to be enhanced in schools that are relatively structured. Teacher morale, for example, is associated with high levels of confidence in the support for them provided by principals and with clear rules about teachers' rights and responsibilities (Moeller 1964). Higher levels of student learning are associated with good disciplinary climates in classrooms (Coleman and Hoffer 1987); with the amount of time spent on task rather than in free-form or classroom management activities (Edmonds 1979); even with the amount and difficulty of the material covered during a term, provided that it is age appropriate (Dreeben and Gamoran 1986).

The Moral Order of Schools

Even so, the management of motivation in performance-oriented bureaucracies is never an easy task, and it is particularly difficult when the people from whom performance is required are children or young adults who are surrounded by others of their own age. Children are naturally full of energy, and they have limited attention spans. Some intelligent children (as judged by the staff) receive more than their share of attention in school, placing others in their shadow. Similarly, some children are able to resist the promptings of emotion and exuberance better than their classmates and are often appreciated by teachers for their restraint, again putting others in their shadow. Those who do not stand out positively or do stand out negatively are inclined to withdraw interest from the school and may encourage others to do so as well. Some students—in some schools, a large proportion—are unable or unwilling to adapt to the school environment and are chronically unhappy in it.

The task of stimulating and channeling motivation is naturally difficult under these circumstances. It is made more difficult because some of the most effective devices used in motivating adult workers, such as monetary incentives for compliance, are not available to school authorities. Teachers and schools consequently work in an emotional terrain studded, figuratively speaking, with land mines of potential student resistance.

In their efforts to stimulate and motivate children, schools rely on organizational blueprints and organizational strategies that go well beyond simple classroom discipline and whatever rapport may develop between teachers and students. These blueprints and strategies are the foundations of the *moral order* of the school. By moral order, I mean a set of shared norms of conduct, orientation, and identity. Elements of the school-constructed moral order include the organization of space and time, the use of differentiating and integrating rituals, the creation of status hierarchies, and the use of standardized membership categories. Some elements of the moral order of schools are not constructed; instead, they emerge through the joint activity of teachers and students in the everyday life of the classroom.

Structure: The Organization of Time and Space. In schools, space and time are organized both to control students and to allow for psychologically useful intervals of separation between staff and students. The physical spaces in which children are allowed are strictly limited, and the school day is cut up to avoid leaving students much time away from the eye of watchful authorities.

Certain physical spaces, the teachers' lounge, for example, are designated for staff alone to regroup and let off steam during class breaks. Other time periods, such as recess and lunch period, are for children to group spontaneously and let off energy. Movement between activities is strictly regulated with particular times regularly designated for special activities such as library, physical education, or computer workshop. Bells organize access to classroom space during the day. Access to certain other school spaces, such as the principal's office or the nurse's office, is restricted to students, who must be directed to them specially by their teachers.

Structure: Rituals. Schools also rely on rituals for shaping and motivating students. *Rituals* are focused gatherings that channel group attention and involvement in a particular direction and generate collective enthusiasm for the moral order. Rituals fall into two categories. *Differentiating rituals* highlight those who best conform to school ideals. These differentiating rituals include tests and award ceremonies. The difficulty with differentiating rituals is that although they affirm the moral order of the school and may increase motivation among some students, they may also decrease motivation among those students whose loyalty to the school is already weak. *Integrating rituals,* which allow for collective identification with the school, balance the differentiating rituals. Integrating rituals focus attention on emblems of the school or activities that allow for the participation of large numbers of students. These integrating rituals include pep rallies and sporting events, dances and other school-sponsored social activities, academic and extramural competitions with other schools, and the celebration of school traditions or school heroes that build sentimental attachments to the school (Bernstein 1975, chap. 2).

Structure: Status Hierarchies. The encouragement of multiple *status hierarchies* also helps to integrate students into the life of the school. In general, loyalty to the school is easier to retain where many roads to status are available than where only one road exists. Most administrators realize this fact, which is why schools affirm their primary purpose through tests and awards to scholars but also encourage the emergence of nonacademic hierarchies of status. In many schools, good looks, athletic ability, and participation in student government provide important alternative avenues to status among the students. One of the reasons high school is often a more pleasant experience than middle school for students is that high schools generally offer more extracurricular activities—and thus more routes to status. Indeed, in the majority of American secondary schools, the most athletic and the most popular students are far more admired than are the top scholars (Coleman 1961; Tye 1985).

Even the nonconformist bohemian and seemingly alienated student "underground" sustains a kind of loyalty to the school. Membership and status in this counterculture make school pleasant or at least acceptable for some students, however rebellious their stance against school authorities. Many intelligent administrators take the position that the student underground is a valuable part of the life of the school, even though these administrators may themselves be a frequent object of scorn among alienated students.

Structure: Standardized Membership Categories. In general, things would go much worse if schools simply bestowed benefits on the quick-witted and motivated few while blasting the confidence of the majority. Indeed, many individual differences in performance are obscured by broad *standardized membership categories* that allow unequal people to be treated more or less equally. The category "high school graduate," for example, is treated as a meaningful element of the American social structure, even though high school graduates include some people who know a great deal and some who can barely read and write. Similar ambiguities emerge from other educational categories, such as "sociology course," "four units of credit," and "credentialed teacher." Some sociology courses are tough; others are easy. Some units of credit are demanding; others are not. Some formally certified teachers know how to inspire and connect; others are inept.

These categories are treated as standard by schools, and precisely because they are treated as standard, they support the moral order of the schooling enterprise (Meyer and Rowan 1978). If high school graduates were seriously compared to one another, or credentialed teachers were examined closely for evidence of equal competence, profound doubts about the system might very well arise. Insofar as people assume that the categories mean something, they do mean something—and the business of schooling goes along with great success, churning out "qualified" graduates, credit hours, majors, and teachers.

The existence of these standardized membership categories also contributes to the ability of schools to maintain motivation. It is easier to maintain motivation where legitimacy is allocated in large measure by membership in a category rather than by differences in individual performance. If "students" were only those who succeed at a good proficiency level, a great many young people would drop out of school and pursue their education where they had a better chance of feeling accepted and appreciated. (Of course, there are limits to how far one would want to push this argument. If the majority of "certified teachers" were no better prepared than the average well-meaning layperson, the category would in all likelihood eventually become meaningless.)

Emergent Elements: The Community Life of Schools. Emergent properties of everyday interaction in school also help to maintain the moral order of schools. In the classrooms of the young, where children remain together throughout the day, a community life usually emerges, a villagelike atmosphere that provides pleasure to those who are villagers, however temporarily. Running jokes, pleasing forms of recognition ("our little detective," "our speedy weaver,"), even absorbing forms of half-serious conflict ("the king of the boys vs. the queen of the girls") create an atmosphere of community. Myths and legends about previous students and teachers also abound, especially about those defined as odd or unsavory by the majority. Sometimes, stories about these characters of school folklore remain long after the original parties have left the school. These myths and legends also help to define a moral order of the school by characterizing the boundaries between the normal and the deviant as defined by the student body. In larger schools, as children move past the primary grades and experience for the first time the continuous breakup of relationships in their hour-by-hour movement through classrooms and subject matters, this kind of community-like atmosphere fades.

Other emergent properties of the common life in schools do not disappear as completely. The most important of these are the rhythms of the school day, week, and year. The energy and attention of teachers and students alike follow these "natural" rhythms as if traveling on the current of a powerful river. Two former teachers, Ann Lieberman and Lynne Miller (1987), perceptively describe the American variant of these school rhythms. A daily routine exists—taking attendance, continuing from yesterday, introducing today's material, winding down, and making assignments. Days are punctuated by interruptions, with some settling down required after each interruption. Mondays are often hard for everyone, and Fridays are hard at least for students who are already thinking of the weekend.

In the annual rhythm, fall is a time of promise, with a downward spiral from the excitement of the new school year through Thanksgiving, and a brief resurgence between Thanksgiving and Christmas. For most, January is brief. February is very long, and the promise of summer stirs first in March. The final weeks are filled with activities, and then "the patterns learned and shared are rudely put to an end on a Friday in June" (Lieberman and Miller 1987). These rhythms are elements of school organization that help define the behavior of all who are involved.

SOCIOLOGICAL PERSPECTIVE ON SCHOOLING

As you may already have sensed, the underlying coherence of schools makes them an eminently suitable subject for sociology. Sociologists are trained to analyze the relationships that define the workings of institutions; the social and historical context in which these relationships exist; and the actual behaviors of people in concrete settings, as opposed to the idealized accounts that people sometimes give of their behavior.

Sociological arguments and theories are built in large part on comparison. If we want to know whether the United States is particularly schooling-conscious, we need to compare indicators of schooling-consciousness, such as per student spending on schools, for this country and others. If we want to know whether the kind of training teachers have makes a difference in how well they teach, we need to compare otherwise similar teachers who have graduated from different kinds of training programs. If we want to know whether class size makes a difference in learning, we need to compare how much is learned, on average, in small and large classes.

Advantages of a Global View

This book is comparative in a broader way than most. Sociology is at its best when it has a truly global focus. From a scientific point of view, the most important reason for taking a global view of schooling is that it allows us to compare more varied data. It is hard to understand the forces playing on schools if we limit our experience to a country in which only a certain number of these forces are at work. For example, let's say a social scientist thought that countries with centralized national ministries for schooling have more equality because budgets and instructional materials tend to be standardized across the entire country. This question obviously could not be answered by looking at the United States alone, because American schooling operates within a system of decentralized, local control. The answer to this question would require a broader canvas of comparison.

Even those who are not scientifically inclined can learn from the experiences of other cultures. The value of global comparisons is not just that the practices of other peoples are intrinsically interesting, although for many people they are intrinsically interesting. Nor do practical interests alone encourage us to look beyond our own shores, even though the world is indeed getting smaller and more interconnected with every passing year. The truth is, even if we are interested only in our own society, we can't always know much about it without thinking about the experiences of others.

Very often, what seems to be a unique problem may be in fact an example of a more general phenomenon. For example, many Americans think of the race problems in the United States as a uniquely American dilemma. However, comparative study suggests that blacks in the United States may be comparable to other very highly subordinated minorities, such as the Oriental Jews in Israel and the Burakamin in Japan (Ogbu 1978). Accepting this conceptual shift raises the further interesting issue of whether any other society has done a better job than the United States in integrating "castelike minorities" through schooling, and, if so, how they have done it.

On the other hand, what appears to be a general pattern—say, the relationship between small classes and higher achievement scores—may turn out to be less general than we imagine. In many East Asian countries, classes of 40 or more are not uncommon, and class size appears to have little relation to achievement (White 1987). This fact raises the further interesting question of what goes into creating an atmosphere in which 40 children can concentrate as one.

By looking at the experience of other peoples, we can also test possibilities that we have contemplated for ourselves. Americans love to think about ways to improve their schools, but the ideas that are proposed often have only the charm of novelty without a supporting practical wisdom. Given the reforms that have been proposed in recent years, we should be able to profit from considering the experiences of societies that, like England, have instituted market-based voucher systems, or, like Germany, have maintained work-related apprenticeship programs for teenagers. To appreciate what it might mean to make standardized testing a more important part of the school experience, we could look at East Asian societies, where achievement is high but adolescents are exposed en masse to the searing ritual of "exam hell" (Rohlen 1983) and are given to fervent prayerful offerings in the hopes of a high score (Zeng 1996).

●●●●●●●●●●●●●●

WHERE ARE THE BEST SCHOOLS IN THE WORLD?

In 1991, *Newsweek* magazine devoted a special section to what it called the best schools in the world ("The Best Schools" 1991). It suggested sending children to Italy for kindergarten, to New Zealand to learn reading, and to the Netherlands to learn math. Once they are literate, children should, according to *Newsweek,* go on for science training in Japan where they will learn through hands-on techniques and wait to learn principles until after they learn practical applications. They should take foreign language instruction in the Netherlands where two foreign languages are required. For high school, children should be sent to Germany. The editors of the magazine lauded the multitrack system in Germany, where only the top third go on to academic study leading to the university, and the majority combine apprenticeship training with job-related academics. The United States is not completely absent from this list of "bests in the world." *Newsweek* considered the United States to excel in arts education and in graduate training.

Articles like this are at least as interesting for what they tell us about contemporary educational ideals as for their specific recommendations. The preferences in this article reflect today's concerns about academic achievement. A different set of choices would almost certainly have been made in the 1960s, when well-to-do people like the editors of *Newsweek* thought schooling should also improve cross-cultural understanding and individual creativity.

Nevertheless, like comparative social science, the article does help to expand our horizons. It encourages us to value a wider range of international experience than we might otherwise be exposed to. It suggests ways the experiences of other countries might be relevant to improving our own institutions.

Careful readers, however, will also be wary of the methods by which this list of "bests" was chosen. Other journalists, with different sources, might well have chosen different schools and different practices. For example, according to international achievement tests, mathematics teaching is apparently at least as effective in Hungary now as it is in Japan. It is also important to remember that the practices of other countries can seldom be imported wholesale into American education. Foreign language teaching in the Netherlands is effective, for example, partly because students in this small country near the center of Europe will inevitably be called on to speak other languages. By contrast, American students grow up speaking English, the language of international business and science, and are consequently relatively insulated from pressures to learn new languages.

•••

A Framework for Understanding Schools and Societies

Beyond comparisons across societies, sociologists rely on theory to help them focus their studies. In a way, sociological analysis can be compared to photography: Like skilled camera work, it requires facility in the use of a number of "lenses." In particular, sociologists must work with the equivalent of wide-angle lenses when they are concerned with very large scale social changes. They must work with middle-horizon lenses when they are concerned with the everyday operation of institutions as they exist at a given point in time. And they must master the close-up, telephoto lens to examine the workings of institutions as they exist in small-group and face-to-face interactions. In the analysis of social institutions like schooling, each of these levels is important.

The broadest perspective can be called the *macrohistorical* level of analysis, the second the *mesoinstitutional* level of analysis, and the third the *microinteractional* level. These levels are not always easy to distinguish, because actions at the higher levels are part of the context in which patterns at the lower levels develop. Nevertheless, they are sufficiently distinct to be discussed separately.[2] Table 1.3 summarizes sociologists' major concerns at each of these three levels.

The Macrohistorical Level. To understand the social institutions we inhabit, we need to know how they came into being. The macrohistorical level of analysis is critical for understanding the development of the current purposes and activities of schools.

Schools have developed for many different reasons, but the most important are to teach the culture of a group, to cement political loyalties, and to prepare young people either for public life or for an occupational craft. In the West, the ancestors of our contemporary schools developed for very different reasons and at very different times. Compulsory primary schools were invented in the early eighteenth century by modernizing kings and emperors,

TABLE 1.3

Levels of Sociological Analysis of Schooling

Level of analysis	Major concerns
Macrohistorical: Development of school structures and purposes	Global origins of school purposes and structures in comparative perspective
	Global development of purposes and forms of schooling
	Consequences of school structures and purposes for society
Mesoinstitutional: Operation of schools as social institutions	Organizational channels and practices for directing energies
	Interests and relationships of major categories of actors
	Environmental influences on schooling
	Consequences of institutional operations for learning, socialization, and sorting
Microinteractional: Staging and inter-action processes involved in class-room instruction	Preexisting structural influences on interaction within schools
	The construction of learning communities
	Interaction-based failures in instructional activities
	Consequences of school interactions for learning, socialization, and sorting

who wanted to teach the rudiments of literacy to their subjects while building an identification among young people in the hinterlands (most of whom had weak attachments to the state) with the language and national heroes of the political center. The predecessors of our secondary schools have an ancient pedigree in the Greek academies, where teaching of philosophy and rhetoric was explicitly rooted in the life conditions and ideals of an aristocracy interested in preparing its sons for public life. The predecessors to today's universities developed during the Middle Ages. They carried on traditions of secular and sacred learning, but were most important for confirming the gentlemanly status of young men entering a handful of "learned occupations" connected to the Church: medicine, law, the clergy, and teaching itself.

Institutions of schooling have always been stamped by the interests and ideals of particular groups and organizations. For instance, the interests of kings and emperors were connected to the origins of primary schooling; the interests of the governing classes of the ancient world were connected to the origins of secondary schooling; and the interests of the Church and the ruling classes of European feudalism were connected to the founding of universities. The historically developed ideologies of these classes and institutions are very often decisive for the functioning of schools. Imagine how different schooling would be if the apprenticeship system of the medieval craft guilds had somehow come to dominate public schooling rather than the liberal arts tradition of the academies and universities.

Schools sometimes change when new class or organizational interests gain power. For example, primary and secondary education in early modern Europe arose when the Protestant Reformation disrupted the Catholic Church's control, and nation-states expanded into this "depopulated" institutional space (Durkheim [1938] 1977). Schools also change when new kinds of connections are made between existing types of schools, when new populations enter old schools, or when new market incentives develop. For example, vocational education became a part of secondary schooling in the United States around the turn of the century, at a time when new populations (mainly from immigrant families) were entering secondary schools for the first time. Those who were already involved in the secondary schools had a market interest in preserving the value of the high school degree, and others had an interest in gaining access to these valuable degrees. In the end, a compromise was worked out: academic education for those headed for higher levels in the academic and class structure and vocational education for many of the new entrants (Cohen 1985; Labaree 1988). Class interests were surely involved here, but so were market incentives, demographic changes, and newly strengthened connections between primary and secondary schools.

Thus, as we look at the multicolored threads that make up the fabric of educational history, we see a smaller number of "golden threads": influences that stand out more strongly than the others. The connection between state power and democratic ideology has been particularly important in our own century as a force in the development of schooling throughout the world. (It was important as early as the 1820s in the highly democratic United States.) Our contemporary systems of schooling reflect the working out of connections between new and surviving forms of schooling; the gradual expansion of student aspirations from lower to higher levels as the previously normal attainment levels no longer satisfy ambitions for upward mobility; the differentiation of curricular tracks to satisfy markets for educated labor; and the creation of standardized models of schooling that flow from the center to the peripheries of power.

Exactly how these forces are manifested in any given country depends on how much power is held by the coalitions that support existing forms of schooling and how conflicts among educators, political parties, and other interests are resolved. The structure of schooling is, therefore, not exactly the same throughout the world. As we will see in Chapters 2 and 3, people's life experiences are very strongly stamped by differences in these structural forms. The haughtiness of pre-World War II British university graduates was distinctly related to the small numbers of secondary school students who had the chance to go on to higher education. These small numbers were an outcome supported by the state's alliance with the "aristocracized" graduates of Oxford and Cambridge. The feverish effort of Japanese students approaching the end of their high school years is shaped by the decisive importance of secondary school-leaving examinations for later success in Japan.

Some sociologists with a macrohistorical perspective write about schooling as something that developed to address the functional requirements of society as a whole. This way of thinking about schooling is obviously rather plausible when the great majority of children attend school. But the historical development of schooling demonstrates the futility of talking about schooling as "functionally connected" to the "needs" of society as a whole. Even today, schools serve the interests of some groups better than others. Those whose interests are not fully satisfied by the dominant form of schooling may have incentives to develop their own schools, as in the case of Christian academies and charter schools today. These alternative schools may then join the field of organizational competitors in the next round of historical development.

Macrohistorical analysis is challenging because it requires looking at institutions not simply in terms of their origins and development but also in comparative perspective. Other societies, with different traditions and different coalitions of power, are a natural context from which to better understand one's own social institutions and their development.

The Mesoinstitutional Level. Most sociological work on schooling is conducted at the middle horizon, or institutional, level of analysis. At the institutional level, sociologists stop the historical clock and focus on institutions as they exist at a given point in time. Institutional analysis is important because it shows us how our institutions are organized and what kinds of forces they respond to in their environments. It can also help us to understand why our institutions don't work as well as they might.

Institutions are conventional and legal arrangements developed to perform particular sets of tasks or to regulate particular activities by limiting the number of ways these tasks and activities are accomplished. Institutions reduce randomness. Marriage, for example, is an institution that regulates sexuality and child rearing by organizing action along a limited set of socially prescribed paths. Schools in contemporary societies can be described as institutions that (1) transmit school knowledge to the young, (2) shape personalities and conduct to conform to a socially approved type (or types), and (3) sort students for positions in the class and occupational structure.

The analysis of institutional life grows out of the essential character of institutions: They are organized to channel energy along socially prescribed lines; they are composed of cooperating categories of actors whose interests are, however, not necessarily always in complete harmony; and they are situated in a larger social environment from which they are not fully insulated. Institutional analysis, therefore, consists of three parts:

1. Analysis of practices related to the realization of the institution's purposes

The reality of school life is strongly colored by the instructional, socializing, and sorting purposes of the schools and the authority and status systems that flow from those purposes. For example, when one looks at schools and classrooms, one sees immediately that spaces are defined, time is divided, groups are created, and routines are developed as a way of reducing random action and providing an order in which learning can occur. Several of these practices were discussed above in the section on the moral order of schools.

2. Analysis of the interests of the major actors in the institution and the ways those interests affect the working of the institution

The three major categories of actors within schools are students, teachers, and administrators. These actors are involved in a partially cooperative enterprise, but it is also what sociologist Robert Park (Park and Burgess 1921) called a relationship of "antagonistic cooperation." Students are mainly the carriers of popular aspirations and popular cultural understandings of schooling, teachers are mainly the carriers of school knowledge and educational standards, and administrators are mainly the carriers of the existing rules of school organization and the interests of the bureaucracy. When differences of interest exist, some degree of tension or even outright conflict can be expected. Teachers, for example, may want students to work harder than students would wish to do if left to their own devices, and students may resist these expectations.

Let's look at just one side of this triangular set of relationships: Many of schooling's successes and failures have to do with the interplay of popular aspirations and bureaucratic interests. In some communities, a lack of interest in education may be offset by the bureaucracy's ardent commitment to high-quality education. In many other communities, these two forces are in harmony and are mutually supportive. But the people's aspirations for success in schooling and the bureaucracy's interest in a constant flow of resources can also lower the quality of schooling. If the community considers schooling successful when most students move unimpeded from grade to grade, it may encourage bureaucratic neglect. Low reading scores may be overlooked or even inflated so as not to make the school and its staff "look bad." In addition, every new thrust of popular democracy generally leads to a new layer of bureaucracy. If interested groups of taxpayers want special education programs or nutrition programs or diversity training programs and have their desires passed into law, the results will be a new bureaucratic office for coordinating these efforts. Eventually, the bureaucracy soaks up a disproportionate share of resources that could be going more directly to instructional purposes (Chubb and Moe 1989).

3. Analysis of the effects of the external environment on the workings of the institution

Although the organizational devices available to schools are more or less similar no matter where they exist, school purposes and activities are nevertheless greatly influenced by the specific environments in which they are situated. First, schools have a specific relationship to other formal educational organizations. They have become linked in a hierarchy with other schools. Primary school is now a universal feeder, but students are split at the secondary level between those who move on in the educational system and those who move out to the labor market. In addition, at any given time, a certain range of alternative schooling types exists in the environment, and these forms are at least potentially organizational competitors. Second, schools are also connected to other groups and organizations. Most important, they are connected to educational organizations (e.g., teacher training institutions, professional associations of educators, and textbook publishers and other providers of instructional materials); to governmental policies and tax laws; to the demographic character, values, and resources of local communities; to the popular culture that influences fashions and attitudes; and to employing organizations through the job market or more direct channels.

These different environmental influences are more or less important depending on the particular school activity under consideration. For example, the quality of teaching in public schools may be highly dependent on the quality of teacher training institutions, which are, therefore, a potentially significant part of the environment in which schools are located. Or consider the relationship between schools and governments. When schools exist within a strongly centralized system of government (as they do in France, Sweden, and Japan), many features of public schooling will be uniform throughout the country—the level of expenditures per student, the course materials studied, and the kinds of training that teachers must have. By contrast, in decentralized systems like the United States, where schooling is a state and local responsibility, quite a bit more inequality and diversity can theoretically exist. Or consider the difference that the kind of community in which a school is located can make: Schools in affluent communities can usually draw on the active support and participation of parents to a greater degree than when they are located in poorer communities.

The Microinteractional Level. Virtually every situation in school involves encounters between people. The microinteractional level of analysis is concerned with what happens in these encounters. Analysis of this immediate experience of schooling is critically important for showing how all its possibilities—mastery of course materials, dutiful compliance, confusion, disengagement, active hostility—are set into motion. The important elements are what people bring into their encounters, the way they present themselves to one another, and the way those presentations are interpreted and acted on.

The background of interaction is usually as important as the process of interaction itself. To use a theatrical metaphor, the staging—scenery, costumes, and props—is as important as the lines exchanged between the actors. The staging represents the preexisting understandings that influence the action on the stage. In the classroom, the "staging" includes the experiences and motives that students, teachers, and administrators bring with them to the classroom; the definition of the situation that prevails in their encounters; and the numbers and kinds of other actors who share the classroom stage. For example, the kinds of interactions that take place vary greatly between classrooms in which large numbers of disengaged students are gathered together and those in which small numbers of highly engaged students are present.

Although the staging of interaction is important, much of the best microlevel analysis—and certainly much of the most dramatic work—focuses on the gestures and spoken lines of the actors, the process of face-to-face interaction itself. Sociologists use videotape, transcripts, and their own observation to home in on how people represent themselves to others through their dress, language, and behavior; how others interpret those representations; and the responses people develop in light of those interpretations. This three-step process—representation, interpretation, and response—occurs simultaneously on both sides of the interaction. Conversations can be thought of as many bits of interaction strung together, and relationships can be thought of as strings of interaction across time.

For example, if a young man wants to project an image of malevolence, he may sport a buzz cut, beard stubble, mirrored sunglasses, tattoo, and a torn shirt, and he may work out to keep his muscles pumped up. He may speak little and, when he does, primarily in short bursts laced with obscenities. Most people will interpret this symbolic display as characteristic of a street tough and will want to steer as clear as possible. The young man's friends, however, may interpret the same representations as the essence of a "stand-up" kind of fellow unwilling to let the world take advantage of him. And the young man's mother might interpret his symbolic actions as a "stage" on the road to adulthood. The young man, meanwhile, is making interpretations of these other people's symbolic representations and is responding to them in light of his understandings.

By showing how both successes and failures of classroom life can arise from the way in which actors interpret and adapt to the symbolic expressions of others, microinteractional analysis can add to our understanding of some of the most basic issues of mass schooling. It is particularly important for showing how effective teachers manage their authority and construct learning communities and for revealing some of the less obvious causes of static and distortion in the teacher-student interchange.

Authority is a basic requirement of classroom life because neither order nor learning are possible without it. However, the management of authority requires considerable skill. Writing in the 1930s, Willard Waller catalogued the various means by which the adults of his time represented themselves as respect-worthy figures (the Old Soldier, the Mother, the Favorite Aunt, the Man about Town) and the repertoire of social control procedures (from raised eyebrows and withering comments to suspensions and expulsions) that teachers of his time used to maintain their control over classroom life (Waller 1932). Since Waller's time, problems in the management of authority have received more attention, particularly as these problems relate to issues of fairness and flexibility. Microlevel analysis has helped to document how teacher expectations may influence students' behavior and how teachers interpret social class and ethnic cultural cues to identify "good" and "bad" students (Rist 1970; Erickson 1975). It has also helped to show how a language of community can be used by educators to include disadvantaged people symbolically and to gain allies, and how, by contrast, a language of technical expertise can be used to deauthorize others, as when teachers use jargon to deauthorize parents as specialists on their children's behavior (Mehan 1993).

Once teachers have established their authority, they must construct a successful community of learners. In the United States, the most effective teachers combine clear task leadership with strong projections of personality and character. They maintain high and challenging standards but also work on maintaining rapport. The expectations of students and teachers can, however, vary greatly from culture to culture. Therefore, different kinds of teachers are effective in different societies. In Japan, teachers expect students to work patiently through their errors and to accept that errors are an important part of learning to be overcome through hard work. The idea that students have greater or lesser abilities is practically irrelevant. Japanese students, in turn, expect their teachers to be technically skilled performers, rather than, for example, encouraging helpers or subject matter specialists (Stevenson and Stigler 1992). As long as these expectations are mutually met, the educational connection is successful.

Throughout the world, confusion and misunderstanding are as much a part of the classroom life as clarity and comprehension. Many of these breakdowns come from disengaged teachers or unmotivated students, who have lost sight of the value of actively participating in the hard work of instruction. Other breakdowns may be due to students' limitations in comprehending the material presented, or teachers' limitations in presenting it well. Clearly, however, breakdowns also occur even when both students and teachers have accepted the legitimacy of classroom effort and are trying to approach their work in a serious way. Take the following example from England of how students in one school were labeled as either "dull" or "intelligent." Working-class children were more likely to ask very basic questions of their teachers and to ask why they needed to learn the material. Middle-class children may have had the same questions but were more likely simply to absorb the material, assuming that eventually they would understand why they were being asked to learn it. Teachers tended to see the first type of students as dull and the second as intelligent. However, another equally valid interpretation would be that the middle-class students had learned to be passive and deferential—that they were, in a sense, less engaged in active learning (Keddie 1971). Many such studies help us to understand why interaction in the classroom so often fails to accomplish as much as it might.

Scientific and Humanistic Faces of Sociology

Sociology is an unusual discipline because it has both a scientific and a humanistic face. It is both a set of propositions about human social relations and a way of understanding and appreciating ourselves and the world around us. Sociologists who identify themselves primarily with the scientific side of the discipline have developed a number of propositions to explain patterns in human social relations. They have also developed a large number of empirically based generalizations about the causes of various social phenomena, such as crime rates, group conflict, upward social mobility, and rates of learning school materials. The scientific side of the discipline has produced many important findings, and you will encounter those that have to do with schooling in this book.

Because of their scientific procedures, sociologists are sometimes in a position to suggest ways to improve our institutions of schooling. For example, by looking at different kinds of teaching under experimental conditions, researchers have developed a clearer sense of the behaviors used by effective and less effective teachers. Similarly, we now have considerable evidence that in the United States and many other countries smaller classrooms and smaller schools help to build a sense of community among students, which, in turn, helps to create a stronger commitment to schoolwork. If these kinds of findings are taken seriously by educators and policymakers, they can lead to improvements in how well schools work.

But the discipline has still more to offer. Max Weber ([1921] 1978), perhaps the greatest sociologist, thought that sociology's major contribution would be the cultivation of human judgment, and perhaps he was right. Sociology allows us to see into the character of our institutions and the consequences they have for our lives. It can also help us to see the forces at play in the actions of others and the ways our own actions may be influenced by a specific set of socially conditioned understandings. Looked at in the right way, sociology offers nothing less than a new way of seeing the world and our places in it.

It is not surprising, therefore, that sociology includes a gallery of institutional landscapes and human portraits, as well as laboratories and data files for testing hypotheses and producing mathematical formulas. The pictures in this gallery can be jarring, because the opportunities and constraints of the social structure often give rise to false hopes and draining struggles. We see, for example, some educational reformers who proclaim success to get attention and resources without actually knowing whether what they do is in fact making a difference. We see intensely "people-oriented" teachers who are led by the uncertain successes of teaching to build walls around their classrooms, depriving themselves of the human contact they prize so highly. And we see the rebels among working-class adolescents who, through their acute sense of moral superiority to the passive rule-followers among their peers, prepare for lives of numbing labor.

Some of the portraits, too, are stimulating, vivid spots of color on a sometimes cold and colorless canvas. Many involve the transforming power of human cooperation and human connections: the electrical charge of a class that is humming along on all cylinders, the graceful gesture of a classmate who captures the dignity rather than the stridency of a moral protest, or perhaps that rare occasion when a teacher interprets a sullen young person as going through a stage on the road to maturity at the same time the young person begins to see the teacher as trustworthy. Although we may be dismayed by the pictures in the sociological gallery as often as we are reassured by them, we do not have to look hard to see a discipline fully engaged with understanding the human condition and human relationships (cf. Geertz 1973, chap. 1).

ORGANIZATION OF THE BOOK

The remainder of this book will take up issues that are important to anyone interested in education and schooling. You will see the guiding influence of the theoretical framework outlined in this chapter—the macrohistorical, meso-institutional, and microinteractional levels of analysis—as well as a global perspective and a reliance on both scientific and humanistic aspects of sociology.

Chapters 2 and 3 provide an overview of schooling in the industrialized and developing worlds. These are the chapters most concerned with the macrohistorical level of analysis. In these chapters, I discuss the rise of schooling and the forms schooling has taken in several societies. I also discuss the major issues facing schools in rich and poor societies.

Chapters 4 through 7 examine the major contemporary social purposes of schools: the transmission of school knowledge, the socialization of personality and conduct, and the sorting of students for positions in the class and occupational structure. These chapters rely primarily on macrohistorical analyses to examine the development of these activities of schooling and on studies at the mesoinstitutional level to illuminate the current issues surrounding them.

Chapter 8 takes up issues related to the teaching and learning of school knowledge. This is the chapter in which the microinteraction level of analysis plays the largest role. Chapter 8 examines the forces outside and inside of classrooms that influence the interaction of teachers and students and the successful transmission of school knowledge.

Part of the interest of sociology stems from what it can tell us about how to improve our institutions. Chapter 9 looks at recent school reform programs in the United States. It brings together evidence about the effectiveness of such reforms as educational vouchers, magnet schools, business partnerships with schools, and community outreach programs. It concludes by discussing the ingredients that go into making good schools.

CHAPTER 2

Schooling in the Industrialized World

This chapter will examine the structure of schooling in the industrialized societies. By industrialized societies, I mean those in which most people are employed in manufacturing and services industries, rather than in mining and farming. Because of the higher productivity of industrialized economies and their domination of world markets for finished goods and business services, people living in industrialized countries have higher average incomes and living standards than people living in developing countries. The industrialized world includes the United States and Canada, the United Kingdom, all of the countries of Western Europe and Scandinavia, the most developed countries of the old Soviet bloc in Central Europe (such as Hungary and the Czech Republic), Israel, Japan, Australia, New Zealand, and several of the emerging industrial powers of the Pacific Rim, including South Korea, Taiwan, Hong Kong, and Singapore.

For the past 50 years, these countries have been able to count on more or less steady economic growth and security from the devastation of war. Most of them have also had the advantage of stable and responsive political systems. These advantages have allowed for a steadiness and regularity in the development of schooling that is not as common in the developing world.

At the same time, specific features of schooling vary considerably among the industrial societies. Consider, for example, key differences among the schooling systems of three countries in the industrial world—the United States, Germany, and Japan—and some of the consequences of these differences.

In the United States, a child beginning school will receive much the same instruction as other children through the end of high school. Some 80-85 percent of the age group will eventually finish high school. Of those who finish high school, the great majority, as many as three out of four high school graduates, will go off to one of 3,500 colleges and universities. School will not be so difficult or demanding for most students that it does not leave considerable time for socializing with friends, for participation in extracurricular activities, and, later, for part-time work. College entrance tests will not keep anyone out of higher education, though they will be used to help determine admissions into a small number of selective colleges and universities. The anxiety these tests create will generally last for only a short time before and after the exam. Most students will want to continue past high school to get the kind of degree that may give them a leg up in the job market, but it will not generally be considered a "life or death" matter if one drops out before completing a degree.

Contrast this relatively open structure, and the easygoing attitude it fosters, with the systems of two other wealthy industrial democracies. In Germany, children are divided at age 10 into three types of schools. This placement will, in the great majority of cases, have a decisive influence on the child's future life trajectory. The bottom track does not lead to college, and the second track leads, at most, to technical colleges with short degree programs. Even graduating from the top track allows entry to college only if the student has passed a demanding secondary school-leaving examination, known as the *Abitur*.

> Upper secondary school in Germany is a serious business. The *Abitur* is normally taken at the end of thirteen years of education, a longer period than in most other countries. The level of knowledge demanded is high. . . . Preparation for the examinations therefore looms very large in the upper secondary student's life in Germany, leaving not much time for extracurricular activities. (Eckstein and Noah 1993:62)

In Germany, even those who leave formal schooling at the end of the compulsory period are busy with school in their teenage years. Nearly all attend "continuation school" part-time while gaining rigorous apprenticeship training in a business or industry. Between school and work, they are adults at a time when American teenagers are still at the beginning of deciding "what they want to do with their lives."

In Japan, the degree of intensity of schooling is greater still, though the structure involves less tracking than in Germany. The great majority of Japanese teenagers take academic rather than vocational studies; a vocational track exists only for the bottom quarter. School is long and intense with as many as 45 students in a classroom and demanding, fact-laden drills a staple of instruction in the upper grades. Extracurricular activities are not discouraged, but students have less time to devote to them than American teenagers. After school, most take additional classes at *juku,* and nearly all also attend these supplementary schools on Saturdays. And no wonder: Performance in school matters greatly for later life success. Scores on secondary school-leaving tests determine who will be admitted to the universities and in what fields.

The rigid pecking order of universities and fields, in turn, determines who will be eligible for the more desirable jobs in Japanese companies and government agencies. Under the circumstances, it is not surprising that a popular saying among Japanese teenagers is: "Fail with five, pass with four"—the five and the four referring to hours of sleep after nighttime study.

What explains the differences that exist in the schooling systems of the industrialized world? And what consequences do these differences have for students? These are the major questions addressed in this chapter. Instead of looking at the content of school instruction, this chapter examines school structure—that is, how school systems are organized. Understanding structure turns out to be a key to understanding national differences in student attitudes, experiences, and opportunities. It unlocks much of what is important in the relation of schools to their societies. I will begin by discussing the historical setting in which contemporary patterns of schooling in the industrialized world developed. In the second part of the chapter, I will develop a typology of schooling systems, using the United States and Germany as the polar cases, and Japan, France, Sweden, and England as examples of intermediate types. I will show that differences in the structure of schooling are connected to differences in the outlook and life chances of students. In the final section of the chapter, I will discuss the social and political forces that have shaped the specific form schooling took in different industrial societies following World War II.

HISTORICAL CONTEXT

The differences among educational systems in the industrial world are best thought of as political responses to increasing social and economic demand for higher levels of educational qualification. Those responses, however, began from two distinct starting points: the assumptions in Europe that schooling beyond primary school is for "elite preparation" and the assumptions in the United States (and other English-speaking democracies of the New World) that schooling serves public purposes and is therefore a general good.

These two different starting points have had an important impact on the direction that system-building efforts have taken. In particular, the premises of elite preparation encouraged more highly structured tracking at the secondary level, as well as relatively restricted access to higher education. The premises of "democratic uplift" encouraged predominantly academic schooling, more flexible and limited tracking at the secondary level, and wider access to higher education.

The Premises of Elite Preparation

The most determined efforts to make primary schooling widely available began earlier in Europe than they did in America. However, it took some 200
years, until the middle of our own century, before schooling in Europe had
much to do with democracy or equal opportunity. From an American perspective, this is an astonishing fact, because democracy and equal opportunity
were important forces in the development of the U.S. schooling system almost
from the beginning.

The first efforts to extend the right of a primary schooling to the masses
were made by European princes in the early 1700s. Occasionally, enlightened
monarchs hoping to elevate the cultural level of their subjects were responsible for these initiatives, as was true in the case of Frederick IV of Denmark,
who created the first mass public schooling in the 1720s. More often, however,
the motives were "profoundly conservative," as in the case of the compulsory
schooling legislation of the leaders of Prussia (a once independent country
that is now part of Germany). Some advanced efforts of instruction based on
drawing out the curiosity of children were adopted in Prussia in the early
1800s, but Prussian educators sought mainly to teach basic literacy and a sense
of identification with and loyalty to the nation-state (Bendix 1968:244-5). Efforts to socialize patriotism, through stories of national heroes and national
achievements, were especially important, because the children of the working
classes might someday be needed by the kings and ministers of Europe for
fighting. In later years, these two motives for maintaining public schools
mixed in complex ways.

The adoption of compulsory public schooling occurred more quickly in
some European countries than others. In the early-adopting states, like Prussia, free and compulsory public schooling was introduced in the early 1800s.
In these countries, political leaders maintained an autonomy from both the
Church and the landed upper classes and had at their service a highly profes-
sionalized civil service bureaucracy. In late-adopting states, like England and
France, free and compulsory public schooling became law only near the end
of the 1800s. In these countries, the state was very closely aligned with the
upper classes, and the upper classes were content to allow the Church to provide rudimentary schooling for the working classes and the poor (Cubberly
1922, chaps. 22-4). Neither early adopters nor late adopters expected children
of the industrial working class or the rural peasantry to go beyond a few years
of primary schooling.

Meanwhile, the upper levels of schooling were monopolized by landowners and the topmost layers of the merchant and professional classes. Indeed, the secondary schools and universities were among the institutions

most closely associated with preservation of the culture of the old aristocratic ruling class. Secondary schools developed as a means of preparing the next generation of the elite for a university education. Although "radical" ideas of extending access to secondary schooling were entertained by European politicians from the 1840s on, these ideas were resisted as encouraging "unsuitable" instruction for the laboring poor (Cross Commission, 1888, quoted in Archer 1979:742). In the representative view of Jules Ferry, a progressive Education minister in the French Third Republic, "confraternity" and "true democracy" required "a first mixing" of the rich and the poor on "the grounds of the school," but such a democracy did not require mixing to extend beyond the basic primary level (Ferry, quoted in Archer 1979:643). Fee requirements and entrance examinations that built on the culture of the leisured classes prevented all but a small number of working-class students from pursuing the academic degrees that were necessary for admission to universities. Only exceptionally talented and motivated lower-class children were sponsored into the elite (Turner 1960).

Strong vested interests naturally developed around the preservation of a very rigorous secondary and higher education requiring high levels of cultivation. The maintenance of educational "quality" in instruction was a deep commitment particularly among secondary school teachers and university professors (Husen 1965; Heidenheimer 1973). Together with their allies in government, they successfully resisted efforts, usually led by Socialist or Labor parties, to expand access to academic secondary and higher education. Even in a country like Sweden, which was governed by the leftist Social Democratic Party for most of the twentieth century, public education did not shift in the direction of untracked secondary schools until the early 1960s, and even then the shift was strongly resisted by secondary school and university faculty (Heidenheimer 1973).

Paternalistic versus Laissez-Faire Governments. One further distinction is necessary to understand the context of school organization in Europe before the era of mass secondary schooling. As a result of state paternalism in the German-speaking and some of the Scandinavian countries, the state and industry played an activist role in the later 1800s, providing job-related training to many who were not destined to continue their studies beyond the minimum level. This state activism was largely supported by labor unions and socialist parties, because of their interest in using the official system for reinforcing the working class and, by extension, the parties who claimed to represent that class. By contrast, governments in countries like England and France, which were dominated by the philosophy of laissez-faire individualism, largely left children and young adults to their own devices in finding work following school. This difference helps to explain the extent of the involvement of different European states in vocational training in later years, and how early European states became involved in organizing schooling with the needs of the labor market in mind.

The Premises of Democratic Uplift

In the colonial United States, literacy was taught primarily in the home or in neighborhood "dame schools." Laws providing for public schooling were on the books as early as the mid-1600s, but this public schooling came to be associated mainly with the poor. In most places, public schools fell into disuse or disrepute. Schools that taught more advanced subjects or occupational skills required fees. Apprenticeships, rather than formal schooling, were a popular means of learning trades and professions (Edwards and Richey 1963, chaps. 1-3).

Interest in publicly supported education for all children increased following the American Revolution, often building on ideas about the requirements for good citizenship in a republic. Nearly all the leaders of the American Revolution were advocates of free and compulsory public schooling for the primary grades, agreeing with New York Governor George Clinton that the state would gain "advantages to morals, religion, liberty and good government . . . from the general diffusion of knowledge" (Clinton, quoted in Welter 1962:24).

The 1830s and 1840s were a period of mobilization for the "common school movement." The most urbanized states took the lead in the development of public schooling, particularly Massachusetts and New York. Communities developed public schooling in a piecemeal fashion, and a wide variety of funding arrangements were tried, including partial public support to supplement fees. Struggles were fought with taxpayers over finance and with churches over control of the curriculum, but by the early 1840s, free and compulsory public primary schools were well institutionalized in New England and the middle Atlantic states. The spread of public primary schooling to the western and southern United States occurred mainly in the 1850s, although attendance remained spotty and facilities primitive in many communities (Edwards and Richey 1963, chaps. 9-10).

Public secondary schooling also got an early start in the United States. The first public high schools were established in Massachusetts in the 1820s and spread to other cities in the next decades. Very few attended these public schools, because admission was usually by examination. Private, fee-requiring academies remained more popular. Nevertheless, by the latter decades of the nineteenth century American educators (and also educators in other English-speaking democracies of the New World) were arguing that all children had a right to secondary schooling, sentiments that would not be common in Europe for more than a half century.

What explains this difference? First, no well-entrenched aristocratic or quasi-aristocratic groups existed in the English-speaking democracies to guard the universities and secondary schools as bastions of a status-linked high culture. (This kind of defense in the United States was limited to a small segment of the system: the elite private preparatory schools and Ivy League colleges.) The enfranchised groups were overwhelmingly small-property owners. The interests of this small-property-owning class, particularly when joined to the evangelical force of Protestant idealism, greatly encouraged use of state power for purposes of creating a virtuous citizenry. The Jacksonian movement helped to extend this spirit in a more democratic direction by advancing the idea of education as the right of all in a democracy. The pragmatic spirit of the small-property-owning classes also encouraged the use of schooling as a means of teaching economically useful subjects.

Horace Mann, the leader of the common school movement in Massachusetts, is a representative figure of American educational ideas during the period. In Mann's view, the current generation is "but the temporary keepers" of the property and civilization of the country. Because the succeeding generations must be saved from "poverty and vice" and prepared for "the adequate performance of their social and civic duties," those who "refuse to enlighten the intellect of the rising generation are guilty of degrading the human race" (Mann, quoted in Cremin 1957:75-7).

The goals of democratic uplift, advanced by educators like Mann, were often explicitly mixed with fears about the customs of new immigrants. Both primary and secondary schools were used for socializing (sometimes known as Americanizing) the more ambitious of the immigrant newcomers along the lines of the civic ideals favored by the country's Protestant and conservative upper classes. Indeed, compulsory schooling laws were enacted earliest in states with dominant Anglo-Protestant majorities (Meyer, Tyack, et al. 1979; Benavot and Riddle 1988).

Economic pragmatism also played a large role in the popularity of public schooling in the United States. Americans looked at mathematics teaching, for example, simultaneously as a way of creating a more rational citizenry and as of practical value in commerce (Cohen 1982). The ideals of civic virtue and economic pragmatism mixed easily in the minds of many eighteenth- and nineteenth-century Americans. The first public high schools, for example, dating from the 1830s, were meant to train a disciplined (but not overly cultivated) elite of young people for managerial and commercial careers (Labaree 1988). The idea of using schooling for practical occupational purposes extended even to higher education beginning as early as the 1860s with the passage of the first Morrill Act. This act created land-grant universities in several states for the purpose of providing practical training in mechanical sciences and agriculture for capable young people from all walks of life. No European university system of the time could possibly have contemplated a similar act. The intellectual elite that dominated the European university systems would never have considered the possibility.

The Rising Demand for Schooling

Those responsible for the development of schooling in the industrial world began from these two distinct starting points, but they encountered the same great source of change: namely, the increasing social demand for schooling.

This rising demand for schooling has been built, to a significant degree, on changes in the kinds of occupations produced by maturing economies. As Martin Trow (1961) first emphasized, expanded enrollments in postprimary schools were strongly correlated with the expansion of white-collar occupations. In industrial societies during the first half of the twentieth century, lower-level white-collar administrative jobs increased and farm and industrial blue-collar jobs decreased. This occupational change was accompanied by expansion of secondary school enrollments, as employers began to look for more qualified workers for the new positions processing words and numbers. More recently, the great change has been the growth of professional and managerial jobs. This occupational change encouraged the growth of higher education enrollments, as employers began to hire still more qualified workers for the new positions involving relatively sophisticated problem-solving skills and more specialized intellectual training. The secondary schools were once in charge of preparing elites for higher education, but they became, in Trow's terms, "mass terminal institutions" in the white-collar era and "mass preparatory institutions" in the professional-managerial era.

Occupational change is probably not the most important factor behind the rising demand for schooling, however. The sociologist John Meyer and his associates (Meyer, Ramirez, et al. 1979) showed that school enrollments around the world, in industrial and nonindustrial societies alike, tend to increase much faster than can be explained simply by occupational changes. At any given level in the schooling system, from primary to higher education, an S-shaped enrollment curve can be traced. At first enrollments increase slowly. Once they reach a "take off" point, however, they increase rapidly, leveling off

FIGURE 2.1

Enrollments in Industrialized Societies, 1950-70

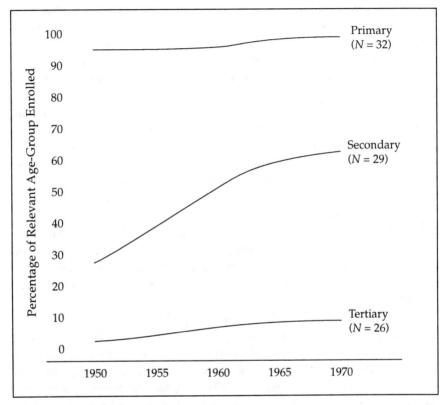

Source: Adapted from Meyer, Ramirez, et al. (1979:51).

Note: Industrialized societies are the wealthiest industrialized countries that won independence before 1945.

only once near-universal enrollment has been achieved. Figure 2.1 provides a graphic representation of the growth of enrollments over time in secondary schooling and higher education.

Thus, an even more important force than occupational change has been changing expectations about how much schooling is "enough"—and the interests of states in responding to changing expectations. The desire for more schooling can be built on many factors other than changing occupational requirements. Some families may begin to see more schooling as providing important social benefits, such as the prospect of mixing with a higher class of people. Others may see it as providing possible opportunities for economic advancement. These families will try to pursue strategies that allow them to invest more heavily in schooling. When enough families begin to make the sacrifices necessary for their children to receive more schooling, higher aspirations become a defensive necessity even for families that are not particularly ambitious. Simply maintaining the family's reputation in the community may require more schooling for the younger generation. Because most people hope that schooling will help them economically, curricula that meet labor market needs will usually attract a strong interest from students.

In addition, the expansion of schooling has often been encouraged by more abstract aspirations; it has come to represent ideas of progress and modernity. Indeed, John Meyer and his associates have argued that the S-curve pattern reflects the interests of both national leaders and ordinary citizens in embracing a "world-wide . . . cultural milieu" that associates educational attainment with higher levels of development and prosperity (Meyer, Ramirez, et al. 1979:52).

Governments have many tools at their disposal to retard and channel demand for higher levels of schooling. These tools include the use of fee requirements, the assignment of students into academic or vocational programs, the adjustment of examination requirements for admission into higher levels, and the creation of qualification levels that may become meaningful in the labor market.

In Europe, national educational policies prevented much change in the supply of places in the upper levels of schooling until after World War II. In the 1930s, for example, less than 5 percent of French students attended secondary schools (Neave 1985). The French began to reform their schooling system in the 1940s and 1950s to allow more students to attend and complete secondary schooling. Policymakers in many other countries, including England and Sweden, contained social demand for schooling in old structures through the early and mid-1960s. Policymakers in most countries added vocational tracks to prepare the majority of students for jobs rather than higher levels of schooling.

Very frequently, secondary school-leaving examinations designed for an intellectual elite kept the proportion of students going on to higher education at a low rate. Over the past two decades, the European countries have adjusted their examination systems to permit a larger pool of students to go on to higher education. In England, for example, the once famously difficult school-leaving examinations were adjusted a decade ago to increase the pool of students eligible for higher education and to reduce the high levels of school leaving at age 16. These changes have had the desired effects: Between 1986 and 1996, the proportion of 18-year-olds qualified for higher education jumped by 50 percent. And school leaving at age 16 dropped even more.

As the old system of class-divided schooling has given way, a new system of planning for labor markets has arisen. Governments respond to changing demands for schooling by channeling it in directions that they see as advantageous to the further growth of the economy and the stability of the state. If health is an expanding field, they will, for example, often build new health curricula or specialized institutions for health training. Private suppliers of schooling also keep labor market opportunities in mind when they plan new courses of study.

In some ways, the pressures for expansion have consequently led to similar changes throughout the industrial world. The differentiation of life fates now occurs later. Where children were once commonly divided by age 10 or 11, they now study similar subjects until age 15 or 16. Most systems now begin occupational streaming in upper secondary school. "Short-cycle" programs of one or two years connected to specific occupations have also been introduced in higher education, along the lines of American community college programs. Most systems also provide many more options for students to change courses of study and to prepare for critical examinations. Thus, we have seen a proliferation of occupational streams and options for continuing schooling.

Nevertheless, some important differences remain. Comparisons bring out the importance of inherited institutional structures, old social divisions, and concrete policy choices acting within the context of common pressures to expand schooling and to rationalize it in relation to the market demand for trained labor.

SIX SCHOOLING SYSTEMS

The best way to appreciate the range of formal schooling systems that exists in the industrialized world is to "tour" several of them. This section examines six systems that contrast in structure: the United States, Germany, Japan, France, Sweden, and England. Together, these systems illustrate a range of educational possibilities in industrialized societies.[3]

Today, all industrial societies have essentially universal schooling in the primary and lower secondary grades. In other words, all children attend school at least through age 15 or 16. All these societies also offer reasonably similar curricula for elementary students, emphasizing the three Rs combined with quite a bit of character and citizenship training.

One important structural difference at the primary level remains, however. Some countries have central government ministries of education; others organize public education in a more decentralized way. France, Sweden, and Japan are examples of systems that remain largely centralized. Standardized national curricula, funding patterns, and personnel requirements are characteristic of these centralized systems. In other countries, financing, administration, and planning are decentralized either at the regional level, as in Germany and Canada, or at the local level, as in the United States.

Many Americans favor local control on the grounds that locally controlled schools may be more responsive to the particular interests and concerns of the communities in which they are located. For example, communities that prize diversity may be able to express those values more clearly in their classrooms than if they operated under a central bureaucracy. It also seems unfair to many people to penalize communities that want to spend more on schooling by making them conform to a central bureaucracy's notion of fairness.

Nevertheless, local control also fosters high levels of inequality between communities in school resources and staffing. Centralized systems spend essentially the same amount on every student, meaning that public school children in wealthy areas receive no more than students in impoverished areas. By contrast, in locally controlled systems, such as in the United States, per student expenditures can vary significantly, because the tax base to support schools differs greatly among communities.[4] In recent years, the richest districts of the state of Texas, for example, spent nine times as much on their students as did the poorest districts in the state (Kozol 1987:223). America's affluent suburbs frequently spend more than twice as much per student as the impoverished central cities they surround (ibid., pp. 236-7).[5]

Although this important difference at the primary level should be kept in mind, the major differences among schooling systems in industrial societies are found not at the primary or even at the *lower secondary school* level (grades 7 through 9, corresponding to the American junior high school years), but at the *upper secondary school* level (grades 10 through 12 and in some countries grades 13 and 14, corresponding to the American high school years). These are the grades in which students begin to approach either higher education or the job market. Major differences are also found in the organization of higher education. Five variations in structure are particularly important:

- The age at which students are separated into higher- and lower-track schools

- The proportion of students enrolled in academic and vocational curricula in upper secondary schools

- The extent to which vocational curricula are strongly or weakly tied into the labor market

- The number of students completing university-level higher education

- The extent to which a separate set of elite universities is directly connected to the top level of corporate and government positions[6]

The American and German systems represent the most distinct structures in the contemporary industrialized world. The American system is the most expansive and open in the world, whereas the German system is the most highly tracked and among the more restrictive at the upper levels. Like the Americans, the Japanese emphasize academic course work and college going, but they have preserved a sharply differentiated elite segment and a distinct although fairly small vocational track, beginning at the upper secondary level, for the least academically promising students. The Swedish and French systems are egalitarian in the early grades, highly differentiated in the middle (with a great many distinct occupational streams), and narrow at the top, producing relatively few university graduates. The English have worked in recent years to modernize one of the more class-divided systems in the world. They have greatly expanded the number of college-going students while attempting to keep more young people in schooling through the provision of "further education colleges" and "education and training" options. They have been forced to design a system all their own—one that most closely resembles the American system at the top while beginning to resemble the German system for those who leave school early.

United States and Germany: Schooling Opposites

Among the wealthiest countries in the industrial world, no schooling systems are as different as the U.S. and German systems. The differences between the two systems are significant from bottom to top. The Americans offer largely academic schooling through high school and send large numbers of students on to higher education. They have the highest college graduation rates in the developed world. The Germans divide children at an early age, provide for vocational apprenticeships for a near majority at the upper secondary level, and graduate half as many young people from university-level education as the Americans do.

German schoolchildren are divided at the age of 10 among three distinct kinds of schools stratified by the degree of "academic esteem" in which the schools (and, therefore, the students) are held (Lehmann 1994). The *Hauptschule* is designed for children who, it is thought, will eventually work in blue-collar, crafts, and lower-level service jobs. The *Realschule* is designed for children who, it is expected, will eventually work in more routine white-collar and technical jobs. The *Gymnasium* alone is for academic study leading to the university and eventually to the more intellectual professions and to executive management.

At the end of the lower secondary years, students receive certificates that allow them to continue schooling or to move into the apprenticeship system.

Three tracks remain: most students from *Gymnasium* continue their general education studies in preparation for the *Abitur* and the university; most students from *Realschule* go into full-time vocational training or enter the "dual system" of apprenticeship training; and most students from *Hauptschule* move into apprenticeships. The most distinctive part of German schooling is the dual system of apprenticeship training. In this system, students spend part of their time working in apprenticeships to learn a trade and part of their time in continuation schools funded by the state. This system has helped to produce skill levels among German workers that have engaged the attention of the rest of the industrialized world. The German system has even become a model for some business-oriented reformers in the United States, who feel that it would serve the interests of many American high school students better than the general education curriculum emphasized in most American high schools.

A passing mark on the *Abitur* signals successful completion of secondary school and provides the necessary admission ticket to higher education. The elite quarter of German students who pass the examination are entitled to enroll in any German university and (with a few exceptions) in any field of study they desire. In this sense, higher education institutions differentiate among students barely at all. Students who make it through academic training in secondary school are considered to have demonstrated their maturity for higher-level study. This situation contrasts markedly with the American system, which is much more open but makes no such confident assumptions about the readiness of students for higher-level study (Teichler 1985; Lehmann 1994).

As in most of Europe, higher education in Germany is publicly supported and tuition free. Even so, less than one-quarter of young people enter one of only 325 institutions of higher learning in the country (Organization for Economic Cooperation and Development [OECD] 1996:279). More than half of these are technical colleges, or *Fachhochschulen*, with shorter degree programs, similar to American community colleges.[7] These technical colleges have been a center of growth in recent years. The first university degree is supposed to take four years, but most students take five years or more to finish it. Less than 15 percent of the age group receive their university diplomas. (Because university students begin their studies later in Germany than in the United States, it is possible to argue that the university diploma is more like an American master's degree than like an American bachelor's degree. This makes the 15 percent figure look rather more impressive.) In Germany, university education is strongly oriented to the arts and sciences, and all German universities are considered equal to one another. Thus, tracking in German secondary schooling allows for a relatively undifferentiated and equal structure of higher education.

Consider the contrasts with the American system. American primary and lower secondary schools are largely untracked. Nearly all American high schools do offer vocational courses, and some have formal vocational tracks. However, vocational courses are weakly connected to jobs, and many wage incentives exist for high school graduates to continue their schooling in two- or four-year colleges. The great majority of students are in the "general" or "college preparatory" tracks or take course work mainly in these areas. No high school graduates are barred by their course of study from continuing their schooling after high school.

From the beginning of the American republic, weak state control over higher education made it relatively easy for a wide variety of groups to open colleges. American higher education now includes a wide range of institutions, from religious colleges of a few hundred students to public universities of 50,000 or more. Altogether, there are some 2,000 four-year colleges and universities and another 1,500 two-year colleges—10 times as many institutions for a population only 3.5 times as large as the German population. Each of the institutions competes for new students, thereby encouraging college attendance. Not surprisingly, a higher proportion of American students go on to higher education than anywhere else in the world. About 40 percent of high school students enter four-year colleges and universities, and another 20 percent enter two-year community colleges. Not everyone survives, of course, but more than 30 percent of the college-age group do now graduate with a bachelor's degree. (A similar "supply side" argument can be made that the extraordinary diversity of religious organizations in the United States encourages higher levels of religious socialization among Americans than would otherwise occur.)

In the United States, students can study a rich array of practical, job-related subjects in college, as well as the standard liberal arts and sciences courses. Students often wait until college to begin to make serious decisions about their work lives. In contrast to the German system, the largely untracked structure of American secondary schooling leads to a highly stratified system of higher education and pushes the hard decisions about career preparation—and the differentiation of life fates—back into the college years for the majority of students (Allmendinger 1989).

The U.S. and German systems are not alone at the poles of schooling organization in the contemporary industrial world. The Canadian schooling system resembles the American system; it too has a comprehensive and academically oriented upper secondary level and a relatively large proportion of high school graduates continuing into higher education (OECD 1996:260-2). Correspondingly, the Austrians, who are geographically and culturally close to the

Germans, have created a structure of schooling that is very similar to the German system and, in fact, produces an even smaller proportion of university graduates (OECD 1996:253-5).

• • • • • • • • • • • • •

THE GERMAN "DUAL SYSTEM" OF APPRENTICESHIP TRAINING

In Germany, tracking begins at age 10 and schooling opportunities are limited for those in the lower tracks. Yet, oddly enough, German workers at all levels enjoy greater income equity than the workers in most industrial societies, including the United States. One important reason for this equity is Germany's dual system. The system is dual because it combines further schooling and on-site apprenticeship training for a near-majority of German youths above the age of 15.

Compulsory schooling ends in Germany at age 15. Not long ago, some 60 percent of German youths moved into the dual system at the end of compulsory schooling, but today the proportion is under half. Most of these apprenticeship programs run for two or three years. They include training for a great variety of occupations, from auto mechanics to banking, though the great majority are in the skilled blue-collar occupations. A typical week includes three or four days of work with a company and one or two days in a local vocational school. Some companies operate on-site schools. The schools emphasize practical skills but include academic material related to these practical skills. McKernan (1994) reported on one lesson involving a procedure for bending metal. While the students were learning this procedure, the teacher was also writing on the board the formulas related to the stress capabilities of the metal. Classroom learning also includes continued exposure to subjects that would be found in an American high school—languages, math, and social studies.

Apprenticeship students are paid an allowance equivalent to 20 to 25 percent of the full wage paid to a journeyman worker. An allowance between $500 and $800 per month is not much to live on, but it is adequate for the large proportion of apprenticeship students who continue to live in their parents' home.

Training under the dual system is meant to be broad, and students in the course of their training usually rotate through a number of jobs. Even so, the upward mobility of German workers with apprenticeship credentials is more limited than in many other industrial countries. The relatively restricted mobility of German workers is compensated by the high wages that prevail in German industry. Many argue that these wages are fair given the high levels of skill typical of workers trained in the dual system.

The high skill levels might also help to explain the historically strong popularity of the system with German employers. All the major industrial and commercial firms take part in the apprenticeship system, even though they have no financial incentive for doing so. Companies support apprenticeship training through dues they pay to one of two national business associations. Apprentices are not required to stay with the companies that train them, and indeed most leave their companies within a year of leaving the apprenticeship program (Maurice, Sellier, and Silvestre 1986). In recent years, the system has come under criticism by employers and some social scientists, primarily for its lack of flexibility (Blossfeld 1992).

•••

Japan: American Style Expansion with Distinct Layers

Since the Westernizing Meiji Restoration in the 1860s, Japanese schooling has sought to combine an Eastern spirit with Western organization and technology (Cummings 1985). Although both Germany and the United States served as models at different times, Japanese schooling has ended up more closely resembling the American system. It is academic in orientation at the upper secondary level, and a large number of Japanese students go on to higher education. As in the United States, most who go on finish their degrees. However, the Japanese have retained a small, but sharply differentiated, vocational sector in their upper secondary schools, and a highly differentiated elite track in higher education.

Early childhood is regarded as an age of innocence, and young children are doted on in a self-conscious effort to build up feelings of trust. At age six, schooling becomes a more intense and organized affair. The primary and lower secondary grades are entirely academic and untracked. The system is centrally controlled; therefore, curriculum, teacher recruitment and pay, and per student expenditures are all equalized across communities.

In the equivalent of the American high school years, Japanese schooling provides academic education for the great majority. Three-quarters of upper secondary school students pursue the academic studies that theoretically permit them to go on to higher education. High schools vary in reputation, and parents try to enroll their children in the best school they can. High schools provide different quality preparation for university entrance examinations (Rosenbaum and Kariya 1989). Ten percent of students drop out during their upper secondary school years, and a relatively small vocational school track exists for the 10-15 percent students who do poorly in their lower secondary school studies. Vocational schools often have direct links to employers.

Access to higher education is controlled by examination. The most important tests are secondary school-leaving examinations, which establish students' eligibility for higher education. Students are also required to take university admission tests to gain entry into particular universities and departments. In spite of the rigorous requirements of testing, larger numbers of Japanese students are now attending both non-university-level higher education (for occupationally relevant training and credentials) and university-level higher education. Over 50 percent of Japanese students go on to higher education—almost as high a proportion as in the United States. In the United States, most enroll in colleges and universities, but in Japan, the majority enrolls in short-cycle occupational training colleges not unlike American community colleges. These enrollments are highly gender based; women are still very much "second class" academic citizens. Over 90 percent of two-year college students are women, and four-year college attendance, even among very good female students, is still not typical.

Of the 25 percent of 18- to 21-year-olds who enroll in universities, nearly all complete their degrees, giving Japan (together with the United States, Australia, Canada, New Zealand, England, and Korea) one of the highest university-level graduation rates in the industrialized world.

The Japanese also maintain a small, elite system of top-ranked public universities for training future corporate and government leaders. These elite public universities are much more exclusively tied to top positions in Japanese society than are such selective American colleges and universities as Harvard, Yale, and Princeton. In the United States, it is not uncommon for a graduate of a less selective institution to become a corporate CEO or top government official; in Japan, this would be a rare event. The apex of this system is Tokyo University. The admission ticket to the best universities and therefore to the occupational elite is outstanding performance on the most demanding of all university admissions tests (Shields 1992; Kanaga 1994).

Although the Japanese schooling structure is comparable in many respects to the American structure, student achievement is generally higher, especially in the most demanding fields of study. Japanese families materially support and morally enforce expectations that children will work hard and achieve good marks in school. Family pride is very much connected to the school performance of children, particularly male children. School is a central interest in Japanese families, and nonworking mothers, who are the majority, often buy their children's textbooks so that they can know exactly what their children are studying (White 1987). The large family expenditures on education—some one-third of total family spending—are perhaps the best indicator of the motivational push provided by the Japanese family (Shields 1992).

Teaching methods also have something to do with the effectiveness of Japanese schooling. Japanese curricular practices emphasize in-depth study and relatively advanced topics. By all accounts, Japanese students concentrate hard in their classrooms, and discipline is not much of a problem in spite of the sometimes large numbers of students in classrooms (as high as 40 or more) and the rather repetitious forms of memorization and drill that are still common.

In spite of these motivational supports, effort would probably not be as high in Japan if academic performance did not matter so much for determining a student's life trajectory. Test performance is tightly connected to college and university admissions, and the college attended and field of study pursued are in turn tightly connected to the jobs students obtain after graduation. Particular colleges are sometimes closely associated with particular firms, and even where they are not, they are closely associated with distinct levels in Japanese organizational life. The Japanese "educational machine" works because of the unusually tight connections between school performance and later life chances and the central role that testing plays in this connection (Rohlen 1983). It is no wonder that Japanese students refer to the period of intense preparation for the testing that will so strongly influence their life fate as "exam hell."

Several East Asian systems resemble the Japanese. The Koreans, for example, have also greatly increased higher education enrollment and graduation rates in recent years. They have a higher proportion of secondary school vocational students than the Japanese, but not as high a proportion as most Western European countries (OECD 1996:297-9). Student performance levels are as high as in Japan for many of the same reasons.

France and Sweden: Egalitarian Bottoms, Complex Middles, Narrow Tops

The French and Swedish systems illustrate the most common way that European policymakers have accommodated inherited structures of elite secondary and higher education to the increasing social demand for equality of educational opportunity and marketable upper-level credentials. These systems provide strictly equal schooling in the primary and lower secondary school grades. In the upper secondary school years, equal education in both countries gives way to highly differentiated and predominantly vocational curricula. Although access to higher education has increased in recent years, relatively few finish with university-level degrees. Educational policymakers have used occupational streaming in the upper secondary and early higher education years to resolve the tension between increased social demand for qualifications and elite resistance to American style democratization of access to higher education. I have included two examples of this structure to bring out some of the more frequent variations within it. The French system is distinguished from the Swedish system primarily by its separation of upper secondary students into separate academic and vocational schools, by its examination system, by the increasing importance of higher education credentials in the labor market, and by its upper layer of *grandes écoles*, which are a separate elite track comparable to the elite public universities in Japan or Oxford and Cambridge in England. It is a somewhat more elaborated and upgraded version of a common structural skeleton.

France. For 100 years in France, the emphasis has been on standard schooling in the primary grades. (High levels of grade repetition maintained a check on quality. Until recently, over half of all schoolchildren repeated at least one grade.) Secondary school, however, remained the preserve of an elite. As late as the 1930s, only 4 percent of French youth were admitted to the *lycees*, the French secondary schools. These students were almost exclusively from upper-middle- or upper-class families (Neave 1985). The French began a long process of democratizing secondary schooling after World War II by adding a common curriculum in most lower secondary schools and by reducing the amount of grade repetition (which nevertheless remains high by American standards). By the late 1950s, Charles de Gaulle and his planners began to make inroads in democratizing secondary education. However, even in 1965, after 20 years of reform effort, only one-fifth of French students studied in the *lycees*, and just half of those were able to pass the *baccalaureate*, which alone allowed admission to higher education. The baccalaureate was widely considered one of the most demanding examinations in Europe (Eckstein and Noah 1993). The majority of students took general education courses (*cours complementaire*), which led to nonuniversity qualifications, or vocational courses.

Today, a small minority of French students begin occupational studies at the end of lower secondary school. At age 16, those remaining in school (more than 80 percent of the age group) are divided by academic aptitude into academic and occupational streams. They are assigned to different schools, *academic lycees* and *lycées professionels*, respectively. Teachers' evaluations are primary in this process, although parents may appeal teachers' recommendations (OECD 1996:275-6).

The majority pursue technical and vocational training at the *lycées professionels*. Students can prepare for a wide variety of occupational specializations in these schools. Well over 200 types of vocational certification can be obtained on completion of studies. At the lowest level, these schools emphasize work orientation for future semiskilled workers. At the highest level, there are specialized courses for future technicians and junior managers, and in the middle, highly specialized courses for apprentice skilled workers. The curriculum at every level of the *lycée professionel* is oriented toward work-related skills (Holmes and MacLean 1989:59).

In recent years, it has become possible for students from the technical and vocational programs to take the exam for the baccalaureate and thereby to become eligible for higher education. The road to the baccalaureate, which once led exclusively through the academic *lycees,* has thus become three roads. Almost half of successful candidates now come either from technical (30 percent) or vocational (15 percent) programs (OECD 1996:275). Combined with larger age cohorts, the new options have led to 10 times as many 17- and 18-year-olds taking the baccalaureate examination as did in 1960. Even with pass rates that have remained relatively constant at 65 percent, the proportion eligible for higher education has shot up proportionately—from 50,000 to some 500,000.

Higher education credentials are becoming increasingly important in the labor market, and more than a third of students in the age group now enroll in higher education. However, most study in short-cycle programs of two or three years, or drop out before completing the work for their diplomas in general university studies. Thus, occupational streaming now cuts across institutional lines; occupational programs in secondary school frequently lead to more occupational training in higher education.

Like the German system, the French system yields relatively few university-level graduates; only 15 percent of the age group finish higher degrees— in other words, half as high a proportion as in the United States and about the same proportion as in Germany. Most academic degree programs are four years or longer, and these long degree programs discourage students from completing degrees, even if they are eligible to do so. Students can exit programs with lower-level credentials after the second and third years. These credentials help in the labor market and are a compensation for those who lack the means or the encouragement to continue. What appears to be American style expansion of higher education therefore turns out to be compatible with German levels of restrictiveness in the numbers of university graduates.

As access to higher education has become less elite, a new internal stratification has developed between scientific and nonscientific specialties. The old literary and humanist culture, which once formed the foundations of elite French schooling, is becoming less popular. Today, the scientific disciplines have the highest prestige and also attract students from the highest socioeconomic backgrounds (Neave 1985).

The top 10 percent of upper secondary school students compete for a rarer prize. Following an extra year or two of preparation, they take the extremely demanding *concours* examination, which alone allows for admission to the *grandes écoles*. The *grandes écoles* are far more important in French society than the Ivy League colleges and universities are in American society. Most of the *grandes écoles* were established during the reign of Napoleon as a way of training elite leadership for the civil service. The *grandes écoles* train students for specific areas, such as engineering and business administration. The state civil service continues to absorb a large proportion of the best students. Graduation from one of the *grandes écoles* more or less guarantees a life in one of the command posts of French society (Suleiman 1978; Neave 1985).

Sweden. Egalitarian reforms at the primary level came later to Sweden than to France. Swedish policymakers abandoned a highly class-divided system of primary and secondary schooling in the 1950s and 1960s under the leadership of Social Democratic reformers. At the primary and lower secondary level, Sweden is now among the most egalitarian of all industrialized societies, making special efforts to provide equal schooling for the major ethnic minority, the Lapps, and for rural students (Swedish Institute 1996). As in France, highly egalitarian policies are possible because of national-level control of curriculum, teacher recruitment and pay, and per student expenditures.

Instead of dividing upper secondary students into separate schools, the Swedish system keeps all students together in "comprehensive" upper secondary schools, the *gymnasieskola*. This allows for somewhat more switching from program to program than is typical in France (Marklund 1994). Even so, the overall emphasis is on differentiation. In fact, the *gymnasieskola* represent one of the most refined streaming systems in the industrialized world. They begin somewhat later than elsewhere in the industrial world (at age 16 or 17) and can continue (depending on course of study) through age 20. The schools were at one time organized into 25 curricular streams—all under one roof— only 6 of which were predominantly academic. These have recently been replaced by 16 programs, only 2 of which are primarily academic. The vocational programs range from vehicle repair and construction to graphic media and business administration (Swedish Institute 1995).

Both rates of college going and rates of university graduation are similar in Sweden to those in France. Approximately 35 percent of the age group will at one time or another enroll in higher education, but only about 15 percent finish university-level degrees. In Sweden, upper secondary school credentials remain more important in the labor market than higher education credentials. Many students who enroll in higher education take only a course or two to improve their upper secondary school qualifications. *Numerus clausus,* or bureaucratically set entry levels, limit enrollment in many fields to numbers that can be easily absorbed by the labor market.

Swedish universities do not offer a separate elite track. Instead, they are modeled along the lines of the unstratified German universities. They are theoretically equal in standing and are expected to admit any qualified student for whom a place is available.[8]

England: Modernizing a Class-Divided System

English schooling was once renowned for the upper-class ambiance of the elite secondary schools and ancient universities and for the "11-plus" examination that divided children among three separate institutional tracks at that tender age. It is no wonder that stereotypes of English schooling tend to emphasize the aristocratic character of higher education, dominated by Oxford and Cambridge, and the desire of most working-class students to leave schooling as soon as they possibly could.

These stereotypes are now badly out of date. However, the formerly class-divided structure of English schooling has created unique problems for policymakers attempting to increase the number of students continuing with their schooling through age 18 and above. In their efforts to bring the system into alignment with schooling in other industrial societies, English policymakers have been forced in two directions. For those who could be induced to stay in school beyond age 16, they pushed in the direction of American style expansion of higher education opportunities. For those who could not be induced to stay in school, they began to expand in the direction of German style apprenticeship and job training.

A generation ago, English schoolchildren were still assigned to one of three types of schools at age 11, largely on the basis of examination results. The majority of students—some 60 percent in the 1960s and 1970s—dropped out of school at the minimum school-leaving age and went off on their own to seek employment. This was by some measure the highest rate of school leaving among the wealthier European countries. Only the most promising students remained to study in the "sixth form" (grades 11 and 12) for the demanding General Certificate of Education "advanced-level" ("A-level") exams (Eckstein and Noah 1993:48-50). Those who passed two of these difficult exams were qualified to enter the universities, but fewer than one in five adolescents made it that far (ibid., pp. 173-4), and not many more than 10 percent completed university-level degrees.

Since that time, virtually every aspect of the system has changed. Beginning in the mid-1960s, the tripartite structure and the 11-plus exam were replaced with untracked comprehensive schools. In the 1970s, the government introduced the further education (FE) colleges to reduce the amount of school leaving at age 16. These colleges provided vocational qualifications and academic options for 16- and 17-year-olds. Not unlike American community colleges, the FE sector now enrolls an increasing number of adults and part-time students. In the 1980s, the government introduced a national curriculum to set standards for a unified, rather than a class-divided, system. During the same period, the government changed the secondary school-leaving examination to allow students with a wider range of course work to take and pass the examination. The government also established a three-year bachelor's degree and integrated the two tiers of higher education—polytechnics and universities—into a unified structure of higher education. Each of these steps can be interpreted as an effort to "catch up" with the rest of Europe from an unpromising starting point.

The results of these policies have been dramatic, although the shadow of the old system remains. Today, the school-leaving group is just under 30 percent. This remains a high proportion by the standards of most European countries, but it is nothing like the 60 percent who left school at age 16 in the 1960s and 1970s. The government now issues "youth credits" to all 16- and 17-year-old school-leavers. These credits provide access to apprenticeship and training programs in a variety of different forms. Some of these forms involve part-time school attendance and provide qualifications for jobs in the middle of the occupational structure. Others provide qualifications for lower-level jobs.

The FE sector enrolls a third of all 16- and 17-year-olds and an even larger number of adults. These 440 FE colleges—equivalent to grades 11 and 12 in the United States—offer a mix of technical, vocational, and academic courses. Many students pursue vocational qualifications for middle-level jobs and move directly into the labor market. However, approximately one-quarter of 18-year-olds who enroll in higher education come from the FE sector. Some adults also eventually enroll in higher education after attending the FE colleges.

Higher education has been correspondingly transformed in recent years. The proportion of the age group attending college doubled in the six years between 1988 and 1994 alone—from just over 15 percent to nearly one-third (OECD 1996:333). Today, only a handful of countries have a higher proportion of college graduates at the typical age of graduation. Thus, a system that was once among the most restrictive in Europe has become one of the more open in a matter of two decades.

The English have accomplished this feat by standardizing the three-year bachelor's degree (a very short degree program), changing the courses required to take the GCE examinations at the end of secondary school, and expanding the path to higher education from the FE sector. Each of these changes has motivated more students to aspire to stay in school for the bachelor's.

English higher education has remained highly stratified in prestige, however, with the ancient universities of Oxford and Cambridge dominating the top rank, the University of London following not far behind, and the old "red-brick" universities and polytechnics lagging well behind in prestige and resources. Admission to Oxford and Cambridge is by competitive examination. Like elite higher education elsewhere in the advanced world, these ancient universities, once known for their aristocratic undergraduates and classical courses of study, have become largely upper middle class, integrated by gender, and increasingly science oriented in the years since World War II (Soares 1997).

• • • • • • • • • • • • •

SCHOOLING IN THE FORMER SOVIET UNION

One of the more unusual of the industrial world's schooling systems no longer exists. The interest of schooling in the old Soviet Union lies in the purposes it served and the tensions that existed within it—particularly the tensions between a class-oriented ideology and the industrial interests of the state.

In the old Soviet Union, experience with manual labor was part of the curriculum throughout the elementary years, and both the brightest and least motivated students were expected to become competent at industrial arts (Bronfenbrenner 1970). Efforts were also made to socialize children into the norms of collective life. Most children's games in the old Soviet Union emphasized cooperative activity, rather than competitive activity. Teachers encouraged competition, but this competition was rarely between individuals, as it is almost exclusively in the United States. Instead, students sitting in a particular row of desks would compete with other groups formed in the same way. In this way, students were encouraged to develop norms of shared contribution to group performance (Bronfenbrenner 1970).

The structure of Soviet schooling was not much different from that of other European systems. Tracking began at age 14 and competitive examinations were used to allocate access to higher education and the elite positions that were connected to graduation from higher education. Ironically, for most of the history of the Soviet Union, schooling provided relatively little opportunity for nonelite segments of the population.

Indeed, schooling was more thoroughly dominated at the upper levels by the leading classes than were the schooling systems of most of the "bourgeois democracies." At least this was true for most of the 70-year history of the Soviet Union.

As is true virtually everywhere, competitive examinations for admission to higher education favored children whose parents had higher levels of formal education (Dobson 1977; Kerblay 1983). This de facto preference appeared to many to violate some of the principles of the "workers' state," and it led to episodic attempts to reform the system so that children from working-class and peasant backgrounds would have greater access.

The major example of politically determined preference was the Soviet "class affirmative action" era of 1927-31. During this period, Joseph Stalin changed admission policies in higher education to give preference to candidates from working-class and peasant backgrounds. Many scholars have interpreted the policy as an effort by Stalin not just to actualize Soviet egalitarian ideas but, more important, to build a cadre of extreme loyalists among the "new men" who were favored by the policies (Fitzpatrick 1979; Bailes 1979). After just a few years, Stalin's experiment foundered on complaints of educators and managers about the "quality" of the new cohorts of university graduates, and competitive testing was reinstituted. Other episodes of class affirmative action occurred under Nikita Khrushchev in 1958-64 and again under Leonid Brezhnev in 1969-70. Thus, educational policy in the old Soviet Union oscillated between overriding concerns with efficiency and overriding concerns with equality. Efficiency concerns, which promoted greater reliance on testing, favored students from more privileged backgrounds; equality concerns favored the situation of the lower classes somewhat. In spite of ideology, efficiency concerns came first for all but 12 of the 70 years of Soviet rule.

• •

Different Structures, Different Consciousness

In some ways, students throughout the industrial world are now participants in a global culture. Blue jeans, rock music, hanging out with friends, and the adventures of increasing independence are great attractions nearly everywhere. However, underneath these familiar activities lie some important national differences in outlook, and these differences are very much related to the design of schooling in different countries.

You may already have pictures in your minds of national student types based on books and articles you have read before: the cultivated British "sixth former"; the hard-driving, *juku*-attending Japanese; the seemingly carefree American. Some writers have argued that these national types are best thought of as products of a unique national character or of particular historical experiences. However, these national characteristics are in fact more clearly related to differences in the organization of schooling itself. Indeed, differences in schooling structures are connected to such diverse features of consciousness in young adults as the perception of status boundaries, the willingness to concentrate intensively, the extent of opportunity consciousness versus class consciousness, and even to levels of confidence about the future.

How can schooling structures be related to something as seemingly nonacademic as where people draw status lines? The answer is that lines of institutional demarcation are also lines of social distinction. In Germany and Sweden, where all universities are considered similarly prestigious, the distinction between the university and nonuniversity educated is what matters. In the United States, where colleges and universities are extremely diverse, status is connected instead to distinctive features of the college attended and to the relative selectivity of the college. In societies like France, Japan, and England, which have very strongly delineated elite tracks, the major status distinction divides graduates of the elite universities from those of the nonelite universities.

The kinds of testing and job linkage structures that develop in schooling systems also have an impact on student attitudes and understandings of the world. The extraordinary discipline of Japanese secondary school students makes sense because exams figure decisively in admission to higher education and higher education figures decisively in one's later career. As Thomas Rohlen (1983) wrote, Japan has built an "ideal educational machine" for harnessing effort:

> A simple but powerful formula . . . has dominated Japanese secondary
> education ever since the establishment of middle schools: the difficulty
> of a schools' entrance exams is the crucial measure of its students' talent.
> Employers choose to allow this criterion of school reputation, rather than
> an individual's grades or subjects studied, to guide their selection of per-
> sonnel for managerial jobs. Entrance exams thus become the route to suc-
> cess. (Pp. 58-9)

The tremendous investment of Japanese parents in the education of their children is, of course, another factor that encourages this intensity. But it too is connected to the strong ties between schooling success and adult status.

Surely, the cultivation and sense of superiority that once marked British sixth formers (those in the final two years of preparation for university) were connected to the fact that fewer than 20 percent passed the advanced-level qualifying exams that allowed for university admission. By contrast, the lesser importance of college admissions tests in the United States and the loose connection of schooling to jobs work together to blunt academic competitiveness in secondary school. In such a system, interests in popular culture and peer group friendships tend to fill the space unoccupied by academic pursuits (Clark 1983).

Not surprisingly, more open systems also tend to give rise to "opportunity consciousness" rather than "class consciousness" (Brint and Karabel 1989:220-5). American students do not experience any obvious blocks to their educational mobility, such as separate vocational tracks or life-defining tests. The sense that the future remains open is pervasive in such a system. The more restricted systems give rise to a sharper sense of what is possible for people of a certain social class. In much of Europe, the vertical vision of the upwardly mobile is consequently relatively rare, and a sense of identification with one's own social class more common.

A sense of the possibility of upward mobility through schooling does not necessarily translate into confidence about the future. Alexis de Tocqueville, a perceptive observer who visited America in the 1830s, wondered why "a cloud habitually hung upon [the] brows" of Americans, who were in the "happiest circumstances the world affords" (Tocqueville [1840] 1981:430). The openness of American society, Tocqueville argued, meant that ambitions were constantly stimulated and many a person's "hopes and desires . . . [inevitably] blasted" (p. 434). A sense of anxiety about the future is still palpable among American students, and it is connected to the open structure of schooling as well as to the general competitiveness of American society. By contrast, the German system of tracking greatly strengthens the connection of schooling to jobs and, therefore, may ease the anxiety that adolescents otherwise feel about whether educational preparation will have a rewarding outcome (Maurice et al. 1986; Hamilton 1990).

EXPLAINING CONTEMPORARY VARIATIONS
IN SCHOOLING SYSTEMS

School "systems" are obviously not designed in the same highly self-conscious way that, say, an automobile engine's system is designed. Nevertheless, it is possible to think of schooling in different countries as systems of interrelated parts. These parts would include, for example, the organization of tracks, the amount of filtering through standardized testing, and the strength of linkages between particular schools and particular jobs.

The parts of schooling systems seem to some researchers to bear a logical connection to one another. For instance, compared to more open systems, more restrictive systems might seem logically to be built on more testing, more student effort (because of the need to pass tests), and perhaps also stronger connections between schooling and jobs (Clark 1983; Eckstein and Noah 1993). Indeed, the studies discussed in this chapter indicate that policymakers can influence the flow of students through a system by introducing occupational options and qualifications, changing the requirements for key examinations, and adjusting the length of time to get degrees.

However, if we look at systems other than the American and German, the coincidence of structural elements is far from perfect. High academic standards would seem to go with low levels of higher education enrollment. But the Japanese, for example, have high standards and relatively high enrollments in university-level education. Moreover, in the Japanese case this unconventional mix is unusually effective. Conversely, the Swedes have been able to maintain a restrictive structure at the higher levels while encouraging openness at the lower levels and de-emphasizing testing throughout the system (cf. Allmendinger 1989).

Therefore, it would be wrong to imagine that a strong underlying structural logic forces the key parts of schooling systems to vary together. The most that one can say is that some loose affinities exist. Table 2.1 indicates how much variation in fact exists between the key parts of educational systems in the six systems discussed at length in this chapter.

To understand why the parts of schooling systems do not vary together in a purely logical way, we must examine how political decisions about schooling have been made in the half century since World War II and, no less important, the social and organizational context in which these decisions were made. Specifically, comparisons across the industrial societies suggest that it is easier to create large-scale changes in centrally controlled systems of schooling, because reform battles need only be won at the top. They also suggest that state efforts to tie secondary schooling directly to highly skilled and well-paid work reduce the amount of credential seeking at higher levels in the system. They suggest further that social factors, such as the strength of class and gender divisions, can influence the shape of schooling reforms by channeling subordinate groups into lower levels of schooling. Finally, they show that the most popular and powerful institutional legacies from earlier periods, such as the *grandes écoles* in France, become embedded and largely unalterable parts of the educational environment.

TABLE 2.1

Differences in Schooling Structures in Six Industrialized Countries

	Tracking in separate institutions	Equity in per capita spending		
Primary and lower secondary schooling				
Japan	No	Yes		
France	No	Yes		
Sweden	No	Yes		
United States	No	No		
England	No	No		
Germany	Yes (at age 10)	No		

	Percentage completing at typical age	Percentage of graduates in academic programs	Secondary school-leaving examinations	
Upper secondary schooling				
United States	75	over 75	No	
Japan	90	75	Yes	
France	80	45	Yes	
Sweden	75	35	No	
England	60	40	Yes	
Germany	90	25	Yes	

	Percentage of age group ever attending four-year college or university	University graduates as percentage of age group	Universities equal in quality	Strength of linkage between elite higher education and top corporate/ government jobs
Higher education				
United States	45	30	No	Moderate
Japan	35	25	No	Strong
England	35	25	No	Strong
France	35	15	No	Strong
Sweden	35	15	Yes	Weak
Germany	25	15	Yes	Weak

Source: Organization for Economic Cooperation and Development (1996:123, 173, 181).

Note: Percentages are rounded to the nearest 5 percent.

Post–World War II Politics of Change

Changes in schooling systems since World War II have been the result primarily of the efforts of governments to accommodate and channel a rising social demand for formal education. In addition, states themselves have been very interested in using schooling to advance national goals, particularly economic development goals. The major decisions have been whether to adopt the American model of general and academic secondary education for most students and relatively open access to higher education, or to retain traditional European tracking structures and, especially, more restricted access to university-level education. Most governments compromised between these two models by increasing access and equalizing curricula at lower levels while pushing differentiated curricula back later in the secondary school years (Heidenheimer, Heclo, and Adams 1983). Indeed, among the industrial societies, only the English-speaking democracies (the United States, Canada, Australia, and New Zealand) and some East Asian countries (such as Japan and Korea) enroll a majority of upper secondary school students in nonvocational studies. Elsewhere, the majority of upper secondary students are enrolled in vocational programs (OECD 1996:173).

Expansive tendencies in the U.S. system were already well established before World War II. Substantially more students graduated from upper secondary school and attended college in the United States than anywhere else in the world. In particular, the large number of colleges and universities already established in the United States before the war encouraged competition for students and consequently high levels of college going. American policymakers reinforced these expansive pressures by adopting social reform goals in the 1960s aimed at improving the opportunities of minorities and women. These commitments led to the creation of relatively generous financial aid programs and affirmative action policies aimed at increasing rather than limiting college enrollments. Few strong ties existed between educational credentials and particular jobs. This competitive situation stimulated a constant interest in higher-level qualifications and high levels of job switching.

The conditions prevailing in Germany following World War II provide a sharp contrast to those in the United States. In Germany, decentralization and a divided reform movement permitted conservatives to contain the rising social demand for schooling within a highly tracked structure. The Germans lacked a crusader who could push reform to the top of the agenda against the fears of conservatives about the quality of academic schooling and the fears of the well-organized left that a reformed system would lead to the more complete subordination of workers. In the more conservative German *Länder* (like American states), the idea of common secondary schooling for all students never gained a strong hearing (Heidenheimer 1973).

Most older teenagers enrolled in the dual system of apprenticeship training combined with course work in continuation schools. The success of the dual system has reduced pressures for expansion at higher levels of the system. The German example suggests that high wages and skills in industry are correlated with reduced demand for higher education, whereas low wages and skills in industry are correlated with high demand for higher education credentials (Maurice et al. 1986).

Germany remains distinctive, but it is becoming less distinctive. Even the Germans have increased access to academic study in secondary school and to higher education, albeit less than most other European polities have. The Germans have also found that the lowest of the three tracks of secondary schooling (the *Hauptschule*) has become increasingly unpopular and difficult to support. This track may fade out in the end. Moreover, in recent years, a debate has arisen in Germany about the costs and flexibility of "dualism," and some corporate and political leaders are now pushing for a complete or partial dismantling of the system (see, e.g., Blossfeld 1992). These efforts could push German schooling in the direction of later differentiation and more credential-based job competition.

In the mid-1960s, with the election of a Labour government, the British belatedly abandoned their system of highly tracked lower secondary schooling. However, they maintained a higher education system very nearly as restrictive as the one in Germany. Social factors largely explain this "halfway" move in the case of England. Class-cultural tensions were stronger in England than elsewhere in Europe, and school institutions reinforced these tensions. The secondary school-leaving exams were difficult to pass for students who did not come from highly cultivated backgrounds, and no provisions were made for more general or vocational training in secondary schools. Not surprisingly, working-class students abandoned the system as early as they could, and higher education remained the preserve of a rather narrowly constituted academic and social elite.

Since the 1970s, the English have engaged in a self-conscious policy of modernization, which has greatly reduced this legacy of class division without yet entirely eliminating it.

The transformation of English secondary and higher education is the most recent illustration of the importance of centralized control. In the 1960s, local education authorities (LEAs) were given leeway to decide about replacing their tripartite systems of secondary schooling with comprehensives and to experiment in other ways with schooling. Although most LEAs adopted the new structure of secondary schooling, some maintained the old tripartite system. The Thatcher government consulted with the LEAs, but simultaneously moved to centralize control over educational policy making. The result has been a complete overhaul of English secondary schooling and higher education since the 1970s: the introduction of the FE college sector and youth credits and apprenticeships for school leavers, the creation of a unified higher education system, changed examination requirements, and a weakening of the influence of Oxford and Cambridge over academic culture in England.

Faced with less serious social cleavages, most European governments adapted more quickly to increased social demand for schooling while continuing to accommodate the quality concerns of academic elites. They did so by democratizing lower levels of schooling while introducing highly differentiated occupational curricula in the upper secondary schools and later in higher education.

This does not mean that reform necessarily came easily. One of the leaders of the Swedish reform movement, Torsten Husen (1965), has described the ebb and flow of a decade of debate over whether to abandon the German style early-tracking system in Sweden. Similarly, parliamentary discord in the Fourth Republic ruined the efforts of reformers to democratize secondary schooling in France. Reform did not come until a new leader, Charles de Gaulle, had a substantial enough majority to subdue his legislature (Monchalban 1994). Nevertheless, once the battles are won in centralized polities, they tend not to be refought. Moreover, reform leads to greater standardization and equalization of instruction in the lower grades—something that does not exist to this day in the highly education-conscious United States.

In recent years, higher education enrollments have been allowed to trend upward in Europe in response to an increasing demand for professional level skills. This has often required adjusting requirements for secondary school-leaving examinations to allow students from technical and vocational programs to take the exams. At the same time, the value of the university degree has been preserved in different ways in different countries. In Sweden, upper secondary school credentials continue to be decisive in the labor market, and students are admitted into the most highly desired academic fields only in relation to expected labor market demand. Many students attend higher education institutions for short, occupationally relevant programs or to take a course or two to improve their upper secondary school qualifications. Other countries have maintained the value of the university degree by retaining long academic degree programs. Degree programs that last five to seven years are strongly associated with lower levels of degree completion—typically under 15 percent of the age group (OECD 1996:179-80). In France, a number of short-cycle degree programs and other exit points have been introduced into the system with the expectation that most students will take the option of leaving without finishing higher-level degrees.

The postwar history of schooling in Japan illustrates the importance of external models, at first voluntarily adopted following initial contact with the

West and later enforced by the American occupation in the years after World War II. The Germans were the most important direct influence at first, particularly in the reconstruction of higher education. The American occupation added to these elements a model that encouraged academic schooling for the great majority of students and, in particular, more equal opportunities at the secondary school level through a common curriculum. At the same time, external models were adapted to a preexisting institutional design: The Japanese, like the French, retained both a relatively small vocational track at the upper secondary level and an elite stratum of public universities whose mission it was to train top elites for industry and government. A social factor, the sharp divisions between male and female roles in Japanese society, has largely kept women out of the competition for the most desirable spaces in higher education and the occupational elite and encouraged a unique development of two-year colleges oriented particularly to the training of women.

Thus, there are no simple answers to the question of how popular aspirations have interacted with state interests and inherited structures to create distinctive national systems of schooling. Good answers are possible if we keep in mind the following essential elements: the two starting points from which contemporary systems developed; the strong social demand for more education that all countries have experienced; and the political, social, and institutional forces that have helped shape this demand into one of a handful of structural designs.

CONCLUSION

Schooling systems in industrialized societies have developed into a small number of specifiable designs. The American structure, like a giant missile staging system, provides a common boost upward for most students. Most students study general or academic subjects until they reach college. The tracks within stages are relatively loose and unstructured, and quite a bit of movement occurs among them. The upward propulsion carries large numbers into higher education, where for the first time consequential forms of differentiation begin. The German system, by contrast, resembles a branching system of train tracks that split a short time after the train leaves its originating station. Trains on the separate tracks carry approximately equal numbers of children destined for different kinds of work. Between these two extremes are systems that differentiate students later than the Germans but earlier than the Americans. Systems like those in France and Sweden start off looking like the American common schooling system, but place most students into vocational courses of study by age 16, narrow further at the level of entry into higher education, and radically narrow as students approach the stage of university graduation. The size of the layers in these systems can vary substantially. Some, such as the Japanese system, push children along together through age 16, and then separate them into a relatively compressed vocational track, a bulging middle track for students engaged in academic curricula, and a wafer-thin layer of elite training. Most systems place a majority of students into programs leading to vocational qualifications but allow movement from these programs into short-cycle higher education and occasionally into university-level higher education.

Contemporary differences in schooling structure do not result from any deep-seated patterns of national character or culture. Instead, they help to create aspects of national "character." Status identities, for example, are associated with the most prominent lines of school differentiation. Systems that produce relatively large numbers of privileged college graduates who are not otherwise differentiated by selectivity levels create status lines based on professionalism and expertise as important status resources. Those systems in which elite tracks are sharply differentiated produce status systems strongly marked by elitism. Other characteristic expressions of identification and emotion—from the extent of class and opportunity consciousness to the extent of intensity or carefreeness among adolescents—are also connected to structures of schooling.

These structures are largely the result of political decisions made by elites beginning from two different starting points and in response to the common pressure of increased social demand for schooling stimulated, in part, by government interests in economic development.

The two different starting points are the premises of democratic uplift and elite preparation. These premises reflect different class and ideological circumstances at the beginning of the age of mass schooling. In the United States, the dominance of the small-property-owning class supported premises of democratic uplift. In Europe, the dominance of propertied and cultivated elites in a more class-divided society supported the premises of elite preparation. These two starting points led to radically different levels of enrollment at higher levels of schooling in the nineteenth and early twentieth centuries.

Specific national responses to the increasing social demand for higher levels of education have been influenced by several distinct political forces: in all countries, by the degree of centralized control over public education; in Germany, Japan, and to a lesser extent Sweden, by traditions of strong state planning to connect schooling and work; and in Japan, by the effective control of the system by the United States (and its model of schooling) following

World War II. Choices about the shape of schooling systems have also been influenced at times by social factors, such as the strength of class divisions in Britain and gender stratification in Japan. They have been influenced, finally, by widely supported institutional legacies, such as the German dual system of apprenticeship training, the French *grandes écoles*, and the large and pluralistic higher education sector in the United States. Within these constraints, policymakers have been able to influence the flow of students through the system, for example, by building new types of schools, introducing new occupational curricula, changing examination requirements, and altering the length of degree programs.

This chapter has emphasized the differences that continue to distinguish national schooling systems in the industrialized world. Nevertheless, it is important to recognize that these systems are gradually becoming more alike over time. Virtually all industrialized countries, for example, require attendance of children for at least 10 years between the ages of 6 and 15 or 16. Most have, in addition, made efforts to democratize secondary schooling and higher education so as to provide greater opportunities for students from less advantaged social backgrounds. Higher education is a fast-growing sector throughout the industrial world.

It is also true that educational ministries in all industrial countries are interested in coordinating school studies with the occupational needs of their economies. In general, they tend to consider the workforce of the future as requiring higher levels of schooling. These similarities reflect a universal recognition of a state interest in an educated citizenry and in the connection of schooling to labor market circumstances. They also reflect the "revolution in expectations" that has been one of the fruits of industrialism and affluence. Under the pressure of these common forces of change, the schooling systems of industrial societies may tend to converge still more in the future. International organizations, such as the OECD and the European Union, have facilitated this convergence by disseminating policy and statistical information among member states and by promoting a common set of educational standards.

Chapter 3 will show that the governments of developing countries have many of the same interests and objectives, but their schooling systems face a different set of circumstances—most notably, greater levels of physical insecurity and economic need among students and many fewer resources with which to provide schooling for all.

Schooling in the Developing World

The developing world includes most of the Southern Hemisphere: Latin America and the Caribbean; the war-torn lands of Southeast Asia (and, at least for the time being, also some fast-developing countries in East Asia, such as Thailand and Malaysia); islands like Papua New Guinea of the southern Pacific Ocean; the southern Asia peninsula that includes India, Pakistan, and Bangladesh; the Muslim countries of the Middle East; and virtually all of Africa.

Some students in industrialized societies envy the rich folk knowledge of rural people in these less developed parts of the world. They feel that this folk knowledge expresses the more cohesive and communally oriented way of life of developing societies and that it is connected to the real needs of people who interact in a simpler and more satisfying way with their environments. These sentiments echo those of the French romantic philosopher Jean-Jacques Rousseau ([1754] 1964). Writing in the mid-1700s, Rousseau criticized the unnaturalness of urban, commercial civilization and exalted the greater sense of integration of societies untouched by the "corrupting influence" of civilization.

However popular these views may be on campuses in the industrial world (and, e.g., among supporters of Green parties in Europe), they have been consistently rejected by the leaders of less developed countries—and for compelling reasons. Most inhabitants of imagined idyllic villages actually live in destitute conditions, lacking the amenities of the modern world from indoor plumbing to VCRs. The reality is summed up well by the historian Daniel Kevles (1995):

> Stripped of the gauzy romanticism of myth, the pre-industrial village was for most people a place of exhausting and unremitting subsistence labor, harnessing men, women, and children to the mind-numbing tasks of farm and household. It subjected most of its inhabitants to local prejudices,

enforced ignorance, and arbitrary power, while leaving them vulnerable to devastating diseases and early death. (P. 4)

Under the circumstances, it is little wonder that modernization has been the great rallying cry of people in less developed countries. *Modernization* refers to the cluster of social processes—economic development, improved communications and transportation, the creation of progress-oriented mentalities—that are both the cause and the effect of movement from poverty-stricken traditional societies to relatively wealthy industrial societies. The leaders of the world's less developed countries have consistently seen schooling for the masses as a symbol of progress and modernity and a means of economic development. In the words of Sekou Touré (1965), the leader of the independence movement in Guinea:

> Man's social behavior and economic activities are directly conditioned by the quality of his . . . education. It is in order to free the youth of this country from all the social evils inherited from the past that [we] are anxious to develop educational facilities and allocate an important share of . . . [the] budget to educational purposes. (P. 125)

The hopes of people like Touré have not been realized very evenly in the contemporary developing world. This chapter considers schooling in the developing world in the context of the aspirations of modernizing leaders and the obdurate problems they face. The chapter concentrates on three major topics: (1) how the schooling systems in the developing world have been influenced by colonialism, politics, and indebtedness; (2) the successes and failures of schooling in the contemporary developing world; and (3) the complicated relationship between schooling and economic development. Some other important topics—such as patterns of teaching and learning in the developing world—will be discussed in later chapters of the book.

BACKGROUND OF SCHOOLING
IN THE DEVELOPING SOCIETIES

To understand schooling in the contemporary developing world, it is necessary to understand something of the impact of colonialism, the hopes inspired by nationalist movements, and the specific problems that hamper development: poverty, traditionalism, and physical insecurity. In more recent years, as we will see, these problems have lessened in some countries but continued or increased in some others. In the latter, very high levels of indebtedness have often limited the ability of governments to improve schooling systems.

The Colonial Legacy

Nearly all of today's developing countries were once colonies—that is, they were under the direct administrative rule of one or another of the European powers. The Americas broke free from European rule in the late eighteenth and early nineteenth centuries, but most countries in Africa, the Near East, and Asia won their independence only in the past 50 years. Between 1945 and 1968, 66 countries gained political independence from colonial rule. Thus, most of the developing world consists of rather new states.

Colonial rulers were mainly interested in raw materials, cheap labor, and acquiescent subjects. Schooling for the masses was sometimes considered helpful for these purposes, but it was a comparatively low priority. In the absence of strong official support, Christian missionaries often introduced formal education as a way of evangelizing the indigenous populations. Some improvements occurred after World War II, perhaps as a reaction to the racism of the Nazis, but they remained in line with colonial, rather than native, interests. Little technical or agricultural schooling was provided, and schooling was infused with the content and ethos of the colonial powers. It also continued to be racially segregated and unbalanced. At the higher levels, schools enrolled the children of virtually all of the rulers but less than 1 percent of the ruled. For example, of the 25,000 secondary students in Kenya in the years before independence, only 8,000 were Africans (Eshiwani 1985).

It is not surprising that the outlooks of rural people in this period were inwardly turned and parochial to an extraordinary degree. When the political scientist Daniel Lerner (1958) asked poor farmers in Turkey to comment on the policies of the government, the farmers looked at him with blank, amused, or quizzical expressions. It was impossible for them to make such a cognitive leap or to understand why they might want to try.

But colonialism did provide fertile ground for the nationalist movements that fought for independence. Typically, nationalist sentiment emerged first among the country's native-born elites, who had been exposed to high-quality elementary and secondary schooling and usually to higher education abroad. These are the people that colonial administrators depended on to help manage the native population and to support colonial government and business enterprise. Nearly all of the leaders of the nationalist struggle in the Third World— Gandhi, Nehru, Sukarno, Nkrumah, Muhammad V, U Nu, Jinna Ben Bella, Keita, Azikwe, Nasser, Kenyatta, Nyerere, Bourguiba, Lee, Sekou Touré—came from the gentry and professional classes and studied at the most important universities in England and France, such as the London School of Economics and the Sorbonne (von der Mehden 1969:72-90). Anticolonial ideas and sentiments, cultivated in discussions at universities like these, were among the perhaps unintended exports of the Western metropoles to their colonies in the rest of the world.

Continuing Problems

Measured in historic terms, life in the Third World today is improving at an encouraging pace. People now live longer on average than before, are more likely to have enough food to avoid hunger, and are more often literate (United Nations Development Project [UNDP] 1994:1-2). Nevertheless, modernizing leaders in these countries continue to be faced with resistant problems related to poverty, traditionalism, and physical insecurity. In some regions (particularly countries south of the Sahara desert in Africa, often referred to as sub-Saharan Africa, and South Asia), these problems are acute.

Poverty. Some 80 percent of the world's population is located in the developing world, but less than one-fifth of its total wealth (UNDP 1994). Virtually every economic and social indicator—trade, living standards, health, schooling, and political stability—shows dramatic gaps along the North-South divide.

Basic literacy, for example, is nearly universal in the developed world but still under half in parts of Africa. In industrial societies, completion of primary education is essentially universal; in parts of Latin America, attrition after the first year of grade school is 40 percent. Perhaps most noteworthy of all: Public expenditures on schooling per inhabitant are on average 20 times lower in the developing world than in the industrialized world. In some developing countries, school textbooks must be shared by as many as 20 students (United Nations Educational, Scientific, and Cultural Organization [UNESCO] 1994:36).

In every respect, the material conditions of schooling in developing countries are far worse than the material conditions of schooling in the industrial world. In low-income developing countries, primary school students may attend an open-air school or study in a shabbily constructed building that lacks such basic educational resources as maps, globes, science equipment, and library books. The teachers in these schools have less formal education on average than high school graduates in the United States. Students may share their classrooms with more than 50 other children, a good many of whom are chronically undernourished, parasite ridden, and hungry.

Even the better-off countries of the developing world have very large pockets of extreme poverty, but the degree of poverty in the Third World varies considerably from region to region and country to country. The developing countries of Asia, Latin America and the Caribbean, and the Arab states are not as desperately impoverished as sub-Saharan Africa and the South Asia peninsula that includes India, Pakistan, and Bangladesh. Indeed, it is frequently better to think of the wealth of countries of the world in terms of a continuum rather than a sharp break between rich and poor. Book ownership is one such graded measure on this continuum. In the industrialized countries, every inhabitant owns on average five books. In the better-off developing countries, every 5 to 10 inhabitants will own one book. In the very poorest countries, people outnumber books by 50 or more to 1 (UNESCO 1994:32).

Poverty of this magnitude is invariably a scourge of schooling. The differences are well illustrated by a study by Uday Desai (1991) of the factors statistically associated with school dropout in an Indian village. Living in a slum and not having educational supplies in the home were two factors—both obvious enough. But two other factors also stood out: not having bathroom facilities in the house and living far from a source of drinking water. In rich countries, we tend to forget how much simple physical energy may be necessary to cope with the basic demands of life. Parents of poorly nourished children are often unwilling to allow their children to attend school. This simple fact is an important explanation of low enrollment rates in the poorest regions of the world.

Traditionalism. Poverty is also associated with another impediment to development: traditional outlooks, which revere "the way things have always been." Edward Shils ([1962] 1975), a sociologist who wrote many articles on the role of tradition in social life, noted that the timeless ways of the past weighed heavily on the ambitious plans of leaders of the "new states":

> Fealty to rulers, respect for the aged, bravery in war, obligations to one's kin, responsiveness to the transcendent powers which make and destroy men's lives—these are [the] virtues [of traditional societies]. . . . [T]he freedom of the individual, economic progress, a concern for national unity and dignity, and an interest in the larger world have little place in the outlook. (P. 496)

Certain groups in Third World countries suffer particularly from these traditional outlooks. Women (and particularly rural women) are acutely disadvantaged in many developing countries, because their role is socially defined to be primary in the private sphere of the family, but entirely secondary in the public sphere (Alrabaa 1985; Robertson 1985). And in most of the Third World, rural populations are far more resistant to changing ancient ways than are urban groups. (People in rural areas often do not see schooling as having much utility for their lives, which may be the more important factor.)

Often the schooling gaps between these more traditionally oriented groups and other members of the society are extreme: More than half of the women in developing countries, for example, are illiterate compared with just over a quarter of men (Psacharopoulos and Tzannatos 1992). In Colombia, only 20 percent of rural children finish primary school compared with 60 percent of urban children, and in Guatemala, even the average male in rural areas has fewer than two years of schooling.

Poverty and traditionalism create the basis for a half-hidden, half-open conflict between schools and families. Children are valuable workers on family farms, especially true where farms are large enough to require the work of many but budgets are too tight for the employment of hired labor. Even in cities, young children can be important auxiliary earners for their families, or they may be turned loose at young ages to fend for themselves. (In the early 1980s, UNICEF estimated that 80 million children worldwide—equivalent to about a third of the American population—lived at least for brief periods on the streets.) Compulsory schooling may be entirely ineffective in the face of these economic incentives and social dislocations. Researchers have attributed a good part of the very high elementary school drop-out rates characteristic of many developing countries to precisely these factors. According to UN estimates, minors in Paraguay, for example, contribute on average one-quarter of the family income, and in rural Indonesia boys can earn as much as 40 percent of the family income as agricultural laborers. Another factor contributing to high drop-out rates is the disconnection between the experience of school life and the experience of home and community life. In her reminiscence of an early visit to rural Mexico, anthropologist Nancy Hornberger (1987) suggests several bases for alienation from schooling: "In the mountains outside of San Cristobal, Mexico, [I wondered] what the Tzotzeil-speaking children think and feel as they sat in the freezing cold morning fog, on unfamiliar school room chairs, listening to a language no one spoke in their homes, required to attend school by an unknown and distant state" (p. 210).

Physical Insecurity. Sheer physical security is also far more likely to be an issue in the Third World than in industrial societies. Physical insecurity can come from war, rebellion, famine, malnutrition, or epidemic. In Cambodia, for example, school enrollments were greatly reduced for some 20 years as an indirect result of the state terrorism of the Pol Pot regime (Kingdom of Cambodia 1994). The situation is not very different in other countries suffering from the devastation of years of civil war, ethnic conflict, or war with nearby neighbors. In recent years, these forms of violence have brought devastation—and cultural stagnation—to Afghanistan, Angola, Haiti, Iraq, Mozambique, Somalia, Sudan, and Zaire, among other countries in the developing world (UNDP 1994:31-43).

Children and young adults cannot concentrate on school lessons where they fear for their lives, or see little hope for the future because of constant warfare. Two U.S.-trained anthropologists, Adel Assal and Edwin Farrell (1992), described the disruptive effects of the civil war in Lebanon during the late 1980s: "[Many students] spoke of the constant sound of guns and bombs. . . . They related experiences of schools closing during bombardments and children manifesting physical symptoms such as stomach aches" (p. 278). Because of the constant movement of the population to avoid unsafe areas, many students were transients, and some of the best teachers left, often for other countries. The numbing effects of war showed up most often among the older children. "As students got older, school became more meaningless. . . . With the passing of play at adolescence, many of these young people seemed to be more lost than they were as children. . . . Boredom appeared to be the state that came with the perception that their lives were being wasted" (ibid., p. 286). If boredom can be defined as an irritated state of disinterest, this finding makes sense. Interestingly, the same kind of effects are seen in U.S. inner-city schools surrounded by threats of instability and violence.

Low enrollments and high drop-out rates are typical of countries in which the problems of physical insecurity are acute. Indeed, several countries hard hit by war—Afghanistan, Ethiopia, Mozambique, and Somalia—experienced negative rates of enrollment growth in the 1980s (Lockheed, Verspoor, and Associates 1990:24). Thinking about the impact of violence and disease in the Third World, I am reminded of the historian Marc Bloch's (1961) conclusions about the end of the European "dark age" and the beginning of European progress in the late middle ages:

> However much may be learnt from the study of the last [barbarian] invasions [in Europe], we should . . . not allow their lessons to overshadow the still more important fact of their cessation. Till then these ravages . . . had in truth formed the main fabric of history in the West as in the rest of the world. Thenceforward the West would almost alone be free from them. . . . [T]his extraordinary immunity . . . was one of the fundamental factors of European civilization in the deepest sense, in the exact sense of the word. (P. 56)

EDUCATION, POLITICS, AND SOCIETY

The structure of schooling in the developing world has gone through two phases. During the first 30 years following World War II—the immediate postcolonial period for most of the Third World—the basic outlines of and rationale for a Western model of schooling were widely accepted. Nevertheless, quite a bit of variation in organization and accepted practices existed. Some of this variation arose from differences in preexisting traditions or commitments to different development philosophies. In addition, the kinds of regimes that held power frequently made a decisive difference. Leftist intellectuals in power built on existing traditions to push mass schooling forward as energetically as they could. In other countries, the landowners and military men who held the reigns of power (either throughout the period or at least for many years) tended to be wary of the costs and the potential control problems associated with a more educated population. They were usually more restrictive than expansionist in their thinking about schooling.

By contrast, the second postcolonial generation (from the mid-1970s to the present) has been marked by the declining influence of the "politics of passion" and by increasing adherence to a new standard model of schooling designed for efficiency and equity under conditions of constrained governmental resources. This new standard model has been energetically promoted by international donor agencies and particularly by the World Bank. Although this model has become popular throughout the developing world, the poorest and most war-torn governments have lacked the resources and the capacity to do much more than aspire to conformity.

The First Postcolonial Generation

Certain commonalities in Third World schooling have existed since the first days of independence, because leaders in the developing world from the start emulated features of the "modern" and "progressive" schooling systems of the West. The sociologist Alex Inkeles (Inkeles and Sirowy 1983) marveled at the pervasive diffusion of a "standard set of concepts, institutions, and practices" that define schooling throughout the world. Even in remote and isolated villages, he observed, schools, teachers, and curricula are organized and act in remarkably familiar ways. "We perhaps take for granted this sort of standardization . . . in a railroad system or an airline," he wrote, "but that such consistency should apply as well in a realm which would seem to permit endless diversity [is] . . . notable" (Inkeles and Sirowy 1983:304).

The following are some of the structures and practices that conform to a standard pattern throughout the world:

- Public responsibility for schooling is a well-institutionalized principle and this responsibility is generally administered by a central ministry of education with a formal inspectorate to oversee the conduct of education throughout the country.

- Schooling systems in every country establish an "articulated ladder" consisting of preschool, primary, secondary, and higher education.
- Attendance is compulsory for several years throughout the world.
- Teachers nearly everywhere are formally prepared and certified.
- The administrative hierarchy of superintendents, principals (or headmasters), and staff is commonplace.
- The length of the school day and the school year are standard within a relatively narrow range across the world.
- The subjects taught in the formal curriculum had a surprisingly high level of consistency worldwide. Primary school curriculum everywhere consisted of approximately 50 percent of the time spent on language skills and mathematics, with language skills receiving the most attention. Science, social studies, and arts were given approximately equal time during the week—about half as much time was spent on each of them as on mathematics (Benavot and Kamens 1989; Lockheed et al. 1990).
- Formal testing is used throughout the world to measure how well students have learned curricular materials.

Inkeles's study of the world's schooling systems circa 1980 found a "marked convergent tendency" over time in nearly half of the 30 aspects of school structure and practice he investigated and a "slower and more moderate" convergence in four others (Inkeles and Sirowy 1983:326-7).

Why were elements of the Western model adopted so widely in the postcolonial world? Some analysts would describe this outcome as one face of Western *hegemony* (i.e., cultural dominance that benefits the Western powers). This interpretation is not quite right. As John Meyer (Meyer, Nagel, and Snyder 1993) has observed in relation to a study of the southern African nation of Botswana, "It is not obvious that the interests of [Western] agencies gain or that Botswana's interests lose in the transactions involved" (p. 467). Like the early promoters of mass public schooling in the West, leaders of the new states envisioned societies made up of individuals who were entitled to have access to literate culture and who could be socialized for active and enlightened citizenship. They also saw schools as contributing to national economic development. From these premises, some common lines of educational action followed. At the same time, it is clear that Western agencies and experts helped to disseminate forms of organization and practices that became part of the "standard model" of schooling.

Varieties of Schooling. Although a number of premises and practices were rather widely shared from the beginning, schooling in the developing world remained diverse in other respects. One reason for variation was that, after independence, governments often adopted distinctive practices of their former colonizers. These were familiar and accepted parts of the school environment for the first postcolonial generation. Thus, secondary school examinations in English-speaking Africa were modeled on the British O-level examinations, and only Anglophonic Africa had the distinctive British institution of the "sixth form" as a prelude to examinations (Foster 1985). In former French colonies, high rates of grade repeating were common, just as they have always been in France (ibid.). Some scholars have noted that students' levels of educational aspiration were higher in former British colonies of Africa as compared to former French colonies, and they argue that this discrepancy reflected the somewhat greater support for native schooling typical of British administrators influenced by missionary initiatives (ibid.).

Governmental policies on vocational education also varied, because some governments evaluated vocational education positively in relation to development goals, whereas others did not. The communist and socialist countries of the developing world, with their ideological commitment to manual labor, were the most strongly wedded to rapid expansion of vocational education (Carnoy and Samoff 1990). In some nonsocialist countries, such as Ghana and Zaire, vocational education was considered the quickest route to developing a modern, technically trained workforce. In other countries, however, vocational education had little appeal because it offended the status aspirations of upwardly mobile young people and their parents. Vocational education was particularly unpopular where national leaders had attended European universities and where upper-class social mores disdained manual labor. Even in countries like Ghana, which championed vocational preparation, implementation was often weak or nonexistent because of the desire for high-status curricula (Foster 1965). Many countries overproduced secondary school graduates in the postindependence period because the demand for academic schooling exceeded the development of white-collar and professional jobs in the economy. Both Egypt and India, for example, produced far more secondary school and university graduates than they could employ, and both, as an unintended consequence, became exporters of high-talent manpower to other countries (Harbison and Myers 1964:183).

• • • • • • • • • • • • •

THE HARAMBEE SCHOOLS OF KENYA

To this day, in the east African country of Kenya, a larger number of secondary schools are operated under community authority than under government authority. These *harambee* (or self-help) schools are unlike educational institutions anywhere else in the world. Whole communities pay for them through donations and self-assessments. They are operated under the authority of local religious or other community organizations. Some are assisted by the government, but most are independent except insofar as curricula and other standards must be approved by the Ministry of Education.

The *harambee* schools grew out of traditions of community organization in Kenya. Residents in an area would join together to provide private, voluntary financial assistance, materials, or labor for a project. Neighbors, for example, might contribute a few shillings toward the construction of a borehole, a cattle dip, or some other facility from which all could benefit (Widner 1992:61-2). When Jomo Kenyatta took power following Kenyan independence in 1963, he institutionalized the *harambee* system as part of his nation-building effort.

School projects quickly became central to the *harambee* movement. In most communities, clan elders, church leaders, primary school committees, and local notables became the focal points in efforts to raise funds for a *harambee* secondary school. The school committees used local materials and voluntary (usually female) labor to get the schools started. They collected donations and sometimes enforced levies on households and local traders. The hired headmasters to administer the schools and continued to contribute through donations and self-imposed levies for the continuation of the schools.

The *harambee* schools have fostered community pride and have frequently been more responsive to community concerns than would be true of bureaucratic governmental organizations. At the same time, however, they have also been subject to abuse not only by intriguing politicians but also by private speculators and nonaccountable headmasters. Businessmen have occasionally operated *harambee* schools as educational franchises, hiring cheap instructional labor and using fees for their own enrichment. Headmasters have sometimes diminished community enthusiasm for the schools by refusing to spend sufficient time listening to questions and explaining their actions (Anderson 1975). More recently, community overreach has become a serious problem. Expensive projects proliferated in the early 1980s, and these often remained half finished because of the financial burdens the projects placed on poorer residents (Widner 1992).

Although high standards were maintained in some of the *harambee* schools, they soon became a distinctly lower tier of secondary schooling in Kenya. Just a decade after independence, the *harambee* schools were attracting only the marginal secondary school students. Those who did well on the primary school-leaving examinations were allowed to enroll instead in the national schools, or, a step lower, in the government-maintained schools (Dore 1975:69-70). As a result, *harambee* school graduates often have trouble finding good jobs. One response has been the development of *harambee* technical institutes, but they have enrolled only a few thousand students each year (Eshiwani 1985).

If there is a lesson in the *harambee* experience, it has to do with the difficulty of maintaining the spirit of *gemeinschaft* in a modernizing society. Started in the spirit of traditional community, *harambee* schools quickly became a means of supplying the social demand for more schooling in a way that did not directly cost the government. They just as quickly fell to the bottom of the Kenyan secondary schooling system, and they also fell prey to a host of modern problems—from the intrigues of party politics to the speculations of unscrupulous business people to the unresponsiveness of hired bureaucratic officials. That they have nonetheless persisted is testimony to the adaptive powers of peasant communities to more modern conditions and to the ability of modernizing politicians to find new purposes for peasant traditions.

••

Countries in the developing world also differed in their levels of tolerance for nontraditional forms of control. In Kenya, for example, the government tacitly supported the *harambee* (or self-help) schools, which ran parallel with the official system and were meant to provide an alternative to government-funded schools. In most places, however, governments sought to bring all educational institutions within its control.

Populist and Authoritarian Leaders. The greatest differences in the educational policies of the new states stemmed from the social and ideological character of the regimes that held power. Mass-mobilizing populist leaders and status quo-oriented authoritarian leaders are no longer familiar political types to people in the industrialized world, where the institutions of market-oriented democracy hold sway, but they loomed large in the postcolonial developing world.

Mass-mobilizing leaders are those who make direct and regular appeals to the aspirations of the poor for a better life and attempt to stimulate the energy of the people for the purposes of nation building and economic modernization. Mass-mobilizing leaders have run a gamut from those committed to revolutionizing society completely to those content to make relatively modest changes in the life chances of the poor. The ideals that inspire mass mobilization clearly vary, but they create three distinctive types of leaders:

- Anticolonial and nationalist leaders operating in competitive democracies. For example, leaders like Mahatma Gandhi of India were motivated primarily by anticolonial sentiments and favored democratic forms of nation building.

- Militant socialist and communist leaders, usually controlling dominant-party or single-party states. These include socialists such as Gamal Nasser in Egypt, Julius Nyerere in Tanzania, and Jomo Kenyatta in Kenya, and communist heads of single-party states like Mao Tse-tung of China and Fidel Castro of Cuba.

- Religious populists, like the ayatollahs of Iran, who are now important in parts of the Arab world.

Status quo-oriented leaders are those whose highest priority is to maintain social order and stability. These status quo-oriented leaders are of three types: representatives of traditional dynastic families, civilian dictators, and military leaders. Even today, traditional ruling families, such as the Al-Aziz As-Sa'ud in Saudi Arabia and the as-Sabah in Kuwait, dominate many of the oil-producing states of the Middle East. Dynastic families also played an important role elsewhere in the developing world, particularly in Latin America and Africa, though they did not manage to hold on to direct power there for long. By contrast, civilian dictators and military men have repeatedly come to power in the Third World when elite interests have been challenged by popular unrest. In Africa, for example, most countries have experienced episodes of military rule, and in about half of the countries military rule has been longer than civilian rule.

The schooling policies of these types of leaders reflect their ideology. The most radical mass-mobilizing governments—those in China, Cuba, Tanzania, Mozambique, and Nicaragua under the Sandinistas—made extraordinary efforts to bring about social and political transformation through schooling. They mounted intensive literacy campaigns, set up thousands of adult education centers, insisted on the combination of vocational and academic schooling (including requirements that urban students work in the countryside), and restricted higher levels of schooling to concentrate on the schooling of the poor. They have usually engaged in highly charged campaigns of political resocialization to create "new socialist men" (and women) (Carnoy and Samoff 1990).

The literacy campaigns were among the most ambitious accomplishments of mass-mobilizing socialist leaders. The first mass literacy campaign was mounted by the Chinese in the mid-1950s at a time when some 85 percent of their largely rural population was illiterate. The Chinese did not achieve universal literacy, but they did, by official estimates, cut illiteracy by two-thirds (Arnove 1986). In Cuba, shortly after the revolution, Fidel Castro closed the schools and sent 250,000 teachers and university students to the countryside with instructions to achieve a fully literate population in nine months. Cuba was already highly literate. The official estimate was that the campaign cut illiteracy from 21 percent to just under 4 percent. (Some scholars argue that the costs of training were so high and the level of literacy achieved so modest that it cannot be classified as the rousing success the revolutionaries claimed; see Fagen 1969:54-5.) Nicaragua under the Sandinistas also launched a literacy campaign (Arnove 1986), though with more limited success. However disputable the official numbers, the literacy campaigns did make a difference in these countries. If goals are highly specific, methods sharply focused, and the population sufficiently mobilized to change, major cultural changes can occur in a very short time.

Most mass-mobilizing leaders have had more modest goals, and they have often had to live with the compromises inherent in democratic government as well. The desire to improve economic opportunities for the poor has, however, been a constant among mass-mobilizing populist leaders—whether socialist or not. As the economists Frederick Harbison and Charles Myers (1964) put it, mass-mobilizing nationalist leaders were invariably interested in "massive and immediate expansion" of schooling (p. 179). Mass-mobilizing leaders in the early postcolonial years spent more on schooling as a proportion of gross national product (GNP) than would have been predicted simply by looking at the wealth of their countries or the levels of enrollment they inherited (Garms 1968).

The policies of status quo-oriented authoritarian leaders provide a striking contrast. Dynastic rulers invariably have wanted to preserve traditional society as much as possible and to allow modernization to take place slowly if at all. They are typically aligned with the largest religious institutions, the large landowners, national and international business elites, and the military, and they are invariably quite distant from the aspirations of the poor. Civilian dictators supported by the military (such as the Duvalier family in Haiti, the Kim family in South Korea, and the Mobuto family in the former Zaire) have also aligned themselves with the interests of national elites. The United States supported many of these civilian dictators during the Cold War, because of their favorable attitudes toward multinational firms and their strong commitments to suppressing communist and socialist movements.

By contrast, military men have frequently come to power promising reform and modernization. They have sometimes acted decisively on these promises, as, for example, in Peru in the mid- and late 1960s (Stepan 1978) and, to a lesser extent, in Ethiopia after 1974 (Liebenow 1987). More often, however, after short-lived efforts to build support through reform measures, they have shown themselves to be far more interested in control and stability than in social reform.

Whereas most mass-mobilizing leaders in the developing world tended to see schooling as an investment in national development, authoritarian leaders tended to highlight the costs of educating the populace and to fear the independence of educational institutions. They generally restricted educational funding and, when they feared unrest, they also repressed academic freedom.

The consequences of authoritarian rule are well illustrated by the history of South American schooling during periods of military rule. Studies of educational expenditures in these countries from the 1950s and 1960s showed that under equivalent conditions, military leaders spent less on social welfare than civilian regimes did. Military regimes were marked, in particular, by rapid increases in social spending to establish legitimacy, followed by equally rapid returns to the status quo (Schmitter 1971). The patterns have been more complicated in Africa, where military governments often succeeded dynastic leaders who were even less interested in schooling (Odeotola 1982). Nevertheless, a leading student of military government in Africa concludes that "studies suggest better development under civilians" than under military rule (Liebenow 1987:153-4). As in Latin America, some military regimes had a reforming disposition at the time they assumed power, but lost it over time.

More recent evidence further confirms the relationship between authoritarian rule and restrictions on schooling for the poor and working classes. When military leaders came to power in the "Southern cone" states of South America (Brazil, Uruguay, Argentina, and Chile) in the 1960s and 1970s, they frequently closed down public schools in many urban working-class districts, fired teachers thought to be hostile to the regime, and reopened schools only gradually when loyalists could be recruited to teach and administer them (Hanson 1996). In countries such as Brazil, Argentina, and Chile, university enrollments were restricted, radical students expelled, dissenting faculty silenced or fired, and university autonomy in matters of self-governance strictly curtailed (Levy 1986).

One consequence of status quo-oriented leadership has been to shift the benefits of schooling away from the poor and in the direction of the well-to-do—more precisely, to those among the well-to-do who were politically conservative or disengaged. These regimes characteristically had a negligent attitude toward the poor and cultivated the wealthier classes so that they could stay in power. In countries such as Argentina, Brazil, Chile, and Uruguay before the movement toward democracy of the late 1980s, children from the most poorly educated families had no more than a 5 percent chance of entering a university, but children whose parents had university educations had a 50 percent chance or more of admission. Because higher education was well supported by the state in the form of free tuition and other benefits, but loans for living expenses were hard to obtain, the state ended up providing larger subsidies for the schooling of the affluent than for the schooling of the poor (Schiefelbein 1985:196).

• • • • • • • • • • • • •

THE "GOLDEN LIFE" OF LATIN AMERICAN UNIVERSITY STUDENTS

Until recently, the image of the university student in South America was very much like the image of the college student in the United States during the 1920s, when few attended—and those who did usually came from upper- and upper-middle-class families. South American universities were seen as places of cosmopolitanism and hedonism in the midst of highly inegalitarian social orders.

The image reflected the unusual circumstances of university students in Latin America, who have traditionally been treated with extraordinary largesse by the state and unusual deference by the larger society. University attendance was (and in most countries still is) free or almost free of charge. In addition, university students sometimes had an astonishing package of fringe benefits: "access to subsidized transportation, housing and food, free health insurance, sports facilities (often likened to country clubs), equipment, free language courses, textbooks, and tickets to many cultural events" (Schiefelbein 1985:204). The rest of society paid its respect to university graduates by addressing them with special titles in everyday life: *doctor, ingeniero* (engineer), *abogado* (lawyer), and *licentiado* (graduate, with the connotation of presumed knowledgeability). Graduates are also traditionally privileged to gather in guilds and unions to lobby those in power to limit certain income-producing activities to only those with specific diplomas (Schiefelbein 1985:205).

The "golden life" of university students would have seemed less unjust to many if the universities were open to students from all social backgrounds. In fact, however, children from high-social-status families were overrepresented more in Latin America than virtually anywhere else in the world. Part-time employment in university towns, scholarships, and loans were not widely available, making higher education too expensive for working-class and poor families. Those loans that were available required collateral that was out of reach of most families.

In addition, entrance examinations in Latin American universities were closely tied to class-linked cultural knowledge.

The golden life is no longer the same. With the coming of the new democratic regimes of the 1980s—and the new spirit of freedom—colleges and universities became open-admissions institutions in many countries: Anyone with a high school degree could attend free of charge. In Argentina, in the 1990s, nearly 40 percent of college-age people were enrolled in higher education (UNDP 1994). In addition, the World Bank and other international agencies have repeatedly called for reduced state support for higher education in Latin America, the introduction of income-weighted tuition, and scholarships and loans for low-income students. Some countries, such as Colombia, have begun to introduce modest tuitions, and other countries, such as Argentina, Chile, and Brazil, have debated the possibility of introducing tuition.

For other reasons, as well, the golden life of Latin American university students is under attack. As enrollments have grown, underemployment and low wages have become common among university graduates, particularly in nontechnical areas (Winkler 1990). In spite of rapidly declining of rates of economic return, students continue to enroll in large numbers in fields like law and humanities. Why? In part, it is because the technical fields require preparation that is generally lacking among secondary school graduates. But socially conditioned expectations related to the golden life may also be important. Students may simply be focusing on the traditional deference accorded graduates and the cachet of being established in a profession—not on the growing likelihood that they will be underemployed.

....

The Second Postcolonial Generation

In the second postcolonial generation, two distinct trends, leading in opposite directions, have been evident in Third World schooling. On the one hand, schooling systems in the developing world are becoming more similar to one another. Some of the convergence is based on the declining politics of passion and the rise of incrementalist "expert" planning. Most of the change, however, is based on the models of school policy promulgated by the World Bank and other donor agencies. On the other hand, countries in the developing world are becoming less similar in their economic and social circumstances, leading to decided improvements in schooling in some countries and stagnating or even deteriorating conditions in others.

The Waning of Left and Right. Today, both mass-mobilizing and status quo-oriented leaders are on the wane in the developing world. Communism and socialism no longer represent inspiring political ideals, charismatic anti-colonial leaders have become national symbols rather than active forces, and state bureaucracies in the developing world have begun to operate much like state bureaucracies elsewhere. Altogether, the politics of passion has greatly subsided.

Insofar as mass-mobilizing leaders can still be found in the developing world, the religious populists of the Arab states are arguably the most important examples. It is, of course, tempting to see these leaders more as status quo-oriented authoritarians than as mass mobilizers, because they strenuously resist change in matters of religious doctrine. Yet in regard to schools, they are far more like other mass-mobilizing leaders than they are like authoritarian leaders. Although they have added religious content into curricula, they have declared no holy wars on the secular culture of the schools. In fact, public expenditures for schooling as a percentage of GNP are now higher in the Arab states than elsewhere in the developing world. They either equal or surpass rates of spending in the developed countries (UNESCO 1993:13). Moreover, illiteracy rates in the Arab states, although still high by the standards of the developed world (particularly among women), declined very significantly in the 1980s (UNESCO 1993:6). Clearly, Islamic leaders are following the path of previous mass-mobilizing leaders, using schooling to foster the cultural development of the masses and nationalist sentiment.

Status quo–oriented authoritarian government in the Third World is also yielding, although not yet completely. In the 1980s, civilian governments took over in all countries in Latin America previously ruled by the military. These new civilian governments have seemingly consolidated the power of democracy, and in the process expanded opportunities for schooling. Some military governments in Asia, such as South Korea, have also given way to civilian control. Military regimes still control large parts of Africa, but democratic forces are making a few inroads. The most brutal and corrupt of the military regimes in Africa, that of Idi Amin in Uganda, for example, gave way to civilian control (Diamond, Linz, and Lipset 1986).

With the development of democratic regimes, incrementalist, "expert" planning has become the norm in the developing world. The premises of this planning, however, have been set by policy analysts outside of the countries themselves, and particularly by analysts associated with the World Bank.

The Role of the World Bank. Those who have tried to explain the remarkable similarities among schools throughout the world have usually emphasized the role of models drawn from the experience of mass schooling in the West and promoted by international agencies and international schooling experts. These well-promoted models provide a kind of cultural grid for the rest of the world (Meyer, Ramirez, et al. 1979; Meyer, Ramirez, and Soysal 1992).

This analysis helps to explain why so much similarity existed in the beginning in Third World schooling systems, but it does not explain very well why these systems have changed over time. In fact, the standard model has changed significantly over the past quarter century. The new elements include an increasing consensus about what kinds of resources and practices are necessary to improve learning, more reliance on private funds to support schooling, a decreasing emphasis on vocational education, and a widely accepted methodology for evaluating schooling policies. These new elements are largely the product of the research and advocacy of the World Bank.

The World Bank, headquartered in Washington, D.C., is an institution financed by the wealthiest industrial countries for the purpose of providing loans and advice to the developing world. Not only have the educational researchers of the World Bank accumulated large amounts of data about the developing world, they have also analyzed it in a rigorous way and come to conclusions about what works and what does not work in Third World schooling. Successful agents of change combine knowledge, a commitment to action, and access to the levers of power (Etzioni 1968). Many research-based efforts to improve institutions have the first two elements, but only rarely the crucial third. This is the great advantage of the World Bank's reform efforts: It not only has knowledge and commitment, it also has the clout to follow through effectively. In a developing world that is more and more loan dependent, its research findings are broadly comparable to the ideology of early nationalist leaders, and its power of the purse broadly comparable to the popular support of the early nationalists.

World Bank researchers do not see eye to eye on every issue, but they have developed a coherent framework for analyzing how schooling funds should be spent given a country's available resources. This framework combines a concern for the efficient use of resources with a concern for equity in the distribution of resources between advantaged and disadvantaged groups. The policy approach might be called "back to basics" at the primary level combined with "let the market decide" at the post-primary level. The World Bank has concluded that most educational policy making has been a disaster, with too much funding of higher education relative to primary schooling, too much funding of vocational education relative to general education, and too little private investment in schooling relative to public investment. It argues that developing countries have had the best results where

- Schooling budgets are allocated largely to primary schooling, especially where primary schooling is not universal.

- Subsidies to higher education are returned to the lower levels of society in the form of special scholarships for the poor.

- Resources for the unschooled are freed by reducing the length of compulsory schooling.

- Private schools are tolerated as a way to reduce the pressure on hard-pressed public resources.

- General education, which is more flexible and less costly, is emphasized over vocational education.

- Social demand—giving people the schooling they want and will pay for—is emphasized above the level of primary schooling (and in the poorest countries, also at the level of primary schooling).

- Wage differentials between graduates of different schooling levels are maintained so as to provide incentives for further human capital development among those who are able to finish primary school (Psacharopoulos 1986).

The World Bank has also expressed consistent views over the past decades about what kind of learning should be taking place in classrooms and how that learning can be enhanced. It has taken a consistently strong stand against vocational education as an ineffective and costly substitute for sound general education. In the view of World Bank researchers, vocational education is an inefficient and ineffective means of economic development. The major contribution of formal schooling to agricultural development has been through the provision of literacy and numeracy rather than through the development of "practical" or "agricultural" curricula in the schools (Psacharopoulos 1987). Quality in learning, according to the World Bank's researchers, can be achieved through trained teachers, adequate instructional materials (especially textbooks), increased time on academic tasks, exams to monitor progress, and provision of basic nutritional requirements (where possible) through school lunch programs (Lockheed et al. 1990). According to World Bank-sponsored research, lavish buildings and equipment, curricular reforms, and even smaller class sizes are not as important to educational progress (Gannicott and Throsby 1992).

Unlike most advocacy groups, the World Bank has the leverage to bring its vision of good schooling into practice—at least into the official policy documents that serve as models for practice. For the most part, the power of the World Bank is indirect. It advocates, but it is rarely so heavy-handed as to insist on conformity with its recommendations as a precondition to the provision of loans. Nevertheless, in their hopes of gaining World Bank support, leaders must take its model into account. This implicit power is supported by the direct contribution donor agencies make to schooling in the developing world. The World Bank is the largest external donor, providing one-quarter of all external support in the world, with annual lending commitments of approximately $2 billion (World Bank 1995:145). This is only a small proportion of the total, but its loss would be missed by hard-pressed governments.

The reliance of Third World economies on development loans, and their high level of indebtedness, is a still more important support for the power of the World Bank. A basic principle of power is that the more one party depends on another for external resources to survive, the more likely that party is to conform to the wishes of the resource provider (Pfeffer and Salancik 1978). Thus, countries badly in need of development loans are more likely to conform to the recommendations of donor agencies than those less in need. Those countries less in need of World Bank development funds—several in East Asia fit this criterion—are in a position to go their own way in schooling policy. Many countries in the developing world are deeply in debt, however. In the most impoverished countries of sub-Saharan Africa, some 20 percent of government revenues goes to debt payments. These countries spend twice as much paying off their debt as they do on health and schooling. It is not surprising that they take the recommendations of the World Bank and other donor agencies very seriously.

The World Bank's recommendations, based on years of study, seem eminently sensible, but room exists for disagreement. For example, although the World Bank consistently argues for freeing resources devoted to higher education for support of lower levels, the governments of some developing countries feel that students simply would not have enough money to attend universities without substantial subsidization. Many African universities are known to have good academic standards. Should they become much smaller and havens for the wealthy? Without substantial state subsidization, they probably would. Perhaps the World Bank's position makes sense given the scarcity of resources available to many African governments, but an argument can be made on the other side.

The power of the World Bank may also be problematic insofar as it directs all schooling policy along a single path. A single, dominating model can reduce variation not only in useful ways (by reducing the amount of wasted effort) but also in potentially problematic ways (by discouraging useful variation). Different structures may be better suited to different national circumstances. Much as in population genetics, variations in social systems can be important for the new directions they suggest, or for their more suitable fit to particular circumstances. Industrialized societies, after all, have developed a number of quite different working structures of schooling. These provide a useful range of possibilities to consider, as well as solutions that may be better adjusted to national circumstances than any single model, in all likelihood, would be.

Diverging Economic Trends. The Third World now includes both a large number of economic success stories and a number of economic "disaster areas." It also includes a middle range of countries, making more gradual or mixed progress in reaching development goals. Figure 3.1 shows historian Paul Kennedy's (1996) two versions of a tour through the contemporary developing world. One is a "cornucopian tour" through the "success belt." The other is a "doomster's tour" through the "disaster belt."

As economic circumstances have diverged in the developing world, so have some schooling circumstances. We can take the middle range of developing countries in per capita income as a baseline. In most of these countries, 80 percent or more of the relevant age group starts first grade, about half complete primary school, and 20-25 percent enter secondary school. Following secondary school, less than 10 percent, however, typically go on to higher education (UNDP 1994:156-7).

By contrast, the higher-income developing countries now enroll virtually all children in first grade, graduate approximately three-quarters from primary school, and send about half on to secondary school. The highest-income countries in the developing world—countries like Argentina, Taiwan, and Kuwait—may enroll 20 to 25 percent of the relevant age group in college, a higher figure even than some industrialized societies. Quite a bit of variation exists in enrollment rates in the low-income countries. In most, however, few students have the family support to stay in school for long—sometimes even to attend at all. Because of governmental budgetary constraints, secondary schools and colleges cannot accommodate everyone even if students did have the wherewithal to continue. The poorest developing countries, therefore, allow natural attrition, combined with primary school-leaving examinations, to limit the number of students continuing on to secondary school. For example, in the poor African country of Mali, less than one-quarter of all children in the relevant age group are enrolled in primary school, only about 5 percent are enrolled in secondary schooling, and less than 1 percent are enrolled in higher education (UNESCO 1991:67).

In the poorest countries, the amount of actual time spent on learning is also much lower. A careful study of actual school time in Haiti in 1984 showed that the official version of the school year was far from the truth. The school day often began late, teachers were frequently absent on Tuesday and Friday market days, and 48 public holidays were celebrated instead of the official 28. With unofficial school closings and delayed openings, the functional school year was only 70 days, 40 percent of the international standard. In a study of 15 village schools in India, two-thirds of the teachers were absent at the time of the investigators' unexpected visits, and the acting teachers "did little more than a keep a semblance of order among the pupils" (Dreze and Sen 1995:125). In Malawi, the school year is 192 days—higher than the international standard—but one-third of those days are during the rainy season, when the roads are impassable and students cannot go to school. One study of class time in a poor region of rural Peru found that only 6 percent of the total time that students were at school was devoted to academic instruction. The rest of the time was spent on recreation periods and sports competitions, waiting during adult meetings, time lost to teacher absences, housekeeping activities, and unsupervised desk work. Some social scientists see a correspondence between the way schools are organized and the roles students will play in later life:

> As can be seen in the descriptions of planting, watering, cleaning, cooking, child care, long walks and so on, Quechua children are expected to handle many practical, physical jobs themselves; correspondingly, they are apparently not expected to handle intellectual jobs, even with the teacher's help. (Hornberger 1987:216)

The Deterioration of Schooling in Low-Income Countries. Schooling in low-income countries has not just stagnated—in some cases, it has deteriorated in recent years. Indeed, the greatest force currently aligned against the standard model is declining economic and population conditions in the poorest regions of the developing world. As economies idle, debt burdens accumulate, and populations continue to grow, the state finds it more and more difficult to keep its institutions operating effectively. Those parts of the world that remain outside the standard model promulgated by the World Bank do so more often because of deficient resources and disorganization than because of ideas or traditions opposed to the standard model.

The mix of economic troubles and population growth has led, in particular, to increasing gaps between sub-Saharan Africa and the rest of the world. Since 1980, deterioration of enrollments and schooling quality has been a fact of life in most of the countries of sub-Saharan Africa. (Botswana, Gabon, and Zimbabwe are notable exceptions.) School enrollments have fallen as a proportion of school-age populations. Per pupil expenditures on schooling have fallen at every level, and much of what remains has been misallocated. Even the capacity to monitor what is happening has been lost:

FIGURE 3.1

Two Views of the Developing World

Doomster's journey

FIGURE 3.1

Continued

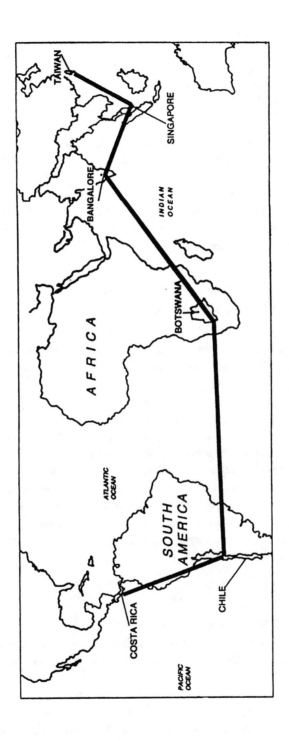

Cornucopian's journey

Source: Kennedy (1996:21-2).

> In sub-Saharan Africa, we are losing track of enrollments, of whether teachers are even getting paid, and of textual and other available materials. Is there any ministry in sub-Saharan Africa that can say that it knows more about what textbooks are currently available than it did 20 years ago? (Heyneman 1993:513)

Some deterioration in expenditures on schooling has also occurred in the countries of South Asia, although enrollments have not declined. These countries (which include India, Pakistan, and Bangladesh) are, of course, the world's other center of concentrated poverty. Because governments can no longer support free, public schooling, in some countries of sub-Saharan Africa and South Asia families are now required to pay at least token fees for use of the public schooling system from primary school on.

SCHOOLING AND ECONOMIC DEVELOPMENT

Key questions among students of schooling in the developing world are: How much is an educated labor force associated with economic development? Is mass schooling a necessary precondition for economic development? Is it more a consequence of development than a cause? Or is it a contingent factor—important in some cases and not in others?

These are questions that have been debated by development scholars for more than a generation. Until recently, two major theoretical perspectives existed concerning the role of schooling in economic development. One is usually known as *dependency theory*; the other, *human capital theory*. These are being challenged and at least partially replaced today by theories of *state-led development*, which emphasize contingencies and view human capital development as one important factor among others. The recent successes of several high-performing Asian economies lend empirical support to the theories of state-led development.

Dependency Theories

In the 1960s and 1970s, many social theorists argued that the Third World suffers because the developed world continues to exploit it even in the absence of colonial structures. Developing countries thus remain dependent on the industrial societies.

One version of dependency theory, the *world systems theory* of Immanuel Wallerstein (1974), argues that countries in the world are connected by the functions they perform in the world economy. "Periphery" states—most of the former colonies of the Third World—supply raw materials to "core" states—the industrial societies—where those materials are refined, combined, and assembled into products. Those products may be sold in home markets or in global markets, including the countries where the raw materials came from. For example, large quantities of sugar cane are harvested in some tropical countries and imported to the United States, where they are turned into sugar and combined with other ingredients to be resold to the rest of the world as candy bars and other products. The "raw material" states of the periphery are poor and backward; the "complex operations" states of the core are wealthier and forward looking.

Exports do not always improve the situation of periphery states, because most profits are restricted to the local land-owning elites and the merchants (who, if foreign, remit profits to the home country). Export earnings therefore provide precious little capital for diversifying local economies. A relatively few people may gain wealth from their roles as overseers and middlemen in world economic transactions, but most of the population remains rural and is engaged in small-scale farming either for subsistence or for local markets. Others are employed as cheap hired labor for multinational agribusiness, mining, or sweatshop industry.

"Semiperiphery" states lie between these two poles. They export some raw materials to the core states, but also produce some products for regional or global consumption. They are economically not as advanced as the core, but they are also not as poor as the periphery. World system theorists would consider countries like Chile and Thailand to be semiperipheral.

Dependency theorists place little faith in schooling as a force in economic development. They argue that low levels of school funding and enrollment are closely connected to the country's location in the world division of labor. International business most needs the Third World to supply cheap labor for extracting raw materials and producing some commercial products. Even nationalistic governments that wish to develop their schooling systems usually do not have enough money to do so effectively. Dependency theorists conclude that resources spent on schooling serve not disadvantaged groups and the poor but rather landowners and local and international business people seeking large pools of cheap but competent labor (Clark 1992).

It is difficult to avoid seeing one obvious flaw in dependency theory: For national and multinational business, expanding markets in developing countries are at least as important a goal as employing cheap labor. In fact, larger markets for the goods and services in which developed countries specialize will not evolve unless the populace in Third World countries have more wealth. It is also true that dependency theorists have not been able to explain very well why some countries move into the core of the world capitalist economy from the semiperiphery and others into the semiperiphery from the periphery. Nor have these theories been able to account very well for the different levels of development among countries that have very similar populations and natural resources.

The evidence indicates that rapid population growth, ethnic and class hostilities, and the corruption of officials have scuttled the development hopes of many Third World countries more thoroughly than the profit seeking of international business ever could. For example, the devastations brought by civil war and tyranny have kept Cambodia stagnant while nearby Thailand, a very similar society, modernizes rapidly. Conversely, far-sighted economic policies, useful strategic alliances, and determined and cohesive leadership have promoted development in countries where world systems or dependency theory would not have expected it. No better explanation exists for why the Czech Republic, for example, should be poised on the edge of economic prosperity while many of its next-door neighbors in the former Soviet bloc continue to flounder.

Human Capital Theories

Human capital theory, the leading rival to dependency theories throughout the 1960s and 1970s, was accepted during those decades by the overwhelming majority of development scholars in the West. Human capital theory assumes that economic development is possible for any country that is fully developed and uses its human resources. Education is at the center of human capital theory, because it is based on the importance of a well-trained workforce for economic development.

In a well-known book, *Education, Manpower, and Economic Growth* (1964), the economists Frederick Harbison and Charles Myers laid out what was by that time the conventional wisdom among development scholars who accepted human capital theory:

> The builders of economies are elites of various kinds of who organize and
> lead the march toward progress. . . . Their effectiveness as prime movers
> depends not only on their own development but on the knowledge, skills,
> and capabilities of those whom they lead as well. Thus, in a very real sense,
> the wealth of a nation and its potential for . . . growth stem from the power
> to develop and effectively utilize the innate capacities of people. Human re-
> source development, therefore, may be a more realistic and reliable indicator
> of modernization or development than any other single indicator. (P. 14)

To develop the innate capacities of the people, it was believed that public investments in formal education were essential.

Social scientists who studied the developing world during this period found moderate to strong correlations between a country's investment in schooling and its GNP per capita (Schultz 1961; Denison 1962, chap. 7; Harbison and Myers 1964). These findings were sometimes taken as support for human capital theory. At the same time, researchers recognized that some countries invested more in schooling than their economic level seemed to warrant and that other countries had comparatively dynamic economies in spite of low levels of investment in schooling (Harbison and Myers 1964). A good many researchers in the human capital school concluded that human resources development alone was not sufficient to produce economic growth. Harbison and Myers (1964), for example, wrote:

> Human resource development is only one of many factors which are associated with economic growth. The availability of petroleum and mineral resources, world markets for particular agricultural commodities, the population-to-land ratio, the stability of political institutions, social and cultural traditions, the existence of a will to modernize and a host of other factors are also influential. (P. 114)

Anderson and Bowman (1965) noted that pre-World War II income levels were a much better predictor of postwar income levels than were prewar schooling levels.

Later scholars raised new questions about human capital theory. Some felt that the less careful human capital theorists had assumed a causal relationship that the data simply did not support. Instead of investments in schooling creating a hardworking and skilled workforce to carry forward economic development goals, it might simply be the case that richer countries could afford to spend more on education (see, e.g., Collins 1979, chap. 2). Some writers even came to question the fundamental assumption of human capital theory—that more educated workers are more productive workers (Berg 1970; Thurow 1973; Blaug 1987). They pointed out that people who were overeducated for their jobs might not be challenged enough to be very productive at all.

State-Led Development Theories

Today, social scientists have largely rejected the dependency and human capital theories in favor of a more complex view of the relationship between schooling and economic development. A well-educated labor force is often an important factor in development, and a poorly educated labor force can certainly be an impediment. However, other factors are at least as essential to sustained economic growth. These include effective economic policies and trade alliances, and the avoidance of war, political tyranny, overpopulation, and overborrowing. Economic development is like making a cake. Several ingredients are required—eggs, flour, sugar—and several others must be kept as far away as possible. Without one of the required ingredients, the cake cannot be baked, and the same is true if any one of the banned ingredients somehow gets into the mix. High levels of schooling are, therefore, best considered both a contributor to economic development and (more reliably) a consequence. Economically successful developing countries tend to invest heavily in human capital development through formal education. The opposite, however, is not as true: Investment in human capital development does not in itself lead to high rates of economic growth. However, it can contribute, if mixed with the right development policies, by helping to create a disciplined and skilled labor force.

In the years following World War II, the most educated nations in Latin America were Argentina, Chile, and Uruguay, and none of those countries moved to the forefront of economic development in their region. Indeed, the social upheavals of industrialization and political conflict produced brutally repressive military dictatorships instead of the rapid growth reformers had anticipated. "Their elegant constitutions were torn up, their congresses closed, their courts rendered a sham" (Skidmore and Smith 1989:372).

We can better understand the relationship between economic and schooling development if we look in some detail at the world's greatest economic success story of the past quarter century: the eight "high-performing Asian economies" (HPAEs). In addition to Japan, these high-performing economies include the "four tigers"—Hong Kong, South Korea, Singapore, and Taiwan—along with Indonesia, Malaysia, and Thailand, which have joined the group within the past two decades. The four tigers are now poised to enter the elite club of fully industrialized, wealthy societies, and the other three developing countries are not far behind. Another Asian economy, "market-Leninist" China, has also shown remarkable economic gains. Figure 3.2 shows patterns of growth and income inequality in several countries of the developing world since the 1960s. The figure shows that the highest-performing economies tend to be concentrated in East Asia and suggests, moreover, that growth in these economies has not been accompanied by the same high rates of income inequality found in the high-growth countries of Africa and Latin America. (It is important to note that data on levels of inequality are controversial; some analysts find the sources of this data to be unreliable. See, e.g., Moll 1992.) This concentration of East Asian economies at the top of the growth charts has en-

FIGURE 3.2

Income Inequality and Growth of Gross Domestic Product, 1985-9

Source: World Bank (1993:4).

Note: Income inequality is measured by the ratio of the income shares of the richest 20 percent and the poorest 20 percent of the population.

couraged social scientists to look for the sources of the "East Asian miracle" (see, e.g., Amsden 1989; World Bank 1993).

The High-Performing Asian Economies. By 1965, Hong Kong, Korea, and Singapore had achieved universal primary schooling, well ahead of other developing economies. Even Indonesia had a primary school enrollment rate of 70 percent. These high enrollment rates continued in later years through the secondary level and are now evident in higher education (World Bank 1993:43-6). In general, enrollment rates at different levels of schooling in the HPAEs have tended to be higher than predicted for their country's income level—meaning that they were investing more in schooling than countries at a similar level of GNP per capita. Between 1970 and 1989, for example, real expenditures per pupil at the primary level rose by 355 percent in Korea, compared with 64 percent in Mexico, 38 percent in Kenya, and just 13 percent in Pakistan (World Bank 1993:45). Remember, however, that per pupil expenditures mainly reflect economic growth, which allows more spending.

Schooling is far from a completely independent part of the East Asian miracle. Educational institutions, like most other institutions in these societies, have benefited from lower birth rates than are found in the rest of the developing world. Lower birth rates mean that resources do not have to be stretched as far, class sizes are manageable, and everyone can be accommodated. They have also benefited from the absence of political conflict, famine, and disease—factors that have limited progress in such nearby countries as Burma, Laos, Cambodia, and Vietnam. They have clearly benefited from good family learning environments, which are built partly on the educational achievements of the previous generation and partly on the comparatively small number of children in each home. Instead of thinking of schooling as an important variable in the development formula, it would be better to think of it as part of a "virtuous circle" of influences.

Without doubt, the most important part of this virtuous circle is economic progress itself. As an economy grows, more resources become available for schooling children. The more people who are educated and the better the quality of the schooling they receive, the better the social environment they provide for the next generation. However, economic policies, not a commitment to human capital development, led the way in Asia. Indeed, it is entirely possible that the economic policies of the HPAEs could have been successful without a strong commitment to formal education.

Japan was the first Asian economy to reach full industrialization, and it provided a model for many of the later-developing HPAEs. Following World War II, Japan promoted the development of several weak industries by offering protective tariffs and formal incentives for introducing advanced technology. It also established so-called rationalization cartels to remove inefficient firms from export markets.

Government policies in the other HPAEs have not been based on a single model, but they have all actively supported export industries and imposed high tariffs on imports to protect domestic industry. In several countries, capital markets were not free. Governments repressed interest rates and directed credit to guide investments. The HPAEs have also developed an effective regional economic alliance for shared growth, with investment flowing first from Japan to the four tigers and more recently from these economies to Indonesia, Malaysia, and Thailand. The success of the East Asian economies is also built on comparatively low levels of social welfare spending, which reduces the threat of overborrowing to finance government debt. (A helpful overview of the policies of governments in the HPAEs is provided in World Bank 1993:79-103.)

Looking at the success of the HPAEs in relation to the rest of the developing world, it would appear that they have truly built the better mousetrap—and that the mousetrap has been built by state-based development elites. Adrian Leftwich (1995) has listed four characteristics of the successful "developmental state" (many shared by fast-growing economies outside of Asia as well):

- A determined and cohesive developmental elite

- Relative autonomy of this elite from intrusive political and military forces

- A competent, powerful, and insulated economic bureaucracy to carry out and monitor policies

- A weak set of social class actors, such as labor unions and local business interests

Export-oriented development (rather than the development of national industries to supply imported products) seems to be a centerpiece of most successful development states, as is the creation of strong trade and investment alliances with other regional powers. For example, Botswana, a successful African development state, appears to have benefited from trade with and investment by South Africa and Zimbabwe.

In thinking about the full implications of the East Asian miracle, it is worth remembering that nearly all of these highly disciplined societies achieved economic success at the expense of political freedom and legal protections for citizens. All four of the little tigers were ruled by dictators, or near dictators, and the harshness of these regimes is legendary. In Singapore, even small infractions, such as spray painting private property, can bring a brutal caning at the hands of authorities, and political dissent is not tolerated. In South Korea, laws authorizing arbitrary arrest and detention and suppression of free association, expression, and assembly—which propped up decades of military rule—have been used by the civilian president, President Kim, against political opponents and labor activists. Schooling in the HPAEs reflects both the competitiveness of their economies and the authoritarianism of their political regimes. Little critical discussion gets in the way of drills on facts and principles, despite the avowed political liberalism of many schoolteachers.

Factors Related to Success. We can now draw some conclusions about the role of schooling in economic development. Schooling can aid economic development, and economic development certainly tends to improve schooling, but the correlations hide as much as they reveal. Low-income countries in the developing world sometimes have high levels of literacy, high primary school enrollments, and good university systems. By the late 1970s, Kenya, the Philippines, Peru, and Chile, for example, all reported primary school enrollment rates well above 75 percent (Carceles 1979), but their per capita growth for the 1965-89 period lagged behind countries such as Indonesia and Brazil, which had yet to reach high levels of enrollment in the primary grades (World Bank 1993:31).

The problems of developing countries stem more often from political turmoil, overpopulation, ineffective economic policies, and foreign debt than from schooling policies. The pitfalls into which developing countries can fall are many, and a strong commitment to schooling provides no magic ladder out. Only when a commitment to human capital development through schooling is combined with political stability, declining population growth, effective policies for the advancement of trade and industry, and macroeconomic stability to prevent overborrowing can a low-income developing society begin to experience strong rates of growth and development.

CONCLUSION

Most countries in the developing world have been independent for only approximately 50 years. They inherited many features of schooling from the colonial powers. In their administrative and curricular structure, schools look very similar the world over. In addition, some particular practices of the colonial powers continued to stamp schooling in the newly independent states. Grade repeating, common in France, was, for example, also more common in the former French colonies.

The first generation of colonial leaders included many mass-mobilizing intellectuals and many status quo-oriented dynastic families and military rulers. The policies of these two groups tended to differ greatly. Mass-mobilizing intellectuals were schooling expansionists. They launched literacy campaigns, invested heavily in schooling, and were responsive to the schooling interests of the poor. Status quo-oriented leaders were more leery of schooling expenditures and repressed dissent that arose among students. Because of their relative indifference to the poor, their schooling policies tended to subsidize the well-to-do.

The second postcolonial generation has been marked by an increasing level of convergence in school policies, but increasing differences in economic conditions. The new standard model of schooling bears the imprint both of the decline of political passions in the Third World and the influence of donor agencies like the World Bank. The World Bank has successfully promulgated a model of schooling that encourages primary schooling and private spending, discourages vocational schooling, and evaluates schooling through a mix of efficiency and equity criteria. In spite of more standard policies, the poorest countries of the developing world have seen their school systems deteriorate as a result of economic stagnation, high indebtedness, and continued population growth. Most developing countries face problems of poverty, traditionalism, and physical insecurity. Where the problems of the developing world are greatest, so are the problems of schooling.

Three theories have sought to explain the role schooling plays in economic development. These are the dependency, human capital, and state-led development theories. The contemporary evidence tends to support the third of these theories, which focuses on the role the state plays in encouraging development through supporting export industries, regulating capital markets, and encouraging regional growth coalitions. Schooling in this theory is a factor of lesser importance in economic development than in the human capital theory, but it is a more important factor than the dependency theory allows. It is less important than state economic policies as an engine of growth, but it can play a role in economic development by helping to create a disciplined and skilled labor force.

In Chapters 2 and 3, I have discussed the structure of schooling in both the industrialized and the developing world. Drawing primarily on the work of macrohistorical sociologists, I have shown why schooling systems have developed as they have and some consequences of different structures. The next part of the book takes up three major functions of schooling in the contemporary world: the transmission of knowledge, socialization, and social selection. The chapters in this part of the book rely primarily on work at the macrohistorical and institutional levels of analysis. Chapter 4 begins this new section by looking at the defining purpose of schooling for most educators, the transmission of knowledge.

CHAPTER 4

Schools and the Transmission of Knowledge

Schooling has three major purposes in contemporary societies: the *transmission of school knowledge* (the topic of this chapter); *socialization*, the training of values, attitudes, and habits of conduct (the topic of Chapter 5); and *social selection*, the sorting of people for higher- and lower-level jobs in society (the topic of Chapters 6 and 7). These purposes underlie the familiar activities of schools. When students read silently at their desks or work on problems at the blackboard, they are studying the knowledge that one generation of educators considers important to transmit to the next generation of students. When they are told by a teacher to sit still, concentrate, and do their own work, students are being socialized—in this case into habits of industriousness and independence. When they are directed on the basis of grades and test scores into more demanding or less demanding courses of study, they are being differentiated in ways connected to social selection.

By transmission of school knowledge, I mean specifically the instruction of the uneducated members of a society by school authorities in the facts, theories, interpretations, and reasoning abilities that are considered to be of consequence for the development of the individual and the larger society. (It is important to keep in mind that just as schooling and education are separate, so the knowledge transmitted through schooling is only a subset of all knowledge in the world.) In modern societies, the transmission of school knowledge occurs through an organized curriculum of subjects distributed over blocks of time in the school day. The *curriculum* can be defined as a "historically specific pattern of knowledge, which is selected, organized and distributed to learners through educational institutions" (Kliebard 1992:181).

As I will discuss it, the study of the transmission of school knowledge consists of two parts: first, the subjects and course content that goes into making up the curriculum, and second, the extent to which this material is in fact successfully transmitted to the next generation. (The sociology of classroom interaction is discussed separately in Chapter 8, because teaching and learning are connected not only to the transmission of school knowledge but also to socialization and social selection.)

This chapter begins by examining the importance of the kinds of knowledge transmitted in schools. It then takes up three key topics: how the school curriculum developed historically, what the contemporary structure of curriculum looks like in different parts of the world, and how well students actually learn course materials. I will also discuss the recent rise of multicultural curricula as a case study of the forces that can influence the creation of new course content.

How Important Is School Knowledge?

It may seem obvious that the teaching of subject matter is the principal purpose of schooling. But is it really the most important purpose of schooling? Undoubtedly, some forms of knowledge—basic literacy and numeracy, in particular—are essential equipment for living capably in the complex organizations of society. But some good arguments can be raised for the view that the transmission of school knowledge is a less important activity of schooling than the other two major purposes, socialization and social selection. Here are some of the more persuasive arguments:

- Both individuals and societies rely on a number of different knowledge systems for orienting conduct.

In adult life, the knowledge taught in school does not necessarily count for more than other forms, such as common sense, popular culture, merchandising, folklore, and belief systems. Nearly everyone recognizes that other knowledge systems compete with school knowledge in everyday life. Moreover, some of these alternative systems of meaning, such as popular culture, have become more important over time.

- Beyond transmitting basic skills of literacy and numeracy, schools do not actually succeed very well in transmitting the lessons of the curriculum.

Some students, of course, pull in knowledge like magnets in a field of iron filings—but not the majority. Little that is taught in school sticks in most students' minds for long. A British book of humor, *1066 and All That*, contends that it is the first truly "memorable history of England," because unlike any other history book it is the only one devoted to what adults actually remember from their school lessons, as opposed to what they are supposed to remember (Sellar and Yeatman 1931). In addition to "103 Good Things and Five Bad Kings," the book includes "Two Genuine Dates." Two of the four dates originally included "were eliminated at the last moment after research . . . revealed that they are not memorable." The book has the cheeky wit to say what most teachers couldn't dare to admit: School knowledge has a short half-life for most students, when it has a life at all.

- Much of what educators count as the transmission of knowledge is actually better interpreted as an aspect of socialization or social selection.

For example, social studies classes are usually accompanied by discussions of how other people see the world. The real lesson is that we shouldn't judge others too fast. The purpose of such classes is more to create socially approved attitudes than to transmit a formal body of knowledge. When mastery of difficult subject matter is closely connected to prospects of moving up the school and social hierarchy, knowledge may become more a basis of stratification than equipment for effective living.

If we concentrate on the majority of the students, rather than the academic elite, we may in the end conclude that the transmission of school knowledge beyond basic reading and calculating is not the most successful activity of the school. Even so, it is important to examine for several reasons:

- The facts, theories, and interpretations accepted by top cultural authorities play an important (though by no means exclusive) role in decision making in modern societies.

In almost every important institutional realm—from the courts to the hospitals to the corporations—decision makers rely in significant measure on formal knowledge in making judgments and developing plans.

- Mastering the school curriculum has practical importance as a means of gaining a livelihood for many people, and it also influences the way many people do their work.

School knowledge is, in this sense, building material for much work, particularly in the upper reaches of the occupational structure. Of course, it is not the only influence on work activities. Even top professionals rely on practical knowledge gained at work as much as they rely on school knowledge, but school knowledge is a backdrop for gaining this practical knowledge and often it is also a direct reference point.

- In every modern society, the subjects taught in school are, partly as a consequence of their importance in the upper reaches of society, surrounded with an aura of special significance.

The prestige of the ideals represented by school knowledge is very often a factor in what people think they *should* be paying attention to, as the popularity of television game shows based largely on school knowledge (such as "Jeopardy") attest. People may refer to it when they are trying to make a serious point or are communicating with high-status people.

- Even those who do not carry the torch of secular learning into their adult lives do often find something of considerable value in their school lessons.

This value may come from a variety of sources—from a useful knowledge of correct grammar and pronunciation, or a way of dissecting arguments, or a flash of insight brought on by a particular work of art. A good many people gain the lifelong habit of reading through school; they become frequenters of libraries and subscribers to periodicals.

These contributions do not, to my mind, quite reach the same level of importance as the contributions of schools to shaping attitudes and ways of interacting (socialization) and to selecting winners and losers in the "stratification sweepstakes" (social selection). But they are important enough to warrant our close attention.

CURRICULUM MAKING AND CURRICULAR CHANGE

Why do children study English, math, basic science, and social studies in elementary school, rather than, for example, business principles, computers, morality, and American ethnic cultures? Or, even further afield, why not car maintenance, popular music, consumer awareness, and science fiction? Asking these kinds of questions leads us to the heart of the social organization of school knowledge.

A common way of looking at the school curriculum is to say that science and mathematics are taught because they explain why things happen in nature, and the humanities are taught because they represent the best that has been thought and said about human beings. (Ideas about increasing sensitivity to our own and other cultures usually provide justification for social studies.) These ideas echo the famous lines of the nineteenth-century English essayist Matthew Arnold ([1869] 1949), who argued that certain subjects and works must be taught because they represent the "best that has been thought or said" and therefore produce a fully humane reason, a mind that is not only logical and efficient but fully open to experience and sophisticated in judgment.

However appealing these sentiments may be, they are not very helpful as a way of understanding what kinds of materials are actually represented in school curricula. They fail to provide an accurate historical grounding and suggest a greater stability than in fact exists. School curricula are not, in fact, very stable over time. New subjects like social science gain ground over time, and old subjects like Greek and Latin decline in importance. Nor, except in scientific fields, are the major lessons taught very stable. Current judgments of intellectual value are not always very similar to past judgments, and outside of a handful of enduring authors, such as Homer and Shakespeare, the reputations of authors and works are nearly always in dispute.

To understand the changing emphasis of different levels of schooling and the rise and fall of subjects, it is necessary to move away from the philosophical humanism of Arnold to the less high-minded but truer realm of social history. This perspective is based on understanding the most important macroforces shaping school knowledge:

- Purposes of different levels of schooling at the time they were originally organized

- Propensities of social actors (such as the upper classes and the state) insofar as they are involved in curriculum making

- Formation of a ladder structure with each level defined relative to the others

- The shift from moralistic to developmental approaches to conceptualizing the relationship between children and society

- Changing numbers and composition of student populations and the ways in which new students provide a rationale for new curricula

- Maneuvering of rival bands of educators for influence on the basis of their commitments to particular forms of schooling

In cooperation with history, sociology can help to explain why boundaries exist between academic and nonacademic culture, why new subject matters come into being, and why they gain and lose standing over time.

The Three Sources of Curriculum

Our contemporary schooling systems did not originate in any single curricular purpose. Instead, three distinct purposes have played a role: rudimentary learning, liberal learning, and occupationally specialized learning. Each purpose is linked to a distinct level of schooling.

Primary schools, which have existed sporadically since ancient times, were developed to teach basic literacy and morality. Primary schools were often in the hands of private individuals or religious authorities. As Chapter 2 explained, our modern state-based mass systems of primary schooling had their origins in the nation-building efforts of eighteenth-century modernizers. Efforts to encourage loyalty to the king or emperor were important, but again the original purposes also focused on the teaching of morality and basic skills of literacy.

Secondary schools have a connection to the ancient world of Greece and Rome. The "liberal arts" ideal played a decisive role. The purpose here was to develop people who were fit to govern by exposing them to the accumulated wisdom of great minds, thereby preparing them for the active life of the citizen (Marrou [1948] 1982).

Universities developed as institutions for skills training in the upper reaches of society. In the East, advanced training for occupational specialization existed since the time of the Han Dynasty (200 BCE). The ultimate aim of professional training was preparation for state service. In the West, universities were a product of the later middle ages. They grew up as bands of students surrounding renowned scholars and teachers (Rashdall [1895] 1936). Their underlying purpose was to provide training for a "learned occupation"—either the clergy, medicine, or law, or the teaching of these subjects. In this sense, the medieval universities were clearly vocational, although they were not narrowly vocational. Because they trained young men for "liberal professions," they were based on the premise that specialized training should be connected to broad learning.

These three levels of schooling originally had very little relation to one another. But in the course of creating the integrated ladder structure of primary, secondary, and higher education that we have today, the originating purposes of the three levels mixed in new ways. Most important, the inspiration of the liberal arts ideal spread to primary education. The specialized curriculum, originally associated with the university, spread in turn to secondary schooling, where it has coexisted, often uneasily, with academic purposes. In addition, since the rise of the German research universities in the nineteenth century, the ideal of research has become an important third element (together with occupationally specialized and liberal learning) in the curriculum of higher education, particularly for graduate and postdoctoral students.

Nevertheless, it is safe to say that the ideal of the liberal arts has had the most diffuse influence on schooling. The ideal of the liberal arts in education is aristocratic in origin, both because its ultimate purpose was to prepare students for governance and because, at the time this ideal originated, only aristocrats had the leisure to study. More particularly, in the West, the liberal arts tradition is born in a dispute between the two kinds of teachers that prepared upper-class students for public life, orators and philosophers (Marrou [1948] 1982; Kimball 1986). For the orators, rhetoric and related disciplines were the culmination of education, because they prepared students for the active public life of the citizen. For the philosophers, scientific studies were most important because they provided training in the truths underlying the appearances of everyday life. Our contemporary humanities come essentially from the first tradition; the sciences originate from the second.

In the Hellenistic world (the world created by the conquests of Alexander the Great), liberal education gained many of the connotations that it has today. *Liberal* comes from the same root as *liberty*, and in this context, it has a similar meaning. It came to mean learning that makes the mind free rather than subject to the influence of others. The old dispute between orators and philosophers as to which form of knowledge was superior achieved a kind of curricular organization in the Hellenistic world, with both branches included among the *septem artes liberalis* (seven liberal arts). The great contrast continued to be between liberal and servile. Education for servility both in the Hellenistic and Roman worlds included all subjects intended to prepare students for a practical trade, rather than for political or cultural leadership.

The ideal of a liberal education, therefore, had more or less from the beginning a status-defining character. I believe it is wrong to reduce this curriculum to its status-defining elements, however. "Liberal culture" has also been rich in quality. The most serious questions of human existence—the nature of love and courage, the meaning of death, the proper balance between public and private life, the consequences of good intentions and mistaken judgments— have been pondered and debated in the works of philosophers, historians, novelists, artists, and dramatists. In addition, the arts of expression have traditionally been taught through exposure to the highest-quality work in the visual and performing arts and in literature and speech. Indeed, it is one of the great triumphs of democratic societies to have aspired at times to make this liberal culture—this education for the freedom of the mind—available to everyone, rather than limiting it to a narrow elite.

Conflict of Ideologies in the Modern Period

As the discussion of the rise of liberal education suggests, it is axiomatic among sociologists that how a society selects and classifies the knowledge it considers to be public "reflects both the distribution of power and the principles of social control" operative in the society (Bernstein 1971:47). The aristocracy and gentry (and those who have inherited their ideals) have clearly lost power over time, and the major new competitors have been the business-oriented middle classes, democratic reformers, and state planners.

The cultural historian Raymond Williams (1961) suggests that curricular changes have reflected the relative power of these groups. Table 4.1 schematizes Williams's argument. (The American curricular historian Herbert Kliebard [1986, 1992] has emphasized essentially the same forces, though he has used different names to characterize them.) When considering arguments about the social bases of curriculum, it is important to avoid the pitfalls of overly deterministic thinking: Although groups are the decisive carriers of different views of curriculum, not everyone in a group lines up in the same way.

TABLE 4.1

A Typology of Educational Ideals

Social group	Ideology	Educational policies
Aristocracy/gentry	Generalist	Nonvocational courses, providing cultivation, character, and judgment
Merchant/upper professional classes	Specialist	Higher vocational and professional courses, providing training for desired occupations and positions
Radical reformers (especially patricians and subordinate professionals)	Democratic	Expansion of "upper-class" education, providing opportunities for everyone to be "an aristocrat"
State planners	Utilitarian	Lower vocational and semiprofessional courses, providing training for positions needed in the economy and the state

Source: Adapted from Williams (1961).

Note that the "generalist ideology" associated originally with aristocrats and gentry encourages broad academic training and the idea of education as preparation for leadership. In contrast, the "specialist ideology" carried by the merchant and professional classes encouraged training for desired occupational and professional positions. Thus, when the commercial or industrial wing of the middle class has the greatest relative power (or when the military or an authoritarian party-state is in power), the study of science and mathematics, which have practical applications in business and industry, is usually favored over humanities studies. The "democratic ideology" of radical reformers (historically, led by patrician elites and nonbusiness professionals) is "expansionist" and argues that the highest-quality education should be available to all. In the early nineteenth century, this democratic ideology was a transforming force in the United States; by the middle of the twentieth century, it became an important force virtually everywhere.

In general, humanistic education, which was once the dominant form of higher learning in Europe, has become more and more associated with subordinate fractions of the middle class (e.g., artists, writers, and teachers). Specialist education has triumphed among the dominant fractions of the middle class: business people, managers, and higher-status professions such as medicine and law (Bourdieu 1984). The cause of liberal arts has been taken up primarily by the democratic reformers, who have aspired to extend "cultural aristocracy" to the masses (see, e.g., Barber 1992). In many countries, the trend has been for supporters of generalist and democratic ideologies to struggle for institutional space against supporters of specialist ideologies. The curriculum has in the process changed to accommodate these two ideas about "the good society"—namely, a democratic ideology that has demanded equality and opportunity based on a common academic curriculum and a utilitarian ideology that has emphasized individual ability and practical training.

Thus, the modern curriculum stands as a compromise between the major influences described in Table 4.1. In general, the movement has been toward teaching skills in the lower grades that prepare students for academic studies, toward mixing liberal arts and practical studies in secondary school, toward limiting liberal arts to the lower division of university-level education, and toward beginning specialist training in upper-division college courses with continuation in graduate and professional schools. The state once used primary education to build "good citizens," but democratizing forces have gradually gained the upper hand in primary education. Aristocratic, generalist traditions once dominated undergraduate education, but the forces of specialization have captured all but the first two years of higher education.

The Rise and Fall of School Subjects

The specific subjects that move in and out of the curriculum are also conditioned by large forces of institutional change. Consider the American secondary school curriculum. Like characters in a play, school subjects enter and depart the stage. Classical languages play a leading role in the early acts, only to retire into the shadows in more recent acts. Physics, algebra, and foreign languages make a later entrance, are relatively silent at first, then slowly swell into important supporting actors before falling back again into the deep shadows near the curtain. "Life adjustment" subjects like money management and personal appearance come in as the curtain rises on the twentieth century and are more or less dispatched by the Cold War period only to reenter in an altered form in the 1960s. If we take a long enough view, we can see a great pageant of comings and goings. What is true for subjects is true at an accelerated rate for authors, ideas, and modes of interpretation.

How do sociologists explain all of these dramatic goings-on? The most important part of the explanation has to do with the reigning definition among educators about the purposes of a particular level of schooling. As understandings of the purposes of a level of schooling change, so do the subjects in the curriculum. At the primary level, these understandings have been strongly associated with a shift from moralistic to developmental thinking about childhood and society. Developmentalism, which has been allied with democratic reform movements, has encouraged the schools to address a wider range of mental and socioemotional capacities in children. These new philosophies gained their strongest foothold at a time when primary schools were becoming institutions providing preparation for further instruction, and shedding their old identity as institutions providing rudimentary and terminal instruction for the young. At the secondary level, these understandings are strongly associated with how many and what types of students are enrolled at different levels in the system. When few are enrolled and those few come from the upper classes, a more elite set of subjects is taught than when many are enrolled. Educators have usually turned to curricular tracking and watered-down courses when working- and lower-class students first enter a level of schooling that has been dominated by middle and upper classes, especially if the level of education is terminal for the majority of students.

Primary School Subjects. Several new subjects have entered the primary school curriculum over time, particularly as it has become a preparatory stage of schooling. These include arts and physical education, mathematics and science, and social studies.

The addition of arithmetic to the primary school curriculum illustrates how children in the Age of Enlightenment were already coming to be seen as capable of enhanced mental development. In some countries, including the United States, arithmetic already had strong advocates by the end of the eighteenth century. Because it was seen as having the power to "improve the logical and rational faculties of the mind," it was closely associated with ideas of civic virtue, and it was championed by such leading figures of the American republic as Thomas Jefferson and Noah Webster (Cohen 1982). France and Prussia (now part of Germany) also adopted arithmetic early. Here arithmetic was associated with ideals of rationality championed by the "enlightened despots" Napoleon and Frederick the Great. However, it was not until the middle of the nineteenth century that most countries adopted mathematics as part of their primary school curriculum. In general, the adoption of mathematics was associated with industrialization (Kamens and Benavot 1992), indicating that mathematics was perceived as having a practical importance in industrializing economies.

Science lagged behind arithmetic as a primary school subject, partly because it represented a threat to countries with national religions. The conflict between the Catholic Church and science created particular resistance to science teaching in Catholic countries. However, by the middle of the nineteenth century, it too had entered the primary school curriculum in many Protestant countries, where it was seen as "adding to the capacities of individuals to be loyal and productive citizens" (Kamens and Benavot 1992:113).

The arts and physical education were a part of classical ideals of education, but not of the original forms of mass primary education. Authoritarian forms of instruction looked to religious and moral training as the basis of "spiritual development." Primary schooling in the eighteenth and early nineteenth centuries was thoroughly integrated with moral instruction and religious imagery (Tyack and Hansot 1982). Explicit moral and religious instruction continues in primary schools today in most countries, but neither is as universally important in the curriculum as arts and physical education have become (Cha 1992:68).

When primary schools became preparatory rather than terminal, the character of children was also redefined. No longer expected simply to conform, they were redefined—under the influence of educational and cognitive psychologists (Kliebard 1986)—as growing organisms with "developing capacities." Under this new cultural understanding, comprehensive schooling came to include aesthetic and physical development as well as basic skills and moral development.

Political change is perhaps more important in the rise of social studies as a substitute for civics and history in the primary school curriculum. This transition has occurred only very recently, beginning in the 1960s and 1970s.

> The construction of national myths, symbols and monuments has given way to the prosaic work of institution-building based on internationally available models. . . . As the sacredness of the "nation" declines, learning facts, names and dates becomes a less compelling task of schooling. . . . [Moreover], other cultures and societies gain credibility as objects of analysis, from whom useful lessons may be drawn. (Kamens 1992:77)

Changing patterns of cross-cultural contact due to tourism and trade are no doubt also involved in the rise of social studies.

Secondary School Subjects. Again, the perceived purposes of the institutions and the kinds of students enrolling in them strongly influenced the curriculum. In a famous article on the transformations of secondary schooling, Trow (1961) noted three major stages in the development of secondary schooling: secondary school as preparation for elites, as a terminal institution for the majority, and as a preparatory institution for the majority.

When secondary schools played a preparatory role for the elite, classical subjects predominated. In the West, these classical subjects included Latin, Greek, philosophy, history and geography, together with a smattering of mathematics and science; in the East, they included classical literary texts, calligraphy, and religious philosophy. Secondary schools became less singularly wedded to liberal arts as they became less elite. Although a residue of aristocratic humanism remained an important force in Europe, many of the subjects that were central to the classical curriculum (particularly Latin, Greek, and philosophy) declined greatly in importance.

As soon as large numbers of middle-class students were admitted, pressures built for a more "modern" curriculum. In Europe, new curricular options based on national languages or math and science were introduced in the early twentieth century, but the classical curriculum retained its centrality until the great expansion of European secondary education in the 1950s and 1960s (Kamens, Meyer, and Benavot 1996:131). Today, the classical curriculum has been superseded by two more modern curriculum packages: one for students concentrating in arts, humanities, and modern languages and one for students concentrating in mathematics and science.

The math and science curricula reflect the perceived relevance of these subjects in the industrial world. Science began to be introduced in Europe in the mid-nineteenth century in lectures and demonstrations, but it did not become a formal part of the curriculum until the 1870s. The introduction of scientific education at higher levels of schooling was resisted by those with a strong stake in the humanistic education of gentlemen. The classical curriculum held out longest in countries like England, in which higher education was highly independent from the modernizing interests of the state. It was not until the turn of the century that scientific specializations became available to secondary students in Britain, and then only in a limited way (Keeves 1986).

By contrast, the transition from the "classical" curriculum to a modern "comprehensive" curriculum in American secondary schools occurred much earlier—more or less simultaneously with the introduction of the first public high schools in the 1820s and 1830s (Labaree 1988). This modern curriculum included courses in rhetoric and English composition, French, German, Latin, astronomy, chemistry, physics, geometry, trigonometry, calculus, political economy, moral science, mechanical drawing, and bookkeeping (ibid., chap. 6). The comprehensive curriculum is closely associated with the democratic premises of American schooling, and it remains far more popular in the United States and in the Americas generally than in Europe or the developing world (Kamens et al. 1996:138).

The secondary school curriculum remained academically oriented for the majority only so long as university enrollments were low and secondary schools prepared relatively small numbers of students either for university admissions or higher-level commercial careers. Once secondary school replaced primary school as the terminal phase of schooling for most students, strong pressures developed for differentiation between academic and vocational curricula.

In the United States, the pressures to create vocational tracks began to develop before the turn of the century. But they were largely resisted until the first decade of the twentieth century, when thousands of new immigrants entered the secondary schools.[9]

By the 1920s, American high schools showed a "tremendous differentiation" of course offerings (Kliebard 1992), with educators everywhere arguing that easier, more practical work be offered to students not bound for college. In the 1920s, five out of six schools offered curricula in "industrial arts" and/or commercial subjects (Cohen 1985). So-called life adjustment curricula were also particularly popular during this period, with students studying such nonacademic subjects as how to manage money, personal hygiene, and dating behavior (Cremin 1961, chap. 9). The educational historian David Cohen (1985) wrote:

> American educators quickly built a system around the assumption that most students didn't have what it took to be serious about the great issues of human life, and that even if they had the wit, they had neither the will nor the futures that would support heavy-duty study. (P. 245)

Secondary schools became mass institutions in Europe later than in the United States. But in Europe, too, a change in numbers led to a change in curriculum. The tradition of elite secondary schooling was modified to include practical training in one of two ways: Either new vocational institutions were established or a lower tier of vocational studies was added in the existing academically oriented institutions. The European systems developed highly segregated streams for specific occupational preparation, though the specific numbers and types fluctuated with economic demand and policy changes.

After World War II, college enrollments in the United States increased significantly, and secondary schools became mass transfer institutions rather than mass terminal institutions. Vocational subjects diminished in importance in secondary schools, because more people were going on to higher education. At the same time, because higher education remained relatively exclusive, more demanding academic subjects such as foreign languages, physics, and algebra gained a brief renaissance. By the late 1960s, college attendance was no longer atypical, however, and the academic quality of students attending higher education was no longer as high. Specifically, vocational curricula continued to diminish, but so did the more rigorous academic subjects. Today, foreign languages, physics, trigonometry, and calculus enroll fewer students than they did in the immediate postwar period (Goodlad 1984; Ravitch 1995).

MODERN GLOBAL STRUCTURES OF SCHOOL KNOWLEDGE

Today, a very high level of agreement exists throughout the world about the subjects that should be taught in primary schools—and even about the amount of time that should be allotted to these subjects. A common core of subjects exists also in secondary schools, although this core plays a major part only for those pursuing academic studies. Even for these students, possibilities for specialization and in the amount of time allotted to different subjects vary quite a bit from country to country. The secondary school curriculum in Europe and East Asia has more specialization possibilities, is more rigorous, and is more sharply stratified from vocational studies than in the United States. Thus, the secondary school curriculum in Europe shows the inheritance of aristocratic humanism in Europe combined with an emphasis on preuniversity specialization. In the United States, the inheritance of democratic idealism remains apparent, although in a substantially weakened form.

Global Curriculum in Primary Schooling

The core subject areas in official primary school curricula throughout the world are national languages and literatures, math and science, social sciences, art and music, and physical education. Moreover, the amount of time allocated to these subjects is surprisingly similar throughout the world, indicating that they are institutionalized on an explicit worldwide model. Language instruction—reading, writing, and grammar—is the dominant curricular category in primary education; virtually everywhere in the world about one-third of class time is devoted to language instruction. Almost all of this instruction is in the national or official language. Mathematics and science have increased somewhat in importance over time, with about 20 percent of class time going to these subjects in the prewar period and closer to 25 percent now. In virtually all countries, math is given at least twice as much class time as science. Most of the remainder of class time is given over to arts and music, social science, and physical education. The time allocated to these subjects has been remarkably stable: approximately 25 percent of class time in the prewar years and 25 percent of class time today (Meyer, Kamens, and Benavot 1992). Table 4.2 shows the amount of time governments have expected teachers to spend on primary school subjects in three time periods, beginning in 1920.

TABLE 4.2

Average Percentage of Total Instructional Time Allocated to Subjects in Primary School Curriculum, 1920-86

Subject	Panel A[a]			Panel B		
	1920-45	*1945-69*	N	*1945-69*	*1969-86*	N
Language	35.3	36.4	31	36.0	33.9	70
National/local	31.0	32.4	31	26.0	25.1	72
Foreign	3.5	4.6	45	9.5	8.3	73
Mathematics	15.4	17.3	37	16.5	18.2	80
Natural science	5.2	7.0	42	7.1	7.9	75
Social science	8.8	8.6	36	8.1	8.1	73
History/geography/civics	8.0	6.2	37	5.9	3.2	74
Social studies	0.5	2.5	45	2.1	4.8	74
Arts	9.2	10.5	39	10.0	10.2	71
Religious/moral	6.9	5.2	37	6.1	5.2	68
Physical education	6.0	7.2	39	6.9	7.1	72
Hygiene/health	0.9	1.0	40	1.4	1.2	70
Practical/vocational	6.2	5.8	34	6.3	5.1	73

Source: Adapted from Meyer, Kamens, and Benavot (1992:49).

a. Each panel refers to a constant set of countries for which data were available in the two time periods.

Although the similarities across the world are impressive, some atypical patterns do stand out. Latin American teachers are expected to spend less time on language instruction and more in social sciences and practical training, such as farming, industrial arts, and housekeeping. The Caribbean is high in math and science and also health studies. Western countries tend to provide more aesthetic and physical education, and Asian countries give somewhat more official attention to moral education (ibid., p. 51). Other subject matter spheres are not as standardized throughout the world. Religious education takes up one-sixth of class time in the Middle East and Islamic North Africa, but has no role in Eastern Europe and only a minor role elsewhere. Whether religion is taught in the schools seems to depend primarily on whether the country has an established national religion (ibid., p. 77).

To some degree, these patterns are based on levels of economic development. Higher levels of development are associated with more time allocated for aesthetic and mathematical education, and less time spent on practical education (ibid., p. 56). The causes of these associations are perhaps self-evident, given the preparatory role primary education plays in developed societies and the increasing importance of mathematical reasoning in industrial and commercial life.

Practical subjects have shown a long-term decline, as primary school has become preparatory rather than terminal in most countries, but they remain important in poorer regions, such as sub-Saharan Africa, Latin America, and southern Asia. In India, one of the poorest countries in the world, practical subjects are expected to take up fully one-fifth of the school day. Practical subjects are also important in Eastern Europe, where they are an inheritance of the Marxist emphasis on manual labor (ibid., pp. 50-2, 75).

Researchers led by the sociologist John Meyer have been largely responsible for collecting these data on trends in curriculum organization. According to their theory, the modern system of school knowledge is based on a vision of modernity, originating in the West, linking individual development and social progress. This common vision of modernity has become institutionalized on a worldwide basis, according to Meyer and colleagues, in large part because developing states have modeled their curricular structures on those of the core states in the world economy. In addition, the core states have taken an active role in helping to diffuse their ideals about the purposes of schooling and methods for realizing these purposes. To be accepted as a fully modern state, according to Meyer and his associates, national leaders feel the need to adopt originally Western notions of how to link rational persons to progressive nation-states through the medium of mass schooling.

Is the global system of school knowledge rooted in an abstract vision of modernity, as Meyer and his associates argue? An alternative explanation might very well emphasize the practical politics involved in emulating the curriculum of core powers or the cognitive advantages of Western style curricular organization. But one point cannot be disputed: Meyer and his team have done an enormous service by establishing just how similar curricular designs across the world have become at the primary school level.[10]

• • • • • • • • • • • •

GRID AND INTEGRATED CURRICULA

The creation of divisions by school subjects is by no means the only way to organize curricula. The sociologist Basil Bernstein (1971) distinguished two types of curriculum organization: one based on analytical divisions of knowledge (or subjects) and one based on integrated groupings of knowledge. These are the *grid* and the *integrated* forms of curriculum organization. The grid curriculum classifies fields of knowledge. It is the kind of curriculum in which people study English in the first period, history in the second period, math in the third, and so on. The integrated curriculum lumps together fields of knowledge for the multisided study of a particular topic. In a unit on Asian civilization, for example, the teacher might draw on studies of ancient Asian science, Asian literature, history, geography—and particularly, ways these various fields interact. Instead of dividing knowledge into analytical components, the integrated curricula attempts to foster understanding of a broad topic by drawing on several disciplines. In the industrialized world, large parts of preschool and early elementary education are based on integrated type curricula. They may offer units, for example, on the way of life of Native Americans or color as both scientific fact and an element of artistic expression. School reformers have sometimes advocated integrated curricula as most appropriate for all grade levels, and some experimental schools have put these curricula into operation. Nevertheless, at the higher levels of schooling, the curriculum has tended to be organized into discrete subject matter areas separated by blocks of time. Teachers have long preferred this grid style on pedagogical grounds; it is easier for them to see the development of mastery (and to attend to deficiencies) when one subject is studied at a time.

Gridded curricula have not, however, always been as rigorously organized as they now are. Before the era of mass schooling, masters worked with students in a much less formal and more personal way. They read works with a student or students, but not in a strictly ordered way and not always during strictly prescribed periods of time. This pattern persists at a few ancient universities, such as Cambridge and Oxford in England. The more rigorous arrangement of the school day into strictly standardized blocks of time based on a sequence of subject matter is clearly associated with the Reformation and, even more so, with the transition from elite to mass schooling under state control. The first appearance of the term *curriculum* occurs in Glasgow, Scotland in 1633. The sense of structural order and discipline may come less from classical sources than from the ideas of the Protestant reformer John Calvin. "Curriculum," writes David Hamilton (Hamilton and Associates 1980), "was to Calvinist educational practice what discipline was to Calvinist social practice" (p. 14).

Public bureaucracy, with its need to coordinate large numbers of students and teachers, shows a strong affinity for more standardized forms of ordering and classification of knowledge (Goodson 1988; Bidwell and Dreeben 1992). Subject matter divisions, along with spatially separated classrooms and standard time units, are the kinds of highly organized, rule-bound practices that bureaucracies "thrive on" (Bidwell and Dreeben 1992:359). It is not surprising, therefore, that the rise of urban mass schooling under public bureaucratic control led to far greater organization and monitoring of curricular divisions.

In our own age of ad hoc social relationships and instantaneous communication, the disciplinary structures of schools and universities stand out as one of the longest-lasting and most stable forms of social structure. In considering these socially constructed divisions of time and personnel, it is hard not to feel that they are inherently limiting in some ways. It is clear that solutions to many problems—from cracking the genetic code to improving social welfare policies—require the skills of researchers from different subject matter fields. In universities, the limitations of disciplinary organization are often circumvented through the creation of interdisciplinary programs and interdisciplinary research groups.

• •

Global Variation in Secondary School Curricula

Comparative studies of secondary school curricula are more limited than those of primary school curricula, partly because much more variety exists at the secondary level. To make comparisons at all, we must collapse the great variety of curricula into a few, more general categories.

Nevertheless, it is clear that essentially the same subject matter core exists at the secondary level of schooling as in primary school. Throughout the world, this core consists of language instruction, mathematics and science, and social studies. Moral and religious instruction, arts and music, and physical education are also prevalent, although they are of secondary importance.

A great contrast exists between the European and American models, however. The European systems include many more occupational specialty programs. The academic programs are more demanding, and the systems as a whole are usually more rigidly stratified than the American system.

Academic Streams. In the old core states of Europe, academic students are divided into separate curricular tracks, or specializations. These can be reduced to three major types: classical, humanities, and math and science. Students enrolled in these curricular specializations take a different mix of course work.

- The classical curricula concentrate on classical languages (Greek and Latin), other languages, and a certain amount of science and math. Instead of social studies, they generally include history and geography. Philosophy is now often required as well.

- Those students who choose the modern humanities specializations tend to take the majority of their course work in modern foreign languages. Languages and literature courses outnumber math and science courses at a ratio of approximately two to one. Classical languages and philosophy are generally minor or nonexistent parts of these curricula. As in primary schooling, social studies has grown in importance compared to the older subjects of history and geography.

- Math and science specializations are a mirror image of the modern humanities curricula. About twice as much time is spent on math and science as compared to languages and literature. In addition, social science tends to be of minor consequence, with hours that would otherwise be allocated to social studies absorbed by additional study in the math and science core.

All three curricula typically include a certain amount of moral or religious education, art and music education, and physical education (Kamens et al. 1996:128-9). In most countries, foreign language instruction is also compulsory, and in some linguistically isolated countries, such as the Netherlands, two foreign languages are required (Bergentoft 1994).

In the developing world, secondary curricula show both the impact of Westernization generally, and in many cases a special interest in science and mathematics curricula, which are thought to contribute to rapid industrialization. Specialized math and science programs have grown significantly in Asia and sub-Saharan Africa. These regions have been dominated by political elites committed to strategies of rapid industrialization (Kamens et al. 1996:134-5).

Math and science curricula are everywhere associated with economic progress. For this reason, math and science concentrations have become more prestigious than classical curricula even in many core European countries like France (Neave 1985), and they have been more prestigious in Japan from the beginning of academic secondary education.

In the United States, separate curricular specializations do not exist, and a comprehensive curriculum dominates secondary schooling. English, math, science, and social studies each takes up one to two periods a day in both junior and senior high school. Math and science (if grouped together) become more prominent in the curriculum than language instruction as early as junior high school (Goodlad 1984:198-200). Arts and physical education are somewhat more likely than the academic subjects to be electives, but they are also taken by most students. Few highly demanding courses are required. Less than a quarter of American students take physics or trigonometry, and only about 10 percent study calculus (Ravitch 1995). Although college-bound students are now likely to have at least two years of language training, less than half of all students study a foreign language for even two years of secondary school and only 10 percent study a foreign language for four years (National Center for Educational Statistics [NCES] 1994).

The elective system in American high schools has sometimes made secondary schooling look more like a shopping mall than a focused curriculum. Today, it is not uncommon to find a hundred or more courses listed on the books at the larger American high schools (Powell, Farrar, and Cohen 1985). Thus, American students can often choose electives from a large menu on the basis of casual interest as much as academic intentions. Lightweight courses, such as "marriage and family," continue to be popular.

Secondary schools in most countries require substantially more compulsory work of students bound for higher education than do schools in the United States, particularly in the upper secondary years (Holmes and McLean 1989). Table 4.3 summarizes the compulsory courses required in the first year of upper secondary school for university-bound students in two countries with national curricula, France and Japan. In addition to having tougher required courses than the United States does, these countries permit a more limited range of electives at first. Electives are common in the final years of secondary school in France and Japan, but they have a very different meaning. They are used to prepare for secondary school-leaving and university entrance examinations in the students' major field or fields of concentration. For example, a Japanese student expecting to specialize in science at the university will typically devote 80 percent of his or her electives to additional science courses (ibid., p. 208).

TABLE 4.3

*Compulsory Courses in the First Upper Secondary Year
for University-Bound Students, France and Japan*

France	Japan
French (5 hours)	Japanese (5 credits)
History/geography (4 hours)	Social science (3.5 credits)
Modern language (3 hours)	Mathematics (6 credits)
Physical science (3.5 hours)	Science (6 credits)
Biological science (2 hours)	Physical education (5 credits for boys, 3 credits for girls)
Mathematics (4 hours)	
Physical education (2 hours)	

Source: Holmes and MacLean (1989:77, 209).

Vocational Streams. Preparatory curricula are, as a general principle, far more focused than curricula leading out into the job market. Indeed, it is very difficult to generalize about secondary school vocational curricula across national boundaries, because of the tremendous diversity in these curricula and because of the frequent changes in streams and options. European secondary schools may have as few as a handful of vocational streams, or as many as dozens. These often include separate streams for commercial subjects (such as accounting and finance), human service subjects (such as social welfare work), and manual subjects grouped by processes (repair) or materials (metallurgy, electronics).

In the United States, the situation is particularly complex because variation exists from state to state and school to school. Some U.S. high schools have separate vocational tracks, but most now include vocational courses as options in a single comprehensive curriculum. The only way to determine which students are concentrating on occupational preparation is to look at transcripts. Those who take 20 percent or more of their classes in occupationally related course work can safely be categorized as "vocational" students. Vocationally oriented students usually sample a range of occupationally related course work, rather than concentrating in any one area (as they would in Europe). They may also take quite a bit of nonacademic course work that is not specifically related to preparation for jobs (i.e., courses in typing, personal finance, or shop).

Tremendous variation exists even from school to school. A very wide range of occupational courses (such as cosmetology, machine repair, and bookkeeping) are offered in some high schools, and hardly any are offered in others. Those schools that send a large majority of their students on to higher education may allocate less than 15 percent of their teachers' time to nonacademic courses. In schools where few students go on to higher education, more than two-fifths or more of the teachers' time may be allocated to them (Goodlad 1984:202).

MULTICULTURALISM:
A CASE STUDY OF CURRICULAR CHANGE

Course content generally changes at a much faster rate than the rise and fall of subject matter disciplines themselves. By course content, I mean the particular authors, works, interpretations, and theories taught in courses like English or social studies. Some have suggested that these changes generally reflect changing power relations or other social conditions (Bernal 1987). Such writers might see a correspondence, for example, between periods of widespread social criticism and the popularity of the Romantic poets in English courses, or between feminism as a force in the political environment and gender as a popular topic in social science. Sometimes these kinds of correspondence between societal conditions and the popularity of cultural works do exist. However, intellectual trends cannot reliably be reduced to their "social causes." New insights are usually at least as important as new social interests or conditions. Therefore, a complex attitude is required: We must be aware of the forces in the social environment that influence the reception of ideas while also appreciating the particular character of the ideas in play.

In general, course content in science and mathematics is more insulated from changing social concerns than course content in other disciplines. Otherwise, no general principles have yet emerged that help to make sense of the complex histories of course content, which researchers have only recently begun to examine in a systematic and dispassionate way (see, e.g., Graff 1987).

Given the limitations of the existing evidence, I will not attempt to provide a comprehensive treatment of course-level changes in the curriculum. Instead, I will examine a single, though particularly dramatic, case of course-level change: the rise of multiculturalism in the humanities and social sciences. In doing so, I hope to accomplish two goals: to illustrate some of the ideas that sociologists use to understand curricular change at the course level and to provide sociological commentary on the most important and controversial curricular change of our time.

The Debate over Multiculturalism

Henry Louis Gates, Jr. (1992), one of the protagonists in the debate over multicultural curricula, wrote:

> Few commentators could have predicted that one of the issues dominating academic and popular discourse in the final [decades] of the twentieth century—[at the same time as] the fall of apartheid in South Africa [and] communism in Russia . . . —would be the matter of cultural pluralism in our high school and college curricula and its relation to the "American" national identity. (P. xi)

Indeed, the debate has been conducted at a high emotional pitch. On one side of the controversy are defenders of traditional great works and traditional "Western values"; on the other, an alliance of minorities, women, literary theorists, and postmodern philosophers who want to revise the established canon of great works and, sometimes also, the scheme of identifications and values they believe underlies it. One side has argued for the permanent relevance of the classics of Western thought, the other at a minimum for the inclusion of new voices, particularly those of women and minorities.

Given that the word *multiculturalism* hardly existed in public discussion in 1980 (see Bernstein 1994:4), the influence it has exercised in a period of less than two decades must be considered nothing short of phenomenal. As the conservative social commentator Nathan Glazer (1997) has remarked, with a tinge of resignation: "We are all multiculturalists now."

By the late 1980s, many U.S. states (beginning with California in 1987) added principles in their curriculum guidelines requiring "multicultural and gender-fair" perspectives (Rosenfelt 1994). The institutionalization of multiculturalism in official policies lent legitimacy to efforts to take account of the contributions and experiences of minorities and women.

The transformation of the curriculum is clearest in primary school. Students now read African and Asian folktales, and they have their imaginative passports stamped with the impressions of countries throughout the world, rather than only those of Europe and America. The customs of many different lands are studied. Walls and hallways are decorated with pictures of famous women and minorities, as well as famous nonminority men.

Many high schools have added minority and women writers to their English curricula, and some have introduced new "world literature" courses. High school textbooks have moved away from a concern with the doings of presidents and prime ministers and begun to play up the contributions of women and minorities. They have also frankly recognized the failings of American society in the integration of racial minorities (Fitzgerald 1979).

The scope of change is also impressive in higher education. A recent survey of some 200 institutions showed that one-third of colleges and universities had multicultural general education requirements, either as part of required core courses or as part of college distribution requirements (Levine and Cureton

1992). One-third of the schools also offered course work specifically in ethnic and gender studies. More than half of colleges and universities reported efforts to introduce multicultural themes into departmental offerings. These efforts were largely in the nature of add-ons to existing curricula, rather than replacements for traditional courses (Levine and Cureton 1992:29). At the same time, entirely new courses have been added, some of which attract a larger number of students than traditional courses. In recent years, the fastest-growing course offerings in university history departments have been Asia, Latin America, and Eastern Europe; Western European and English history courses have declined in number (Frank, Schofer, and Torres 1994).

•••••••••••••

THREE MULTICULTURALISMS

Despite the prevalence of multicultural course content, the debate over multiculturalism continues to be intermittently rancorous, largely because three very different visions all go under the same *multicultural* label.

The most moderate of these visions—"Multiculturalism 1"—is in favor of *cultural expansion.* It is essentially another name for the American tradition of cultural pluralism, albeit with a stronger interest in the representation of women, minorities, and Third World cultures than of the contributions of European immigrants. This variant of multiculturalism advocates exposure to different cultures, but it does not necessarily advocate a devaluation of works traditionally considered to be classics of Western thought. This is the variant of multiculturalism to which many well-established advocates of multiculturalism, such as Henry Louis Gates, Jr., self-consciously subscribe.

"Multiculturalism 2" adds a dimension; it is *culturally relativistic* in addition to being culturally expansionist. Its advocates see all cultures as having a similar validity, and they therefore protest against an education based on the rank ordering of texts or cultures. For this second type of multiculturalist, the ideal curriculum would draw more or less equally from the works and histories of many different peoples.

The distinctive characteristic of "Multiculturalism 3" is that it is *ethnocentric.* It seeks to show the oppression of subject groups, and it is self-consciously opposed to dominant groups, whose privileges are often seen as the result of the exploitation of subject groups. Most of these "multiculturalists" are not really multiculturalist at all; they usually want to focus more or less exclusively on their own particular group and have very little interest in exploring the cultures of other groups. Afrocentrists, "critical race theorists," and some types of feminists fit into this camp (see, e.g., Asante 1987). The experience of minorities is seen as separate and antagonistic to the dominant order, not common to a larger national or human experience.

Because this has become a thoroughly muddled debate, perhaps the best solution would be to dispense with the term multicultural altogether and to substitute in its place three terms: cultural expansionism, cultural relativism, and ethnocentrism. These clearer terms would not solve another great problem, however: the tendency to meld more moderate forms of multiculturalism into less moderate forms. Thus, the cultural relativist asks, "If we want to expand the representation of groups in the curriculum, why shouldn't we also treat each one as equal in importance?" And, the ethnocentrist asks, "If every group is essentially equal in importance, why not focus on the special contributions of the particular group with which I personally identify?"

• •

Forces Encouraging Multicultural Curricula

Multiculturalism triumphed with such swiftness in large part because the cultural expansion version of multiculturalism (see sidebar) resonates very strongly with American society's long-standing appreciation and acceptance of cultural differences. The dominant ideology in the United States is market-oriented individualism, which leaves everyone alone to mind his or her own business. This is not a very strongly unifying ideology in a nation of immigrants, and it is, therefore, not very surprising that ideals of cultural pluralism have been a part of the American creed since even the American revolution (see, e.g., de Crèvecoeur [1783] 1912). Multiculturalism, in this sense, can be interpreted as simply stretching a traditional cultural value to include those who have, for no particularly good reason, been left out up to this point.

Some of the other forces encouraging the swift adoption of multiculturalism are also obvious enough. Both the university and the larger society have changed dramatically in their demographic composition since the 1950s. American society is still mostly white, but the white proportion dropped from 90 to 75 percent between the censuses of 1950 and 1990, and by 1990 white males made up only about a third of the population. Most legal immigrants no longer come from Europe, but from Asia and Latin America, and the fastest-growing groups are the three major racial and ethnic minorities (Riche 1993). Colleges and universities have also changed in ways that make both the student body and the faculty look more like that larger society. The new academic generation—those who have not yet reached the tenure stage—is more than 40 percent female and almost 17 percent minority (Finkelstein, Seal, and Schuster 1995).

Generational conflict is another factor, as Gates (1992) observed: "Ours was the generation that took over buildings in the late 1960s and demanded black and women's studies programs and now, like the return of the repressed, has come back to challenge the traditional [curriculum]" (p. 19). Indeed, much of the impetus behind multiculturalism can be found in the political protest and identity politics of the 1960s. Consciousness raising through appeals to group pride (e.g., "black is beautiful" and "gay pride") became a central part of political mobilization during that period. Many of the battles between multiculturalists and their critics remind outside observers of nothing so much as a superannuated version of Sixties generational conflict with older, but still angry, protesters confronting stooped, but still unbending, defenders of traditional values. The relative insecurity of liberal arts scholars in a university world now dominated by the natural sciences and the powerful professional schools comes into play as well. The desire to change the world is generally felt more keenly by those whose own circumstances are unsettled, especially if those circumstances have become less secure in a short period of time.

These forces create an environment conducive to change, and legal requirements, of course, provide a strong lever of change. Even so, something is very odd about this situation: Educators seem curiously eager to jettison a cultural heritage that seemed not long ago to define what it meant to have a fully mature consciousness. The great African American novelist Ralph Ellison once wrote that he found mental "freedom" by reading Marx, Freud, Eliot, Pound, Gertrude Stein, and Hemingway as a boy in Macon County, Alabama. By freedom, Ellison meant exposure to artists and writers who offered a broad and profound sense of life, its possibilities, and its dilemmas. However, the notion that the great thinkers of the Western tradition have special relevance to our civilization no longer rings true even to many of the brightest high school and college students. Why is that?

The conservative writer Nathan Glazer (1997) has argued that multiculturalism is the price American academic culture is paying for its failure to integrate African Americans. Although it is clear that the alienation of minorities often fuels movements of collective cultural assertion, Glazer's is not a fully satisfying explanation. Multiculturalism is, after all, on the agenda throughout the world. For a more complete answer, it is necessary to look for the deeper social and economic currents that may be working under the surface controversies.

Globalization is one enormously important factor. Since the end of the Cold War, we have seen the full internationalization of capitalist exchange and the internationalization of the business elite. Japanese, European, and North American firms are tied through complex networks of joint ownership, joint capitalization, and franchising. Financial markets have become fully internationalized among the richer powers, with changes in one stock exchange affecting the other major exchanges. Travel and tourism continue to grow as a part of the global economy, and other forms of international exchange—from scholarly conferences to food and musical influences—also become commonplace. It is not surprising under these circumstances that multiculturalism has triumphed perhaps most quickly in elite institutions, including the once-stodgy private boarding schools. These schools, like other elites spheres, have become internationalized over the past several decades. They admit increasing numbers of international students, and the parents of native-born students see, through their own experience, that their children will be living in a more globally integrated world.

Less obvious, but perhaps equally important, is our collective loss of faith in the emancipatory potential of difficult or ambiguous lessons. Ralph Ellison had this faith, but few students now do. As the number of students in higher education has grown, colleges and universities have begun to become mass rather than elite institutions. The market value of a college degree has for some time been more important to entering freshmen than concern with values of education itself (Cooperative Institutional Research Program 1987). In a world of instantaneous information and relatively easy circumstances, difficult or ambiguous lessons may seem hardly worth the effort, especially if they are unrelated to future job prospects. This is true to an even greater degree if a mature consciousness, a consciousness aware of complexity and ambiguity, is no longer necessary equipment for social acceptance among highly educated people.

Thus, whatever the truth of the new works in the multicultural canon, this curricular change would never have been effected without large-scale social change (globalization, credentialism, the shift away from ideals of cultivation involving "difficult works"), demographic changes both in the university and in the larger society, and vigorous political and moral struggles on the part of intellectuals interested in advancing multiculturalism.

The rise of multiculturalism is an instance of multisided causation. In some other cases, curricular change has been more exclusively influenced by the persuasive power of new theories or by the funding priorities of government and foundation officials.

SCHOOLING'S LIMITED SUCCESS IN
TRANSMITTING KNOWLEDGE

If the transmission of knowledge is widely accepted to be a key purpose of schooling, it is fair to ask how successfully it is done. At one time, schools were content to transmit academic knowledge only to a small elite. By historical standards, therefore, the ambition and performance of schooling are impressive. Nevertheless, contemporary schools have had only modest success in transmitting the lessons of the curriculum to the majority of students. This limited success suggests that exposure to course materials may be more effective as a vehicle for practicing a handful of general mental operations (such as focusing, memorizing, applying rules, dividing wholes, and connecting parts) than it is for conveying specific information.

Nonintellectual Interests of Students

The acquisition of school knowledge is undoubtedly very important for the top 15-20 percent of students. These students develop at least a degree of proficiency in their studies. It is also important for society insofar as it profits from the work of this academically oriented stratum.

Schools are much less successful in transmitting knowledge to the majority of students, however. The facts are clear enough. Students do not remember much course content after the final test has been given (Collins 1979:17-9). What little that is remembered continues to erode at a fast rate. When they look back on their schooling, most people have vague memories of liking or not liking particular instructors, but they remember very little of the material covered in class and cannot clearly identify concrete knowledge they acquired.

Nor do the majority of students consider learning to be the most important part of their schooling experience. Instead, they speak more often of the opportunity to see and be seen with their friends. Moreover, in the status system of adolescent society, academic success ranks low. Athletic and dating success are more esteemed, and in some national studies membership in the academic elite actually ranks lower than membership in a gang as a badge of status (Tye 1985). Even college students largely reject intellectual identities. Those who take a real interest in their course work often do not retain intellectual interests after they finish their schooling. Without support from a larger circle of friends and acquaintances, the intellectual interests developed in school tend to fade (Feldman and Newcomb 1969; Withey 1971).[11] In many countries, including the United States, judgments of admirable qualities in others are much more likely to focus on economic success or moral character than on cultivation and intellect (Lamont 1992).

Declining Performance? Indeed, the poor performance of American students on national educational assessments became a cause for widespread alarm in the 1980s. Diane Ravitch and Chester Finn's *What Do Our 17 Year Olds Know?* (1987) was one of a number of studies and commission reports that called attention to the troubled state of learning among American high school students during the period. Ravitch and Finn reported average scores in the failing range on two national assessments: Only 54.5 percent correct in history and 52 percent correct in literature. Among the dispiriting findings for educators was that only one-third of the students could identify the date of the Civil War within a 50-year time frame, and only about the same proportion could identify the theme of George Orwell's novel, *1984.* Other reports of the era showed that 30 percent of high school seniors could not locate Great Britain on a map (Sowell 1992). Student performance, particularly in secondary school, declined significantly between the mid-1960s and the late 1970s, a consequence in part of less demanding curricula.

Assessments like these have been given on a national basis to 4th, 8th, and 12th graders for some 25 years now through the National Assessment of Educational Progress (NAEP). The results of these assessments have improved in recent years (see the discussion in Chapter 9), but performance levels overall have remained low. For example, in the 1990s approximately 40 percent of American students at all grade levels scored at a level "below basic competence" in mathematics, and only 20 percent in any grade level reached the "proficiency" level that the assessment's governing board considered within reach of *all* students (Ravitch 1995:79).

International Comparisons

Do American students perform less well than students in other countries? Although differences exist among students from different countries, the evidence suggests that the "1066 and all that" effect is relevant throughout the world. It is hard work to master school knowledge, and the payoffs for this hard work are by no means self-evident to many students. School knowledge is not especially memorable to most students—whether they are attending classes in Bangkok, Paris, Johannesburg, Cleveland, or Kyoto.

International educational assessments have been conducted since the mid-1960s in the core subjects of reading comprehension, mathematics, and science and also in a few other subjects. These international assessments provide evidence about how well U.S. schools are performing in relation to schools in other countries.

Special precautions have to be taken when interpreting the findings of these studies, because a variety of technical problems limit the comparability of scores across nations (see, e.g., Husen 1979; Inkeles 1979; Noah 1987). For example, not all countries have sampled their schools adequately or looked at an exactly comparable set of students. If variables such as the poverty rates in different countries or actual exposure to tested materials are not included in the reporting of results, the gross results may be misleading to compare (Berliner and Biddle 1995:51-63). Perhaps most important, performance on standardized tests may not reflect the actual knowledge of students very well. The observational studies of anthropologists such as Jean Lave (1988) show that the ability to express knowledge is highly contextual. The same students who give random, uninformed responses on tests may show a quick grasp of mathematics when they are laying carpets in their family business or playing number games with their friends.

Nevertheless, if they are taken with the proper number of grains of salt, some of the findings of the assessments can be used as indicators of how well schools are doing in the area of transmitting knowledge. No country is consistently superior to all others across all subjects and age levels. Instead, the "winners" and "losers" in these assessments shift quite a bit from test to test, grade level to grade level, and year to year. Not surprisingly, the largest differences are between students from industrialized countries and students from developing countries. Students in some East Asian countries (e.g., Japan and China) and some Central European countries (e.g., Hungary and the Czech Republic) have performed well on most tests of mathematics and science.

It is important to keep in mind that scores on these tests are not based on percent correct. A score of 500 does not mean 50 percent correct. Instead, they are designed to produce a normal distribution. Average scores also vary from test to test. In recent tests of eighth graders, for example, the average score in mathematics was 509 and the average score in science was 522. In the math test, a score of 655 put a student in the top 10 percent and in a science a score of 656 put a student in the top 10 percent (NCES 1996: 23).

International assessments for grades 4, 6, and 8 show that students from high-income countries average in the 500 to 600 range on tests of mathematics, science, and reading, while students from low-income countries average 100 to 150 points lower (Ravitch 1995: 83-9; NCES, 1996). In some developing countries, like Burkina Faso, scores suggest essentially random responses to test questions. The international results also show a much wider range of scores within developing countries, reflecting in part the very large differences in quality between urban and rural schools (Lockheed, Fonancier, and Bianchi 1989).

The Results in Context. Most popular accounts of these tests have emphasized the poor performance of American students. In fact, when American students are compared with students in other industrialized countries, they have often scored near or at the top of tests in reading comprehension. They are generally closer to average among students from industrialized countries on tests in science, and they score comparatively poorly on tests of mathematics (Carson, Huelskamp, and Woodall 1992). (However, American nine-year-olds recently scored near the top of the latest mathematics assessment.)

Because international test results have been irresponsibly reported and irresponsibly used, the alarm about the failure of American schools compared with other systems can legitimately be characterized as a "manufactured crisis" (Berliner and Biddle 1995). This does not mean, however, that American students—or students from any other country—are necessarily performing that well.

The mathematics and science tests bear the closest scrutiny. Mathematics and science are enormously important subjects for technologically advanced societies. They are the best single indicators of students' ability to succeed well in higher education and in the more challenging jobs in the occupational structure. Moreover, because mathematics and science are universal languages, the problems of translation that otherwise plague test constructors are minimized.

On tests of mathematics and science, students from several East Asian societies (notably, Japan, Korea, Singapore, and Hong Kong) have usually outperformed American students by a considerable margin, and students from some Central European countries (notably, Hungary and the Czech Republic) have also generally scored higher than American students. Even in the highest-scoring countries, national averages typically fall below 67 percent correct.

Explaining Cross-National Differences. Country differences in average scores can be explained by a combination of factors internal and external to the schools. The most important factors internal to the schools are the kinds of materials that are taught and the methods used to teach them. A well-focused curriculum, which requires exposure to higher-level knowledge and skills but does not attempt to cover too many topics, usually leads to better average performance (NCES 1996:37-8). Teachers who have sufficient time to plan lessons, who talk to each other frequently about their work, and who incorporate problems connected to students' everyday life experience are also more likely to have a positive effect on learning. (See also the discussion of teaching and learning in Chapter 8.) Both individual classrooms and societies can vary on these dimensions.

The most important factors outside of the schools are parents' investment in their children's education, the availability of alternatives that draw children away from schooling, and the consequences for later life of school achievement. If parents invest time, effort, and money in their children's education, they will tend to encourage good performance. If regular times are set aside for homework and few alternatives exist—either in informal socializing or work opportunities—as a distraction from study, more students are likely to concentrate effectively on their schoolwork. Finally, a strong link between school performance and later opportunities also focuses attention on school. When children do not feel that schooling is relevant to their futures, they will not take schooling as seriously. Again, both individual classrooms and societies can vary in these ways. Figure 4.1 provides a graphic representation of the forces I have described as relevant to different levels of performance on international mathematics and science assessments.

The example of Japan indicates that schools are most effective in transmitting school knowledge when students have the opportunity to learn demanding materials, have strong support for schoolwork, and have strong incentives to achieve. Even the East Asian societies have not, however, created the perfect schooling machinery. Recent research shows that Japanese adolescents now have competing alternatives available to them. They watch about as much television as American students, and they actually do less homework than American students (NCES 1996:57-67).

In math and science, the biggest differences between American students and students from higher-scoring countries is that American students are asked to cover too many topics and have fewer opportunities to learn more demanding curricular materials than their counterparts in East Asia and Central Europe (NCES 1996, chap. 3; Berliner and Biddle 1995:54-8). The findings of international assessments, far from demonstrating the dismal state of learning in the United States compared with other countries, actually support those who think that American students and American schools are not much worse than students and schools in other countries—and may in fact perform somewhat better when they have access to comparably well-designed learning materials.

International Tests and Economic Competitiveness

Nevertheless, newspaper editors and politicians like to use international comparisons to sound alarms about the threat that poor school performance poses for the future prosperity of the country. These kinds of warnings have in the past been effective for focusing attention on schools, but they are not based on sound arguments (see Collins 1979, chap. 1; Blaug 1987; Berliner and Biddle 1995). International comparisons in fact tell us next to nothing about the likely trajectory of national economies.

FIGURE 4.1

Model of National Achievement in Educational Assessments

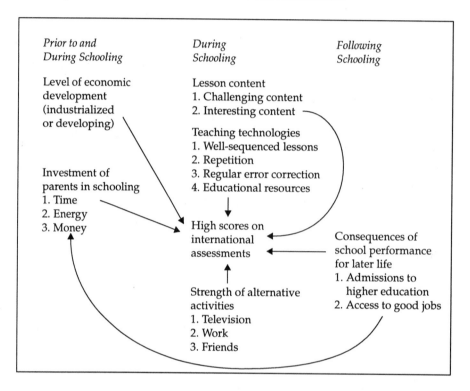

Consider just two counterfactuals: It is well known that the performance of American high school students took a nosedive in the late 1960s and throughout the 1970s (Ravitch 1995, chap. 3). Yet by the time these mediocre students began to take leading roles in the economic life of the country, the economy was humming along quite nicely. The United States rebounded from the economic slump of the 1970s in large part because a devalued dollar made U.S. industries more competitive in those industries in which it had lost market share (Berliner and Biddle 1995:92). The schools were responsible neither for the slump nor for the rebound. By contrast, the economic troubles of the 1970s occurred under the watch of the supposedly diligent students of the 1950s. In fact, it is unlikely that scores on standardized tests of school knowledge have any clear relationship to how well or poorly advanced capitalist economies perform. The evidence suggests that swings in the advanced economies have causes all their own.

Support is also missing for the related notions that a more knowledgeable citizenry will necessarily raise the level of public discourse or that it will raise the tone of popular culture. If political discourse has deteriorated—and who can say with certainty that it has?—this deterioration has much more to do with the vastly increased scale of government operations and the gulf that consequently separates citizens from their leaders. Similarly, if public taste has fallen—again, who can confidently say that it has?—this almost certainly has more to do with the enormous capacity of popular media to stimulate the eardrums and galvanize the eyeballs.

In short, if the results of international comparisons cause people to feel dissatisfied with the state of knowledge transmission in the schools, they should justify improvement as desirable in its own right, rather than because it will magically boost competitiveness, strengthen the political order, or improve public taste. It can be argued that better learning is desirable because learning alone has the capacity to improve students' faculties of logic and judgment and to deepen their experience of the world. If improvements can eventually be shown to have positive spillovers in other arenas, so much the better.

Scores on international assessments are probably not completely unrelated to national economic circumstances, however. In all likelihood, they do tell us something about the level of mobilized human energy, or industriousness, in a society. It follows that international comparisons may be more important for developing countries than for industrialized societies. In the latter, industriousness becomes part of the fabric of organizational life; it is regulated by what Max Weber called the "iron cage" of rules and incentives and, in some companies, also by technological surveillance. Better retention of school knowledge surely would not produce modernized economies overnight in the developing world. But together with political stability, wise use of resources and relief from debt burdens, it might help to place the upcoming generation of students on a better footing to meet future development goals.

CONCLUSION

The transmission of knowledge is the most obvious purpose of schooling. To investigate the transmission of school knowledge, it is necessary to examine how subject matter materials become part of the curriculum and how successfully these materials are transmitted to students.

Contemporary structures of school knowledge originate in three separate concerns: the state's interest in providing rudimentary literacy and numeracy training, the aristocracy's interest in preparing its offspring to govern, and church and professional interests in occupational specialization. These were important historical bases, respectively, of primary, secondary, and university education. Over time, primary schooling has broadened to encompass a wider range of mental and socioemotional capacities; secondary schools have become divided between academic tracks leading to the university and occupational tracks leading to the job market; and liberal arts have migrated upward to control the first two years of higher education. In addition, research has been added as a capstone to higher education in graduate and postdoctoral training. In general, these changes reflect the growing importance of specialist ideologies at the higher levels of schooling. They are also closely connected to organizational changes (particularly the creation of articulated ladder structures linking the three levels of schooling) and demographic influences (especially the increasing number of students moving from primary to secondary schooling and then on to higher education). Some cultural trends, such as the rise of "progressive" child development philosophies, are also involved in these changes. These have greatly influenced curriculum at the preschool and primary levels.

Today, primary school curricula are very similar throughout the world. Most schooling concentrates on national language and literature and, to a lesser degree, math and science. The arts, physical education, and social science are also represented throughout the world, though they are not allocated as much time in the curriculum. John Meyer and his associates (Meyer, Kamens, and Benavot 1992) have argued that this global curriculum structure reflects an originally Western, but now globally institutionalized, vision of modernity linking individual development to national purposes. Secondary school curricula are more varied, however. European academic tracks feature more specialization and intensity than American academic tracks and also a higher level of distance from vocational tracks. Here we see the residue of the nineteenth-century ideals of elite preparation in Europe and democratic uplift in the United States.

By historical standards, the capacity of contemporary schooling to transmit knowledge is impressive. In the early part of this century fewer than five percent of Europeans even received secondary education. Nevertheless, schools have not succeeded in bringing the majority of students to high levels of achievement. Only 15-20 percent of students in most industrialized countries show real proficiency in the mastery of school subjects. Students from industrialized societies tend to perform better than students from developing societies on these tests, but no countries consistently outperform all others. In general, American students score high on tests of reading comprehension, and

East Asian and Central European students score high on tests in mathematics and science. In recent years, American students have begun to catch up in these subjects. Differences between countries largely reflect the greater opportunity students in East Asia and Central Europe have to learn more challenging and better focused course material. Factors external to the schools also help to explain country differences in student performance. High levels of parental support for learning, the existence of regular times for study, and strong rewards in the job market for good school performance all contribute to better scores.

The results of national and international assessments have often been irresponsibly reported and used for political purposes. Contrary to many published reports, no convincing links have been established between a country's average score on international education assessments and its level of economic competitiveness, civic virtue, or public taste. Inaccurate and biased reports about student performance on international assessments have raised the level of public concern about schooling, but they have also misled many people about the true sources of economic and social problems.

CHAPTER 5

Schools and Socialization

The early-nineteenth-century American school reformer Horace Mann observed that it is easier to create a republic than to create republicans (Mann, quoted in Cremin 1957:14). By this, Mann meant that the self-restraint and virtuous conduct that make representative government possible do not necessarily come naturally to those born into republics and must therefore be created by society's institutions, particularly its schools. Mann's observation suggests the important role schools have long played in the socialization of children.

Sociologists use the term *socialization* to describe the efforts of a group that considers itself the carrier of the society's accepted ways of life to shape the values and behavior of another group which is considered to be less-than-completely integrated into those ways of life. In the school context, adult authorities are usually the socializers and students the socialized. However, students can also try to socialize adults into the ways of student society. (If they are successful, this would be an example of "reverse socialization." The effort of school authorities to socialize students is undoubtedly one of the major activities of schooling. Think of how often students' attention and behavior is organized in school around explicit or implicit norms of conduct. Every time a teacher says "I need your attention," she is socializing students to be responsive to authority. Every time she hands back a paper with a smile or a frown, she is socializing students to value work well done in the eyes of the school.

Schools play a secondary role to families in socializing children. The powerful mix of emotional intimacy and consistent attentiveness typical of family life cannot be duplicated by the more impersonal institutions of society. Families create the capacity for trust and self-control out of which healthy egos develop. Even so, schools are organized in ways that are particularly conducive to the formation of personalities for a public world in which intimacy and attentiveness are not always in generous supply. Schools specialize in the creation of people who can adapt to impersonal work environments and who can pursue their interests in action with and against people who are neither kin nor intimate friends. Without lengthy exposure to the socializing environments of the school, most children would not be as well prepared as they are for adult life.

This chapter begins by describing the three types of socialization that can take place in schools and then sketches the historical development of schools' socializing role. The remainder of the chapter analyzes two distinct sites of socialization in contemporary schools: the classroom and the "playground." By playground, I mean all school spaces outside the classroom—the hallways, playgrounds, lunch rooms, and extracurricular activity rooms. Classrooms are the spaces in which lessons of industry and work-related achievement are principally taught. Playgrounds are the spaces in which friendships and coalitions are formed and broken, status hierarchies are expressed and challenged, and children learn to balance self-assertion and self-control in informal social life. If teachers are the primary socializers in the classroom setting, the dominant boys and girls are the primary socializers in these outside spaces.

THREE DIMENSIONS OF SOCIALIZATION

Socialization is more than instilling values and standards of conduct. Think of socialization as involving three dimensions: efforts to shape behavior, moral values, and cultural styles. The differences in these dimensions become clearer when we consider how students who conform primarily on one of these dimensions are characterized. Students are described as "well disciplined" by authorities if they conform behaviorally, "good" if they are seen to conform morally, and "well adjusted" if they conform culturally.

Behavioral Conformity. Training for behavioral conformity involves activities related to the body, its mechanical actions, and its accessories. In schools with strict disciplinary environments, students may, for example, be required to sit erect with their eyes on the teacher, to raise their hands before talking, to stay in their seats unless they are excused, to have their pencils sharpened at all times, and to have their textbooks with them in class. If students are punished for failing to comply with these requirements, the school is attempting to use its powers of control to socialize for behavioral conformity.

Moral Conformity. Training for moral conformity involves activities related to the production of an internalized sense of "right action." Teachers may talk about the importance of such virtues as honesty, kindness, courage, hard work, or fairness. They may also assign reading materials that illustrate the consequences of not being guided by these virtues. At higher levels, more complex moral issues may be raised, involving the collision of two "goods" or finer judgments of others' actions. Clearly, training for behavioral and moral conformity are overlapping in practice. Most schools expect a movement from external discipline based on behavioral control to self-discipline in conformity with key moral values. Nevertheless, it is possible to have a high level of behavioral conformity without much in the way of moral conformity, as the various cheating and harassment scandals in the military academies demonstrate.

Cultural Conformity. Training for cultural conformity, or acculturation, is more a matter of learning approved styles and outlooks. In the better Parisian secondary schools, for example, students are expected to express themselves vividly, with memorable phrases and sharp wit (Bourdieu 1988). If a student makes a very witty remark in class, the teacher will smile in appreciation or attempt an equally witty riposte. By contrast, in secondary school in a Central European republic, it may be more important for students to demonstrate conspicuous thoughtfulness: to probe beneath the surface appearances and to ask questions that get to the heart of a difficult problem. These styles and outlooks reflect the cultural logic of a particular group or time or place. It is, for example, reasonable to expect that centers of learning in cosmopolitan capitals like Paris will reflect the quick pace and brilliant surfaces of archetypal urban life, whereas those in relatively isolated regions show a gravity that frequently appears unduly stiff to urban sophisticates. Students of acculturation tend to be cultural relativists; they try to understand the social logic that produces distinctive cultural styles, but they do not necessarily think that cultural styles and outlooks have any universal validity.

Even when schools emphasize all three types of conformity, they may be more successful in one area than others. For example, military cadets are required to conform to an enormous number of behavioral rules. If they don't salute in a crisp fashion, they can be sent back to barracks. If their boots don't show a "spit shine," they can be forced to clean out latrines. Because well-executed response to orders is vitally important in the military, behavioral conformity is a top priority. By contrast, faculty in art schools may expect students to take pride in thumbing their noses at behavioral and moral conventions, as the famous battle cry of bohemia, *"éepater les bourgeois"* (literally, shock or flabbergast the middle class), demands. But acculturation is unavoidable even in this nonconformist environment. To be accepted by other bohemians, would-be bohemians will necessarily conform to the expressive style and outlooks typical of their set. They may need to be able to talk knowledge-ably about obscure poets or musicians and to shift smoothly between attitudes of enthusiasm for the offbeat and worldweariness in the face of the familiar. A would-be bohemian who does not act in these ways is not very well suited for bohemian life.

Discussions of the role of schools in socialization are often muddled by the failure to keep these three dimensions distinct. Many contemporary conserva-tive critics, for example, suggest that schools are failing in the area of sociali-zation because they have stopped emphasizing moral virtues. In the introduc-tion to his best-seller *The Book of Virtues* (1993), former U.S. Secretary of Education William Bennett wrote:

> Where do we go to find the material that will help our children in [the] task [of developing moral literacy]? The simple answer is we . . . have a wealth of material to draw on—materials that virtually all schools and homes and churches once taught to students for the sake of shaping character. That many no longer do so is something this book hopes to change. (P. 11)

Although he raises an important issue in this passage, Secretary Bennett is high-lighting one dimension of socialization while playing down the other two.

Schools need to develop a certain minimum level of behavioral conformity, and they can't help but acculturate students in some way. Nor have they aban-doned the field of moral instruction as completely as Bennett and other critics contend. The specific socialization messages and the techniques used to social-ize have, however, changed greatly over time.

SOCIALIZATION IN COMPARATIVE AND HISTORICAL PERSPECTIVE

School socialization environments can be described as fitting one of four major ideal types:

- The village/communal pattern is based on relatively lax behavioral con-trol, relatively low levels of explicit moral training, and accommodation to the rhythms of village life.

- The industrializing pattern is based on very high levels of behavioral train-ing, high levels of training for moral conformity, and acculturation primar-ily to the world of mechanical production.

- The bureaucratic/mass consumption pattern is based on impersonal con-trol through rules and routines, relatively lower levels of moral discussion, and many more choices. Students are acculturated to a double-sided world of bureaucratic organization and mass consumption.

- The elite pattern has existed at the upper reaches of all societies, but the specific forms of elite socialization have varied greatly from society to society because of differences in the outlooks of the groups decisive in the formation of the schools, the geographic location of the schools, and other factors.

Table 5.1 compares these four socialization environments.

TABLE 5.1

School Socializing Environments

	Dimensions of socialization		
Type of environment	*Behavioral*	*Moral*	*Cultural*
Village/communal	Relatively lax	Relatively weak emphasis	Accommodation to rhythms of village life
Industrializing	Strong explicit emphasis	Strong explicit emphasis	Preparation for world of industrial production and nation building
Bureaucratic/ mass consumption	Embedded in rules and practices	Relatively weak emphasis and more pluralistic	Preparation for impersonal organizational life, cultural pluralism, and consumerism
Elite	Largely implicit (based on behavior modeling)	Relatively strong and highly ritualized	Preparation for world of power and status

Qualifications about the Typology. It is important to avoid overly sweeping generalizations about how uniformly schools in any society fit into this typology. First, cultural understandings of childhood often have an independent influence on how societies organize their socialization practices. Some societies, such as contemporary Japan, draw a strict separation between the years of innocence and the years of responsibility. Early childhood is seen as a period of experimentation in which children require indulgence and unconditional support. They are not expected to conform to a highly disciplined style of life until later childhood (Stevenson and Stigler 1992). These views have been common historically in many European countries as well (Cubberly 1922).

Second, the socializing environment in primary and secondary schools always differs somewhat. The personal authority of teachers over students is much more typical of primary schooling than of secondary schooling today. Choices are far greater in secondary schools. Therefore, the bureaucratic/ mass consumption pattern is always more apparent as a relatively pure form at the secondary school level.

Moreover, within countries, the dominant socialization pattern does not necessarily sweep away the others. In some cases, a mix of elements may be present. Laurence Wylie (1974) describes a village school in the south of France in the 1950s that seems to mix elements of the village/communal and industrializing patterns. A favored child is allowed to wander unimpeded from classroom to classroom, where he is affectionately hugged by each teacher. The teachers do not have the same expectations for every child and are tolerant of those who are not succeeding. At the same time, the teachers maintain, and the parents insist on, a rather strict climate of authority in the classroom ("Children must never dispute the word of the teacher") with "severe punishments" in the few cases of lying or stealing (Wylie 1974, chap. 4).

Finally, the circumstances of the local economy or the social class composition of the school may create significant variation within a country. In the United States, the bureaucratic/mass consumption pattern now predominates in most middle- and upper-middle-class communities. But the other three socialization environments can also be found in various places. The elite pattern continues, of course, in private day and boarding schools (and even in advanced placement tracks of some suburban public schools). The village/communal pattern is apparent in some of the poorest rural areas of the country— for example, among Mexican farmworkers in the Central Valley of California or in the poorest sections of the Mississippi delta. The industrializing pattern can still be found in many urban working-class schools. In these working-class schools, students are closely monitored for behavioral conformity and are expected to follow a large number of detailed rules. The environment is more highly moralized, and work assignments are typically based on rote memorization, filling in answers on rather undemanding worksheets (Bowles and Gintis 1976; Anyon 1980; Cookson and Persell 1985). Parents tend to be the instigators of such class-conditioned socialization. Upper-middle-class parents expect more self-directed and creative schoolwork for their children; working-class parents demand tough discipline and strict compliance with the teacher's direction (Kohn 1972; Anyon 1979; Lareau 1987).

Although some variations in school socialization environments exist in all countries, the majority of schools will typically resemble one of the three major types more than the others. (The elite pattern is by definition rare; see the sidebar.)

As societies change, so do the dominant patterns of socialization in schools. The first transformation is from the relatively free-flowing village/communal pattern to an industrial pattern characterized by very stringent demands for behavioral control and moral conformity. Today, the majority of schools in the wealthier societies have made a second transformation: from the industrial to the bureaucratic/mass consumption pattern. Some of these changes are the result of conscious emulation of the leading organizations in society; some an unconscious reflection of changing expectations in the larger society.

•••••••••••••

SOCIALIZATION IN ELITE SCHOOLS

One of the great advantages of elite schooling is in the area of social training. Through modeling the behavior of fellow students, children at private preparatory schools are able to acquire a refined sense of the accepted demeanor of publicly expressed power in a democracy: good spirits and an easy manner with obvious social inferiors; an aloof attitude (which can be aggressively expressed, if necessary, through snubs and smirks) toward social inferiors who encroach too closely; and true frankness only with recognized social equals.

Socialization in elite schools often reflects the activities and circumstances of the groups that were decisive either in the founding of the schools or during the schools' most important transformations. In the United States, private day and boarding schools were founded, for the most part, in the late nineteenth century by old, prominent families, largely as a way of maintaining social distance from the large numbers of new rich who had risen during the "Gilded Age." These schools, located in rural areas of New England, inculcated the values of American "old money": a very high level of self-control; taboos on discussions of money; a constant admonition to be involved in service activities for the public good; experience in juggling many activities; an efficient, businesslike approach to assignments; the expectation that knowledge is to be used rather than simply memorized; and a sense of entitlement to the privileges and power of high social status (Cookson and Persell 1985).

By contrast, British public schools (which are the same as American elite private boarding schools), also located outside of London, reflected the imprint of the colonial administration of the British Empire, with its emphasis on sports as a proving ground for the battlefield, chapel as an essential feature of a world-transforming Christian mission, and earnest effort in the classroom. In the most prestigious of the public schools, such as Eton, it also showed the imprint of dandyism on the English aristocracy (McConnell 1985).

In Germany, the values of the *bildungsbergertum*—the educated upper-middle class—strongly shaped German elite education following the university reform of the early 1800s (Ringer 1969). This class, which sharply distinguished itself from the business-oriented upper-middle class, emphasized internal cultivation and external civility. It was highly intellectual and sought to distinguish the "higher court" of cultural values from the self-interested behavior of everyday life (Ringer 1992).

Acculturation in French elite education, by contrast, was shaped by Parisian wit and civil service precision, as these became embedded in the teaching traditions of the *grandes écoles* founded by Napoleon for the purpose of forming a military, industrial, and administrative elite for state service (Suleiman 1978). The *grandes écoles*, located in and around Paris, exercised a tremendous influence on the socializing patterns of the French academic secondary schools, not least of all because French secondary school teachers were trained at one of them, the *École Normale Superieure* (Bourdieu 1988).

• •

The First Transformation: From Village to Factory

The least developed countries are those in which the routines of public life are also least entrenched, and where the intimate cultures of family and village still take precedence. The classroom environment in such countries tends to be relatively informal, and expectations for attendance, attentiveness, or performance cannot be easily enforced. Individual transgressions, such as poor performance and spotty attendance, are readily forgiven. Not much can be expected of teachers, either. A good example comes from Nancy Hornberger's (1987) fieldwork in rural Peru: "Over the seven day period, out of 50.5 hours spent at school by the children . . . 30.5 hours were [spent out of the classroom] as follows: 16.5 hours in recreation periods, 4.5 hours in sports competitions, 3.5 hours waiting during adult meetings, 3.5 hours in which teachers were absent during school, and 2.5 hours in line-up activities" (p. 211). She goes on to add that a fifth of the classroom time consisted of housecleaning activities, such as sweeping up the classroom.

At somewhat higher levels of economic development, the classroom climate changes. Few countries have managed to achieve sustained economic growth without the industrialization of schoolchildren. The informal ways of the village are replaced by readiness and exertion at industrial work. The value of strict obedience to authority is communicated to students through strict classroom discipline, and classroom life is consequently harsh. Many countries provide a warm and nurturing environment for early primary schooling, with rugs and overstuffed furniture easing the transition from home to school. Regimentation takes over in the later grades. In some countries, such as Germany in the later nineteenth century, the influence of factory style discipline was heightened in the upper primary grades and secondary schools by a nationalist ideology that stressed preparation for war (Ringer 1979, chap. 2).

Of course, not all countries leaped into the modern era on the heels of industrialized schools. In slow-industrializing countries, the era of mass schooling preceded industrialization. In these countries, socialization took a different path at first. In the early 1800s, the Swiss German reformer Johann-Heinrich Pestalozzi preached that all children could develop their intellectual and moral capacities, if schools encouraged them to do so. He introduced methods of teaching in parts of modern Switzerland and Germany that aimed to inspire children's interest in learning, rather than to fill their heads with mechanical drill. This effort to adapt schooling to the natural interests and development of children dovetailed in these countries with the state's interest in separating formal schooling from religious control and connecting children to a new model of "modern" personality and national purpose.

The English, by contrast, developed mass schooling after rather than before industrialization. The industrialization of schooling also goes to the greatest lengths in England. At the same time that Pestalozian ideas were adopted in the German-speaking world, the English were beginning experiments with monitorial instruction, or the Lancasterian system. The system is named after Joseph Lancaster, who developed a plan in which one teacher, assisted by several of the brighter pupils, could teach from 200 to 1,000 students in one school. The pupils were sorted into rows, and each row was assigned to a monitor. The teacher first taught these monitors a lesson from a printed card, then each monitor took his row to a "station" at the wall of the room and proceed to teach the other children what he had learned. The Lancasterian schools were organized in a largely mechanical fashion. "The *Manuals of Instruction* gave complete directions for the organization and management of monitorial schools, the details of recitation work, use of apparatus, order, position of pupils at their work and classification being minutely laid down"

(Cubberly 1922:341). The schools were very popular between 1810 and 1830 in England and other early-industrializing countries, but fell out of fashion by 1840. The low expense of monitorial schools could not compensate for their inability to sustain the interest of hundreds of children at a time.

In many eastern cities in the United States, the first free schools were Lancasterian schools, and indeed Lancaster spent most of the last 20 years of his life organizing schools in the United States (Cubberly 1922:360). Even after the popularity of the monitorial system waned, schooling in the United States remained highly repressive. No doubt Puritan asceticism, aligned with industrial work discipline, influenced the unusual severity of schooling in the United States. Children were relentlessly schooled to be obedient, regular, and precise in their habits. Classrooms were organized not so much to stimulate the intellect as to create well-disciplined workers. The phrase "toeing the line" still had a literal meaning. Joseph Rice (1893) visited hundreds of urban classrooms in the eastern United States to collect data for his book on the public high school at the turn of the century. In one school described by Rice, during "recitation periods" (periods in which students demonstrated that they had memorized a text), children were expected "to stand on the line, perfectly motionless, their bodies erect, their knees and feet together, the tips of their shoes touching the edge of a board in the floor." The teachers, according to Rice, paid as much attention to the state of their toes and knees as to the words coming out of their mouths: " 'How can you learn anything' asked one teacher, 'with your knees and toes out of order?' " (p. 98).

Disciplinary practices varied, of course, but they were generally strict. At Philadelphia's Central High School, two evaluations were taken every hour—one for scholarship, the other for conduct. Demerits for disciplinary infractions (such as laziness or insubordination) were deducted from the student's grade point average at the end of term, influencing class rank and chances for promotion. In 1853, the principal of Philadelphia's Central High School described this system of discipline:

> The whole machinery of the school, like an extended piece of net-work,
> is thrown over and around (the student), and made to bear upon him, not
> with any great amount of force at any one time or place, but with a restrain-
> ing influence just sufficient, and always and every where present. Some of
> the most hopeless cases of idleness and insubordination that I have ever
> known have been found to yield to this species of treatment. (Quoted in
> Labaree 1988:18)

Teachers, too, were tightly controlled. In smaller communities, in particular, female teachers were told what they could wear, where they could travel, how late they could be out, and whose company they could keep. In many places, they were prevented from marrying or joining early feminist organizations. Men had more leeway in most communities. Nevertheless, rules such as the following from one southern California school were not uncommon: "Any teacher who smokes, uses liquor in any form, frequents pool or public halls, or gets shaved in a barber shop will give good reason to suspect his worth, intention, integrity, and honesty" (Oak Glen School, 1873).

Nineteenth-century classrooms were also more highly moralized places than they are today. The schools taught a bundle of virtues that reflect three primary moral traditions: the *Judeo-Christian moral code* of honesty, decency, tolerance, love of goodness, and kindness; the *Protestant work ethic* of industry, enterprise, planning, and frugality; and *republican-nationalist "civil religion"* of patriotism, bravery in battle, love of freedom, respect for the rule of law and the Constitution, and responsible participation in the institutions of political society.[12] The explicit moral teachings of the schools reflect the schools' historical interaction with several waves of dominant idea systems. The first and second of these waves occurred more or less simultaneously. From the eighteenth-century beginnings of mass schooling in Europe, children were taught to be good and patriotic subjects and also to follow the moral norms of the Judeo-Christian tradition (Bendix 1968). A third wave, which followed the rising tide of capitalism and industrialism in the early nineteenth century, encouraged thrift, sobriety, and hard work. The waves of social change brought on by the rise of the nation-state and industrializing capitalism left similar imprints in the socializing objectives and practices of schools throughout the world.

In the United States, most children in the mid- and late nineteenth century learned to read from the McGuffey Readers where "the rules were always clear: Never Drink, Never Smoke, Work Hard, Tell the Truth, Obey Authority, Trust Providence" (Tyack and Hansot 1982:27). "Like a church with its Bible, the rural school with its McGuffey Readers was to be a small incubator of virtue" (ibid., p. 4). Leading educational historians have argued that such rules were based on a tight interweaving of the "absolutist morality of the evangelical movement," the faith in "civic virtue" of eighteenth-century Republicanism, and "entrepreneurial economic values." The common school supported capitalism "by rationalizing wealth or poverty as the result of individual effort or indolence, and by making the political economy seem to be not a matter of choice but of providential design" (ibid., p. 24). These schools were the natural seedbeds both for hard-driving entrepreneurs and their hardworking and abstemious laborers.

The same emphasis on behavioral conformity and moralism found in nineteenth-century American schooling can be found today in industrializing parts of the developing world. Consider the following, admittedly rather extreme, description of disciplinary practices in modernizing Lebanon:

> Those who received failing grades were asked to line up in the front of the room. The teacher took a long, thin wooden stick and slapped the first boy's open palms. Others were slapped across the face, on the hand, or across the body with the wooden stick. . . . Once the punishment was meted out, the teacher began explaining the answers to the quiz in his seemingly relaxed, friendly manner. (Howard 1970:129)

Well-adjusted students in these authoritarian systems are, at least publicly, not very willing to criticize the harshness of their teachers. One boy explained why teachers hit: "He hits us because his conscience will hurt him when he doesn't help us to discover the good path. . . . Truly, the teacher is a candle that melts and melts to light the road of virtue, love, and goodness. He is the messenger of civilization" (ibid., p. 130).

The Second Transformation: From Factory to Office and Shopping Mall

In later stages of capitalist development, the industrializing pattern gives way to the bureaucratic/mass consumption pattern. This second transformation is at the heart of Americans' school experience today, particularly in secondary schools. A number of forces came together following World War I to produce the new pattern, which was less obtrusive in behavioral control, less highly moralized, and less single-minded in concerns with production. Instead of preparing students for factory work, schools began preparing them for work in bureaucracies and for a consumer-oriented life of choice and variety. These forces arrived somewhat later in Europe and the rest of the industrialized world than they did in the United States.

The Progressive Era's (1896-1918) emphasis on administrative solutions to social problems played the midwife in this transformation. The triumph of "scientific managers" moved the schools out of the hands of people who were obsessed with personally rooting out evil and put them into the hands of people who favored structural forms of control. With the right rules and organizational practices, educators like George Strayer and Ellwood Cubberly believed, it would be unnecessary to install a miniature tyranny in each classroom. Authoritarian methods were, in any event, coming under criticism by developmental psychologists, who saw them as creating a regime of fear in the classroom rather than an environment conducive to active exploration and learning.

At about the same time, schools came to be seen as institutions responsible more for the development of mental abilities than for the development of character. Secondary schools had always been more purely cognitive in orientation, but conflicts over what constitutes "good character" in a country newly self-conscious of its multiethnic population led both primary and secondary schools to tread more gingerly on moral topics than they once had.

If the movement toward a more student-oriented ethos began in social engineering and the desire to avoid controversy, it ended in full-fledged consumerism. First, schools were seen as a place to have fun as well as to work. Later, they were seen as places to choose among subject matter alternatives rather than to conform with standardized curricula.

Toward Consumerism. As early as the 1920s in the United States, profiles in popular magazines of "heroes of production" (i.e., business, scientific, and political leaders) were giving way to profiles of "heroes of consumption" (sports and entertainment celebrities) (Lowenthal 1957, chap. 4). At the same time, football became popular and began attracting increasing numbers of students to college (Riesman and Denney 1951). Sports and then other extracurricular activities (band, glee club, etc.) became a focal point for high school students in the 1920s and 1930s. David Cohen (1985) quotes one high school principal of the period observing the difference in interest generated by extracurriculars and regular instruction: Extracurricular activity "pulsates with life and purpose," the principal noted, whereas the formal curriculum "owes its existence to a coercive regime, loosely connected and highly artificial" (p. 257).

In the curriculum, social engineering justified as consumerism began in the early 1900s. Educators were determined to "meet the needs" of secondary school students who would not be attending college by providing more practical course work. Under the influence of the "life adjustment" philosophy popularized after World War I, this emphasis on student interests gradually branched out to incorporate students in academic and general education tracks. Courses were provided to students to prepare them for balancing a checkbook, dating, driving, and raising children. After a swing back toward academic rigor in the Sputnik era, consumerism flowered again in the late 1960s and 1970s. The U.S. Department of Education counted thousands of course titles on high school campuses at the end of the 1970s, with the vast number in relatively nondemanding "general education" programs, such as movie making, health education, and driver's education (Angus and Mirel 1995).

At the height of the era of student consumerism in the late 1970s, three social scientists, Arthur Powell, Eleanor Farrar, and David Cohen, studied a dozen American high schools and published their findings in *The Shopping Mall High School* (1985). How different their portrait is from the factory-like regimes described by Joseph Rice only a century earlier: "Most educators are proud of the mall-like features of high schools. 'The nice thing about [our] school,' a teacher explained, 'is that students can do their own thing. They can be involved in music, fine arts, athletics, sitting out on the south lawn—and nobody puts them down for it.' " Here three crucial features of "the shopping mall high school" are nicely summarized:

- *Variety.* The schools offered a wide variety of consumer opportunities, from curricular opportunities like fine arts to extracurricular opportunities like sports to noncurricular opportunities like hanging out with friends.

- *Choice.* The schools placed choice in the hands of the consumer. The customer had real power not only to decide what to take and where to go but also how much effort to expend. Many schools, Powell and his associates found, allowed negotiated "treaties" between students and teachers rather than strict requirements handed down from above. If teachers agreed to keep requirements at an achievable minimum, students agreed to comply with the course requirements and to remain civilly attentive. The specific nature of the agreements were open to implicit or, in some cases, explicit bargaining.

- *Neutrality.* The schools were neutral about the choices students made. One choice was more or less as good as another (Powell et al. 1985:11).

Powell and his coauthors exaggerated the movement toward consumerism, perhaps to bring out the changes as dramatically as possible. The term *shopping mall high schools* is misleading: The socialization pattern found in today's schools includes socialization *both* for a world of consumer choice and bureaucratic regulation. Consider the ways organizational abilities are emphasized in the schools: Students make appointments, manage time, fit things into their schedules, and are urged to plan and to keep themselves on track. Nor are production pressures ignored quite as much as the image of the shopping mall suggests. Teachers assign homework and expect it to be in on time. Bells ring and corridors clear. Tests, papers, and grades remain an obsession. Preparation for life in a highly organized society thus remains at the center of the school's socialization mission, along with preparation for a life of variety and choice.

Evidence from Other Industrial Societies. The same transformation from the factory-like regimen of the nineteenth-century school to the bureaucratic/ mass consumption model of today can be seen throughout the industrialized world. However, in Europe this transformation began only well after World War II, when secondary schooling became for the first time a form of mass rather than class education, and it is only now beginning to develop in the industrialized societies of East Asia.

In the United States, the new environment was created by administrators looking for ways of appealing to the interests of new students while adjusting to the modern world of corporate organization. In Europe, students themselves demanded change, often against the resistance of academically oriented administrators. Student demands for more choice and variety in schooling became popular slogans during the student uprisings of the late 1960s. These demands built both on the large numbers of students moving on to higher grades and the greater affluence of the industrialized world in the second postwar generation. Student protest led to significant curricular change (Boudon 1979).

The changes could be seen even at Wylie's (1974) village school in southern France. When he revisited the village in the 1970s, Wylie was amazed that "the belief in hierarchy has given way to a concern for each individual's will, a mutual respect, a tolerance of differences that I would never have thought possible. . . . In most families there is acceptance, though tinged perhaps with nostalgia, of the young people's new independence" (pp. 382-3).

In East Asia, the changes came even later, but they have now arrived. Merry White (1993) described Japanese secondary school students as grumbling about the rules that regulate school life, concerned with the choices they are offered, and very interested in exploring cultural styles associated with "independence." Socializing and consumerism are as much at the center of Japanese adolescence as are the academic expectations of the schools. The schools have not compromised much to take these new realities into account, but they may very well be forced to do so in the future.

The new socialization pattern is an American original, but it has gained strength because it corresponds to the impersonal bureaucratic regulation, weakly connected fates, and mass consumption priorities of late-twentieth-century life in all advanced societies.

SOCIALIZATION INSIDE THE CLASSROOM

Today's schools continue to buzz with socializing messages in the classroom and on the playground. But some of the most effective means of socialization are not part of the verbal buzz. Instead, they either frame the boundaries of acceptable behavior or are embedded in the very fabric of school routines. I will now look in greater detail at the practices of classroom socialization in contemporary schools and the extent to which these practices are successful in channeling behavior, belief, and orientations along school-approved lines.

Techniques of Socialization. It is helpful to think of classroom socialization as organized around a core of relatively effective rules and routines surrounded by rings of less insistent (and therefore less effective) moral instruction.

The core consists of rules backed up by sanctions and routines of schooling that acculturate students to the worlds of impersonal organization and consumer choice. These embedded routines include such everyday features of schooling as lining up, working independently, choosing among electives, and taking tests. Sociologists have sometimes used the term *hidden curriculum* to describe lessons of socialization that are embedded in the very fabric of schooling: in its official categories and constantly repeated routines.

Surrounding this core are rings of moral instruction. One ring consists of explicit moral instruction—the overt teaching of moral virtues that is found mainly in the elementary grades. Another ring consists of less explicit moral instruction. Some of this instruction occurs through exposure in later grades to the moral lessons of literature and history. Some occurs through observation of the exemplary actions of teachers and principals. Figure 5.1 diagrams this conception of classroom socialization.

The Core: Impersonal Rules and Embedded Practices

Teachers and principals do not force today's students to behave by whacking them across the bottoms or pulling the short hairs on their necks. Instead, students are socialized into an impersonal order in which rules and routine practices construct the boundaries of legitimate conduct; within those boundaries, students are relatively free to act as they wish. Because these rules and practices are built into the very fabric of schooling, they are taken for granted. They therefore direct students' orientations to the world through a powerful, if largely invisible, force—not unlike a magnetic force field.

School Rules. School rules define the serious infractions that require punishments: hurting other children, insulting teachers, being disruptive in class, cheating, and the like. School rules may also prescribe where students can be at different times during the day, and the conditions under which they may leave their classrooms. Rules represent the prerequisites of bureaucratic life: being where you are supposed to be, doing your job, interacting in a peaceful way with co-workers, and accepting the authority of bosses.

FIGURE 5.1

Zones of Socialization in Contemporary Classrooms

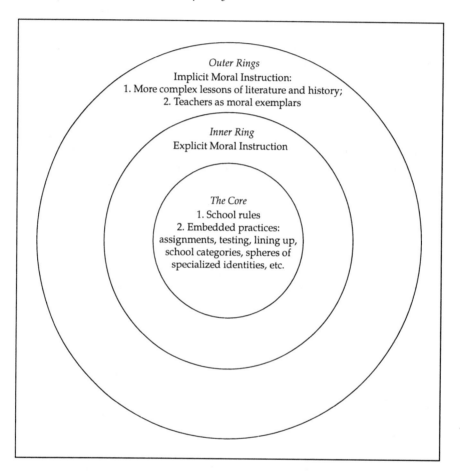

The number of socializing rules in schools varies by society and level of instruction. In the United States, primary schooling is very heavily encased by rules. Secondary schooling depends, to a greater degree, on the internalization of these earlier experiences with rules. This pattern is the norm in most of the developed world. In Japan, however, children remain strongly embedded in group-centered moral life through primary school and emerge into an impersonal, rule-bound setting only with the arrival of secondary schooling (White 1993). In the developing world, rules are frequently equally elaborate in primary and secondary schools.

Embedded Practices. In addition to explicit rules, sociologists have uncovered a number of embedded practices that also play a role in socialization for the world of consumer choice and bureaucratic regulation.

The routine practices of offering choices are the key to the consumer side of classroom socialization. The trend toward consumerism may have been reaching its outer limit at the time Powell, Farrar, and Cohen published their study of shopping mall high schools (Ravitch 1995:48-58). Even so, the choices available to students at secondary schools do continue to resemble the variety of choices they face on a Saturday shopping expedition: dozens of extra-curriculars, scores of electives, hundreds of social networks and possible identities, and only a relatively small number of common requirements.

Many other routine practices of schools are relevant to socializing students for life in bureaucratically organized settings. These encourage students to renounce their immediate impulses and gain patience; value individualism and individually earned achievements; deal effectively with authority and evaluation; and orient themselves to bureaucratic ways of seeing the self and others. These begin in primary school and continue to be embedded in schooling throughout secondary school.

Children are naturally egocentric and inclined to demand the regard of others and the freedom to pursue their own interests as they see fit. Schools as institutions are just as naturally opposed to allowing the natural egoism of children free expression. All of the "lining up" at school—for a turn at the water fountain, in anticipation of lunch or recess, for dismissal at the end of the day—requires students to learn patience. Because groups at school are relatively large, more patience and waiting for others is usually required than at home. Things happen at school not because students want them to happen but because it is time for them to occur. The denial of desire that schools require is "cumulatively important." The crowded condition of classrooms makes delayed gratification inevitable, as well as requiring students to deal with delays, denials, interruptions, and distractions (Jackson 1968).

School practices also socialize students into a life of evaluation based on individual performance. The three-step pattern of assignment, performance, and evaluation—repeated over and over in schools—reinforces the disposition to distinguish one's own efforts and feeds directly into the value of "success" in modern societies. Evaluations at school are more formal, more performance based, more public, and more consequential for adult status than those at home. Rewards are also generally for individual rather than group achievements. Because evaluation is so important in school, it teaches not only the norms of hard work and individual achievement but also various stratagems for managing evaluation while protecting the ego. As Philip Jackson (1968) pointed out, students learn how to enhance praise, how to publicize positive evaluations, and how to conceal negative ones (p. 26). Those who are evaluated poorly may learn to disengage, to "play it cool," to not get involved, and to mask cheating.

School practices also socialize acceptance of authority. Every time a teacher invokes a rule, makes an assignment, or calls for an answer, her or his authority is reinforced. Obedience and even docility are part of the life of labor, and the transition from classroom to factory or office is made easily by "those who have developed 'good work habits' (which is to say responsiveness to authority) in their early years" at school (Jackson 1968). The spatial and temporal organization of schools itself expresses authority relations. Students are not allowed free access to certain spaces: the principals' offices, the teachers' lounges, the counseling rooms. Even their access to classrooms is controlled by the staff. Students are required to be out of hallways and off the grounds at certain times.

At least two other modes of orientation required by bureaucratic life are also taught in schools. One is the habit of considering oneself a member of some larger category of people. Another is the habit of expressing only a facet of one's total personality. These can be thought of as norms of orientation toward *categorical statuses* and *specialized competencies,* respectively (cf. Dreeben 1968).

In schools, categories of people often matter more than individual personalities. Members of the "red group" may be first in line to use the computer during a particular week, and members of the "blue group" the next week. Third graders as a group may be given certain rights and responsibilities, such as the right to use certain equipment on the playground and the responsibility to clean up the playground on certain days. Through these repeated processes of grouping, schools give students experience in making social comparisons in categorical rather than particular terms. Pupils learn to distinguish between persons and the social positions they occupy. This orientation is important in bureaucratically organized societies, where people are constantly being asked to view themselves as members of particular categories—such as those with a particular level of taxable income or having a similar job grade—and to accept the duties and privileges consistent with those categories.[13]

Students also learn to express only specific, situationally relevant parts of their personalities. The whole person rarely matters in the school classroom. What counts is how good a math student the person is, or how good a social studies student. The whole personality is divided into parts, and students learn that only one or a few features of their whole personalities may be relevant. This type of understanding, too, is important in bureaucratically organized societies. It is not, for example, very important to a passenger whether a pilot is good company or likes sports as long as he or she can fly a plane properly.

Schools and Families as Sites of Socialization. Schools are suited structurally to prepare people for impersonal bureaucratic environments in ways that most families are not. In particular, school classrooms have two advantages over families for this purpose:

- Classrooms are the first performance-oriented bureaucracies in which children spend a good deal of time. Unlike families, classrooms are explicitly defined as performance-oriented places, and they are typically organized by relatively distant and titled authorities. Teachers are, in this respect, children's first "bosses" and schoolwork their first "job."

- Classrooms include many more children than families do, and the relationships that develop are broken at the end of the school year. Children do not have the same teacher every year or continue with exactly the same children. The large groups in classrooms and the annual discontinuity of classroom life limit the deep emotional attachments characteristic of families. The interest of teachers is, by necessity, limited to specific aspects of the child and is somewhat more distant emotionally. This impersonality becomes more true as children progress from the early primary grades to the later primary grades, and it is more or less completely true by the time children reach secondary school.

Table 5.2 shows these differences between families and classrooms. Because parents are usually more concerned with the whole child and have a personal, direct authority in the household, "families lack the resources and competence to effect the psychological transition to adult life" in impersonally organized settings (Dreeben 1968:85).

TABLE 5.2

Structural Differences between Classrooms and Families

Classrooms	Families
Yearly promotion	No yearly promotion
Relatively large size	Relatively small size
Heterogeneous composition	Homogeneous composition
Broken relationships	Unbroken relationships
High child to adult ratio	Low child to adult ratio
Narrow, homogeneous age grouping	Mixture of several ages
Narrow range of activities and events	Wide range of activities and events
Little privacy	Some privacy
Specific treatment of individuals	Diffuse treatment of individuals

Source: Adapted from Dreeben (1968).

The Outer Ring: Moral Instruction

It is often assumed that moral instruction has been completely drained out of public schooling. No doubt, some schools have become leery of stepping on toes in a pluralistic society, and others may feel that the traditional types of moral instruction are old-fashioned. Nevertheless, moral instruction has not disappeared from the public schools. Most primary schools continue to be full of moral exhortation—to work hard and plan well, to be honest and faithful, to be courageous and kind, and so on. And many continue to use stories involving well-known heroes (such as George Washington and his apocryphal cherry tree) or familiar fables (such as the ant and the grasshopper) to inculcate traditional moral virtues. Teachers (by overwhelming majorities) say that schools should teach common core moral values, such as honesty, punctuality, responsibility, and industriousness (Farkas and Johnson 1996). And social studies and reading textbooks continue to emphasize such traditional values as "honesty, courage, compassion, persistence, bravery" (Sharp and Wood 1992).

At the same time, traditional moral instruction has been augmented by at least two values that have become more important in American society over time. One is the value of "fairness," which connects directly to the tensions between sharing, equality, and merit that schools must try to resolve. The question, "Is that fair?" has become central to the moral life of many a school classroom. The other new value is "respect for diversity." Some 96 percent of teachers say they believe in "teaching respect for others regardless of their racial and ethnic background," and nearly every schoolroom now includes posters of famous women and minorities, along with the white men who once presided almost exclusively. Textbook studies confirm a dramatic increase in concerns with pluralism and the contributions of the many groups that make up American society (Fitzgerald 1979; Wong 1991; Elson 1964). This is not to say that the balance between the old and the new has always been worked out perfectly. When schoolchildren are asked to choose a famous person to research, men such as Abraham Lincoln and Thomas Edison may be left off the list altogether in the name of diversity.

Oddly, we do not yet have a definitive study of changes in moral instruction over time. The educational historian David Tyack (1996) suggests it is possible that "the national [identifying symbolism] has been enlarged rather than abandoned." But it is also possible that moral education supporting the old Protestant-republican-entrepreneurial culture has grown significantly thinner over time while respect for group differences has grown significantly thicker. Such a change would be a near-perfect demonstration of Émile Durkheim's thesis that societies move from states of cohesion based on a common and

obligatory moral order (which he termed *mechanical solidarity*) to states of cohesion based on pluralistic and balance-oriented moral orders (*organic solidarity*), as their social structures grow more complex.

Cross-National Variations. Some important cultural variations exist in the
organization and content of moral education provided by schools. One of
these differences is the extent to which schools create curricular boundaries
around moral education. In most of the developed world, moral instruction is
interlaced with the regular curriculum. In the United States, for example, discussions of Abe Lincoln's honesty take place in relation to lessons in American
history. By contrast, many developing countries, as well as many developed
Asian countries, devote explicit time every day to moral or religious education. Imagine an American student taking a test on morality in public school,
which is commonplace in Singapore, Hong Kong, and elsewhere in East Asia.
Separate periods for moral instruction presumably produce more commitment to moral norms, although they may create more transparent forms of
hypocrisy as well.

Another important difference has to do with the location of control over
moral instruction. In a few countries, the primary responsibility for enforcing
behavioral and moral conformity is the student group, rather than the teacher.
In Japanese nursery schools, for example, teachers do not pull children out of
the group for misbehaving. Nor do they talk to children about behavior problems. Instead, they rely on other children in the class to censure those who are
misbehaving. As Catherine Lewis (1995) notes: "[These] practices may promote strong internalization and ultimately high compliance while maintaining the role of the teacher as a benevolent, though perhaps not quite indulgent,
figure" (p. 84). In other words, group-based authority may increase the legitimacy of behavioral norms while allowing teachers and school administrators
to be seen in a more sympathetic light than they might otherwise be.

A similar emphasis on peer authority can still be found in British public
schools (called private schools in the United States). Sixth-form leaders (students of 16 to 17 years old) are selected to help the staff organize and discipline
younger students. These "prefectures" both train selected students in habits
of command and encourage student leaders to use their energies on behalf of
the staff rather than on behalf of their potentially rebellious classmates. At
Eton College, for example, the most famous of the British public schools, pre-
fects are members of the Eton Society, also known as "Pop." The members of
Pop wear fancy waistcoats, braided tailcoats, stick-up collars with white bow
ties, check trousers, and a floral buttonhole. They enjoy tremendous prestige
among the younger boys. In the past, members of the Eton Society could hand

out whippings without the authorization of any housemaster, but corporal punishment by boys was banned in 1970. Today, members of the Eton Society must rely on the "symbolic violence" of words to keep their charges in line. Nevertheless, as one observer has noted, "Boy power is still strong and anyone coming [to Eton] from another school is struck by the weight and importance of boy opinion," represented at its pinnacle by the members of Pop (McConnell 1985:212). Just as in the case of Japanese peer authority systems, the prefectorial system has long been credited as one of the hidden reasons for the cohesiveness of British elites.

The content of moral instruction also varies considerably around the world in response to particular political, religious, and pedagogical traditions. In the former Soviet Union, for example, respect for manual work, a centerpiece of Communist ideology, filtered into moral instruction in numerous ways. Heroes of labor were celebrated, special times were set aside for manual labor, and the moral virtues of workers and peasants were celebrated (Bronfenbrenner 1970). In Japan, "principles of the Shinto and Confucian moral order, such as loyalty, filial piety, the discipline of group life, industry, cleanliness, physical strength and perseverance" are reinforced "by means of school rituals, courses of study and extracurricular activities" (Fujita 1986:330). In Israel, the rabbinical tradition of aggressively questioning what one reads, exploring paradoxes, and commenting on commentaries shows up in the qualities of mind that leading academic secondary schools try to cultivate. Singular individuals are also sometimes important. In areas of Europe (particularly Italy and Germany), for example, the progressive pedagogy of the Swiss school reformer Pestalozzi encouraged moral teaching based on a sense of the splendor and balance of nature.

Secondary Schooling and Moral Complexity. As students move up the ladder of formal schooling, moral instruction either diminishes greatly or becomes increasingly implicit and complex. It diminishes most completely for students who enroll in general or vocational programs in secondary school. Industrial work values may continue to be stressed (Oakes, Gamoran, and Page 1992), but otherwise moral instruction fades from the official curriculum. By contrast, moral instruction increases in complexity for students who enroll in the academic programs, particularly those who take a large number of courses in humanities. Exhortations to be honest, hard working, courageous, and kind are replaced by far more challenging lessons, just as simple addition is replaced by more complex mathematics.

The moral instruction of the humanities works at a higher level than the illustrated lists of virtues that today's critics of schooling wish to add to the curriculum. Not every student has the capacity to take moral lessons from literature and history, but these lessons are the stuff out of which the higher forms of moral judgment are created. The widely assigned George Eliot novel *Middlemarch*, for example, expresses several of the more demanding perplexities of moral life: how, for example, a dedicated scholar, for all his knowledge and hard work, can suck the blood out of life, and how an otherwise admirable doctor can desire to please his beloved wife so much that he goes deeply into debt to support her expensive tastes. Through examples such as these, motivated students can learn that even widely proclaimed virtues can at times go too far or fail to be sufficiently balanced by other virtues. Students may also learn that many situations in life involve not a choice between right and wrong, but between two rights. In *Huckleberry Finn*, for example, the meaning of civilization is debated from many sides. Is it obedience to the law and cultivated manners? Or the ability to empathize with the personality and situation of others, regardless of reigning conventions? What happens when the two come into conflict?

Teachers as Exemplars. Most schoolteachers are aware of their role in socializing the young and try to express values through their actions in the classroom. In the primary grades, for example, they usually express the values of kindness and empathy. They have, as Phillip Jackson (Jackson, Boorstrom, and Hansen 1993) observes, "a knack for discerning latent grace in the awkward gesture" and "applaud those who try no matter how slight their success" (p. 259).

Teachers have different strengths as exemplars, and what they have to teach is therefore more evident to some students than to others. One teacher may make precision and clarity important values in her classroom and express respect for these values through the carefulness of her handwriting, the persistence of her correction of imprecise language, her attention to detail in the working through of a proof. Another teacher may express the moral importance of truly engaged activity by throwing his whole body into a lecture, by beaming with pride when a student gives a good answer to a difficult question, or by cheerfully brushing off an annoying interruption. Another may express the moral importance of digging beneath the surface by patiently leading students ever deeper into a short story, by suggesting alternative interpretations, or by engaging in Socratic questioning of students' answers.

Dramatic gestures frequently aid in the expression of moral values. An erect posture, a concentrated energy, a poised piece of chalk at eye level—all can express a kind of heightened respect for precision. A thoughtful stroking of the chin, a dramatic "aha!" and a long pause before sweeping away a shallow interpretation—all can convey a heightened respect for digging deeper.

How Successful Is Moral Instruction?. Moral conformity is not as easily gained as behavioral conformity or acculturation into bureaucratic/mass consumption ways of life. If moral teachings support the practices and social circumstances of students' families and local communities, they are likely to be accepted. If they do not, they may be treated with a good deal of skepticism, or even flatly rejected. The dominant moral culture of schools reflects the social conditions of people who have some authority in society (or identify strongly with those who do) and who are, in addition, not extremely cosmopolitan or worldly in outlook. It is, therefore, most congenial to those who are upwardly striving or located in the broad middle of the social structure. At a minimum, it always confronts opposition on at least two fronts: from the practical opportunism of the "have-not" classes and from the worldliness of upper-class sophisticates (see Bourdieu 1984; Collins 1988:208-25).

Even where the moral teachings of the schools are accepted in principle, they may not have a strong impact on behavior, because the temptations of selfishness, dishonesty, laziness, and cowardice are always great. Moreover, the organizational side of schooling sometimes undermines even simple moral lessons. Schools, for example, subscribe to the value of honesty, but often inadvertently reward cheats who are motivated by the equally high importance schools attach to achievement. Schools preach equality of opportunity, but are notorious for tamping down the ambitions of lower-status children. Many schools proclaim the importance of sturdy independence, but they do not generally approve of nonconformity that upsets the staff's authority.

SOCIALIZATION OUTSIDE THE CLASSROOM

The school playground is an enormously important part of childhood socialization, and it is perhaps too little appreciated. If classrooms are an introduction to bureaucratic life, the playground is an introduction to informal social networks. School experiences outside the classroom prepare children for adult life by teaching them about self-assertion and self-control among friends and colleagues. The values of the classroom and the playground often coexist peacefully, but in some secondary schools, adolescent values crowd out school values.

Like the classroom, the playground has important structural features that are different from those found in students' homes:

- On the playground, adult authority is present in the form of monitors, but this authority is in the background. Adult presence prevents anarchy, but adult distance allows a maximum opportunity for group-directed activity.

- Many children mix on the playground, and freely chosen interactions with a relatively large number of children are, therefore, theoretically possible. The members of school play groups are usually similar in age, but are usually not close neighbors or family members. Age similarity limits the social distance between children, but the aggregation of many acquaintances creates a wide opportunity for cementing, altering, and breaking relationships. The variety of possible contacts allows children to develop increasingly refined judgments about the possibilities and problems of social interaction.

Because they are spheres of monitored, but largely self-directed, activity involving a variety of interaction possibilities among others who are neither very close nor very distant, playgrounds have advantages over close friends and family for the development of skills in informal social relations.

The Playground and Informal Social Life

On the playground, children must learn to deal with bullies, tag-alongs, tattletales, false friends, snobs, and other familiar childhood types. Deciding how to react to these types refines judgment. How does one deal with aggression from another child—by confronting the child, raising a coalition, or trying to avoid the harassment? Under what conditions should a higher authority be appealed to, and when is this action interpreted as failing to stand up for oneself? When does friendship fall over the line into dependency? How much should acquaintances be trusted with valuable information—when does such information cement a friendship and when does it increase one's vulnerability? How much effort should one make to win the friendship of an aloof but desirable child? When should one speak out and when should one wait to assess the situation further? How can one express pride in abilities and achievements without fostering resentment among others? Through confronting these issues, children may become skillful navigators of relationships.

Without a great many experiences in dealing with these issues, children would be less well prepared for adult life. These lessons clearly apply to informal relationships with friends, potential mates, and other community members. But they are no less applicable to informal social relations at work. Much occupational activity can be thought of as "political labor," in which people take and avoid taking stands and in which they maneuver to make useful alliances, to avoid encumbering connections, and to defuse potential conflicts (Collins 1979, chap. 2).

Some sociologists have long seen the experiences of the playground as an important socializing complement to the experiences of the classroom. Talcott Parsons (1959), for example, pointed out that not all important jobs in industrial societies require high levels of academic ability. Social skills are particularly important in many managerial and sales jobs—and also in promotional and public service work. In Parsons's view, those who gain status on the playground but not in the classroom form the pool of future occupants of all jobs that require high levels of social skill and emotional labor (e.g., salespeople, public relations people, entrepreneurs, actors and actresses). They are also the future central organizers of adult friendship networks. Those who gain status in the classroom but not the playground form the pool of future occupants of jobs that require high levels of scholarly and analytical ability (e.g., scientists, engineers, professors, print journalists, civil servants, technical managers). Those who gain status both in the classroom and on the playground are future achievers in elite spheres of occupational and public life (e.g., corporation executives and upper-level managers, college presidents and deans, doctors, lawyers, research entrepreneurs, politicians). Finally, those who lack status in both domains are unlikely to become socially dominant personalities (unless they are unusually late bloomers).

Although it provides opportunities for experimenting with identity, the playground is far from an unstratified domain. Indeed, some inequalities are more apparent on the playground than in the classroom. Although teachers usually try to mix boys and girls, for example, boy and girls overwhelmingly separate along gender lines on the playground. In primary schooling, the dominance of boys is evident in their ability to control large, open play spaces, to label girls as ritually polluting (girls are primarily responsible for "cooties" on most playgrounds), and to invade spaces occupied by groups of girls. Thus, the playground can be a space in which some social relations—particularly gender and gender-related aggressiveness—are reproduced in a more faithful way than in the classroom (Thorne 1995). Status systems based on skills and attributes prized by the dominant children rule the social order of the playground. The social divisions of the playground—cool/uncool, jock/brain, tomboy/sissy—overlap with meaningful divisions in adult informal social life. Because these social divisions draw a high level of verbal attention from children, they exalt some children more regularly and wound others more deeply than adult social divisions usually can.

For all of its verbal violence, the playground is nevertheless an arena of experimentation and change. It is a place where children practice making and breaking friendships and where they try out new identities, which may prove rewarding. It is a place where children watch on the border of socially organized spaces and make forays across the borders at times, as when a popular boy decides to play with the girls for a day or girls join the boys' kickball game. It is a place where children learn to use verbal aggression to fight unwanted labels, as much as to enforce the existing status hierarchy.

Adolescent Society and the Schools

As children grow into teenagers, friends become an increasingly central part of the incentives to attend school. Because of the nonacademic interests of most adolescents, many adults fear that the influence of adolescent culture undermines adult authority and does not adequately prepare children for adult life. It is a worry that goes back to the 1950s as a research concern (see sidebar) and may indeed be a perennial issue. These worries, however, are prone to overstatement. Most adolescent friendship groups are not as deeply alienated as adults fear. Even those teenagers who are deeply alienated may not stay that way; many alienated adolescents grow up into well-adjusted adults once they take on the responsibilities of jobs and families. In addition, adolescent friendship groups reinforce many of the same values as adults. For example, adolescents socialize emotional control by criticizing those who do not show it and calling them "crybabies." And, in most cases, if teenagers do not act with acceptable honesty or show up at appointed times, they will be loudly criticized until they conform or are forced to find new friends.

●●●●●●●●●●●●●●

JAMES COLEMAN AND ADOLESCENT SOCIETY

Before 1950, few young people had enough discretionary time and money to develop their own tastes, their own popular heroes, and their own sense of values. They were either children, under their parents' tutelage, or adults out on their own. The relatively autonomous stage of adolescence—with its emotional passages, strong peer identifications, and ritualized rebellions against adult authority—hardly existed. Some of the key forces bringing youth culture into existence were the freedom afforded by mass ownership of automobiles, the ability of teenagers to find part-time work while attending school, the relaxation of social mores to allow for earlier and less supervised dating, and the lengthening of the time children were expected to remain in school. In the 1950s, these forces came together to create for the first time a sense of adolescence as a separate stage of life. Young people developed their own popular heroes, such as Elvis Presley and James Dean, and they were serviced by multi-million-dollar popular culture and apparel industries. Similar forces were leading to the spread of a youth culture throughout the wealthier liberal democracies, with capitals of youth culture in London, Amsterdam, Berlin, and Paris.

About this time, educators began to worry about the harmful effects of adolescent culture on the academic commitment of the young. Many educators felt that the status hierarchy of young people reinforced values—

such as sexual attractiveness and rebelliousness—that made the work of schooling more difficult. As in the Chuck Berry song, students couldn't wait for the last school bell to ring, so that their "real lives" could begin.

James Coleman (1961) was the first sociologist to examine the influence of American adolescent culture in an empirically rigorous way. Coleman's study of 11 Indiana high schools in the late 1950s confirmed the importance of alternative status systems running parallel to the official status system of the schools. In the American Midwest, Coleman found, it was not so much ducktail haircuts and souped-up cars that posed the major threats to the academically oriented status order of the school. Instead, it was the more conventional alternative interests of teenagers: athletics and the opposite sex. Coleman asked high school students whom they admired most: outstanding students, outstanding athletes, or the students who were most popular with the opposite sex. Both athletic and popularity stars were far more likely to be admired than academic stars.

The "leading crowds" set the tone in the schools that Coleman studied, and they had the effect of accentuating values generally prevalent in their communities. In communities where academics had little status, the leading crowds were even less interested in academics.

Coleman expressed grave concerns about the influence of adolescent society, but unlike the more rigid educational moralists of his time, he did not see adolescent society as a monolithic evil. Adolescents were not entirely cut off from adult society; their status systems recognized the values of adult society in many ways, not least in their tendency to ascribe highest status to the "all-around" boy and girl. Moreover, the effects of the adolescent society varied across the genders (girls were more responsive to adult authority than boys), from class to class, and from community to community.

• •

Variation in the Influence of Adolescent Society. For the culture of adolescent alienation to penetrate deeply, the separation between the world of adults and the world of adolescents must be great and the amount of time adolescents spend exclusively with friends their own age must also be great. Both national and class differences are evident in the level of separation of the two worlds.

In Sweden, for example, greater balance has existed among the reference groups influencing adolescent identities: the family, the school, the local community, and the friendship group. No single force has been as dominant as peer groups now are for many American adolescents. In Sweden, these four socializing forces each have had distinct times during the day and week in which they were considered legitimately central (Andersson 1969). In Japan, where schooling takes up such a large amount of time and consciousness, the role of the peer group is circumscribed throughout secondary school. In college, friendship groups play a much larger role, however. Some who have studied Japanese society argue that the primary function of college friendship groups is to prepare young adults for the intense work group culture of Japanese business and professional life (White 1993, chaps. 4 and 6).

In the United States and many other societies, however, adolescent society has for some time had great autonomy. The discretionary income that comes from part-time work, the freedom that comes from access to cars, and the distinctive sensibility that comes from the fashions disseminated by the popular culture industries all contribute to this autonomy. Moreover, adolescents spend most of their time out of school with one another. Thus, in the United States, the separation between the world of teenagers and the world of adults is great, and the time spent with peers is also great.

If anything, the importance of adolescent peer groups has grown over time. In addition to cash, cars, and pop culture, another important element has been added: With more two-earner families, the amount of interaction between parents and children has declined. When not in school, most children now spend their time with friends or alone, "fooling around" or watching television (Boocock 1972:10; National Center for Educational Statistics 1996:66-7).

The sources of status in adolescent society remain strongly nonacademic.[14] In a study of several thousand junior high school students, Tye (1985) found that "good-looking students" were identified as the most popular students in school by nearly two out of five students. They were followed by "athletes" (23 percent). Even "gang members" (15 percent) were considered more popular than "smart students" (14 percent). Academically oriented students are not at the bottom of high school status hierarchies—the large, neglected mass of unpopular and unknown kids are at the bottom—but they are also far from the top (see also Clasen and Brown 1986).

Social class is a strong influence on the extent to which peer values become all-consuming in the life of adolescents. Even in the United States, the dominant pattern in the middle and upper-middle class (and also among upwardly mobile minorities) is *compartmentalization* of peer and adult influences. Peer values tend to dominate in areas related to informal social life and discretionary consumption: styles of language and emotional expression; dating practices; and preferences in movies, clothing styles, music, and the like. Adult values tend to dominate in areas of long-range planning: the importance of keeping up good grades, going to college and preparing for high-paying and high-status jobs, and selecting acceptable people for dates (Boocock 1972:230-9). Some more thoroughly alienated middle-class rebels exist, but in many suburban schools they have too few compatriots to form a self-sustaining critical mass (Willis 1979). In others, they band together as a nihilist or bohemian minority.

Counterschool Cultures. Although overstated, the concerns of adults about adolescent alienation are not entirely unfounded. Perhaps one-fifth to one-quarter of all adolescents are deeply alienated from adult middle-class society. And schools in the poorest communities must usually deal with much higher proportions of these alienated students.

Antischool peer groups are increasingly common among adolescents who have little adult supervision and are not planning on attending college. The compartmentalization of peer group influence gives way to a more thorough *encapsulation* of adolescent experience by the values of one's friends; in other words, adolescents become the central arbiter of all facets of behavior and orientation. This level of immersion in adolescent culture is strongly associated with the kinds of "problem behaviors" that are so disliked by adults: smoking, profanity, and vandalism among younger teens; drug and alcohol use, school dropout, and early pregnancies among older teens (Jessor and Jessor 1977). More or less complete antischool peer group control is the dominant ambience in many nonimmigrant working- and lower-class schools, and also in cliques of "tough" and "unpopular" kids in middle-class communities.

Sociologists have raised several objections to conventional ways of explaining the rise of counterschool cultures. Rather than drawing exclusive attention to deficiencies of character or family life, as many polemicists do, they have tended to look at disparities between the probable life trajectories of students and those assumed by the schools. Students who are most attracted to the counterschool culture are those who see no linkage between their current school activities and their anticipated adult status and activities (Stinchcombe 1964; Willis 1979; MacLeod 1987).

For boys and girls oriented to working-class jobs or a nonworking married future, the legitimacy of the *educational exchange* often fails completely. The educational exchange can be described as the exchange of respect and deference for valued knowledge: Students conform to gain knowledge that is valuable to them; teachers provide knowledge to gain conformity that is valuable to them. On the students' side, knowledge itself is of primarily instrumental value; it leads to qualifications, which in turn lead (so students hope) to higher status and income. When this chain breaks down, so does the foundation on which the socializing role of the school rests. When the breakdown is profound, the school is likely to confront an active counterschool culture.

The most provocative sociological portrait of a counterschool culture is Paul Willis's (1979) study of "Hammertown boys" in the midlands of England. Willis makes the point that the most defiant boys he studied were the ones with the strongest sense of dignity and self-respect, not the most "defeated." The kids who were upstanding and wouldn't take "bull" joined the "lads"; those who were passive and compliant were part of the group the lads called "ear'oles" (for ear holes, that group's most prominent physical and moral characteristic, according to the lads). The lads were in some respects more realistic than the ear'oles. They refused to accept the official ideology of "equal opportunity" when the world as they knew it offered little real opportunity. Ironically, the lads—with their boisterous high spirits, quick wit, and determination to have "laffs" at the expense of teachers and ear'oles alike—paved their own paths into a life of insecure manual labor. They weren't tracked into lower-class jobs so much as they tracked themselves into those jobs. Their sense of moral superiority to students who passively conformed led them to embrace forms of labor that they considered a valid alternative to the tight controls of white-collar jobs. However, the form of work they chose would eventually tear at their high self-esteem.

England has had an aggressive and rather oppositional working-class adult culture, so it is not surprising that in America, where this sense of class opposition is largely missing, counterschool cultures reveal more drug- and alcohol-laced withdrawal than active rebellion. An American counterschool group studied by Jay MacLeod (1987) shared many of the values of Willis's lads, but had more trouble escaping the dominant culture's definition of success. Their outlooks were more pessimistic and resigned than those of Willis's lads. Unlike the lads, they saw no hope in working-class jobs for the expression of an independent spirit, and they expressed their alienation not by holding the authority structure up to ridicule but by consuming "huge" quantities of alcohol and drugs.

Can Alienation Be Reduced? Some argue that the best approach to reducing adolescent alienation is to control the influence of counterschool cultures through tight security and strict enforcement of rules. These steps help schools in depressed neighborhoods to muddle through, but they are, by definition, unlikely to create any real sense of connection between alienated students and the school authorities who oversee them. At a time when many are aware of the problems of adolescent alienation, it is not surprising that calls for more job-relevant secondary schooling on the German model of apprenticeship training are also growing stronger. But unlike the German "dual system," vocational schooling in the United States, with its low status and uncertain connection to the job market, has not provided adolescents with a strong sense of purpose or motivation to succeed (see, e.g., Grubb and Lazerson 1975; Grasso and Shea 1979).

An alternative solution worth considering, according to MacLeod (1987), is for schools to try to stimulate thinking while being more realistic about the life chances actually facing alienated young people who, quite realistically, do not believe that the ideal of equal opportunity applies to them. Schools should provide more teachers who can relate to the students in nonstigmatizing ways and provide assignments that are materially relevant to these students' likely life trajectories. The one teacher who was able to reach MacLeod's alienated working-class kids dressed in a T-shirt and jeans and gave them assignments for papers on such topics as the origins of the Harley-Davidson motorcycle and the experience of life in prison.

Clearly, the mild hedonism of the adolescent society of the 1950s has given way to a more sullen and disenchanted mood in many economically depressed communities today. The growing gap between rich and poor is an important backdrop against which this new mood has developed. And MacLeod's suggestions notwithstanding, confident solutions to the problem of adolescent alienation are in short supply.

CONCLUSION

Schools may attempt to control behavior, moral values, and cultural orientations. These three dimensions of socialization overlap in practice, but are analytically distinguishable. It is possible to define four historically important school socialization environments: the village/communal pattern, the industrial pattern, the bureaucratic/mass consumption pattern, and the elite pattern. These patterns can be found at different stages of a country's economic development and, within countries, also in schools primarily serving different social class populations. Socialization practices in the industrial pattern are particularly harsh. They are based on personal control, rigidly organized work discipline, and a highly morally charged classroom setting. In the United States, the transformation of schools from the village/communal pattern to the industrial pattern occurred in the mid- and late nineteenth century, and the transformation of secondary schools from the industrial to the bureaucratic/mass consumption pattern occurred in the 1920s and 1930s. Elsewhere, the second of these transformations occurred only well after World War II.

Classrooms and playgrounds provide distinct sites of socialization at school. The first is most relevant for socialization into institutional life, and the second is most relevant for socialization into informal social networks. School classrooms and playgrounds are organized in ways that allow them to acculturate students in ways that families cannot duplicate. In the classroom, the impersonality of adult authority and the annual breaking of relationships help to acculturate students to the demands of bureaucratic life. On the playground, the relative distance of adult authority and the presence of many nonintimate peers provide opportunities for children to learn to maneuver in informal social networks.

Classroom socialization practices in contemporary schools can be conceived of as involving a core of rules and routine practices and outer rings of moral instruction. The core of rules and practices create effective pressures for behavioral conformity and acculturation to bureaucratic and mass consumption ways of life. Embedded practices (such as lining up, working independently, making curricular choices, thinking of oneself as a member of a larger category, and being examined for special competencies) are often discussed by sociologists as elements of the "hidden curriculum" of schooling.

Although schools have been accused of renouncing moral instruction, primary school teachers continue to represent some ethical, entrepreneurial, and patriotic values in a positive way. Two new values have, in addition, become part of the moral curriculum: fairness and diversity. In secondary schools, students have the opportunity to learn more complex moral lessons by reading history and literature. Teachers also model much behavior that can properly be considered moral. Students resist the socializing messages of the schools if they are too discordant with the culture of their homes and neighborhoods. The organizational pressures of schooling, moreover, sometimes conflict with or even undermine their moral teachings.

The playground is the site of socialization for informal life in social networks. Here students learn skills in self-presentation, friendship making, conflict making, and conflict resolution. These skills help adults to maneuver in informal social networks. Although playgrounds offer many opportunities for developing these skills, they are also stratified in many of the same ways as adult society. Indeed, social divisions of gender and aggressiveness, at least, are stronger on the playground than in the classroom.

Peer influence increases as children grow into teenagers, but the degree of influence of adolescent society varies. In most middle- and upper-class communities, regardless of country, adolescent lives tend to be compartmentalized, with parents and other adults having the largest influence on long-term plans and peers having the largest influence on immediate life experiences and styles of expression. Antischool peer cultures exist primarily among teen-agers whose long-range life plans have least to do with schooling and who are therefore alienated from the basic educational exchange: opportunities to ac-quire valuable knowledge in return for behavioral compliance. It is likely that the number of alienated adolescents has grown over time as adolescent and adult societies have become more separate and as the income gap between rich and poor has widened.

CHAPTER 6

Schools and Social Selection: Opportunity

In contemporary industrial societies, schools have come to play an extremely important role in selecting people for positions in the occupational structure. Moreover, the schools' role in social selection has increased substantially since the 1930s. In the early part of the century, schooling was not that important to finding work. Most people did not finish high school, and men either inherited the family farm or trade or went off on their own to find work as they could. But now schools are central in the process of sorting and allocating people to jobs. This is true in every industrialized society. Not every child learns the course content or the socialization lessons of schooling, but every child is by definition subject to the schools' performance assessments. For this reason, social selection is the most consequential function of contemporary schooling. School performance from first grade through high school can lead one squirming six-year-old toward a life as a jet-hopping executive and another toward a life of shifting from one low-paid job to another.

The connection between schooling and social selection has become so important that I will devote two chapters to it. Schools are important both for social mobility and for the reproduction of inequalities. These can be thought of as separate social processes that work differently among different groups and in different countries. This chapter will concentrate on the theme of opportunity. The directing questions will be, who "gets ahead" through schooling, and to what extent has the increased importance of schooling in the sorting process provided greater opportunities for people from less advantaged backgrounds to rise? Chapter 7 will concentrate on the theme of inequality. The key questions in that chapter will be, how do the circumstances of lower social classes, ethnic minorities, and women contribute to the reproduction of inequalities through schooling, and to what extent do school structures such as tracking reinforce these inequalities?

The first part of this chapter describes the forces that have made schooling increasingly important in the process of social selection. This section focuses on two key changes: (1) the expansion of education, which encourages a connection between schooling and opportunity consciousness, and (2) the tighter connection between educational credentials and jobs. The second part of the chapter explores the characteristics of people who succeed in schooling and are thereby able to convert their educational credentials into good jobs. Many people believe that educational expansion has substantially improved the opportunities for children born into lower-status families, but the social science evidence suggests that this is not as true as we would like to think. A high level of stability exists across generations in the relationship between fathers' social status and children's educational attainments.

THE INCREASING SIGNIFICANCE OF SCHOOLING IN SOCIAL SELECTION

"To get ahead in life, you need an education." Most of us have heard this familiar refrain from our parents. Income and labor market statistics bear out its truth. U.S. college graduates in today's labor market, for example, will earn by midcareer about twice as much as high school graduates (the difference between $70,000 and $35,000 a year) and three times more than high school dropouts ($23,000 a year) (U.S. Bureau of the Census 1994a). Over the past 20 years, income differences by educational level have increased rather dramatically (see, e.g., Katz and Murphy 1992; Murnane, Willett, and Levy 1995).

Opportunity Consciousness and Educational Expansion

To understand how and why schooling came to play such an important role in the process of social sorting, we should first understand how the idea of opportunity became linked to schooling. As you will recall from Chapter 2, the United States was a forerunner in this area, partly because schools became important in the Americanization of the millions of new immigrants who came into the country in the nineteenth century and partly because reformers believed that schooling could build skills and democracy at the same time. Even in the United States, however, expansion of secondary schooling was slow. As late as 1910, only 15 percent of Americans adolescents graduated from high school. But by 1940, high school graduation rates were already above 70 percent, and 15 percent of the college-age group were going on to higher education. These rates were three to five times higher than anywhere

else in the industrialized world. Since World War II, opportunity consciousness has become linked to schooling throughout the world.

Schooling and Opportunity in the United States. The primary reason why
U.S. secondary school enrollments grew slowly at first is that schooling was
not so tightly linked as it is today to how a person fares in life. Only 150 years
ago, the United States was a nation dominated by small-property owners—
farmers and shopkeepers—most of whom knew how to read and write but
had little in the way of formal education. Although opportunity was an important part of the national creed, opportunity was not at first associated with
"upward social mobility"—much less with upward mobility through schooling. In the early days of the American republic, opportunity meant the possibility for a person to "grow to the full measure of his capacity" free of the
limiting ties of feudal relations. This full measure of capacity had non-
economic as well as economic connotations—referring to competence, character, and satisfying social ties, as well as to material well-being (see Lasch 1995,
chap. 3; Wuthnow 1996). The idea of opportunity as the chance to move up in
the world only gradually entered American consciousness, and it did not become a very important view until the middle of the nineteenth century (Lasch
1995:66-74).

Just before he became president, Abraham Lincoln ([1859] 1953) expressed
the increasingly popular ideal of the "self-made man": "The prudent, penni-
less beginner in the world, labors for wages awhile, saves a surplus with
which to buy tools or land for himself, then labors on this own account another
while, and at length hires another new beginner to help him" (pp. 478-9).
Note, however, that business, not education, was the major road to opportunity for the self-made man. The self-made man grew his business or his farm
by outthinking and outworking his competitors but not necessarily by getting
more schooling than his competitors. Luck sometimes played a role, too, as in
the Horatio Alger stories that were so popular in the decades following the
Civil War.

The expansion of schooling was closely connected to an entirely new kind
of "opportunity consciousness" than the one Lincoln expressed. With the rise
of mammoth corporations and the closing of the frontier at the end of the
nineteenth century, the fate of the self-made man became increasingly threatened. The country was no longer dominated by small-scale entrepreneurs,
farmers, and shopkeepers. More and more people were becoming employees
of large organizations. Clearly, if the American dream of individual advancement was to survive under these new conditions, other pathways to success
would be required.

Schooling at first seemed an unlikely avenue. Businessmen regularly condemned college training, with its emphasis on fine thoughts and high-flown sentiments. They claimed that it made young people unfit for the "real world" (Wyllie 1954:101-5). Even so, some far-sighted philanthropists began to perceive the nation's school system as a replacement for the faltering promise of business entrepreneurship. Andrew Carnegie (1889), for example, believed that schools and colleges should be made into "ladders upon which the aspiring can rise" (p. 663). In the late nineteenth century, the country's schooling system hardly fit anyone's idea of a well-built ladder. Professional schools did not require the completion of four years of college, and colleges did not require the completion of four years of high school. Over the next generation, however, the patchwork of American schooling was reorganized into the ladder structure that people like Andrew Carnegie advocated, thereby providing a mechanism to keep the American promise of opportunity at the very moment when fundamental changes in the economy were threatening to destroy it (Brint and Karabel 1989:3-6).

A suddenly awakened thirst for learning doesn't explain why young people began to graduate in large numbers from high school in the years between the two world wars, and why they began to attend college in large numbers after World War II. Instead, the most important factors were changes in the occupational structure and the increasing incentives for investment in education. Between 1900 and 1940, white-collar jobs almost doubled in the American labor force: from one out of six at the turn of the century to almost one out of three by 1940. Between 1940 and 1970, professional and managerial jobs also rose: from one out of seven to almost one out of four (U.S. Bureau of the Census 1975:139).

Shortly after World War II, American sociologists began noting that the "channels" of upward mobility through business ownership and shop floor advancement were drying up and that higher education was in the process of taking their place (Warner 1949). Some young people enjoyed schooling for its own sake, but many more then as now were primarily interested in using higher degrees as tickets to the better jobs in society, jobs that were becoming more plentiful during this period. And the government, convinced of the need for a more highly educated labor force, encouraged this view by supporting the building of secondary schools and colleges and by providing financial aid support, first in a limited way and then quite lavishly, for those who wanted to attend college but lacked the economic means to do so.

After World War II, the number of students attending college skyrocketed, helped at first by the federal government's loans and by scholarships for returning soldiers. In 1940, about 15 percent of 18- to 21-year-olds attended either a two-year or a four-year college. Just 30 years later, in 1970, the figure was well above 40 percent (U.S. Office of Education 1944:4; Peng 1977). Not everyone who enrolled in college after World War II graduated; in fact, only about half did. Even so, this kind of growth represents a tremendous increase in college enrollments, particularly given the nearly threefold increase in the numbers of 18- to 21-year-olds between 1940 and 1970 thanks to the postwar baby boom.

Of course, higher education did not completely replace entrepreneurship as an avenue to economic success. In fact, entrepreneurship has shown a healthy resistance to displacement by large organizations—and has grown a little in recent decades. Many self-made men and women can still be found, particularly in immigrant communities. Some 10 percent of the American labor force are business owners, most of them owners of small businesses with a helper or two. Nevertheless, building one's own business is a risky and arduous task. Business people must weather downturns in the business cycle, shifting patterns of consumer preferences, and changes affecting their business location. They may be aroused at night by phone calls reporting fires or theft. In view of the uncertainties of entrepreneurship, a large proportion of business people prefer that their children pursue the less risky path of professional training rather than following in their parents' footsteps as entrepreneurs.

Schooling and Opportunity Worldwide. Demand for secondary and higher education grew much more slowly in the rest of the world than it did in the United States. As you will recall from Chapter 2, although the first systems of mass schooling developed in Europe, higher levels of schooling were, except in very unusual cases, off limits for the poor peasantry and working classes throughout the nineteenth century and the early part of the twentieth century. European systems of secondary and higher education were set aside for those who could pay high fees and pass rigorous examinations. It is reasonable to call the European systems of secondary and higher education "status confirming" systems, because they helped to unite the upper classes as a common "status group," culturally very distinct from the masses of people who had only rudimentary schooling (Collins 1977). Even in 1940, few European countries graduated more than 15 percent of young people from secondary school or sent more than 3 to 4 percent on to higher education (Craig 1981:185-6).

Loyal to their traditions of high-quality, elite schooling, European educators fought the expansion of secondary and higher education as long as they could. Nor did politicians, themselves products of elite schooling, agitate very often for expanding secondary and higher education. But the same forces that led to change in the United States wore down the resistance of European educators and politicians a generation later. Once again, occupational change was an important factor. As corporations and state institutions grew, so did the need for white-collar workers. Perhaps even more important was the developing sense among politicians and ordinary citizens alike that schooling could be used as a "ladder of ascent" to a better economic future and to full participation in the modern world (Meyer, Ramirez, and Soysal 1992).

Once governments decided on the necessity of mass schooling at the lower secondary level and later at the upper secondary level, the growth of enrollments in most countries had an almost self-propelling quality that outstripped whatever might have been expected due to occupational change alone. No doubt parents' defensive strategies are partially responsible for the vast growth of enrollments; at particular points, it becomes necessary to send children to school, if only to protect them from social and economic disadvantage. But a change in consciousness—the growing sense that schooling could provide opportunity—also helped to propel the educational revolution in some countries. This change in consciousness can be likened to what occurs in a large-scale social movement or religious "awakening." It was especially apparent in the Third World, where mass schooling was stimulated less by economic interests than by social and political ideals. Schooling had once been considered irrelevant to life (or even a resented feature of colonial subjugation), but it came to be viewed as *the* way to integrate people into "the grand project of nation-building" and individual development (Fuller and Rubinson 1992:12).

The Rise of the "Credential Society"

The desire for more opportunity can be enough to increase the numbers of students attending higher levels of schooling, but it does not in itself improve the likelihood that such hopes will be realized. Only a tightening link between educational qualifications and jobs can do that. The other facet of the schools' changing role in social selection, therefore, has to do with the rise of *credentialism*. By credentialism, social scientists mean the monopolization of access to the more rewarding jobs and economic opportunities by the holders of educational degrees and certificates.[15]

All societies have mechanisms for allocating people to jobs. A few have been even more inclined than the United States to use schools for this purpose. For instance, educational credentials played a more important role in social selection in societies like the Soviet Union than they did in the United States—and they also became important for this purpose earlier in the Soviet Union than they did in the United States. Because entrepreneurship was not an alternative, socialism allowed ambition only one channel: through schooling. From the time of the great bureaucratization of Soviet society in the 1930s, the only means by which ambitious young people could succeed was through higher education credentials (and for the truly ambitious, Communist party membership in addition). As one Soviet émigré to the United States put it, "In the USSR, there is no capital except education. If a person does not want to become a collective farmer or just a charwoman, the only means [he or she has] to get something is through education" (quoted in Geiger 1968:156).

In most of the industrialized world, however, educational credentials played a smaller role for a longer period of time than in the United States. In-house promotion was the major avenue of advance for those who were ambitious. Middle managers and technicians were plucked off the shop floor, not off graduation procession lines. For example, in England—a very late developer of mass higher education—rates of upward mobility were not much different in the 1940s and 1950s than in the United States, but many more mobile people rose due to recognition for good performance on the job. They did not take higher-level jobs by virtue of their educational credentials (Kerkhoff, Campbell, and Wingfield-Laird 1985).

Credentials and Social Stratification. Today, most societies are moving toward credential-based systems of social selection like the one that has become so familiar to us in the United States. An interesting vignette developed by sociologists at the University of California, Berkeley shows the kinds of changes that have been typical over three generations: more white-collar jobs and higher educational requirements (but not necessarily more economic security in recent years). For their story of three generations, Claude Fischer and his colleagues (Fischer et al. 1996) chose a man in the middle of the income spectrum from people born during the Great Depression and then looked at the characteristics of similarly situated men from the preceding and succeeding generations. Using this procedure, they came up with three generations of fictitious Smiths. The man they called "John Smith, Sr." was born in 1915, dropped out of school, and started working in a steel mill at age 14. He was occasionally unemployed, but had steady work through and beyond World War II. He eventually retired with an annual income from pensions and social security checks of $15,000 in 1990. The man in the middle from the next generation, "John Smith, Jr.," attended Rutgers University for two years and then took a management trainee job in Chicago. He never experienced a period of unemployment and moved up the corporate ladder through three firms into higher management. In 1990, the family had an income of $65,000. The man in the middle in the next generation, "Johnny," graduated from a good college and landed a sales job in a computer firm. His toehold in the middle class was less secure, however, than that of John, Jr. At the age of 25, at a time when his computer-generated father had been married for four years and was working his way up the corporate hierarchy, Johnny was still working as a sales rep and was uncertain when, or if, he would be promoted (Fischer et al. 1996:208-9).[16]

Although higher educational credentials have become increasingly prevalent, they are important only in certain spheres of the job structure—and not even in all of the most important spheres. Some people without educational qualifications continue to start successful small businesses (Steinmetz and Wright 1989). Many other businesses are handed down within families (Robinson-1984; Robinson and Garnier 1985). Among small-business owners and farmers, schooling consequently plays a less important role as an investment in the future (Ishida, Muller, and Ridge 1995). Similarly, access to jobs in quite a few skilled trades (e.g., plumber or electrician) is regulated more by family networks than by formal training structures (see, e.g., Bailey and Waldinger 1991).

Higher educational credentials are required for professional occupations and for most nonclerical jobs in large organizations, both corporate and nonprofit. Sociologists sometimes use the term *universalistic* to describe the impersonal, standardized criteria that figure so prominently in the personnel administration of large organizations. Qualifications count more, at least at the entry level, than social background, social contacts, or an impressive exterior. Indeed, protections against discriminatory selection practices are written into hiring policies. In these important and growing spheres of the occupational structure, social stratification by means of educational credentials is quite clearly on the rise both in this country and elsewhere (DiPrete and Grusky 1990).

These jobs represent a very large proportion of the most prestigious and best paying jobs in today's society: everything from actuary to zoologist. Even in the once less credentialized sphere of business management, credentialism has taken over. Almost no one is promoted up the ranks into top management these days without a college degree (Useem 1989). Since the 1960s, a master's degree in business administration from a top-ranked business school has become an important ticket of admission to the executive suite (Useem and Karabel 1986).

With the advance of credentialism, higher education degrees have become important even for some jobs that may not be very intellectually demanding. For example, a health records technician degree from a community college may be required for those who want to help large hospitals and health maintenance organizations keep track of their patient, doctor, and insurance records. These kinds of jobs were once learned at work, but now they often require two years of postsecondary study. Admittedly, medical records are more complicated than they once were, but it is debatable that they are complicated enough to require two years of formal study in an institution of higher education. Wherever large-scale organization exists, so do credential requirements. Is a college degree necessary to manage a video store or fast food franchise? Probably not if the intellectual demands of the job are all that count, but most franchise managers do nevertheless have college degrees.

Educational Credentials as Reliability Signals. It is not obvious that educational credentials should have become so important for allocating people to jobs. After all, employers may have to pay more for educated people, and educated people might not do a particular job better than less educated workers could if they were trained properly on the job (Berg 1970). A good many studies have shown that credentialism discriminates against capable people who have abilities to do jobs just as well as those with degrees, but not the economic resources to obtain the required credentials. Some irreverent social scientists have taken delight in showing that education may actually be a disqualification for some jobs—for example, that aloof and cerebral psychoanalysts may do less good for patients than untrained people who are able to show empathy and act like understanding friends (Hogan 1979). A few critics have gone so far as to argue that credentialism is usually unnecessary and continues primarily because people in positions of power look at highly educated people as similar to themselves, as a kind of cultural kin (Collins 1979, chaps. 1-3).

The critics of credentialism do make an important point: Outside of a few highly technical occupations, academic preparation does not appear to be very specifically tied to the skills most jobs require. English majors may have characteristics that make them desirable employees, but those characteristics don't usually have much to do with their knowledge of Shakespeare or James Joyce. What's more, the information learned in school isn't remembered long enough by most students to do them much good on the job. Most English majors cannot provide off-the-cuff quotes or interpretations of more than a few passages at most from Shakespeare once they have finished their course work. Course knowledge in other fields has a similarly short half-life once final examinations have been turned in (Collins 1979:17-9). Nor are grades in school more than modestly correlated, if at all, with success in work life (Klitgaard 1985; Capelli 1992; Dye and Reck 1989).

But the critics of credentialism err in arguing that credentials must therefore be unrelated to job performance. The advance of credentialism has been propelled primarily by the needs of large organizations. For these organizations, credentials are useful as signals that their holders are more likely than other people to behave in organizationally valued ways (Spence 1974; Thurow 1972). Perhaps the most important characteristic that educational credentials signal is the ability of a job applicant to concentrate in a disciplined way on assigned problems—something that students obviously must do over and over if they are to succeed in school. Other organizationally desirable traits include reliability (showing up every day on time and in a work-ready state), the ability to handle nonroutine or self-directed work, and the ability to conform to the direction and desires of superiors. From the employers' point of view, it is a good bet that those who have survived all of the paper writing, problem sets, and examinations of a college education have developed these qualities to a greater degree than those who have not had such discipline-producing experiences (Squires 1979; Crain 1984). This may privilege the already-advantaged, but the privileges are based not on cultural similarities so much as on signals of reliability and willingness to conform.

As one moves up organizational hierarchies, the steadiness and deferential attitude taught by schooling may be even more important. Organizational careers are "fundamentally an apprenticeship in cooperation. . . . The essential point about jobs at the top of the hierarchy is not an unusual degree of skill but the costliness to management of error and the likelihood of error being made" (Blackburn and Mann 1979:108). Therefore, employers are usually less concerned with skill than such characteristics as discipline, steadiness, and responsibility.

Thus, the growth of large-scale organizations is one important force behind the growth of credentialism. People who run these organizations have incentives to find efficient ways to process people and to fill positions. Educational credentials have proved to be the most cost-effective way to limit the pool of eligibles and to aid in the hiring of people with organizationally valuable qualities. Once credentials are established as a requirement for hiring, inflationary pressures are strong, because students and their families have a compelling interest in obtaining resources that promise them greater opportunities. The modern democratic aspiration for upward mobility can thus "ratchet up" credential requirements above what they might otherwise be.

The result has been the proliferation of specialized occupational jurisdictions off limits to anyone without the accepted educational credentials. Professional associations, governments, and educational institutions have each played a role in carving the job structure into this jigsaw puzzle of occupational jurisdictions controlled by the holders of specialized credentials. All these institutions have had a stake in the expansion of the "credential society": Professional associations are judges in the university accreditation process and want to guarantee "high-quality" performance so as to maintain their respectability, governments are important in the regulation both of occupations and colleges, and educational institutions provide the medium of exchange—degrees and certificates—that keeps the wheels of the system turning (Abbott 1988; Brint 1994, chap. 2).

Beneficiaries of the Credential Society

We have now seen why the expansion of formal education and the rise of credentialism have substantially increased the importance of schooling in the process of social selection. In a much more bureaucratic, impersonal system of organization, educational credentials have come to play the stratifying role that family resources and reputation once played. Statistical studies confirm that although family background was once the most important determinant of an individual's life chances, educational attainment is now more directly decisive (Jencks et al. 1979; Featherman and Hauser 1978; Hout 1988).

Not surprisingly, as schooling has become increasingly important, questions about the fairness of the system have also grown more persistent. On the surface, the new system for sorting people into jobs seems fairer than the old. It seems to provide greater opportunities for able and hardworking children from lower-status families to move up while requiring children from higher-status families to at least prove themselves in school if they want to maintain their advantages. Among those who approve of the credential system, schools are sometimes likened to an elevator in which everyone gets on at the same floor but, depending on how well he or she does in school, gets off at a different floor corresponding to a particular level of occupational prestige and income.

Yet almost from the beginning of the age of credentialism, some sociologists worried that exactly the opposite would occur: that advancement through schooling would be less fair to those closer to the bottom of the class structure than advancement through hard work or business enterprise had been. In 1949, the sociologist W. Lloyd Warner observed that the intense intellectual competition of the modern schooling system could easily deflate working-class aspirations more often than it nurtured and rewarded them. Warner (1949) observed that his own studies of social stratification offered something less than categorical encouragement to those who would like to believe that because the occupational route is no longer as open as it once was, education is providing an adequate substitute (pp. 25, 29).

One important question, therefore, is how much schools are involved in altering inequalities from one generation to the next and how much they are involved in reinforcing the advantages and disadvantages that children from different social backgrounds bring with them to school. Do schools really operate like elevators, giving everyone the same opportunity to get on at the ground floor and to go up as far as their ability and effort allow them? Or are they more like conveyor belts stacked one above the other, depositing people on floors not too dissimilar from the ones from which they began?

Two very different perspectives, corresponding to these two different images, have developed in response to questions about the distribution of opportunity in the credential society. The first can be described as a perspective based on the idea of *meritocracy,* and the second as a perspective based on the idea of *social reproduction.*

Theories of Meritocracy. The term meritocracy was coined by the British sociologist Michael Young in his satire *The Rise of the Meritocracy* (1958), which is about an acutely unhappy society of the future. In this society, people with high measured IQs rule with an increasing sense of entitlement while those with low measured IQs toil miserably without a saving sense of the unfairness of the world. (In Young's satire, a populist revolt, led by women who have been left out of the meritocracy, eventually overthrows the system.) But meritocracy is usually used today in a positive sense, and it has come to mean rule by the most intellectually able. Although effort is usually included as a criterion for membership in the meritocracy, other possible "merits" (e.g., of character) are usually not addressed.

The ideas were in circulation before the term was coined. James Bryant Conant (1938, 1940), then president of Harvard University, wrote two important articles at the end of the Depression era laying out the rationale for a radical change in the organization of the social selection process. His ideas closely corresponded to the modern idea of meritocracy. Conant argued that democracy did not require a "uniform distribution of the world's goods" or a "radical equalization of wealth." What it required instead was a "continuous process by which power and privilege may be automatically redistributed at the end of each generation" (Conant 1940:598).

Conant and other midcentury meritocrats considered schools to be the primary mechanisms of this redistribution. The midcentury meritocrats assumed that talent was not concentrated at the top of the social class structure but was rather widely distributed throughout. By giving every student—from the most humble to the most privileged—an equal educational opportunity at the beginning of life, society would be in a position to fairly select only those most qualified by brains and sweat to occupy the "command posts" at the top. Even better, this "aristocracy of talent" would be recreated fresh in every generation.

The idea of meritocracy combined a principle of "aristocratic" leadership and a principle of democratic selection, or equality of opportunity. To the extent that the theory of meritocracy is true, we would expect the people at the top of the job structure to be those who are the most intellectually able and hardest working and that these people will come from a wide variety of social backgrounds.

Theories of Social Reproduction. From the opposite side of the debate, theorists of social reproduction have responded that Conant's "automatic redistribution" at the end of every generation does not occur. Instead, they have argued, the "aristocracy of talent" is another name (although a misleading one) for inherited and socially transmitted status. Those already advantaged by the social order are precisely the ones who are most likely to be selected by it in the next generation under the cloak of "meritocracy." For these theorists, the supposed fairness of meritocracy does not exist because the schooling system frequently fails to see the potential of those who do not inherit the language, culture, and values of the upper classes. In the words of perhaps the best known American theorists of reproduction, Samuel Bowles and Herbert Gintis (1976), "To reproduce the labor force, the schools are destined to legitimate inequality, limit personal development to forms compatible with submission to . . . authority, and aid in the process whereby youth are resigned to their fate" (p. 266).

Social reproduction theorists argue that the class structure limits society's ability to identify merit. They point to examples like the following: Imagine a girl born into a Spanish-speaking family in southern California. Let's assume that she has high cognitive potential. Nevertheless, linguistic differences may make a child shy in front of native speakers (Rodriguez 1982). She may have little in the way of consistent structure in her household, and this may make it difficult for her to adjust to the highly structured school environment (Clark 1983). Lack of support for intellectual activity in the home may lead her to look for attention and praise in more consistently validated areas of life—such as religion, socializing with friends, or feminine craft arts (Bourdieu 1984). The children she plays with may care as little about school as her parents do, and they may even mock her if she expresses an interest in school (London 1979). Her parents may feel uncomfortable talking to teachers and may therefore avoid school conferences or "working the system" on their daughter's behalf (Lareau 1987). This girl may be born with great potential but become less "meritorious" over time.

Social reproduction theory began in Europe as a critique of the social class biases in the schooling system (Bernstein 1961; Bourdieu and Passeron 1977).

However, critically minded social scientists quickly began to argue that the educational deck can be equally or even more completely stacked against racial and ethnic minorities (Rist 1970; Ogbu 1978) and women (Byrne 1978; Hall 1983).

To the extent that the theory of social reproduction is correct, we would expect to see a high level of status transmission through the schooling system, rather than "automatic redistribution" of high-status jobs to the "best and the brightest" of every generation regardless of their social origins. Moreover, if social reproduction is a primary function of schooling, cognitive ability should count less than social background as a predictor of who gets ahead in both schooling and jobs.

Social Background, Ability, and Opportunity

When we examine the opportunities for social mobility that schooling provides, it is important to separate the effects of occupational upgrading from the effects of educational expansion. In all industrialized societies, many lower-status jobs in farming and manufacturing have been gradually eliminated and higher-status jobs in the professional service sector and business management have increased. Largely because of this change in the occupations that are available, more people have experienced upward occupational mobility than downward mobility in recent generations. Between 1900 and 1970, upward occupational mobility exceeded downward mobility by two or three to one in most industrialized societies (Erikson and Goldthorpe 1992, chap. 6).

People in industrialized societies have experienced other improvements as well. More people, for example, now work in relatively pleasant environments: clean offices and salesrooms rather than grimy shop floors. The cost of many consumer goods has declined relative to real incomes, increasing the standard of living. Thus, more people have the sense that their lives are improving compared with those of their parents.

People also see that they have completed more education than their parents did. They are tempted to attribute positive changes in their work lives and standards of living to the educational levels they have achieved. But this attribution is not necessarily correct. A generation ago, the sociologists Seymour Martin Lipset and Hans Zetterberg (1956) pointed out that occupational upgrading was occurring in all industrialized societies, despite radically different historical experiences, widely varying forms of government, and sharply divergent schooling structures. Subsequent studies have affirmed that similar kinds of occupational changes do occur in all industrialized societies and that these changes occur whether a society has a restrictive or expansive system of higher education (Featherman, Jones, and Hauser 1975; Erikson and Goldthorpe 1992). For example, Switzerland, which graduates less than 10 percent of each age cohort with university-level degrees, has experienced occupational upgrading similar to that of the United States, which graduates 30 percent of each age cohort (Organization for Economic Cooperation and Development 1996).

Someone has to fill the new professional, technical, and managerial jobs even if educational systems do not expand at all. Indeed, in countries with few university-level graduates, less educated people often do continue to fill these higher-level jobs (Erikson and Goldthorpe 1992:303-4).

•••••••••••••

How Much Mobility?

Whether all industrial societies have similar rates of occupational mobility is a much-debated question in sociology. Seymour Martin Lipset and Hans Zetterberg (1956) provided one of the first answers to this question based on comparable cross-national data. Against the views of some American celebrators of American uniqueness, Lipset and Zetterberg argued that the level of mobility found in the United States was not substantially different from that found in a number of European nations. All modern societies seemed to show high rates of mobility, with more upward than downward mobility. Once industrializing societies reached a takeoff point, according to Lipset and Zetterberg, fairly common rates of mobility could be expected.

Later researchers discovered much more variation in the employment and occupational structures of industrial societies than Lipset and Zetterberg projected. Different occupational structures provide different distributions of occupations and therefore affect the rate of mobility. However, the nature of flows between occupational classes are similar (Grusky and Hauser 1984). When sociologists look at flows from father's to son's occupations among just three major classes (professional/managerial, small business/routine white collar, and blue collar/farm workers), they find between 40 and 60 percent of men have changed from their father's occupational class (Erikson and Goldthorpe 1992). Of these changes, upward movements exceed downward movements by between two and three to one—occasionally by more than three to one (ibid., chap. 6).

In the United States, 55 percent of men born between 1900 and 1970 moved within the three broad class categorizations and 45 percent were stable. Among men who were mobile, upward mobility exceeded downward mobility by almost three to one (40 percent upwardly mobile; 15 percent downwardly mobile). These rates, for the most part, fit comfortably within the range of other industrialized societies (Erikson and Goldthorpe 1992:330).

Today, the Lipset/Zetterberg thesis has been amended more than abandoned. Occupational structures are not as similar as Lipset and Zetterberg suggested, but flows among occupations appear to be similar across a wide variety of industrial societies (Featherman et al. 1975; Grusky and Hauser 1984; Erikson and Goldthorpe 1992). Like Lipset and Zetterberg, more recent researchers have found that mobility does not consistently increase with level of industrial development, nor is greater fluidity associated with the nature of schooling or political systems. One additional finding stands out: Occupational mobility is greatest for countries where the level of economic inequality is lowest. In this area, too, it may be that the greater the equality of condition, the greater the equality of opportunity (Erikson and Goldthorpe 1992:388).

• •

One would think that school-based selection would at least be fairer than systems in which higher levels of schooling are more completely monopolized by the upper classes. But the evidence on this point is not as compelling as this logic suggests. Researchers find quite a bit of individual-level mobility, based in part on superior school performance, combined with considerable continuity in the amount of class advantage. Neither social reproduction theory nor meritocratic theory in their strong versions adequately accounts for these findings. Instead, we see schooling as an increasingly important demonstration arena in which both brains and socially transmitted status characteristics attract positive notices—and in which neither is sufficient to ensure the highest levels of success.

How we weigh the evidence, however, depends on whether we take individual characteristics or group patterns as our unit of analysis. The factors that bear on individual life opportunities do not necessarily tell us much about the circumstances faced by most people born into a given group. Therefore, it is important to look both at studies of individual achievement and group differentials.

Who Gets Ahead? Individual-Level Studies

Most of the studies of "who gets ahead?" have examined the individual-level characteristics that seem to make a difference in the kinds of jobs and incomes people eventually attain. These *status attainment studies* measure the independent effects of various attributes, such as social background or measured ability, by holding other variables in the model statistically constant. Thus, if we are interested in the independent effect of father's occupation on adult attainments, we would compare people who are similar in every way except for their fathers occupations—people who, for example, have the same race and gender, the same cognitive abilities, and equivalent educational credentials.

These individual-level studies using data from the United States show that most of the variation in people's adult occupational and income status cannot be predicted by characteristics like social background, cognitive ability, and educational credentials. Some of the unexplained variation in life fates has to do with the ups and downs of companies, industries, or regions (Haveman and Cohen 1994). Indeed, a good case can be made that although it is theoretically possible for school systems to select people on strictly meritocratic grounds, it is not possible for market economies to do so. This is because markets do not reward according to the same standards of merit as schools, but simply according to the economic value of goods and services offered (Goldthorpe 1996). Some of the variation (perhaps quite a bit) has to do with being in the right place at the right time, and similar factors of good or bad fortune. People are subject to the vicissitudes of history, accident, employers' whims, and their own bad decisions. Many unmeasured individual differences are presumably involved.

Both social background and measured cognitive ability show up as important explanatory factors for that part of the variation in people's adult attainments that can be explained—primarily because they both influence the likelihood that a person will obtain high-level educational credentials. If a child has high test scores, he or she is more likely to end up with good educational credentials, even if the child was not born into a high-status family. The opposite is also true: Growing up in a high-status family means that a person is likely to end up with good educational credentials, even if he or she does not have particularly high test scores or top-flight grades.

But measured ability has been more important than background for recent cohorts, especially for recent cohorts of men. Grades and test scores are the best single predictors of educational attainment (measured by number of years of schooling or highest degree level). Even so, background never disappears entirely as a factor. Family background helps to predict test scores, and it also has a modest direct effect on how much schooling a person is likely to receive regardless of the person's test scores (Jencks et al. 1979; Featherman and Hauser 1978).

Even at the height of the equal opportunity era in the United States, bright children whose fathers had blue-collar occupations were less likely than other children to obtain a college degree. According to the U.S. General Social Survey, unskilled blue-collar children with the highest IQs (measured here as the top 14 percent on a word-recognition test) who reached college age in the 1950s and early 1960s had a little more than a 50 percent chance of completing college (see Table 6.1). This is a very good chance, but it is not as high as the 80 percent likelihood of graduating enjoyed by people with the same high level of verbal intelligence and professional or managerial fathers.[18] And it is not even as good a chance as the 70 percent chance of completion enjoyed by children of all IQ levels who were lucky enough to be born into families in the top 10th of the occupational scale (Hout, Raftery, and Bell 1993:46).

TABLE 6.1

*Chances of Completing College by Father's Occupation and GSS[a]
Word Recognition Score, U.S. Men and Women, Born 1946-60*

	Chances of completing college	
Father's occupation	Students with median scores	Students with top 14 percent of scores
All occupations	20%	70%
Professional	38	81
Manager	26	82
Clerical/sales	18	65
Skilled blue collar	15	60
Unskilled blue collar	12	54

Source: General Social Survey data were tabulated by M. Hout (Hout, Raftery, and Bell 1993).
Note: Measured verbal intelligence is based on a 10-item word-recognition test.
a. GSS = General Social Survey.

Other factors also show an independent influence on educational attainment once background and ability are statistically controlled. Until recently, girls from working-class families did not usually attend college, even if they were very bright (Sewell and Shah 1967). Other factors bearing on educational attainment include having an intact two-parent household, having families and friends who value education, taking academic courses (particularly academic courses in math and science), and having strong personal aspirations to succeed (Sewell, Haller, and Portes 1969; Sewell and Hauser 1975; Jencks et al. 1979; Jencks, Crouse, and Mueser 1983).

High-level education credentials, in turn, are the key to obtaining prestigious and well-paid jobs. The people who tend to move up are those who have the habits and skills that bring success in school: regularity, diligence, and reasoning ability. Not all credentials have the same weight in the market, of course. Business and technological disciplines are more highly valued, and the credentials of minorities and women tend to purchase significantly less in the way of high-status jobs and high incomes than do the credentials of nonminority men (Treiman and Roos 1983; Goldin 1992).

The person with the best chance of later life success, then, is a nonminority male born into an intact, two-parent, high-status family that values education; who has high tested intelligence and is surrounded by high-aspiring peers; and who takes lots of academic courses, especially in math and science, gets good grades in school, and maintains high achievement aspirations. Each of these characteristics makes at least a small independent contribution to explaining status attainment in later life. People who hold leadership positions in extracurricular organizations as adolescents also tend to have greater occupational success (Jencks and Associates 1979, chap. 5; Willingham 1985; Howard 1986). People who do not have these characteristics certainly do get ahead at times, just not as frequently.

Other factors that might plausibly seem important in later life success don't show up as statistically significant influences. These include good looks (as rated by peers), good personality ratings from teachers and peers, and even attendance at "high quality" secondary schools (see, e.g., Sewell et al. 1969; Featherman and Hauser 1978; Jencks et al. 1979; Campbell 1983).

These individual-level studies tell us many interesting things. The findings should be enough to make us wary of sweeping indictments of the "class system" or the "race system,"as well as laments about the impossibility of breaching their barriers. In the industrialized world, many thousands of people do breach their barriers every year. The aspirations of one's families and friends—and one's own drive to succeed—make a difference even for people who are not born into very high-status families. Most people know someone like a former student of mine, Tobi, who was born into a working-class (and non-English-speaking) family but spent hours and hours in the library in an effort to be the best prepared student in class. They also usually know someone like another former student, Karen, who came from a wealthy and prominent family and had many rare life experiences (her family's name was attached to a performance hall on campus) but never felt the deep, inner need to work hard enough to stand out.

Perhaps most important, these studies tell us that people who finish higher-level degrees—whether due to family expectations, high intelligence, or just sheer persistence and ambition—have a "leg up" in the labor market even if they are not otherwise advantaged. If a person had to choose just one characteristic on which to rank above most of his or her peers—and was required to be average on all other characteristics—the best choice would be to have high-level educational credentials. Although it seems counterintuitive, this would be a better choice than being born into a wealthy family, scoring very high on tests of intellectual ability, being exceptionally good looking, or having an unusually charming personality (Jencks and Associates 1979).

Comparative Studies of Status Attainment. For many years, the samples and measures used in status attainment studies in different countries were not comparable and therefore impossible to analyze in a rigorous way (Treiman and Ganzeboom 1990). Even today, consistently measured variables in comparative studies are limited to a small number of potential influences on attainment. Most comparative studies of status attainment look only at family origins, educational attainments, and adult status. Some studies have also looked at gender influences. The influence of cognitive abilities, aspirations, family size, race and ethnicity, and other factors that have proved to be important in the American case cannot be investigated.

Nevertheless, some very general cross-national patterns are now evident. One is a pattern of underlying similarity in the process of status attainment. As in the United States, educational qualifications are now more important than social origins throughout the industrialized world in determining how likely people are to succeed. Social origins nevertheless always help to determine how much education a person is likely to obtain. For the most part, the association between class origin and education falls into similar patterns across the industrialized nations. However, the formerly socialist countries of Hungary and Poland were apparently able to dampen the influence of social origins on middle-level educational attainments (and during some periods also on higher-level qualifications) by encouraging able working-class students (Ishida et al. 1995; Muller 1996). Conversely, France stands out for the persistent strength of the ties between higher-status families and the upper levels of the educational system (Garnier and Hout 1976; Muller 1996).

Gender also plays a role in mobility opportunities throughout the world. Although (as we'll see in Chapter 7) access to higher levels of schooling have become more and more equal between men and women, economic returns to education for men and women remain substantial, varying from near equality in Germany and parts of Eastern Europe to large gaps in the United States and Japan (Treiman and Roos 1983).

Although educational qualifications are important in all industrialized countries, relatively few countries have stratification systems as strongly based on educational credentials as the American system is (Erikson and Goldthorpe 1992). It is not surprising that social reproduction theory originated in England and France. Until recently, mobility through schooling was distinctly limited in those countries (Kerkhoff 1974; Garnier and Hout 1976). Countries with smaller higher education systems continue to rely considerably on promotion from the shop and office floor.

In the developing world, social background remains a greater influence both on educational attainment and adult status than in industrialized societies. In countries such as India and Brazil, the class structure is less differentiated, higher levels of schooling are out of reach of the great majority, and stratification remains more deeply rooted in family standing (Kelley 1978; Treiman and Yip 1988).

Who Gets Ahead? Group-Level Studies

The findings for groups do not necessarily point in the same direction as the findings for individuals. One reason for this is that all the characteristics that make a difference for individuals are correlated. People born into high-status families are more likely to be pushed to achieve and to have friends that are similarly motivated. They are more likely to attend schools that place a strong emphasis on academics. And for reasons that partly reflect the economic and social advantages of a high-status birth, they are also more likely to do well on standardized tests of intelligence.

This last point is perhaps the most important. It is not possible to completely isolate measured "intelligence" from social background. Even if we accept IQ scores as good measures of intelligence—something that many leading scientists no longer do (see, e.g., Sternberg 1988; Fischer et al. 1996, chaps. 2 and 3)—we find that IQ scores are substantially conditioned by the social environment. Families can transmit good nutrition, intellectual stimulation, confidence in test-taking situations, and high levels of comfort with "official" linguistic and cultural codes, or they can transmit the opposite qualities. All these qualities can and do influence standard measures of intelligence.

Because all of the important factors in the "opportunity equation" are correlated, it is not easy to use individual-level studies to make final judgments about the fate of social classes. An example of the level of correlation between several key individual-level characteristics is shown in Table 6.2 for American white nonfarm males in the 1960s. The data are from one of the world's best studied surveys, the first Occupational Change in a Generation Survey (OCG I), supplemented by IQ correlations from other surveys.[19]

TABLE 6.2

Estimated True Correlations, Background and Status Characteristics of U.S. White Nonfarm Males, Aged 25-64, Surveyed in 1962

	1	2	3	4	5
1. Father's education					
2. Father's occupation	.640				
3. Education	.426	.485			
4. Early adult IQ	.358	.382	.680		
5. Occupation	.250	.440	.648	.502	
6. Income	.214	.287	.353	.349	.441

Source: Jencks et al. (1972:322).

Note: Education is measured by highest grade attained; occupation is measured using the Duncan scale of occupational prestige; early adult IQ is based on the Armed Forces Qualifying Test (AFQT), given to men usually between the ages of 18 and 26; income is annual monetary income of respondent. AFQT scores were not available on the original survey. The correlations are based on the results of other surveys. Original data from Occupational Change in a Generation I (OCG 1) have been corrected for measurement errors by Jencks and Associates (1972: 330-36).

To measure how much social reproduction exists at the group level, we want to know whether social class advantages have been reduced by the expansion of education, have remained stable, or have increased. To answer these questions, it is necessary to look at the level of correlation between social origins and educational attainments over time (Ishida et al. 1995).

There are many reasons to believe that group differentials may not have narrowed much in spite of the vast expansion of schooling. High-status parents will be anxious to improve the opportunities of their children and will do what they can to give their children advantageous experiences, such as searching for the best schools in town, and perhaps extra resources like tutoring. Parents from upper-status families may be able to transmit advantageous cultural knowledge and experience just as effectively as they transmit economic resources (Bourdieu and Passeron 1977). And they may be able to provide economic and motivational support for staying in school that lower-status parents cannot provide.

School systems, too, respond to increased demand for credentials in ways that do not necessarily reduce class advantages. Educational expansion may be accompanied by a more differentiated structure of tiers and quality levels, and lower-status children may be channeled (or channel themselves) into lower tiers of the system while upper-status children are channeled (or channel themselves) into the higher tiers. The introduction of upper secondary school vocational tracks in many European countries and vocationally oriented community colleges in the United States are notable examples of this process. Educational expansion may primarily encourage a transfer of class differences to higher levels of the system. Thus, when lower-status children become better represented in high school, college may become the key to higher social status. When they begin to enter colleges in larger numbers, the system may shift again to a higher branching point. At this point, graduate training may become the key to higher social status. Only a small proportion of students from lower-status backgrounds will survive to graduate school, whereas a high proportion of students from upper-middle-class families will. In these ways, increased educational attainments may be completely compatible with stable (or even increasing) levels of class reproduction (Boudon 1974).

Findings of International Comparisons. Most studies of group differences find declining correlations between father's status and children's educational attainments over the course of the century. But this decreasing correlation can be misleading. It doesn't necessarily mean that class inequality has been reduced at the highest levels of the system where credentials are most valuable. Instead, the lower correlation largely reflects the decreasing variation in the amount of schooling children receive and the higher average levels of schooling in the population.

Robert Mare (1980) first proposed a method for distinguishing between quantitative results due to the expansion of schooling and those due to the selection and allocation of students. He did so by viewing the educational attainment process as a sequence of transitions (e.g., between elementary and lower secondary school and between lower secondary and upper secondary school). At each stage in the sequence, a student can either make a transition or discontinue. The odds of making any transition can then be computed by social background characteristics over a series of cohorts.

A recent study of 13 industrialized societies found that in 11 of the countries, class differences in transition rates to higher levels of schooling remained highly stable over time, in spite of a rapid rise in the average level of educational attainment in all 13 countries. The countries in the study were the

United States, Japan, Israel, Canada, Great Britain, France, Germany, Italy, Sweden, the Netherlands, Hungary, Czechoslovakia (before its division), and Poland (Blossfeld and Shavit 1993). Only two countries, Sweden and the Netherlands, showed a clear pattern of decreasing class inequality over time at higher levels of schooling. In addition, the United States showed decreasing levels of inequality for some recent cohorts (Hout et al. 1993; see also Featherman and Hauser 1978:238-52). Thus, "whereas the proportions of [students from] all social classes . . . have increased [at higher educational levels], the relative advantage associated with privileged origins persists" (Blossfeld and Shavit 1993:22).[20]

Ironically, the results of this study suggest that the societies ideologically most committed to eliminating class differences often failed most completely to eliminate them at the higher levels of schooling. For instance, leaders of the former Soviet Union periodically instituted periods of "class affirmative action," which substantially changed the composition of the educated classes, but only for brief periods. Findings from elsewhere in the former Soviet bloc suggest that policies designed to increase the opportunities of students from working-class families were usually undermined by political corruption before they could be institutionalized. The advantages afforded by university education were so great that anxious parents used the various means at their disposal—from intimidation to bribery—to win places for their children or for those of important clients. In Czechoslovakia and Hungary, corruption was commonplace, usually in the form of favors done for children of powerful officials, but sometimes also in the form of outright bribes, or "thank-you money" (Mateju 1993; Szelenyi and Aschaffenburg 1993). Corruption was so widespread, in the words of one critic, that far from suffering any disadvantage, "the elite and its successors were allowed to operate almost entirely free from meritocratic competition" (Mateju 1993:257).

Even in Japan, a country noted for its apparently meritocratic test-centered system of educational selection, the patterns do not indicate lesser rates of social reproduction than elsewhere in the industrialized world. In fact, sons from professional and managerial class families in Japan have a very low probability of downward mobility. More advantaged parents typically buy additional private tutoring for their children in the attempt to ensure the kinds of educational successes that are necessary for white-collar employment.

These findings indicate that educational expansion is compatible with little change toward a greater equality across social classes in the distribution of the *most valuable years* of schooling or the *most valuable degrees* (Blossfeld and Shavit 1993:3). Yet the findings do not completely support social reproduction theory. Although the odds of making higher-level transitions are greater for students from high-status families, they are not always as high as social reproduction theory suggests they should be. In the United States, for example, men in the postwar college cohorts had a 20 percent greater chance of obtaining a college degree if their fathers came from the highest 10th of occupational prestige than if they came from the middle of the occupational structure—the difference between a 70 percent and a 50 percent chance (Hout et al. 1993:47). Class advantages can be generally stable over time without being extremely large. Nevertheless, these findings indicate that many high-status families are effectively pursuing the path outlined by social reproduction theorists: converting economic advantages into cultural advantages that help their children go further in school than others usually do and then reconverting school credentials into economic advantages.[21]

The Scandinavian Difference. This leads to an interesting question: Why have class inequalities decreased in Sweden and the Netherlands when they have not, for the most part, decreased elsewhere? In those countries, working-class students have more nearly caught up to middle-class students in their chances of achieving higher levels of schooling. These comparative findings show quite clearly that no universal law exists that "states that privileged classes always find ways to maintain their relative advantages" (Jonsson 1993:126).

The narrowing of class inequalities has occurred in Sweden and the Netherlands in spite of a relatively low rate of university graduation. Access to higher education has become more equal, but the effects of this change are not as noticeable, because relatively few people graduate. Instead, the key changes have been at the level of secondary education, where social origins have counted much less as a determinant of who completes secondary school. They have also counted much less over time as a determinant of who is enrolled in academic as opposed to vocational programs.

In all likelihood, changes in the conditions and attitudes of Scandinavian workers themselves have been most important. Jonsson (1993) writes that the greater chances of working-class people over time are attributable primarily "to an equalization in living conditions . . . due to decreasing income differences [and] . . . welfare state redistribution." In addition, "those characteristics of manual labor which limit workers' ability to give practical support and encouragement to their children . . . [exhausting work, long hours, etc.] have become less common or severe" (p. 126). Sweden and the Netherlands also have had unusually high commitments to equality of opportunity: They are both societies in which an egalitarian, Social Democratic influence in governmental policy (including educational policy) has been very important. These cases suggest that equality of opportunity may be greatest where equality of conditions is also greatest. (See also Erikson and Jonsson 1996.)

A Note on Ethnic Inequalities. Some highly subordinate ethnic groups are analogous to lower-class populations. These include groups like the Maoris in New Zealand, Koreans in Japan, and Oriental Jews in Israel. In fact, the opportunities of highly subordinate minorities may be even fewer because they cannot easily shed the features that mark their low status. The conditions encouraging greater ethnic equality in these circumstances are similar to those that have led to class equalization in Sweden and the Netherlands. Greater ethnic equality requires strong support in society for equalized conditions and governmental policies aimed at reducing inequalities in housing, schooling, and jobs. The most successful cases of reduction in inequalities between majority groups and highly subordinate minorities are those in which subordinate ethnic groups have already gained significant power in at least one institutional domain, such as government, the military, or religion. In Malaysia, a comprehensive government effort has reduced once-large inequalities between the Chinese, Indian, and Malay populations at the same time that educational attainments for all three populations have increased (see case study).

• • • • • • • • • • • • •

ETHNIC MINORITIES AND EQUALITY OF OPPORTUNITY

Ethnic minorities often have the same limited opportunities to advance as lower-class citizens do. Their opportunities may even be worse, because they cannot easily shed the features that mark their low status. The few countries that have improved educational opportunities for ethnic minorities have generally made it a priority to do so. They have usually made it one feature of a more broadly based reform plan. And they have usually also built on relatively weak ethnic status boundaries, with some inconsistencies in power across sectors.

Malaysia is a notable recent success story that illustrates these principles. The Chinese and Indian populations in Malaysia have traditionally controlled most of the wealth in the country, and the indigenous Malays have generally held political power. After years of tension and some racial rioting, the country's New Economic Policy (NEP) was introduced in 1971. The NEP mandated Malay representation in the economy through ethnic ownership quotas, hiring quotas, participation in the armed forces, and educational scholarships. The government also funded rural development, including irrigation and infrastructure projects. Between 1970 and 1990, the proportion of corporate assets owned by Malays rose from 2 percent to 20 percent, and the incidence of poverty declined by 35 percent (United Nations Development Project 1994). Where ethnic groups are completely unintegrated into the more prosperous spheres of the market economy and where sharp and consistent lines of ethnic and cultural stratification exist, even comprehensive government programs do not usually improve the educational opportunities of minorities. Countries such as New Zealand and India, for example, have attempted at times to implement far-reaching plans to improve the condition of their primary disadvantaged minorities, but with little success. The difference seems to be in the relative status of the minorities in question. When minorities are very completely subordinated, reform polices will not be implemented with enthusiasm by the dominant group or embraced with enthusiasm by the disadvantaged group. The emotions of superiority and shame surrounding social boundaries in these systems have thus far proven too much to overcome.

•••

The Rise and Fall of Equalized Opportunity in the United States. Sweden, the Netherlands, and Malaysia are not the only societies that have experienced an equalization of opportunities for higher-level transitions as educational enrollments have expanded. During the period between 1945 and 1980, class inequalities in educational opportunities were also greatly reduced in the United States. The American path was based not on greatly improved conditions for the working classes but on a rapid expansion of higher education accompanied by very substantial state subsidies for lower-income and minority students. As Hout and Dohan (1996) put it,

> The Swedish path [to equality of educational opportunity] goes directly through existing class barriers, lowering them over the course of the century; the American path goes around them, expanding the system so much that class-based selection is irrelevant, because so few students are mustered out. (P. 229)

Between 1960 and 1975, the proportion of women and minorities in higher education increased rapidly—from 37 to 47 percent in the case of women and from 4 to almost 10 percent in the case of African Americans. The 1975 figures approximate the two groups' proportions in the population at large. The proportion of college students from lower-income families also increased somewhat during this period, although less substantially (Peng 1977; Karen 1991). Graduation rates changed in the same direction as enrollment rates. African Americans and women graduated at rates similar to white males, and even differences in graduation rates by social class narrowed somewhat, especially between students from the top two quartiles of the income structure (Mortenson 1995).

Why did more women, minorities, and working-class kids go to college during this period? Both economic optimism and state support were at work. Real incomes were rising, and the long stretch of general prosperity supported an optimistic outlook among working people. They became more willing to invest in the possibility of an even better future for their children (particularly if they didn't have to invest too much). Moreover, thanks to the powerful post-war economy, professional and managerial jobs were growing at a much faster rate than other jobs. Young people and their parents were more willing to make the sacrifices required to attend college because they knew that good jobs would probably be waiting for them at the end of their stay.

Meanwhile, the government provided the means by which those who finished high school could go on to college without suffering crippling economic burdens. Public colleges and universities were well supported by state governments and required only nominal fees for attendance. The best public university system in the country, the University of California, for example, required students to pay fees of just $84 a year in the mid-1950s (less than $500 in 1997 dollars) (Liaison Committee of the Regents of the University of California and the California State Board of Education 1955:405), and these fees increased only moderately through the 1970s. For those who had trouble making the payments, generous financial aid packages were available. The G.I. Bill allowed World War II veterans to attend any college that would admit them. From the mid-1960s through the end of the 1970s, the federal government also provided subsidies for low- and middle-income students to attend college. These subsidies were complemented by extremely high levels of institutional aid. Financial grants-in-aid from all sources reached a peak of $20 billion in 1975-6 (Congressional Budget Office 1992:7).

These efforts had a measurable impact. The sociologist Michael Hout (1988) found that the effect of social origins on the subsequent career success of young men dropped by 50 percent between the early 1960s and the early 1980s. Hout attributed this change to the increased openness of higher education and the strong advantages of college degrees in the labor market. Although employers hiring at lower educational levels remained sensitive to applicants' social backgrounds, employers of college graduates adopted universalistic selection practices. Thus, for the first time, college degrees eclipsed social background as a source of subsequent career advantages.

In the United States, the age of increasing educational opportunity ended around 1980 (Lucas 1996; Mortenson 1995). College enrollments continued to grow, a tribute to the growing importance of college degrees as qualifications for good jobs. But racial and especially class inequalities in college graduation began to increase. For African Americans who enrolled in college, graduation rates in the later 1980s fell to about half the rate for whites (General Accounting Office [GAO] 1995:6). Similarly, after narrowing in the 1970s, the disparities between students from high- and low-income families widened (ibid.; Baker and Velez 1996). After 1980, virtually all the growth in the numbers of graduates came from the top quarter of the income structure. Graduation rates for students from the top quartile of family income approached 80 percent, but graduation rates from the second quartile of family income remained in the high 20 percent range (Mortenson 1995) (see Figure 6.1).

Students from the bottom half of the income distribution and minority students, in particular, were increasingly priced out of four-year colleges and channeled into two-year community colleges (McPherson and Schapiro 1995), where they were prepared primarily for "semiprofessional" occupations (Dougherty 1987; Brint and Karabel 1989). Moreover, for a majority of lower-income and minority students, college attendance became a part-time endeavor (Baker and Velez 1996). These part-time students had markedly lower chances of finishing college because of competing family and work responsibilities.

Selective private colleges raised tuitions to unprecedented levels, but they also offered generous financial aid packages to qualified but financially needy students. In this sense, meritocracy remained in place at the elite schools. Nevertheless, with financial aid costs skyrocketing and competition for the best students increasing, even elite colleges and universities began to pay a little more attention to applicants' ability to pay and less to the obstacles they had overcome to achieve outstanding academic records (Delbanco 1996). More important, the applicant pool also changed. The elite schools began to attract a more homogeneous applicant pool: highly qualified children of quite well-to-do parents. Qualified children from less well-to-do families became less likely to apply, stymied by tuition "sticker prices" that climbed close to $30,000 per year at the more selective schools. Thus, the elite schools began to enroll more of both the brightest and the richest students than they did between 1960 and 1980. In the mid-1990s, approximately 40 percent of incoming students at very selective private colleges and universities came from families earning incomes of $100,000 or higher compared with 15 percent of students in higher education overall (Higher Education Research Institute 1996).

Some saw these growing class and racial inequalities as an ironic outcome of the triumph of meritocracy itself. This argument was popularized in Richard Herrnstein and Charles Murray's best-selling book, *The Bell Curve* (1994). By giving opportunity to less advantaged students from all social backgrounds, Murray and Herrnstein argued, the postwar meritocracy "creamed off" the most able children from lower-status families, leaving an increasingly large cognitive gap between the social classes in America.

FIGURE 6.1

*Estimated Chances for a Baccalaureate Degree by Age 24
by Family Income Quartile, 1970-94*

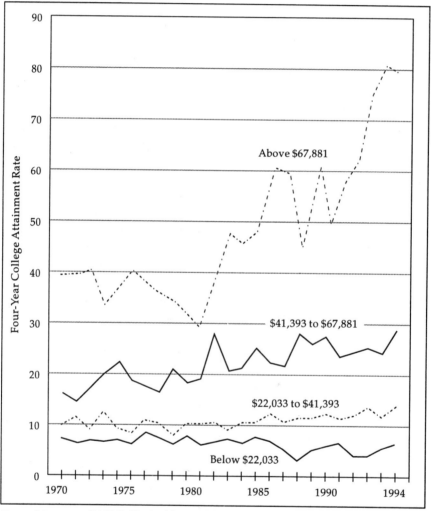

Source: Mortenson (1995:1). Used with permission.

This argument turned out not to hold up to serious scrutiny. Very high test scores are not as concentrated at the top of the class structure as Murray and Herrnstein suggest. In the United States, sociologists found a *narrowing*, not a widening, of cognitive differences between social class and racial groups as one moves from older to younger cohorts (Weakliem, McQuillan, and Schauer

1995; Hauser et al. 1996). This increasing cognitive equality may be largely the result of a more similar cultural environment experienced by lower- and upper-income Americans thanks to television and the movies, or it may be largely the result of lower average intellectual standards of entry in the now much larger professional and managerial occupations. In either case, the reemergence of gross inequalities in educational outcomes cannot be attributed to the concentration of good brains at the top of the class structure.

Instead, essentially the same forces that explain the equalization of opportunities in the postwar era also explain the declining opportunities of lower-income students since 1980. The economic problems of lower-income Americans have contributed significantly: The real incomes of non-college-educated Americans have stagnated since the early 1970s. Optimism about the future has decreased as has the ability to make the kinds of economic sacrifices required to send children to college for four years. Students are now very often forced to wait for college until they are older and to attend part-time while they are working 30 to 40 hours a week (Baker and Velez 1996). And many students from lower-income and less educated families are now limited to attending low-cost two-year colleges, where they are surrounded by part-time and vocationally oriented students.

The public resources available to support equality of opportunity at the college level have also declined. At the better private universities, tuitions are now substantially more than half the average family's total yearly income. Without substantial scholarship aid, children whose families are not in the top few percent of income cannot afford to attend these colleges, no matter how well qualified they may be. Even at public universities, fees have risen at nearly three times the rate of inflation since 1980, much faster than the incomes of all but the very rich. To make matters more difficult still for financially needy students, in the early 1980s loans replaced grants as the primary form of federally provided student financial aid (Congressional Budget Office 1992:7). Studies show that this shift has had little or no impact on high- and middle-income students but has appreciably affected low-income students. Many low-income students must now enroll in less expensive schools or drop out altogether (GAO 1995). These changes in financial aid had a particularly marked effect on black families, who have been reluctant to borrow to finance college (Hauser 1992).

CONCLUSION

Social selection is the most important function that schools perform today. The importance of schooling in social selection is a recent phenomenon, however.

It has depended on the rise of an opportunity consciousness, the attachment of this opportunity consciousness to schooling, and the tightening of the connection between schooling and jobs through credentialism.

In this new system, educational attainment has become the single strongest correlate of getting ahead in adult life. All other factors being equal, it is more important to have high-level education credentials than to be born into a wealthy family, to have high measured intelligence, or to have good looks or a charming personality.

Two theories have developed to explain the connection between schooling and later life success. One theory argues that modern societies are meritocracies in which the brightest and hardest-working people tend to succeed, regardless of their backgrounds. The other argues that educational expansion makes little difference on the level of social reproduction in society. This level of social reproduction is thought to be both rather high and essentially stable, whether or not higher education is relatively restricted or relatively inclusive.

Both individual-level and group-level studies help to evaluate these theories. Individual-level studies are based on comparing the life trajectories of people with different sets of characteristics. These studies indicate that high test scores are the most important influence on educational attainment. Other factors also help people to complete higher-level degrees: support from family and friends, taking and doing well in demanding courses, and high personal aspirations.

Social background is an important influence, but it works primarily through these other variables. It is associated with high test scores for reasons that have partly to do with the ability of high-status parents to provide more stimulating cognitive environments. Higher-status parents also provide the motivation that leads children to do well in school, to surround themselves with supportive peers, to take harder courses, and to adopt high expectations for themselves.

Individual-level characteristics associated with higher attainments are correlated with one another. Group-level studies therefore provide a different perspective—one that emphasizes the distribution of opportunities between classes rather than individual variation within classes. Group-level studies suggest that class inequalities in attaining the most valuable levels of education do not typically decrease with the expansion of schooling. In most countries, correlations between social origins and high-level educational attainments have remained remarkably stable since the beginning of the twentieth century in spite of a rapid rise in the number of years most people stay in school. Sweden and the Netherlands are two exceptions to this rule, and they suggest that equality of opportunity may be greater in countries where equality of conditions are also greater.

The ideal of meritocracy requires, by definition, both rigorous selection procedures and energetic efforts to search as widely as possible for talent. The realization of this vision requires a set of societal supports, which include, at a minimum: (1) equalizing or at least improving economic conditions for all classes and strata in society, (2) high state subsidies for public higher education relative to the absolute costs of attendance, and (3) widespread availability of financial grants-in-aid for qualified lower-income students.

The American experience since World War II demonstrates the importance of these societal supports. The era of equalized opportunities peaked between 1945 and 1980. Once these supports disappeared or declined in the 1980s, so did college graduation rates for lower-income and minority students.

CHAPTER 7

Schools and Social Selection: Inequality

The study of those who are not selected in the school sorting process is, in some ways, even more important than the study of opportunity, although it is not always as comforting to contemplate. For every few who get through school successfully, many are left behind at every critical stage. In the United States today, for example, one-fifth of high school students do not make it as far as graduation, a figure that rises above 50 percent in the poorest minority communities. By the time the academic race finishes with the awarding of graduate and professional degrees, well over 90 percent of each age group has fallen by the wayside.

As we saw in Chapter 6, neither meritocratic nor social reproduction theory adequately explains the distribution of opportunities linked to schooling. Too many extra-meritocratic factors figure into the status attainment process to sustain meritocratic theory, and too much mobility through schooling occurs to sustain social reproduction theory. These theories might plausibly work better in the explanation of school-based inequalities. It is possible that the people who fail in school are more homogeneous with respect to ability or background than those who succeed. However, the theories provide no clearer understanding of inequality than they do of opportunity.

This conclusion is perhaps a little surprising. The ranks of the academically successful seem, after all, to be erected on the backs of those the school system defines as not able or not willing to master the curriculum—those who read haltingly, calculate badly, perhaps begin to consider most instruction a "joke." Certainly, the inequalities of schooling are meant to be built on inequalities of academic ability and motivation.

But meritocratic theory continues to be flawed by its definition of school success as merit and school failure as lack of merit. Some genetic advantages exist that help people in school, but even genetic advantages have to be activated and directed. Nurture (or the social environment) is, therefore, a factor from the beginning.[22] In a neglectful environment, even relatively strong innate ability can fail to be recognized and stimulated. In an attentive and stimulating environment, even modest inborn ability may be maximized. The advantages of privileged groups help them to illuminate and direct sparks of acuity among their children. This is the major reason why good students are as common as crickets in some communities but rare specimens indeed in other communities.

We often use the term *intelligent* to describe children who perform well on standardized tests. In doing so, we fail to appreciate the extent to which good test results are socially produced. Just as important, we also fail to recognize that tests measure only certain kinds of intelligences. Charles Darwin's son observed that Darwin used to say of himself that he "was not quick enough to hold an argument with anyone" (F. Darwin, quoted in Baker 1974:447). Darwin may have thought slowly, but he clearly thought well. Among other qualities, tests measure the ability to solve problems quickly, to check answers and not to guess, and the ability to stay calm under pressure. These might be better described as test-taking abilities than as intelligence. If they are indicators of intelligence, they are only facets of that complex concept. The underlying idea of intelligence includes a great many qualities that tests do not even attempt to measure—for example, the ability to change behavior to respond to challenging new situations, the ability to accurately judge the costs and benefits of different courses of action, and perhaps most important, the capacity to think deeply and creatively about problems. These kinds of intelligences can be very relevant to life success.

Thus, although many people are conditioned to think of tests as measuring intelligence, this label is not completely appropriate. What tests do measure are kinds of intelligences and personal qualities that are particularly relevant to contemporary school systems, because schools, like tests, reward quickness, answer checking, calm nerves, and a good storehouse of cultural knowledge. (For a particularly good discussion of intelligence tests, see Block and Dworkin 1976.)

The problems with social reproduction theory are equally great. In its readiness to show that the educational deck is stacked against subordinate groups, social reproduction theorists often neglect important differences among these groups, important differences in the institutional structures they face, and important differences in the adaptive strategies they develop for making the best of their circumstances. Not all social inequalities are reproduced through schooling. It is true that low-income people and members of some minority groups face long odds in the school system, but what of another disadvantaged group, women? In many countries, their educational attainment has reached near parity with men in just a generation (Jacobs 1995). Nor do subordinate groups face the same set of conditions in schooling systems. Schools may bear considerable responsibility for maintaining inequalities when they allow children to get past the first few grades without a solid basis in reading and writing (Farkas 1993) and when they employ tracking structures that contribute to demoralization rather than to learning (Oakes 1994). But members of some subordinate groups enter schools that aim to equalize opportunities—schools, for example, in which tracking is de-emphasized and resources are equalized.

The view of schooling and inequality developed in this chapter is based on examining the interplay of group circumstances and institutional structures. The chapter concentrates on groups rather than on individuals, because larger structural patterns are most evident when groups are the unit of analysis. Group circumstances include the resources members of groups bring with them to school and the prevailing definitions of the group's place in society. Institutional structures include school tracking structures, labor market structures, and government policies (like Head Start or affirmative action) that are related to the reduction or persistence of inequalities. This view looks at human beings as actively developing strategies to improve their circumstances. Through their adaptive strategies, groups and their individual members can move closer or further away from the schooling system over time.

Figure 7.1 shows the factors that contribute most to explaining inequalities in school-based selection. Each of the factors ideally requires careful attention, and this chapter won't be able to address all five completely. In particular, I will not discuss the genetic side of academic ability, and I will only touch on the important subject of how government policies can affect educational inequalities.

SOCIAL DIFFERENTIATION AND THE SCHOOLS

The first step is to think about what people from different backgrounds bring to the schools, and the best place to start is with groups on either side of the most important social divides. The three major bases of social differentiation are social class, race and ethnicity, and gender. Age is also an important base of social differentiation, but it is less significant in the case of schooling, because schooling is organized around the experience of age cohorts.

Social class, race and ethnicity, and gender are not fateful to the same degree for educational attainment. The specific circumstances of subordinate groups bear on their success or failure in school. These group circumstances

FIGURE 7.1

Factors Affecting the Development of Educational Inequalities

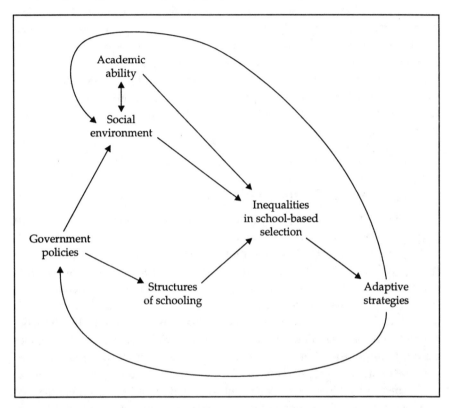

are based on the resources the group brings to schooling and how positively or negatively the group is viewed by the larger society.

Public schooling is a system that requires and rewards intellectual commitments and intellectual activity. Thus, the group resources and experiences that are most directly important to success in school are cultural resources, attitudes about schooling, and motivational follow-through. Beneath these immediate influences usually lie deeper layers of economic and social support.

Society's attitudes are also important, because they influence the social distance between the dominant groups in school and members of subordinate groups. High levels of social distance, which make it very difficult for members of a subordinate group to succeed, are at work in all societies with well-defined class, racial/ethnic, or gender divisions of labor. Social distance is communicated in many ways—from parents telling children that "he's not the kind of boy you want to be friendly with" or "girls don't do that" to teachers subconsciously lowering their expectations for a particular kind of student.

These two factors—group resources and societal definitions of the group's characteristics—can obviously vary from group to group and society to society. In fact, lower-class groups are nearly always highly disadvantaged in schooling; racial and ethnic groups are sometimes even more disadvantaged than lower classes, but are sometimes minimally disadvantaged; and, at least in some contemporary societies, gender differences may not be very disadvantaging at all, at least not in the realm of schooling. For these reasons, I characterize class as a constant divider, race and ethnicity as a varying divider, and gender as a declining divider.

Social Class: The Constant Divider

Social class is essentially a product of the distribution of valuable resources in society and not, for example, of a particular ethnic group's historical experience. Among the most valuable resources are income and wealth, power, and prestige. Almost all societies distribute resources unequally, and so social class is the most consistently present social influence on educational inequality.

Social class is usually measured by indexes of socioeconomic status (SES). These indexes are based on weighted combinations of parental education, occupational prestige, and income. The features of SES that matter most for school performance and attainment are parental education and, to a lesser extent, parental occupation. It is parents' own knowledge and their ability and motivation to pass it on that is most important. A parent without a secondary school degree might be able to buy an encyclopedia or a computer for her children, but this is no substitute for the daily usage of good grammar, advanced vocabulary, and computational skills that an educated parent can provide.

Social Differences within Classes. Of course, not all people in the same social class face exactly the same circumstances. The urban and rural working classes, for example, are not in exactly the same circumstances. Because their environment demands greater efficiency and organizational ability, urban working people in virtually every society acclimatize better to the schooling system than do peasants and farm workers. In addition, schooling is more relevant for urban occupations than for rural occupations and urban schools are generally better supported than rural schools. For all these reasons, the lowest rates of school completion and the lowest test scores are found in rural areas throughout the world (United Nations Development Project 1994).

Differential patterns of association can also make a difference among individuals belonging to essentially the same social class. "The child in a well-endowed community gets the benefits of the locale regardless of his or her family's particular situation" (Fischer et al. 1996:83). Working-class children who attend predominantly middle-class schools are placed in an environment that places more value on completing school than most predominantly working-class schools do. It is not surprising that graduation and college attendance rates are higher for working-class students who attend predominantly middle-class schools (McDill, Meyer, and Rigby 1967; Fischer et al. 1996). Conversely, children living in a neighborhood of particularly concentrated poverty have a greater likelihood of associating with alienated peers simply because more of these kinds of people are available for interaction (Wilson 1987, chap. 2).

Family structure and family size can also make a difference in what happens to people from the same social level. For both emotional and financial reasons, people from broken homes suffer greater disadvantages than others. More children in a household means less attention and less effective economic support for each child (Downey 1995; Fischer et al. 1996:78).

Social Class and Educational Advantages. These specific conditions must be taken into account, but they do not diminish or override the persistent influence of social class. Parental social status is strongly associated with how people think about and act in school. Students from more advantaged homes and neighborhoods are more likely to

- Enter school with a base of knowledge and values that encourage school success
- Be surrounded by an atmosphere of parental support for and active involvement in schooling
- Have the economic resources to purchase instructional materials and educational services (e.g., computers, tutors, tuitions) that are not available to students whose parents have less money
- Present themselves in ways that teachers associate with "good students" (e.g., standard, unaccented English; neat appearance; nice clothes; good manners) and that teachers reward accordingly

This last point merits additional discussion. However hard they may try to be open-minded and clinical in their judgments, middle-class schoolteachers and counselors often feel more comfortable with students who look and sound like themselves. They may feel indifferent—even averse—to students who do not. Many of these feelings are based on quite explicit status symbols: nice or worn clothes, good or poor grooming, deferential or boisterous manners.

Speech is often another factor. Teachers frequently make status associations on the basis of students' use of proper grammar and wide vocabularies. These linguistic abilities are typically the products of class environments more than innate intelligence. Training for public speech is itself class conditioned. The sociologist Basil Bernstein (1961, 1975) has shown that middle-class and working-class speech patterns differ appreciably in the degree to which subject and object references are made explicit or left implicit. A middle-class speech pattern, for example, "The boy threw the ball through the window and the window broke," makes all subjects and objects explicit. The working class pattern, "He threw it and it broke," leaves subjects and objects implicit. In Bernstein's terms, schools are built on the middle-class *elaborated speech code* rather than the working-class *restricted speech code*. Teachers often judge users of the restricted code to be less intelligent than users of the elaborated code.

Lower-status people tend also to be less comfortable interacting with authorities—including teachers. A study by the sociologist Annette Lareau (1987) revealed the power of some of these "hidden advantages" of class. Lareau studied parents' involvement with their children's schooling in two communities. In the predominantly working-class community she studied, she found that parents weren't much involved with their children's educations—not because they didn't care, but because they were ashamed of their own weak academic skills (such as a limited vocabulary or poor spelling). They were also likely to defer to teachers as "the experts." In the predominantly middle-class community she studied, on the other hand, the educational skills and occupational prestige of parents matched or surpassed those of their children's teachers. Middle-class parents were not afraid to intervene on their child's behalf—for example, to bring up problems in the classroom or to request particular teachers for the following year. They also had the necessary economic resources to manage child care, transportation, and time off for meeting with teachers; to hire tutors; and to become intensely involved in their children's schooling. Different social classes, Lareau suggests, have the same affection and concern for their children, but different capacities for acting on these concerns.

Differences in Class Outlooks. Class advantages and disadvantages set boundaries on ways of looking at the world and one's place within it. The French sociologist Pierre Bourdieu (1979) used the term *habitus* to characterize these recurring patterns of class outlook, which are inculcated by families and reproduced over time. For Bourdieu, habitus is a constellation of outlooks expressed through beliefs, values, conduct, speech, dress, and manners. It is a product of a class situation and reproduces a class situation through its influence on social interactions.

The habitus of different social classes bears heavily on schooling success. Most of the very poor do not have the resources or the stability to treat schooling in a completely disciplined way. Their circumstances of life are frequently disorganized and stressful, and it may be difficult for them to give schooling their full attention. People who have grown up in relatively stable family circumstances fail to comprehend just how unstable life can be for Americans in the bottom three to four deciles of family income. One of the most startling findings of a careful evaluation of one educational reform program in inner-city Milwaukee was that even the very highly motivated parents who enrolled their children in the program ended up moving at such a high rate (more than 50 percent changed schools from one school year to the next) that the impact of the program itself could not be truly evaluated (Witte, Bailey, and Thorn 1993). Bad nutrition, poor health, insecurity, and anxiety are common products of severely disorganized and stressful lives. So, too, are irregular effort, confusion, alienation, and defensive boredom.

For the children of stably employed workers, habitus encompasses a somewhat wider range of possibilities. The class habitus oscillates between conformity and rejection of authority. There are those who choose a conformist path, but usually lack enough ease with intellectual materials to be considered promising scholars by their teachers; those who choose a path of rebellion, having "laffs" and goofing off at the schools' expense; and those who withdraw behind a vaguely resentful wall of silence (Willis 1979; MacLeod 1987).

The creation of an identity as a "student" is no mean task even for very able working-class children if they have not been exposed to intellectual activity and high academic expectations in the home. Consider some of the hurdles that are involved in creating a "good student" identity: meeting difficult challenges successfully, accepting labels (ambitious, smart) that may seem ill fitting, overcoming doubts, and negotiating the skepticism or outright hostility of friends and family. The writers Richard Hoggart (1957) and Richard Rodriguez (1982) have provided rich portraits of working-class "scholarship boys" who soak up knowledge like a sponge, rack up awards for scholarship, but have no sense of intimate connection to the works they so compulsively absorb. Many are tempted to give up the chase, and do give it up (Strauss 1959; London 1979).

Moving up the class structure, we see the habitus of organization men and women. Students from these middle-class families exhibit more frequent and more accomplished conformity with institutional expectations—a matter-of-fact, businesslike approach to institutional life. Habits of regular behavior learned in the family allow for an easier negotiation of school demands, and higher parental expectations about schoolwork create an atmosphere of support for good performance in school. Relatively few students at this social level may be truly academically oriented, but most will be able to perform up to an acceptable academic standard.

At the top of the class structure, many children have the resources and confidence to see themselves not just as vessels to be filled with knowledge but as active participants capable of using knowledge for their own purposes (Anyon 1980; Cookson and Persell 1985). They learn to advance their interests in an assertive way and to act on the school world as much as they are acted on by it.

● ● ● ● ● ● ● ● ● ● ● ● ●

Preparing For Power

The "St. Grottlesex" prep schools in New England are the most prestigious private secondary schools in the country. They include such famous names as Andover, Exeter, St. Paul's, St. Mark's, Lawrenceville, Groton, and Choate. These schools are the core of the elite tradition in the United States. The families of as many as 40 percent of each school's students may be listed in *The Social Register*, the arbiter of elite social status in the United States. Other students come from newer generations of intellectually or economically prominent families.

In their study of selective private boarding schools, Peter Cookson and Caroline Persell (1985) found that these schools are designed, above all, to socialize students from upper-class backgrounds for future power. Students are required to read deeply and widely, to learn to interpret from a variety of angles, to see knowledge as something that can be used for practical purposes. Students are encouraged to build facilities, write plays, and apply ideas to controversial public policy issues. Students are constantly set against other star athletes, writers, and orators in competitions for extracurricular glory. Famous graduates, from presidents on down, come to visit, so that students can be close enough to touch power and personally observe the manners and attitudes of the powerful.

Even the landscape and architecture at these schools is designed to give students a sense of being special:

> Andover students can read in the wood-panelled Oliver Wendell Holmes Library, look at works by American artists such as Eakins, Homer, and Whistler in the Addison Gallery . . . or just relax in the . . . Cochran Sanctuary, sixty-five acres of landscaped beauty which includes a brook, two ponds, and natural wild areas as well as manicured lawns and flower beds of rhododendron and laurel. (Cookson and Persell 1985:45)

A headmaster reported the following statement from one of his charges: "This school requires quality in what I do, because I have leaded glass windows in my bedroom" (ibid., p. 48).

● ●

During the course of schooling, there are literally dozens of ways to disengage from the schools' demands for performance. The great majority of students do fall away from the demands of schools, either early or late in their careers. Social class influences the rate at which these disengaging behaviors are expressed. People with fewer resources for succeeding in school tend to express them earlier rather than later. These patterns of disengagement include frequent daydreaming, frequent expressions of anxiety in performance situations, rejection of curricular materials outside a narrow sphere of interest, interpreting the classroom primarily as a stage for comic antics, and emphasizing social relationships as the only important feature of school life. Other patterns of disengagement are class conditioned in a more essential way. Self-protective, sometimes truculent defiance in the face of an unfamiliar academic culture is more common among the working classes and the poor, and self-flattering attitudes of moral or intellectual superiority to the schools are more common in the upper classes.

Worldwide Differentiation by Social Class. Class advantages and disadvantages are very much the same the world over. Even socialist regimes did not succeed in integrating the poor. The political scientist Walter Connor (1979) examined "obstacles to mobility" through education in the former Soviet Union, a state devoted in principle to promoting the interests of workers and peasants. He found that the children of the peasantry were disadvantaged in a number of ways:

- Peasant children lacked the heat in their bedrooms that would allow for uninterrupted study.
- Peasant children were less often disciplined for poor school performance than more privileged children were.
- Educated adult role models were absent.
- The interests of fellow students did not facilitate academic involvements.
- Peasant schools were poor in resources.
- Work competed for students' attention.
- Teachers were less able and experienced because of the low status of peasant schools.
- Stipends in higher education were inadequate, and students from families that could not supplement the stipends often had to take extra jobs. (Connor 1979:207-11)

The magnitude of the problems faced by the lower classes varies from one country to the next, but the type of problems are not fundamentally different. Differences in class circumstances nearly always lead to differences in school-related background knowledge, attitudes about schooling, and motivation in relation to schooling. As we saw in Chapter 6, Sweden and the Netherlands are among a handful of cases in which class circumstances have equalized over time, but in these cases equalization of economic conditions between the classes has been more influential than changes in school structures.

Race and Ethnicity: The Varying Divider

In the United States, race has been our most obvious social divider, and race relations have been our most troubling problem as a society. Ethnic hostilities are also much in the news in other parts of the world. American students thus often assume that racial and ethnic differences are always the most important basis of social inequality. This is not true. Racial and ethnic differences can, at times, be more consequential than class differences (as they are in the United States), but they can also be much less important. The group's circumstance depends largely on the cultural resources, attitudes about schooling, and motivations that its members bring with them to the schools. It also depends on the dominant social definitions of the group's position.

Social scientists (and biologists) have become increasingly skeptical of the concept "race," because so much genetic variation exists within races and particularly because race is often used to "biologize" (and therefore seemingly make more permanent and unalterable) what are actually social and cultural differences. Thus, sociologists use the terms *majority group* and *minority group* to refer to people differentiated by race, ethnicity, or certain other social variables. These terms refer to the amount of power held by a group, not the sheer numbers of people in the group. It is possible for a minority group like blacks in South Africa during the apartheid era to be numerically larger than the majority group. However, because race is still firmly a part of everyday language and is also important for discussions of racism, the term *racial and ethnic minorities* is used here.

Why do race and ethnicity sometimes matter so much and sometimes so little in a group's ability to take advantage of schooling opportunities? The sociologist Stanley Lieberson (1961) argued that ethnic groups migrating voluntarily to a new land have strong incentives to assimilate to the culture of their new country. Although relations might very well be tense for awhile, in the long run the new group could expect to be integrated into the host society. By contrast, he argued, racial and ethnic groups conquered by a technologically superior power are unlikely to be assimilated as easily, both because the majority group is unlikely to fully accept those it has conquered and because the colonized rarely accept their conquerors. In our own country, those groups that have suffered most at the hands of European settlers—conquered groups (the Native Americans) and once-enslaved peoples (the African Americans)— have been less completely assimilated into American society, including the schooling system, than groups that have voluntarily migrated.

Lieberson's (1961) theory explains a great deal of variation in ethnic relations across societies. However, it probably fails to take sufficient account of the power of restricted economic opportunities, exclusionary laws, and cultural prejudices. These forces can sometimes make even voluntary immigrants into social outcasts, resulting in the kinds of deep antagonisms so often associated with conquest. Therefore, we should think as often of the social conditions groups currently face as of their original circumstances.

The Situation of Highly Subordinated Minorities. Some minorities are better off than others. As compared to other minorities, those that are most disadvantaged are restricted by employers to the lowest-level jobs in society, live in highly segregated communities cut off from the rest of society, and are represented in the culture of the majority group in highly prejudicial ways. They are often considered violent, unclean, stupid, immoral, or promiscuous.

One problem for members of these "highly subordinated minorities" is that no way of acting helps to improve their situation. If they are agreeable, they are scorned as servile. If they are assertive, they are criticized as overbearing. If they are good-natured, they are regarded as fools. If they are cautious, they are condemned as untrustworthy. With success, these responses change, although they often change in a very uneven and grudging way.

Highly subordinated minorities develop responses to their situation that are characteristically different from those of less poorly treated minorities. They frequently reject the legitimacy of the institutions of the dominant groups and emphasize solidarity among themselves. Members of highly subordinated groups often develop a sense of themselves as victims and outcasts. Because they are denied status in the terms valued by the larger society, men from these groups, in particular, frequently develop an alternative status system based not on "respectability" but on "reputation" for eye-catching behavior.

> You earn a reputation by how well you talk, by how tough you are, by your willingness to fight even if you lose, by how successful you are with women, by the dollars in your pocket and your willingness to spend them, and by your ability to lead others, no matter the direction. (Gibson 1991:180-1)

As a consequence, high levels of criminal activity and apathy are usually found among highly subordinated minorities, greatly reinforcing the majority group's low opinion of them.

In societies with highly subordinate minority groups, both class and eth-nicity are important determinants of life chances, and neither is reducible to the other. Some members of minority groups may attain middle-class status, but they will tend to be less well accepted and to perform less well on educa-tional assessments than middle-class people from the majority group. Simi-larly, lower-status minorities will face distinct disadvantages compared to lower-status people from the majority group.

Highly subordinated minorities are found in many societies besides our own. They include West Indians in Britain; Maoris in New Zealand; Buraku-min, Okinawans, and Koreans in Japan; Gypsies in the Czech Republic; Arabs and Oriental Jews in Israel; and the Irish in Great Britain (Ogbu 1978; Fischer et al. 1996:192). Consider the following characterization:

> Members of [this] minority, many of whom were brought to the country
> as slave labor, are at the bottom of the social ladder. They do the dirty work,
> when they have work. The rest of the society considers them violent and
> stupid and discriminates against them. Over the years, tension between
> minority and majority has occasionally broken out in deadly riots. In the
> past, minority children were compelled to go to segregated schools and
> did poorly academically. Even now minority children drop out of school
> relatively early and often get into trouble with the law. Schools with many
> minority children are seen as problem-ridden, so majority parents some-
> times move out of the school district or send their children to private schools.
> And, as might be expected, the minority children do worse on standardized
> tests than majority children do. (Fischer et al. 1996:172)

Who are they? Koreans in Japan, members of the same group that dispropor-tionately number among the top achievers in the United States (Lee 1991).

No matter where or how racial stratification systems develop,[23] members of highly subordinated minorities invariably perform less successfully in school than do other minorities. Although the available data are not perfectly comparable, in every case reported these groups show a pattern of low com-mitment to schooling, low test scores, and low levels of educational attain-ment. (See the summary in Fischer et al. 1996:191-4.) Frequently, these out-comes are taken by members of the majority group as evidence of the minority group's intellectual inferiority. However, the real causes are social: The restricted economic opportunities of these groups discourage a sense that schooling is a bridge to future possibilities. Their high levels of residential segregation foster isolation from the outlooks of more advantaged groups. And their stigmatized identities create feelings of resentment and alienation from the authority structures of the larger society, including the schools.

Gradual improvement in the circumstances of these groups is certainly possible, as the cases of African Americans in the United States and Oriental

Jews in Israel demonstrate. But improvement requires a very high level of commitment both by the government and by leaders in the minority communities. Only a few societies have succeeded in approximating multiethnic integration and equality. Most of these societies are found in Latin America, where both the sometimes violent racial mixing typical of colonial era Iberian society and the humanistic philosophy of the Latin American Catholic Church have played a decisive role (van den Berghe 1970, chaps. 2, 3, 6). Even countries such as Brazil, with generally strong records of integration and intermarriage, have not achieved full social equality between racial groups. Like many Latin American countries, the United States has been self-consciously pluralistic and has had a generally good record of inclusion, although African Americans remain much less completely integrated than other groups.

Even in self-consciously pluralistic (or melting pot) societies, new groups usually experience ferocious discrimination at first. The United States provides a wonderful example of long-term absorbing power combined with fierce short-term prejudice. The historical record shows that members of immigrant groups were regularly taunted by other children (and not infrequently by their teachers) for their foreign dress and manners and ridiculed for their unfamiliar accents. A memoir by the literary critic Alfred Kazin (1951) powerfully conveys the sense of strangeness that many immigrants felt and the anxiety induced in them by adult authorities (first represented by teachers and principals):

> It was never learning I associated with that school: only the necessity to succeed, to get ahead of the others in the daily struggle to "make a good impression" on our teachers, who grimly, wearily, and often with ill-concealed distaste watched against our relapsing into the natural savagery they expected of Brownsville boys. . . . It was not just our quickness and memory that were always being tested. Above all . . . it was our character. . . . [T]he very sound of the word as our teachers coldly gave it out from the end of their teeth, with a solemn weight on each dark syllable . . . immediately struck my heart cold with fear—they could not really believe that I had it. (Pp. 17, 20)

Members of new immigrant groups usually appear not just lacking in "character" but also in intellectual ability, a conclusion that IQ tests are only too happy to validate. During World War I, for example, the average IQ score of U.S. enlisted men who were Polish immigrants or their children was 85—a full standard deviation below the population average (Sowell 1981:9). These low test scores were more a function of unfamiliarity with the dominant language and culture than anything else—men of Polish heritage now score above average on IQ tests. Nevertheless, earlier in this century many teachers and school administrators stereotyped Polish and other immigrants as dimwitted and fit only for manual labor.

Variable Rates of Assimilation. One important reason that ethnicity is properly characterized as the "varying divider" is that some immigrant groups become assimilated and move up the socioeconomic ladder faster than others. The success of fast-rising minorities is often attributed to their superior drive or intelligence. However, "model minorities" typically come to their new country with a host of advantages not enjoyed by other groups, quite apart from their drive and intelligence.

Faster-climbing groups almost invariably bring urban skills (and related attitudes and motivations) with them to the new country. Although they were very poor, most immigrant Jews, for example, were urban people, merchants or artisans. In more recent years, Cuban, Korean, and Indian immigrants have come largely from merchant and professional backgrounds. These types of immigrants are well prepared for an urban, commercial society; they bring habits of conduct and experiences that help them succeed (Steinberg 1981). By contrast, slower-climbing groups have invariably come out of agrarian settings and traditional peasant cultures. This is true of the Irish, Sicilian, Mexican, and African Americans. Cultures that celebrate study of the written word, usually for religious reasons, are also extremely helpful in preparing children for success in schooling. By contrast, oral cultures, for all of their glorious banter and song, provide a much less advantageous preparation (Sowell 1981). Keeping just these two factors in mind, it comes as no surprise that the mercantile, Torah-studying Jews were one of the faster-climbing groups in American society, or that the agrarian, oral culture Irish experienced a slow and difficult advance (Steinberg 1981; Sowell 1981).

The sheer number of immigrants is another factor that helps to explain the variable rates of assimilation and advance among ethnic groups. Prejudice "unfurls like a flag" with larger numbers (Lieberson 1980). The phrase "Yellow Peril" was coined in response to the large surge of Chinese immigration in the late nineteenth century, not the small surge of Japanese immigration during the 1890s and 1900s. Indeed, the groups that have had the most difficult time making their way in American society have been part of the largest immigrations. The nearly 2 million Irish who came to the United States between 1830 and 1860 were the largest immigrant group until the massive, 4 million black migration from the South to the North in the 30 years between 1940 and 1970 (Sowell 1981:211). In the United States, the main immediate effects of very large immigrations has been to reduce the level of prejudice against earlier-arriving groups while intensifying opposition to the new group and placing it squarely at the bottom of the social ladder (Lieberson 1980).

Some groups encourage behavior patterns that lead to greater success in schooling. A typical pattern for children from Asian immigrant families is to study around the dinner table with older children helping younger children.

These patterns of intense cooperative learning continue into college, where Asian children often form"study gangs," whose members organize their lives around common classes and shared academic goals (Miller 1995:276).

As Chapter 4 showed, schools have become far more attuned to ideas about ethnic pluralism than they once were. New emphases in the curriculum may help to make members of minority groups less alienated from school, but they will not solve the dilemmas of racial and ethnic stratification. Because new curricula seem to address the problem, they may even direct needed attention away from more important realities, such as economic skills and work-related habits, residential isolation, and stigmatizing representations (and self-representations) of the minority group outside of schooling.

Gender: The Declining Divider

For most of human history, women have had much less power than men. Their status was tied to the reproductive cycle and enforced both by social expectations about women's role and, not infrequently, by the physical strength of men (Blumberg 1984). Not until the 1820s and 1830s, with the upsurge of liberal and democratic ideals in Europe, were the first public calls for women's emancipation heard. Even though women made faster progress in the United States than elsewhere, through the 1950s they remained in a distinctly inferior position and were often frustrated by the narrow circumferences of their lives (see, e.g., Friedan 1963). Given the long history of women's subordination, it is amazing how much things have changed in a generation. Indeed, the changes have been so striking that we can fairly ask whether gender might become irrelevant as a factor in social selection within the next half century.

From a global perspective, women are in a particularly complex situation today. In societies where women continue to be kept out of the public arena, they have essentially the same disadvantages as lower-class groups. They may lack the economic resources, the social ties, and the cultural experiences to compete with men. A few societies restrict women almost completely to the private sphere of family life. By contrast, middle- and upper-middle-class women in more gender-equal societies have the cultural background to navigate their way in society. They are increasingly developing the economic clout and supportive social ties that help as well. In their performance as students, women may even have some distinct advantages, owing in part to the concern with culture and social relationships that are part of traditional feminine roles. Yet a couple of distinct disadvantages of gender also continue to exist, even in contemporary industrial societies. Most important, women look different from men and are therefore easier to discriminate against where discrimination is most advantageous to men.

Patriarchy and Gender Inequality. Differences in women's situations depend most on whether they live in patriarchal or less patriarchal societies. *Patriarchies* are societies in which men dominate more or less completely. Women are excluded from the public and business life of the society and are restricted to the family circle. Their main role is procreation and child rearing. In patriarchal societies, stereotypes about women's "incompetence" in male spheres abound, and men often get away with using physical force in relations with women.

Although elements of patriarchy remain in every society, some societies have minimized these elements considerably over the past several generations. Factors that have led to the eclipse of patriarchy include having fewer children, typical of families following industrialization, and the technological advances that allow women to better control their fertility. They also include the rising expectations that come with women's participation in the paid labor force and with their increasing levels of formal education (Huber and Spitze 1983). A self-reinforcing cycle occurs: As women's child-rearing demands decline and their contribution to family income increases, their power in family decision making and the allocation of household tasks also increases (Gerson 1985). Effective organization is another important reason for the changing circumstances of women. Encouraged by the broader social changes, women's organizations have lobbied effectively to change negative stereotypes, to improve women's opportunities in the workforce, and to expand legal protection against male violence (see, e.g., Stromquist 1993).

The world, consequently, is now divided between what we might reasonably call patriarchal and much less patriarchal (if not quite "postpatriarchal") societies. The defining characteristics of patriarchy are still very much evident in the poorer countries of the Middle East, in nearly all East Asian societies, in South Asia, and in most of Africa. On the other hand, the United States, the other Anglo American democracies, large parts of Europe, and most Latin American societies can be considered less patriarchal. Gender discrimination has not entirely disappeared in these societies—far from it!—but parity has been reached in some important spheres of social life, and the overall climate for women is no longer suffused with the assumptions of male control.

Patriarchal and less patriarchal societies show clear differences in how much educational opportunity women can expect. In the developing world, the largest disparities in the educational enrollments of men and women are found in African and Middle Eastern countries and the smallest disparities in Latin America (Stromquist 1989). Asian countries generally fall in between but still provide relatively few opportunities for women at higher educational levels. Women's college enrollments are, for example, half of men's in both China and India (United Nations International Conference on Population and Development 1995).

The poorer Muslim countries are the most notable examples of gender inequality. Girls represent just two-fifths of school enrollments, even at the primary school level (United Nations Educational, Scientific, and Cultural Organization 1994:6). By Islamic tradition, girls are sequestered at puberty, prohibited from contact with the opposite sex, and prepared for engagement and "pure" marriage to a chosen man. To symbolize their conformity to these traditions, girls begin wearing veils to shield their faces from men. This induction to the traditions of purdah leads, predictably, to early withdrawal from school (Shah and Eastmond 1977). Beyond puberty, education is distinctly secondary to the social pressure on Muslim women to become wives and mothers. However, these cultural and religious prohibitions may be greatly reduced by increasing wealth or by more egalitarian governments. For example, in oil-rich Kuwait, more women than men are enrolled in higher education, and women are overrepresented even in science and engineering (United Nations International Conference on Population and Development 1995).

Correlates of Gender Inequality. One fine study of gender and schooling by Roger Clark (1992) has shed considerable light on the forces that create and reinforce gender inequalities in the developing world. The study showed that countries with higher per capita incomes were more likely to have greater gender equality in schooling. As we have already seen, economic progress is strongly associated with conditions that make women's lives less restricted.

On the other hand, Clark (1992) found that high levels of multinational investment were negatively associated with greater gender equality. (This may be because multinational investors feel more confident when men fill the high-status occupations and also discourage state labor regulation that would improve the conditions of women.) Countries with many ethnic groups generally had less gender equality, too, perhaps because it is politically difficult to extend educational opportunity when many ethnic groups are competing for preeminence. And Islam, with its religiously grounded proscriptions against women, showed up as a strongly negative influence on gender equality in the countries where it was the dominant religion.

In the industrialized world, a great deal more equality exists between men and women. In secondary school and higher education enrollments, women are either equal to men or actually overrepresented compared with men. This pattern holds in the countries of Catholic southern Europe (Spain, Portugal, Italy, and France), in several Scandinavian countries (including Denmark, Norway, and Sweden), in most of the former socialist countries of Central and

Eastern Europe (including the Czech Republic, Poland, and Russia), and in Britain, the United States, and the other English-speaking democracies (Canada, Australia, and New Zealand) (United Nations International Conference on Population and Development 1995). For most of these countries, women's educational parity is relatively recent. An exception is the United States, where women reached parity with men in secondary school and college attendance beginning in the late 1800s, partly because of the high female enrollment in teacher training colleges (Jacobs 1995).

By contrast, Germany and the countries closely connected to it geographically and culturally (Austria, Belgium, and Switzerland) remain notably unequal with respect to women's opportunities in higher education and, to a lesser degree, in secondary education. Gender inequality in education is the norm to an even greater degree in the richest countries of East Asia (Japan and Korea). But even in these countries, the tendency has been toward greater equality in educational access over time (Carceles 1979; Jacobs 1995).

Vestiges of Discrimination. Although women now experience fewer disadvantages in educational access and educational attainments, they continue to experience many disadvantages in how they are treated in schools. Classroom interaction is one area of continuing unequal treatment.

The *microbehaviors* of support in the classroom tend to favor boys over girls. As early as elementary school, boys show a more assertive style of commenting in class and also take up more physical space. Perhaps because of their very audibility and visibility, teachers tend to give boys more "air time" and to allow them to interrupt more often than they do girls (Sadker and Sadker 1994). These patterns continue in higher levels of schooling. Studies of college classrooms show, for example, that instructors are more likely to maintain eye contact with men, to allow men to give longer answers in class, to allow men to complete answers without interruption, to nod and gesture in relation to men's remarks, and to amplify on men's comments. It is even common in some classrooms for instructors to attribute remarks made by a woman to a man (Hall 1983; Wilkinson and Marrett 1985).

These differences in treatment have not stopped women from reaching parity with and in a few areas even surpassing men in school performance and educational attainments. Women, by their training, are well prepared to succeed in school. First, women's traditional specialization in matters related to the arts and culture equips them well for success in the schooling system, where these interests are well supported (DiMaggio and Mohr 1985). Second, to the extent that women are the chief enforcers of social norms in the family, they are well attuned to the emphasis on conformity that is typical of classrooms the world over. Indeed, in some countries, the schools' emphasis on culture and conformity may be considered "effeminate" by men from working- and lower-class backgrounds, further helping to guarantee the preeminence of women in the educational sphere (Gibson 1991). In places where women are no longer restricted by patriarchal assumptions, these circumstances enhance women's ability to navigate the schooling system successfully. They also explain why women, although still very much disadvantaged in society at large, are in an enormously stronger position than lower-class and minority groups when it comes to success in schools.

Substantial economic inequalities remain even in countries in which women have reached educational parity with men. Many of the college majors that lead to high-paying and high-opportunity jobs remain largely male preserves. Engineering, agriculture, economics, mathematics, earth sciences, and many of the physical sciences remain predominantly male fields. Even controlling for ability, gender remains a crucial element in choice of major (Davies and Guppy 1996). Women continue to be weaker in math and science-related fields, and male resistance may also be somewhat greater in those fields, because the potential rewards are also somewhat higher. Some progress is evident even in field selection, however: In the United States, such formerly male fields as medicine, law, business, and biology have largely "desegregated" over the past generation (Jacobs 1995).

Women also remain highly disadvantaged in converting educational credentials into high pay. At most educational levels in the United States, they earn on average about 70 percent of men's earnings; the same ratio holds for female and male Ph.D.s as for female and male dropouts. Field concentrations partly explain these differences at the higher educational levels, but they obviously can't help to explain the differences at lower levels. Instead, the inequities in earnings reflect the fact that occupations are more sex segregated than schools and that predominantly female occupations are poorly paid compared with predominantly male occupations (Reskin 1993). Some of the inequities also reflect the more interrupted work lives of women and their lesser chances of receiving specialized on-the-job training, which can perhaps be considered indirect consequences of male power.

Most economists attribute the rest of the difference in the pay of men and women to the direct effects of discrimination (see, e.g., Osberg 1984, chap. 7; Goldin 1992). The amount of job-related discrimination against women appears to be even higher in the developing world than it is in the industrialized world. Recent estimates from Latin America, for example, indicate that between 60 and 80 percent of the difference in women's and men's wages is due to discrimination rather than to differences in such "human capital" variables as formal qualifications, training, and work-related experience (Psacharopoulos and Tzannatos 1992). These figures are significantly higher than comparable estimates from the United States, which run in the range of 50 to 60 percent (Mincer and Polachek 1974; Osberg 1984:126-8).

There are good reasons to believe that gender will become a less significant factor in the future, even in the area of jobs and salaries. One is that as women gain ground, men's sensibilities change, however slowly and unevenly. Moreover, as the pool of career-oriented women increases, men have more difficulty hiring and promoting men on grounds other than demonstrated competence. Women's organizations and women's support networks contribute to equalization of opportunity by continuing to challenge discrimination in an active way. Education is not yet as useful a stepping stone to well-paying jobs for women as it is for men, but in most industrial societies it might very well become as useful by the time the next generation of girls reaches working age.

SCHOOL ORGANIZATION AND TRACKING STRUCTURES

Social circumstances shape the resources and expectations that children bring with them to school. Society also looks at different groups through the lens of more or less disparaging stereotypes. But an analysis of schooling and inequality should not stop with students' social circumstances. The structure of schools themselves frequently reinforces and accentuates social inequalities. Societies differ in how they distribute resources to schools and in the tracking structures they employ.

In the developed world, incremental improvements in school resources can have a large effect on learning (Heyneman and Loxley 1983). In the industrialized societies, the issue is more complex, because most schools have at least the minimal instructional materials. Not long ago, resources were considered a secondary influence on school achievement in industrialized societies. The social composition of schools mattered greatly, but resources hardly at all (Coleman et al. 1966). This conventional wisdom has been challenged in recent years. As researchers used more sophisticated methods to examine the distribution of resources *within* schools, they discovered that schools distribute resources unequally between programs, thereby influencing how much learning occurs among different groups of students (Bryk and Raudenbush 1988).

Variations in the organization of classroom interactions are discussed at greater length in Chapter 8. But it is important at this point to anticipate a few of the themes of that chapter concerning the association between classroom organization and school-related inequalities. The most important findings are that lower-class and minority students typically receive less instructional time, less demanding and lower-quality educational materials, and less imaginative teaching than other students. They are frequently held to much lower standards than other students (Dreeben and Gamoran 1986). It would be wrong to blame teachers for this state of affairs. Without doubt, teaching is a tough job in classrooms marked by student apathy and low achievement (Good and Brophy 1987:365). Nevertheless, when little is expected of students, those who are disadvantaged by virtue of their social circumstances can be expected to fall still further behind.

Track structures are another force that often works to accentuate inequalities between students. Often students and their parents choose lower-track placements, but many schools actively track students through counseling and assignments. Counselors want to do the best they can for students. Sometimes they will recommend that a student "try out" a less demanding curriculum and then later transfer to a more demanding curriculum. But students rarely transfer back, and they begin to surround themselves with less motivated peers. In places where opportunity consciousness is (or could be) strong, tracking can justly be described as a way of "cooling out" less advantaged and less successful students by encouraging them to lower their expectations to conform to the assessments educators have of them (Clark 1961).

In the sociology of schooling, the term *track* always refers to hierarchical structures that lead toward more or less advantaged destinations. As Chapters 2 and 3 showed, all societies differentiate their educational systems into hierarchical tiers and tracks. In some cases, differentiation occurs early in the schooling system; in other cases, it occurs later. Some systems differentiate on the basis of formal tests, whereas others allow students and parents an apparently wide latitude of personal choice.

In the minds of most educators, tracks in grade school exist primarily to meet the needs of differently prepared and differently interested students. They may also exist to serve a market for specialized and especially "high quality" educational services (as in the case of private schools). Tracks at higher levels exist for some of the same reasons and also to prepare children for adult occupational possibilities.

Tracks of many different types are ubiquitous in schooling. In American society alone, all of the following can plausibly be considered school tracks:

- "Ability grouping" in primary school
- Vocational, general education, and college preparatory curricular tracks in secondary school (where these divisions still exist)
- Basic, regular, and honors course levels in secondary school

- Expensive private primary and secondary schools as compared to public primary and secondary schools
- The quality or reputational level of public secondary schools
- Two-year as compared to four-year colleges
- Vocational as compared to academic programs in two-year colleges
- The quality or reputation of colleges and universities
- The quality or reputation of graduate and professional schools.
- Even different college major and graduate or professional degree programs might plausibly be considered tracks, insofar as they lead to different destinations that can be hierarchically ranked.

From the perspective of studies of inequality, there are two important questions to ask about school tracks. The first is whether lower-status children are unfairly channeled into lower tiers and curricula. The second is whether tracking affects children's life chances net of other important factors—that is, whether tracking makes a difference over and above what we would expect on the basis of the child's background and measured academic ability alone. To examine the first question, we can continue to look at schooling from the point of view of what happens to groups. To examine the second, however, we will have to look for the net impact of tracking as a variable among others in individual-level studies of attainment. The research indicates quite clearly that lower-status children are most likely to end up in lower tracks. It also indicates that tracking often does have at least modest negative net effects on learning opportunities and later life chances. This is a strong statement, because it takes considerable statistical power for any variable to show effects once student background and ability measures are taken into account.

Movement of Low-Status Children into Low-Status Tracks

As we've seen, children from higher-status families usually bring more school-related knowledge and higher aspirations with them to school. And most other tracking structures, even if they do not rely exclusively on ability and performance measures, do depend considerably on such measures to help determine track assignments, or to provide guidance for parents.

Because children from lower-status backgrounds are more likely to have lower grades and test scores, they are also more likely to be assigned to lower tracks (Oakes, Gamoran, and Page 1992). Quite a bit of variation exists in the forms of tracking—tracks may be rigid or flexible, comprehensive or limited—

so it is hard to know precisely how much class and racial stratification exists in track assignments. Nevertheless, estimates from the early 1980s in the United States suggest that low-SES students are approximately twice as likely as high-SES students to participate in vocational programs in high school (National Center for Educational Statistics [NCES] 1985:58). They were also highly underrepresented in math and science courses, and black and Hispanic students were severely underrepresented (ibid., p. 32). These track assignments and track choices, in turn, are strongly correlated with subsequent school trajectories. Students in college preparatory tracks have been three to four times more likely to enroll in four-year colleges compared with students in general and vocational tracks (Peng 1977; NCES 1985). By contrast, students who take high proportions of vocational course work in high school are more likely to drop out (Mann 1986).

Simple cross-tabulated comparisons like these can be revealing, but remember, not all social scientists consider these figures useful, because they do not control for factors like parental status and measured ability that influence attainments in tracked and untracked systems alike. Thus, even if dropouts tend to come from vocational tracks, it does not follow that vocational tracks cause dropout. It may be that students who would drop out under any circumstances tend to enroll in vocational tracks (Mann 1986:4).

Are tracking structures fair? Educators often feel that ability-based tracking is in the interests of students and teachers alike. They argue that it is only logical to group students with similar abilities and interests, because learning is enhanced when people are able to learn at a comfortable pace—that is, when they are neither held up for the "slower" children nor forced to keep pace with the "faster" children. Educators (and parents) who approve of tracking also argue that different methods and curricula may be appropriate for students at different "ability levels." In theory, lower-track students are expected to gain confidence when they are not forced to compete with students who learn at a faster pace. The evidence, as I will show, is not very supportive of these beliefs.

Tracking may also not be necessary to achieve the efficiencies that its advocates value. Even in primary school, where tracking does often show positive effects for both "fast" and "slow" groups, it is not the only way to achieve efficient learning. Studies of cooperative learning programs, where faster learners help to teach slower learners, suggest that these kinds of programs, if they are carefully designed, can benefit both groups. They give faster learners a chance to learn the arts of explanation and slower learners exposure to more able and motivated children (Cohen 1984; Slavin 1994; Slavin and Oickle 1981).

Inequities in Track Assignments. Whether we regard ability-based tracking as efficient and necessary or not, we should recognize that tracking is not based on performance alone, even in cases where performance-based tracking is the stated intention. Minorities and lower-income children have a greater chance of being assigned to lower curricular tracks in some American secondary schools, even after ability and performance are taken into account (Oakes 1994). This bias is based in part on stereotypes that exist among counselors and teachers about the likely prospects of lower-status children and in part on the successful lobbying efforts of higher-status parents to have their children placed in higher tracks, even if their grades and test scores do not seem to warrant it (Oakes 1994). In these cases, the issues of fairness are especially troubling.

Even where track choices are left up to parents and students themselves, children from lower-status backgrounds may "track themselves" in ways that influence their long-term life chances. Here Pierre Bourdieu's (1979) concept of habitus is once again useful. In many cases, decisions are made on the basis of "practicality consciousness," a form of consciousness strongly conditioned by class circumstances. Children from lower-status groups may feel the need to obtain job-related training, because they do not see any real likelihood of attending college. Money is another aspect of practicality consciousness. People who cannot afford four years of college will often try to save money by starting at an inexpensive two-year college. However, no more than 15-20 percent overcome this unpromising start to eventually graduate with a baccalaureate degree (Dougherty 1994).

In other cases, the power of social expectations is decisive. Although Japanese women perform as well as men in most educational fields, patriarchy is still a strong enough factor in Japan to shape expectations about appropriate courses of study. For this reason, women predominate in Japanese two-year colleges, whereas men predominate in four-year colleges and universities (OECD 1995).

Tracks That Increase Inequalities

To understand whether tracks independently affect students' life chances, we must consider whether school tracks have an impact on children's trajectories over and above what would be likely to happen to them if the tracks did not exist. To make this calculation, we would compare what happens to students of similar backgrounds (and, in more sophisticated studies, also similar measured ability levels) who are in tracked and untracked systems or who have moved into different track locations. For example, to discover whether beginning in a two-year rather than a four-year college has independent effects on students' life chances, we would have to compare the odds that students with similar backgrounds and ability levels will graduate if they enroll first in a two-year, rather than a four-year, college. (In evaluating these studies, remember that "mental ability" is itself partly created in the specific sociological conditions of family and community life and should not, therefore, be accorded the same kind of rocklike character as a physical fact.)

When the problem is set up this way, it turns out that many tracks do have a net effect on students' life chances, although not all do. Tracks appear to widen inequalities primarily when motivational intensity differs greatly between higher and lower tracks and when higher tracks are very tightly and directly connected to more desirable locations at the next level of schooling or in the world of work. In addition, tracks that are very strongly stereotyped as having high or low prestige may also widen inequalities between students above what we would expect on the basis of students' characteristics alone. Where prestige rankings are highly crystallized, they confer symbolic values on students in the minds of educators and employers.

Early-Branching Systems. Among the most disadvantageous forms of tracking are the early-branching systems that were once characteristic of most European schooling systems and that continue to be found in the German-speaking world. The inequalities that result are demonstrably large. Most studies have shown that the abolition of early-tracking systems significantly improves the performance and the educational chances of children from lower-status backgrounds (Husen 1965; McPherson and Willms 1987). For many years, working-class students were less strongly represented in preuniversity programs in Germany than in any other country (Husen 1971). This is not surprising. At age 10, many children have not had a complete chance to prove themselves before they are channeled away from academic opportunities.[24] As I noted in Chapter 2, however, the good jobs connected to the apprenticeship system in Germany compensate for the academic disadvantages that working-class children face.

• • • • • • • • • • • • •

TORSTEN HUSEN AND THE SWEDISH EDUCATIONAL REFORM

In the years immediately following World War II, no country in Europe moved more decisively away from the traditional European pattern of early tracking than Sweden. A large share of the credit for the reform of Swedish schools in the 1950s and early 1960s goes to social scientists and especially to their leader, Torsten Husen.

The tools of social science came to Sweden first in education departments, rather than in psychology, sociology, or the other social science disciplines. Thus, the institutional infrastructure for a large-scale research effort on education existed before policymakers developed a strong interest in reorganizing Swedish schools. At the same time, research and policy making were assumed to go hand in hand in Sweden, perhaps because many Swedish academic social scientists had become leaders of the long-time governing party in Sweden, the Social Democrats.

The reform movement was fueled by two key studies. Using military service records, Husen discovered a large reservoir of highly able working-class men whose circumstances had not encouraged them to continue schooling. A colleague of Husen's, Kjell Harnqvist, followed a sample of all fourth-grade students for 10 years, estimating "talent loss" on the basis of the large number of able lower-class students who did not enter the academic ladder (Husen 1965).

Reformers, however, faced a powerful opponent. Most Swedish professors and academic secondary school (*gymnasium*) teachers resisted reform ideas. The majority of educators expected the movement toward comprehensive schools to harm everyone involved. Comprehensive schools would, they felt, place excessive academic demands on less able students, and more able students would be held back by mixed-ability classrooms.

Nevertheless, in 1950, the Swedish parliament passed an educational act providing for a nine-year test of comprehensive schools. Swedish social scientists, under Husen's leadership, studied the consequences. The most interesting and important of these studies capitalized on a naturally occurring experimental situation. The City Council of Stockholm decided to implement pilot comprehensive schools in the southern part of the city while retaining the dual system for a short time in the northern part of the city. The two parts of the city had socioeconomically similar populations, so any differences in student outcomes could not be attributed to class differences. Holding the students' social backgrounds and initial ability levels statistically constant, Nils-Eric Svensson found that the comprehensive system performed better overall. The brighter students suffered no negative consequences, and the lower-ability students performed better throughout their school years than their peers in the tracked system (Husen 1965).

Husen and his colleagues had ingeniously questioned the assumptions underlying the selective system, and their results were finally accepted without reservation. The Education Act passed by the Swedish parliament in 1962 mandated comprehensive schools for all students be-tween the ages of 7 and 16.

••

Ability Grouping. The most familiar tracking structure in the United States is the common practice of ability grouping in elementary and secondary schools. Many different forms of ability grouping exist in elementary schools—be-tween classes, within classes, and other combinations. At one time, most high schools had separate college prep, general education, and vocational tracks. It is now more common for students to be assigned by course levels—that is, to honors, regular, or basic courses.

Studies of the consequences of ability grouping have not always yielded consistent findings. At the elementary level, ability grouping may raise mean achievement levels a little over what mixed-ability grouping would accom-plish (Oakes et al. 1992:590-1).

The story for secondary school tracking is clearly different, however. The best contemporary evidence suggests that high school tracks and course levels motivate upper-track students and discourage lower-track students. Learning is enhanced for upper-track students, who are surrounded by well-motivated peers and often have more dynamic and effective teachers, as well (Gamoran and Mare 1989). Upper-track students are also exposed to "higher status" knowledge and learn to approach the material in more sophisticated ways (Oakes 1985; Oakes et al. 1992).

Upper-track students do not, however, appear to gain as much as lower-track students suffer. The weaker competition does not improve the self-esteem of lower-track students. Instead, the simple material, dull worksheets, and unmotivated peers that are characteristic of the lower tracks tend to in-crease their levels of boredom and apathy (Oakes 1985). Drop-out rates among lower-track students are approximately 10 percent higher than would be ex-pected for otherwise similar students in untracked schools (Gamoran and Mare 1989). In addition, formal vocational programs show few signs of help-ing students find employment related to their training, avoiding unemploy-ment, or securing higher wages than other high school graduates, and they are particularly detrimental to the work prospects of poor and minority students (Eckstrom et al. 1987). Disengagement and delinquent behavior are charac-teristic of students in lower curricular tracks (ibid., p. 56).

Similar course-level tracking systems in other countries have had similarly negative consequences for lower-track students. Gamoran (1996), for example, studied the elimination of highly selective "O-grade" courses in Scotland and their replacement by "S-grade" courses that any student could take. He found a "marked increase" in the English and mathematics learning of Scottish students, increased exposure to science, and reduced within-school inequalities in educational attainments. These changes could be attributed at least in part to the new, more equal system.

Both motivational concentration and institutional linkages help to explain these patterns. Tracks concentrate engaged and disengaged students more than would otherwise be the case. Engaged students are further reinforced by being surrounded by like-minded classmates, whereas the effects are opposite for disengaged students. Moreover, basic course levels and vocational tracks in high school are often stigmatized and have few strong connections to desirable jobs. The incentives to finish a vocational program, under the circumstances, are relatively weak. If we are interested in learning and opportunities, the old saying "It's better to be a big fish in a small pond than a small fish in a big pond" leaves a lot to be desired. Although the challenges to the ego are greater in the more competitive big ponds, it's usually better to be a fish of whatever size in a big pond.

Other Track Structures That Matter. Motivational concentration and institutional linkages also explain why some other tracks matter over and above what we would expect on the basis of student characteristics alone. Elite private secondary schools continue to have a modest independent effect on enrollment in selective colleges, even after student background and ability is controlled (see Karen 1991). The motivational climate in these secondary schools is highly focused on achievement and encourages an active relationship to knowledge. Network links between these schools and selective private colleges and universities are also actively maintained. Counselors stay in close touch with admissions officials at selective colleges and universities, and they may even socialize with them. They counsel students on how to prepare winning applications, and they follow up themselves by urging admissions staffs to give their top students careful consideration. Furthermore, the competitive and upper-class climate of the schools encourages selective colleges to think of prep school students as the kind who are likely to do well (Cookson and Persell 1985).

Similarly, studies of the most selective private colleges show that graduates have significantly increased chances of entering top-rated graduate and professional programs and attaining high incomes, even after background and test scores are controlled (Kingston and Smart 1990). The same forces of motivational press, institutional linkages, and prestige stereotyping seem to be involved.

We can also see the importance of these forces by looking at cases in which they are missing. For example, community colleges, one of the least advantageous tracks in the American educational system, combine poor motivational climates and relatively weak linkage structures. Increasingly, community college students work part-time and have (at most) only one foot in the educational system. Most of the students have done relatively poorly in high school, so they do not reinforce a strong academic learning climate among their peers. Because most students attend part-time and none live on campus, the schools also tend to lack cohesive campus cultures. Students therefore feel little attachment to the goals of the college. Although community college officials purport to create strong channels both to four-year colleges and to good jobs, the linkages are neither as strong nor (in the case of jobs) as desirable as these officials suggest. The transfer function has eroded at most community colleges, and the kinds of semiprofessional and technical jobs available to community college graduates are not usually very high paying. Community colleges do help some "late bloomers" to develop intellectually, and they do give job skills to quite a few students who might otherwise lack them. Nevertheless, studies show that average-ability students from middle-income families have significantly better chances of finishing their degrees and ending up with higher-paying jobs if they start at four-year rather than at two-year colleges (Monk-Turner 1990; Dougherty 1994).

However, vocational tracks that are strongly linked to good jobs can help students in later life. Arum and Shavit (1995) show that students in vocational programs that offer skills strongly demanded by employers stay in school longer and earn higher pay than students in general and generic vocational tracks. This finding is consistent with similar findings for the German "dual system" of apprenticeship training, which is well supported and linked to good jobs (Maurice, Sellier, and Silvestre 1986).[25]

ADAPTIVE STRATEGIES OF GROUPS

People do not simply accept in a passive way the circumstances they encounter. Faced with a range of opportunities and constraints, they develop strategies, either consciously or subconsciously, to make the best of their circumstances (Bourdieu 1979). At any given time, the choices people make about where to invest their time and energy reflect the relative advantages they have and the options available to them. In relation to schooling, these strategies can be seen as investments and disinvestments in schooling, in types of schooling, in the labor market, and in particular occupational "beachheads" already occupied by members of the group.

As we saw in Chapter 6, one condition that affects investment decisions is the availability of alternative resources for making a living. It is not surprising that investments in schooling are lower than would otherwise be expected among the children of owners of small businesses and farms (Ishida, Muller, and Ridge 1995). These people do not usually have the same incentive as children from nonpropertied groups to use schooling as a means of gaining economic security. (As the offspring of people who are used to "running things," it's possible that they may also tend to sympathize less with the authority structure of schooling.)

The choices people make partly reflect the existing state of the credentials and labor markets. Indeed, in contemporary capitalist democracies, market forces are perhaps the most pervasive influence on individual and group strategies. Improving labor markets increase the supply of credential seekers, and declining labor markets decrease the supply of credential seekers.[26] We tend to think of this market orientation as a modern phenomenon, but historical research suggests that it has been influential since the seventeenth and eighteenth centuries, at least among groups able to afford secondary and higher education. As the historian John Craig (1981) observed, European societies experienced a growing demand for clergy and teachers thanks to the Reformation and Counter-Reformation, and the growth of centralized power increased demand for bureaucrats. This led to an early surge in higher education enrollments. The later stagnation of higher education reflected the greater returns to entrepreneurial activity.

Group strategies sometimes aim to maintain the market value of those degrees to which the group has better-than-average access. An interesting example of this process is described by David Labaree (1988) in his study of one of the first high schools in the United States, Central High School in Philadelphia. Central High was for many years the only high school in the city. It was highly selective; students had to pass very rigorous exams to be admitted. Even once admitted, students had no guarantee of finishing. Only about a quarter did finish. But those who finished the degree generally found very good employment in the Philadelphia business community. Many went on to become civic and business leaders in the city.

The high market value of the degree helped create strong and ultimately successful pressures for more high schools and more high school degrees. This plenitude reduced the value of the high school degree, however. In an attempt to create a new kind of credential-based market monopoly, the high school curriculum was eventually divided into college preparatory and vocational tracks. Much educational history can be written as a conflict between strategies for limiting access to valuable credentials, popular agitation for access to these credentials, fears (and realities) of declining market value in the face of increased access, and new strategies of monopolization developed by those whose position has thereby been threatened. This dynamic expresses a common conflict between market monopolies and democratic politics (Collins 1979; Labaree 1988).

At any given time, schooling may appear to be a relatively more advantageous setting for some groups than work, or work may appear to be more advantageous than schooling. In the United States, for example, African Americans and women have tended to invest heavily in education as a means of improving their access to desirable jobs. In a race- and gender-sensitive age, they faced a more favorable climate in schooling and in the credentialized sectors of the labor market than they did in the noncredentialized sectors. At similar ability and income levels, white males have been more likely to invest in work than schooling, because their relative advantages were typically greater there.

Hispanics, by contrast, have adopted a more mixed strategy. Those from the least educated families, seeing limitations to their advancement through schooling due to linguistic and cultural disadvantages, have developed strong niches in skilled trades and entrepreneurship (Bailey and Waldinger 1991). Given these strategic investments, it is not surprising that Hispanics have the highest secondary school drop-out rates of any group in American society (U.S. Department of Education 1995:110). At the same time, native-English-speaking Hispanics have invested as heavily in education as other minority groups (Alexander, Pallas, and Holupka 1987).

Strategies sometimes reflect the more specific mix of resources that students bring to schooling. At higher levels in the educational system, students from well-educated families who are not top achievers themselves more often move into humanistic fields, such as literature and art history, where their early family-based cultural advantages can pay off in the prestige market, if not so much on the earnings scale (Bourdieu 1984). By contrast, very high achievers from less educated families tend to move into high-paying technical fields, both because they lack the school-related knowledge to succeed in many humanistic disciplines and because they are usually less attuned to prestige competition than to economic security (Davies and Guppy 1996).

At the broadest societal level, mobility strategies depend on how closely linked schooling is with employment. In countries such as England and the United States, which have relatively weak links between schooling and work, a wider range of mobility strategies comes into play. Family resources may be concentrated on education or, alternatively, on securing noncredentialed jobs in skilled trades or entrepreneurial business. By contrast, in countries such as

Hungary, Japan, and Germany where stronger education-to-employment links exist, a narrower range of mobility strategies is sensible. The best strategy (and the one most frequently followed) is for families to invest heavily in furthering education and job-related training before employment (Erikson and Goldthorpe 1992:304-5).

CONCLUSION

Neither meritocratic nor social reproduction theories are entirely adequate for explaining patterns of inequality in school performance and educational attainment. Meritocratic theory embraces an unwarranted tautological definition of merit (i.e., those who succeed are meritorious), and social reproduction theory is too sweeping and blunt-edged to be fully satisfying. A better explanation can be developed by focusing on the interaction of group circumstances, institutional channels, and adaptive strategies. Group circumstances include both school-relevant resources, such as cultural knowledge and motivational commitments, and the stereotypical definitions of groups in the larger society. Institutional channels include school tracking structures, labor market circumstances, and government policies.

Social class, race and ethnicity, and gender are major bases of differentiation in societies. These social divisions are not, however, equally fateful determinants of school success and failure. Social class is strongly related to school performance and attainment nearly everywhere, because it is consistently associated with the distribution of cultural resources and motivational attitudes. Race and ethnicity is a varying divider. In some cases, it is even more important than class; in others, it is of marginal importance. Highly subordinated minorities are restricted in employment, segregated in housing, and stigmatized in the dominant culture. These groups invariably perform poorly in school. Racial and ethnic groups that, by contrast, assimilate rapidly are usually those that come to a host society voluntarily and with urban, commercial skills. Often, they also have religious traditions that place strong emphasis on the written word. Gender is a declining factor in educational inequality. Girls are often well socialized for the cultural emphases and orderliness of schooling. In addition, the power of patriarchal social structures has declined in the industrialized world as women have gained control over fertility, won legal rights, and begun to participate more regularly in paid employment.

Tracking systems are developed to improve school efficiency by grouping students with similar abilities or interests. School tracking structures can, however, sometimes reinforce and accentuate social inequalities. This is especially true for tracking structures that are highly concentrated in terms of motivational climate, are strongly connected to either high- or low-status jobs, and have strongly crystallized levels of prestige in society. Early branching systems, rigid ability grouping in secondary schools, and vocational tracks in secondary and higher education are among the most likely to reinforce and accentuate social inequalities.

It is wrong to think of groups as passively conforming to their social fates. Instead, they develop strategies to improve their circumstances by weighing the relative advantages of investing in schooling or work, and different kinds of schooling and work. These investment and disinvestment strategies cumulate into the distinctive paths by which groups make their way in the structure of social stratification.

CHAPTER 8

Teaching and Learning in Comparative Perspective

Extraordinary teachers come in a great many types and temperaments. Some, like Mr. Bixby, Mark Twain's guide to the mysteries of the Mississippi River, are irascible and demanding, content only with seemingly impossible feats. Others, like the nun who overcame the writer Richard Rodriguez's fear of reading as a child, are patient and quietly persistent.

> At the end of each school day, for nearly six months, I would meet with her in the tiny room that served as the school's library. . . . [T]he old nun would read from her favorite books, usually biographies of early American presidents. Playfully she ran through complex sentences, calling the words alive with her voice, making it seem that the author somehow was speaking directly to me. . . . I sat there and sensed for the very first time some possibility of fellowship between a reader and a writer. (Rodriguez 1982:60)

Still others are charming and enthusiastic. Louisa May Alcott describes Jo's mentor in *Little Women*, the German philosopher Freidrich Bhaer, as "turning only his sunny side to the world."

For all their differences, writers' descriptions of extraordinary teachers feature a highly personal relationship between teacher and student. Often, the lessons come in private tutorials—on the river, in the practice room, or in the professor's office or lab. And they come at a time when the student is eager to learn. Frequently, the student's old ways have proved insufficient for mastering a new situation, and the student is therefore particularly open to changes. The full force of the teacher's personality and understanding are focused on a mind willing to be transformed.[27]

Literary portraits of the more impersonal setting of schooling often convey exactly the opposite impression. Teachers are usually depicted as dull, mind-numbing pedants or vengeful persecutors surrounded by anxious and fearful children. Consider, for example, George Orwell's ([1952] 1968) memories of his boarding school life at St. Cyprian's School in England around the time of World War I:

> The [headmistress] was a stocky, square-built woman with hard red cheeks, a flat top to her head, prominent brows and deep-set, suspicious eyes. Although a great deal of the time she was full of false heartiness, jollying one along with mannish slang ("*Buck* up, old chap!" and so forth), and even using one's Christian name, her eyes never lost their . . . accusing look. It was difficult to look her in the face without feeling guilty, even at moments when one was not guilty of anything in particular. . . . Your home might be far from perfect, but at least it was a place ruled by love rather than by fear. . . . At eight years old you were suddenly taken out of this warm nest and flung into a world of force and fraud and secrecy, like a gold-fish into a tank full of pike. Against no matter what degree of bullying you had no redress. (pp. 331, 349)

Of course, some great teachers are also found in larger group settings. We have only to think of such virtuosos of the classroom as Jaime Escalante (portrayed in the movie *Stand and Deliver*), who exhorted, joked, and goaded his class of mostly working-class Latino students to top marks on the Educational Testing Service's advanced placement calculus test. Some books, such as *Goodbye, Mr. Chips* and *To Sir with Love*, have explored the transformations extracted from jaded and cynical students by great classroom teachers.

But in the United States we do not normally expect schools to be places where the joys and deep pleasures of learning prevail. The most comprehensive study of schooling in recent years depicts a "general picture of considerable passivity among students and emotional flatness in classrooms" (Goodlad 1984:113). Why is that? What prevents so many classrooms from fulfilling the empowering promise of education? And why do some classrooms overcome the odds to hum along with energy and purpose?

This chapter takes a close-up view of the interaction between teachers and learners. Even so, larger structural influences must be addressed, because they bear on the character and quality of classroom interaction. This chapter will therefore start from outside the school before moving into the classroom. It begins by examining the identities and interests that teachers and students bring with them to the classroom. It then discusses preset features of school and classroom organization that affect teaching and learning. They include the bureaucratic setting of teaching, the uncertainties of success in instruction, the number of students in the classroom, and the way that the school day is divided. Only after the stage is fully set does the chapter take up the lines and gestures of the actors themselves and show how they lead either to learning or boredom and frustration.

Teachers and Students beyond the Classroom

To understand life in classrooms, we must first look beyond the classroom doors. Both teachers and students bring with them certain experiences that are relevant to what happens in the classroom after the school bell rings. The key is to think about what kinds of experiences foster high energy and expectations and what kinds of experiences diminish interest and energy or draw it away from the classroom.

Social Circumstances of Teachers

Before teachers ever set foot in a classroom, they are first recruited and trained. Partly because of the people who are recruited and the rigor of their training, teachers step into the classroom with a certain status in society. These circumstances have an influence on how teachers teach and the kinds of expectations they hold for students.

Comparative studies show that American teachers once ranked near the bottom of the scale of teacher preparation and status in the industrialized world. Teaching now recruits higher-quality students than before, but the preparation of teachers remains poor in many places. In the absence of further reforms of teacher training, we should not expect great improvements in the way that schools work.

Personalities and Preferences. Teachers who were themselves good students and who were trained in rigorous academic programs are usually enthusiastic about academics and will set somewhat higher standards for their students than will teachers who were not good students. However, in the United States, schoolteachers are recruited mainly from the middle two quarters of high school students and from the bottom half of college graduates. The college entrance test scores of education students are consistently lower on average than those of students in any other discipline (Stevenson and Stigler 1992). These scores have been going up in recent years, but they remain substantially below the national average (Berliner and Biddle 1995:103-5).

Prospective teachers also have distinctive preferences that influence their choice of career. People who go into teaching do not indicate as much interest in "making money" as those who go into high-paying fields or as much interest in "working with ideas" as those who go into science, medicine, or academic specialties. Instead, their most common characteristic is that they enjoy "working with people" (Davis 1965; Lortie 1975). More than 80 percent of teachers say their major satisfaction comes in "making a difference in the life of a child" (Lortie 1975; Kottkamp, Provenzo, and Cohn 1986). Nor do secondary school teachers think of themselves primarily as subject matter specialists.

Recent studies suggest that no more than a third of American teachers are subject matter oriented. These subject matter specialists gravitate toward private schools and wealthier suburban school districts. Most teachers say they are primarily interested in the rewards that come from seeing children develop and mature (Kottkamp, Provenzo and Cohn 1986).

The dominant "people orientations" of American teachers have some decided benefits. American teachers may be more approachable and sympathetic toward children than their counterparts in much of Europe and East Asia. As the sociologist Philip Jackson and his colleagues (Jackson, Boostrom, and Hansen 1993) observe:

> American teachers tend to look for strengths rather than weaknesses. They take what students say in class—their contributions to a discussion, for example—and turn these remarks around until they make better sense, asking questions about them or rephrasing them in a way that makes them more substantial than they were when first stated. They applaud those who try, no matter how slight their success. They have a knack for discerning latent grace within the awkward gesture. (P. 259)

At the same time, because they are often themselves quite removed from the spirit of academic learning, American teachers' expectations for students are generally not as high as those of their European and Asian colleagues. Think of how different doctors, the archetypal clinicians, are from American teachers in this regard. For most doctors, all that ultimately matters is that their patients improve. They diagnose what ails the patient and then prescribe remedies in light of the diagnosis. Few teachers regard their students in such a clinical spirit. For many, pleasures come not just from seeing intellectual growth but also—and often primarily—from nods and smiles and similar signs of affirmation. Rewards may also come from seeing children improve in their social skills, becoming "better adjusted" to their peers. These approval-based satisfactions are not necessarily inappropriate, but they are very different from the more exclusive interest in academic mastery that is typical among teachers in other industrial democracies.

Recruitment and Training. Teacher training in the United States was until recently notorious for its lack of rigor as compared to training in other industrialized countries. On this subject, the frustrations of critics sometimes reached the boiling point. According to one, "The worst of the ed schools are certification mills where the minimally qualified instruct the barely literate in a parody of learning" (Kramer 1991:220).

This observation is no longer as true as it once was. Most prospective teachers take 20 to 30 percent of their courses in education and the rest in other fields (Berliner and Biddle 1995:107). Education courses vary considerably in quality, but education schools have improved their standards in recent years by offering more rigorous courses and by introducing minimal grade requirements and proficiency examinations (ibid., pp. 107-8). Even so, it remains true that prospective secondary school teachers who are education majors take fewer classes in their subject matter specialty than other majors would.

Half of the prospective teachers in the United States do not sit for competitive examinations to receive their teaching degrees. To receive their certification, all they must do is pass their course work and participate in a minimal amount of classroom observation and practice teaching. In an effort to improve standards, many American states now require teachers to pass proficiency examinations, but these tests do not require competence above what would be typical of an attentive high school sophomore. In the California test, for example, math questions are limited to basic computation and elementary algebra and geometry (Green 1988).

Very different patterns of teacher recruitment and training are characteristic of Europe and Asia. Training is usually different for those who teach lower and upper grades. In no place do primary school teachers think of themselves as subject matter specialists. However, in many places they are recruited from among the better secondary school students, and they also usually express an interest in the intellectual development of their students more than in their social and emotional development.

In Japan, for example, prospective teachers do not stay as long in school as American teachers do, but they are more highly selected. Only the top fifth of candidates for teaching jobs pass rigorous screening examinations and are able to obtain the jobs they seek (Stevenson and Stigler 1992). Japanese teachers also spend much longer observing experienced teachers before they are given their own classrooms. In Japan, 20 hours of in-service training is required during the first year after certification.

In Germany, requirements are still stiffer. Primary school teachers and teachers in nonacademic secondary schools are now almost all university graduates. Specific requirements for certification vary somewhat from state to state, but all states require prospective teachers to study two academic subjects in addition to education. They then take a first state examination in their academic subjects and in education. During the practical phase of their training, following graduation, prospective teachers practice as student teachers for two years and prepare for a second state exam, which they must pass to be certified (Bailey 1995).

Even greater differences in training separate secondary school teachers in Europe and Asia from American junior high and high school teachers. In France, Germany, and Sweden, prospective secondary school teachers take their training at universities and major in academic subjects rather than in education. They generally have to pass rigorous national examinations as well. In Germany, less than half pass these examinations. The second state exam consists of a thesis on an educational topic, two observed and graded lessons, and an oral exam (Stallmann 1990). By this point, teacher training has lasted for seven or eight years. Even so, teachers must continue for three years or more on probation before they receive tenure (i.e., secure employment over the lifetime). During this time, they are evaluated periodically by school supervisors and administrators (Bailey 1995).

Social Standing. Partly because of how they are recruited and trained, teachers have a markedly higher social status in most of Western Europe and Japan than they do in the United States. This status, in turn, helps to bring very able people into the profession. In the United States, teaching is a respectable occupation, but it does not carry the same prestige as most professional occupations. Some of the low social status of children (who are both loved and disdained for their lack of adult responsibility) rubs off on those who teach them.

In other industrialized countries, secondary school teachers and college professors are considered to be involved in fundamentally similar work, which they pursue in a fundamentally similar spirit, as intellectuals. Public opinion polls in Germany, for example, place teachers in the top 11 occupations that deserve respect (Bailey 1995:39). High status is communicated in the terms used to refer to teachers. The Japanese term for teacher, *sensei*, implies great respect and applies equally to teachers at all levels, including university professors. In France, where secondary schools are tightly linked to the universities, secondary school teachers are referred to as *professeurs.*

This high status is associated with concrete forms of recognition as well. In Japan, teachers by law must be paid 10 percent more than other civil servants of the same seniority levels (White 1993:90). The average teacher earns about the same as the average engineer (Berliner and Biddle 1995:103). (In the United States, the average teacher earns about 60 percent of the salary of engineers.) In Germany and France, teachers are paid as high-ranking civil servants and, in Germany, their pay includes supplements for spouses, children, and housing. Teachers' pay in the United States varies considerably from community to community, but starting salaries are among the lowest of professional occupations and do not climb quickly. Among primary and junior high school teachers with 15 years' experience, salaries average only a little over $30,000 a year (Organization for Economic Cooperation and Development 1996:149). (See Figure 8.1.)

FIGURE 8.1

Annual Teacher Salaries in Public Primary and Lower Secondary Schools, 1994

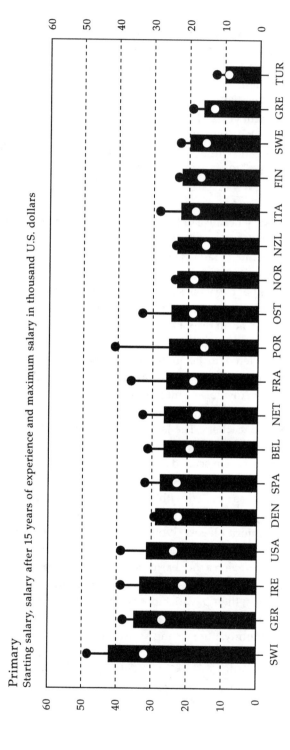

Primary
Starting salary, salary after 15 years of experience and maximum salary in thousand U.S. dollars

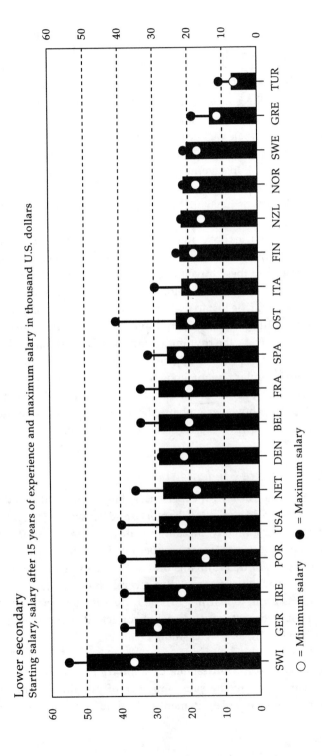

Lower secondary
Starting salary, salary after 15 years of experience and maximum salary in thousand U.S. dollars

○ = Minimum salary   ● = Maximum salary

Source: Adapted from Organization for Economic Cooperation and Development (1996:146).

Note: SWI = Switzerland; GER = Germany; IRE = Ireland; USA = United States; DEN = Denmark; SPA = Spain; BEL = Belgium; NET = Netherlands; FRA = France; POR = Portugal; OST = Austria; NOR = Norway; NZL = New Zealand; ITA = Italy; FIN = Finland; SWE = Sweden; GRE = Greece; TUR = Turkey.

Teachers in the Developing World. Poorly prepared and poorly qualified teachers are a far more important problem in the developing world than they are in the industrialized world. Indeed, in the absence of more qualified teachers, teachers with incomplete secondary education are common in primary school classrooms. As the educational researcher Marlaine Lockheed (1993) has noted, "Where teacher education requirements are low, many primary school teachers have a weak background in the subjects they are teaching" (p. 29). In Nepal, nearly a third of primary school teachers have not even set foot in a secondary school. In several African countries, as of the early 1990s, a majority of primary school teachers were not graduates of secondary schools (Lockheed 1993). Those who have little education are frequently unfit to teach effectively.

Teachers in poor countries have other hurdles to overcome. Most seriously, they cannot always show up for work. They may have to travel long distances to work or to be paid, and these travels contribute to absences. Supervision of family festivals and religious celebrations sometimes keep teachers out of class. Months at a time can be lost to teacher strikes, which are relatively common. Some countries allow for maternity leaves but do not make provisions for substitute teachers. Thus, the rhythms of natural and communal life, along with the inefficiencies of poorly working bureaucracies, make education in the Third World a more irregular phenomenon than it is in the United States. Here the occasional snow day is something that children look forward to for months and substitute teachers, however embattled they may be, do show up in a predictable way for work when the permanent teacher is ill.

Social Circumstances of Students

Just as teachers come to class with experiences that influence their attitudes and behavior in class, so do students. Chapters 6 and 7 discussed the influence of social class, race and ethnicity, measured ability, and family motivational climates on students' outlooks toward schooling. These factors are without doubt the most important determinants of how well equipped and well disposed students are to achieve in school. But several other factors also bear on the interest students bring to learning. These factors include the importance of schooling for job prospects, outside-of-school activities, and community pressures for achievement, as well as student learning styles.

Job Prospects, Nonschool Activities, and Community Pressures. Throughout the world, students share in the same universe of possible feelings about school. Some enter school full of excitement and confidence, with a reasonably clear sense of what is expected and parental support for their efforts. Others enter school with great trepidation, confused about what is expected of them and unclear that they will be able to succeed. Still others seem to be in trouble from the beginning, either because they are resentful of adult authority or because they would simply prefer to be otherwise occupied.

Societies vary in the proportion of "engaged" students to "disengaged" students. Students in the United States say they are relatively satisfied with their schools and teachers but often report that they are bored or uninterested in what is going on in class. Students in Asia, by contrast, report much stronger positive feelings about school and seldom report feelings of boredom or restlessness (Stevenson and Stigler 1992:61-7). In cross-national comparisons, the amount of student disengagement appears to depend primarily on three forces: the extent to which school performance is relevant to success in adult life, the number and demands of outside-of-school involvements, and the level of pressure exerted by parents and communities.

In places where school performance is not particularly relevant to adult success, student engagement with schooling is comparatively low. Particularly in societies with anemic economies, few children have the cultural tools or the freedom from economic want that encourages them (or their parents) to be highly committed to schooling. With opportunities for higher levels of schooling limited, many also do not see the relevance of postprimary schooling to their later life chances. As school-based opportunities for mobility increase, so does the importance of schooling in the life of the young. A longitudinal study comparing three villages in Papua New Guinea, for example, found that only in the community with an increasing number of middle-class jobs linked to schooling did children perceive schooling as a particularly valuable activity. In the villages relying on traditional economic activities related to fishing, school drop-out rates were high and young people indicated little interest in schooling (Pomponio and Lancy 1986).

Psychological disengagement from schooling can also be high in the most advanced economies. American students have, until recently, been prime examples of the problems that exist when democratic openness is not accompanied by strong community pressure to maintain high standards. Except for a minority of academically motivated students (perhaps 10-15 percent of the age group), "getting by without working hard" became something of a norm among American secondary school students between the mid-1960s and the early 1990s (Powell, Farrar, and Cohen 1985; Steinberg 1996). Nor was this essentially a phenomenon of class or ethnic disadvantage. Although acute levels of disengagement were more common in lower-class and ethnic minority groups, they were a prominent feature of middle-class school environments as well.

As students have become aware of the increasing income and status gap between college graduates and those without higher degrees, schooling has become more interesting to American students (Public Agenda 1997). Even so, students still must balance the demands of schooling against the attractions of other activities. Many American students admit to coasting during school hours. Between one-third and two-fifths of American students report that when they are in class, they are neither trying very hard nor paying attention (Steinberg 1996:67). A statistic like this might mean that "coasting" attitudes are "socially expected" more than that they are an accurate reflection of true sentiments, but social expectations are themselves revealing because they show what passes as acceptable and appropriate in a culture.

In terms of time allocation, schoolwork ranks below part-time work and social life for most teenagers. American teenagers spend on average 15 to 20 hours a week on afterschool jobs—not, as one myth has it, because their families depend on the money but because they, understandably enough, want to support an active consumer lifestyle. They spend another 20 to 25 hours a week on socializing with friends. About 15 hours a week are spent on extracurricular activities, such as sports or music. And another 15 hours a week are given over to watching television (Steinberg 1996:164).

Student engagement is higher in most of Europe and Japan in large part because adolescents rarely have afterschool or weekend jobs. But student engagement is also higher because schooling is widely perceived as crucial to job prospects and particularly because families and communities maintain strong pressures on children to succeed in school. Where parents and the community insist that school is the main priority, student engagement usually remains high. Where the community does not do its job, secondary schools inevitably suffer the consequences of "warehousing" many bored and disenchanted students. The "common school" tradition of countries like the United States, Canada, Australia, and Japan clearly depends on a community that helps to keep motivation high.

Learning Styles. American educators have pioneered studies of student learning styles. Some of these studies focus on cognitive functioning; others on cultural differences. These studies provide a persuasive picture of children who bring a range of cognitive habits to classrooms that are very often organized in a cognitively single-minded way.

The term *cognitive styles* refers to how children absorb and process information. Cognitive psychologists are certain that children acquire different styles and strategies of learning, but they do not agree on how best to think about these differences (see, e.g., Presseisen et al. 1990). Some students are predisposed to learn through reflective observations and others through active experimentation with materials. Some need to think about lessons in terms of their own concrete experiences; others move readily to abstract concepts. More active learners may feel bored in class unless they are engaged in handling materials, asking questions, or making comments. More reflective children sometimes feel uncomfortable and anxious in such a challenging environment and learn better by reading alone or listening to teachers lecture (Boocock 1972:129-33). Experienced teachers mix their methods of instruction to accommodate both more active and more reflective learners.

Theories of *cultural differences* in learning styles are more controversial, because they have become linked to campaigns to transform curriculum and pedagogy in predominantly minority schools. However, they are not greatly different in substance from the cognitive theories. The same differences that cognitive theorists root in personality and brain functioning, cultural theorists root in life circumstances. The term cultural differences, therefore, refers to ways of apprehending the environment that are conditioned by the life practices and assumptions of an individual's reference group. Some researchers have argued that both social class and ethnicity create cultural differences in learning styles.

One theory contrasts "analytical" and "relational" learning styles, the first associated with higher-income white and Asian homes and the second with lower-income and especially lower-income Latino and African American homes (Cohen 1969; Hale-Benson 1982). These terms are used to describe two ways of thinking:

- The analytical style emphasizes the ability to remove objects from their context and to group them together on the basis of some common property. For example, a tree, a cucumber, and a flower might all be grouped together as "vegetation." Students comfortable with the analytical style can look at a sentence, identify the noun from the context of a sentence, and generalize about the properties of nouns—where they come in sentences, what relationship they have with other sentence elements, and so on. The analytical style also emphasizes growth in breadth and depth of general information.

- The relational style is "self-centered in its orientation to reality" and tends to lump objects together rather than splitting them apart. "For example, a comb, lipstick, pocketbook, and door might be grouped together under the conceptual umbrella of 'getting ready to go out' " (Boocock 1972:109). In this way of thinking, no single object is an example of the context that encompasses it; each has meaning only in connection with the other objects in the relevant context. Students inclined to the relational style would tend to think of nouns, verbs, adjectives, and other grammatical elements as having a meaning only in the context of the sentence as a whole.

These two cognitive styles are thought to be rooted in the forms of communication employed in different home environments. The analytical style is encouraged by parents who are used to distancing themselves from their immediate surroundings and use grouping and abstracting to experience the world. Similarly, the relational style is thought to be the product of simultaneously more communal and more egocentric forms of life experience prevalent in lower-income and minority neighborhoods.

It would be wrong to think of the analytical style as intrinsically superior in every respect to the relational style. There is such a thing as too much analysis and not enough "feel" for a context.[28] Nevertheless, research on learning styles becomes problematic when it is too closely tied to political projects to transform schooling. Schools do favor the analytical style, but they do so on pragmatic and egalitarian grounds. As the political scientist Andrew Hacker (1990) wrote:

> The abilities and outlooks associated with the analytical style can no longer be adequately thought of as "white" or "Western" or "European," but are in fact part of a dominant global culture, which stresses not only literacy and numerical skills, but also administrative efficiency and economic competitiveness. (P. 24)

Curricula and teaching based on the relational style may, therefore, inadvertently encourage students to remain ill equipped for success.

Schools can, however, do more to encourage students who bring a more relational style to school. Research by Robert Slavin (1980) and others has shown that lower-class and minority children learn better in cooperative learning environments, where members of a group all work together on a lesson. They may also appreciate more continuous feedback. One reason that the cooperative learning approach works well with lower-class and minority children is that it makes these children feel less lonely in the classroom. Another may be that it "fits" the more communal forms of life in their families and neighborhoods.

SOCIAL ORGANIZATION OF CLASSROOM LIFE

Teachers and students come to classrooms with socially conditioned ways of seeing the world, and they meet in a space that is itself socially structured. The most important aspects of the social organization of classroom life are the bureaucratic setting of mass schooling; the "ecological" features of the class-room (such as the number of students in class, the way instructional time is divided, and the methods of grouping students); and the prevailing instructional culture in different countries.

Craft Production Ideals, Bureaucratic Realities

In a well-known essay on organizations and social structure, the sociologist Arthur Stinchcombe (1959) made a distinction that helps to explain why most literary memoirs of outstanding teaching are set outside of classrooms. The distinction is between two types of production systems:

- *Craft production,* in Stinchcombe's terms, involves the use of a variety of unstandardized materials, many nonroutine processes, and the creation of individualized products. Fashion design, custom-made furniture, and specialized computer software programs would be examples of craft production industries. Craft industries usually have few levels of management, and managers are generally considered to be less important in the operation than the craftspeople or professionals who conceive and execute the work.

- *Bureaucratic production* involves a standard set of raw materials, routine processes, and standardized products. Paper mills, smelting plants, and automobile assembly plants are examples of industries organized along the lines of bureaucratic production. Because production processes are relatively routine, coordination and control are typically more relevant concerns than creative work with the materials themselves. Managerial hierarchies are steep, and managers are more important in the operation than the people who make the products.

Schooling should ideally be organized as a craft production industry. The "raw materials" in this process are students, and they are obviously highly unstandardized. They come into schools with many different personalities, interests, capacities, and motivations. The processes that teachers need to use to reach and transform these students are certainly varied as well. Some students require constant prodding, even expressions of exasperation to get them involved. Others might require imaginative, hands-on play. Still others might need large amounts of emotional support coupled with high expectations. Even the final products will not be precisely the same; they should be "custom built." Certainly, graduates should meet minimum standards of knowledge, maturity, and self-confidence, but individual talents and interests ought to be given a wide opportunity for development as well.

Nevertheless, schooling is actually organized more along the lines of bureaucratic production. Students are grouped together in batches and treated as more or less standard vessels into which knowledge is poured. Teachers have too little time to get to know each student personally, and they must think in terms of methods that work better on average in large groups. The teacher's authority is central in such a setting rather than the learners' progress. In addition, the classroom is organized by the large number of rules that may be necessary to keep order in a grouped setting, but which discourage the disorderly discussions out of which important insights and debates frequently develop.

The deep personal connections that are a vital part of memorable educational experiences do not usually have the time and space to blossom in bureaucratic settings. The care and creativity we associate with craft production is, consequently, frequently overshadowed by the efficient processing structure we associate with bureaucratic production. Few students receive as much personal attention as would be desirable. This tendency becomes more and more pronounced as students move from primary grades, where they spend all day with the same teacher, to higher grades, where they pass from one teacher to the next as they follow their class schedule.

To organize schooling as a craft production industry would require one-on-one tutorials and small-group sessions rather than classes of 30 or so students following a single teacher's lectures and questions. This change would require much more money than any society has been willing to spend on schooling. (Elite universities, such as Oxford and Cambridge in England, are the only places where personal tutorials are more common than instruction in large groups.) Because teachers work with large groups of students all at once, they tend to rely on a standard set of teaching techniques, primarily seat work and lectures interspersed with questions. Under these circumstances, they cannot know whether every student who is physically present is also mentally engaged. Their success as teachers is measured primarily by whether they cover the curricular material and whether their students move along without causing too many problems—and perhaps also by their subjective sense of how well their students are doing.

•••••••••••••

HOW MUCH HAS TEACHING CHANGED?

Ever wonder whether teachers in your parents', grandparents', and great-grandparents' generations taught the same way as teachers today? Many people assume that teachers were stricter in "the good old days," more likely to "stick to the book," and perhaps, more unforgiving of errors. Yet no one has really known. No one, that is, until Larry Cuban decided to find out.

In his book *How Teachers Taught* (1993), Cuban, a former high school social studies teacher and school administrator, looked at a tremendous amount of data to decide how much had changed over the course of a century. He examined photographs of teachers and students in class. He looked at textbooks and books used by teachers as resources. He gathered student recollections of their classroom experiences. He gathered teacher reports of how they taught. He combed through reports from journalists, administrators, parents, and others who visited classrooms. He looked over student writings in school newspapers and yearbooks. He collected research studies of teaching practices. And, finally, he read descriptions of classroom architecture. From these sources, he gathered detailed descriptions of over 1,200 classrooms for the years 1890 to 1990. These descriptions were embedded in a larger set of data that indirectly revealed teaching practices in almost 7,000 other classrooms.

Cuban divided teacher-centered classrooms from student-centered classrooms and he also allowed for mixed forms. In the teacher-centered classroom, activity follows a strict routine of lecturing, board work, and seat work. Students are not free to move around the classroom, and they sit in rows with attention focused on the teacher. Cuban found that highly teacher-centered instruction is most common today, especially at the secondary school level, and it was also most common 100 years ago. However, some hybrids dating from periods of reform have slowly changed the character of American classroom life at the primary school level. Today's primary schools have more activity centers, more field trips, and more student movement around the classroom. Some student-centered reforms have not been adopted, however. Few elementary school classrooms, for example, allow for joint teacher-student decisions about what to study.

In Cuban's view, the need to maintain the teacher's authority explains why some student-centered reforms have fallen by the wayside. Teachers have become less strict and less formal, but they continue to feel the need for control over the essential aspects of classroom organization. Therefore, they implicitly differentiate between an inner core of instructional authority and an outer periphery of social relations. The core includes the lesson content, lesson techniques, and tasks to be done. The periphery includes the arrangement of classroom space, the amount of student movement, the amount of ability and interest grouping, and the amount of classroom noise tolerated. Teachers have felt the need to defend their clear authority over the core features of classroom life but not as much over peripheral features. As Cuban (1993) observed, "Substantial numbers of teachers, concerned with maintaining order and limiting classroom noise, yet attracted to the new ideas about children and their development, struck compromises between what were viewed as essential teacher prerogatives . . . and the new beliefs" (p. 269).

•••

The Ambiguous and Uncertain Work of Teaching

The sociologist Dan Lortie (1975) provided a now-classic analysis of teaching in a bureaucratic production setting that increases our appreciation of the difficulties of the task. As compared with other professions, Lortie noted, schoolteaching is distinguished by four characteristics: work with large, heterogeneous groups of students; work that requires high levels of group concentration but is marked by many interruptions; work that has multiple goals rather than a single, overriding goal; and work that is performed in an environment generally lacking in collegial support. The first three of these distinguishing characteristics make the work of teaching objectively difficult. The fourth leads to a sense of isolation that reinforces the uncertainties of teaching and has some unique consequences of its own.

1. Large groups, mixed abilities

In our bureaucratically organized schools, teachers typically work with groups of 30 or more students. These students have a mix of abilities, motives, and interests. Even when they are predisposed to learn, they may learn in very different ways. Obviously, under these circumstances, a teacher cannot know with any certainly that he or she is getting through to every student. Even if the teacher is getting through, the payoff for the student may not come immediately. A great teacher may, so to speak, turn over the soil without harvesting the crop; lessons may need to "sink in." Moreover, even very good teachers inevitably fail with many of their students. And, to make matters worse, even when teachers seem to be succeeding, they may not be succeeding very well. Those children who seem to be doing well may simply be good students who would do well no matter who they had as a teacher.

This situation, Lortie argued, creates a pervasive sense of uncertainty among teachers. Some two-thirds of the teachers Lortie interviewed said they encountered problems in assessing their work, and most of those felt the problems were serious. As one told Lortie, "I feel very inadequate and hopeless at times." Another said, "It's only every once in awhile when you do see progress. . . . You can go on for an eternity with nothing" (Lortie 1975:143-4).

2. Permeable boundaries

The objective difficulties of single-handedly teaching large, mixed-ability groups are compounded by the many interruptions during the average school day. For learning to occur in a bureaucratic setting, students must concentrate together on the lessons. However, teachers often find it difficult to control the boundaries around their classrooms. P.A. announcements may break in at any time. Distractions, from clanging ambulances to bellowing marching bands, may be within earshot of the class. Parents may arrive to ferry a child to an appointment, disrupting the flow of activity. The children themselves may be difficult to control or quiet down. These interruptions make it difficult to preserve the high levels of concentration that allow students to learn and practice most efficiently.

3. Multiple goals

The mixed goals of schooling in the United States create conflicts in the minds of many teachers about what they should expect from their students. Academic goals are by no means the only goals that schools care about. Schools also want their students to be socially well adjusted, to be good citizens, and to be able to develop their specific talents (e.g., in music or art). Increasingly, schools are also asked to provide nutritional, emotional, and moral support to children whose families are unable to do so.

Although academic goals are usually most important, they may not be the most important goal for every student. Many teachers are unclear about what priority they should give different kinds of child development goals. Teachers wonder if they are doing their job acceptably if, for example, their students seem to be self-assured and self-controlled but aren't making great progress academically. Conversely, those who feel that their students are making progress academically may feel insecure if they don't detect evidence of social and emotional progress as well.

4. Isolation from colleagues

Unlike therapists, social workers, doctors, and others in human services work, teachers are essentially on their own. Therapists-in-training talk to their supervisors about every patient encounter, but teachers rarely interact with their principals or with other teachers on matters of practice. Principals rarely visit classrooms or review class notes. Nor do teachers have a strong collegial culture with respect to the sharing of craft skills. Team teaching is rare, and, perhaps because of the uncertainties of the craft, conversations in the teacher's lounge only occasionally take up issues of practice. As Lortie (1975) observed, "Teachers say that their principal teacher has been experience; they learned to teach through trial and error in the classroom. They portray the process as the acquisition of personally tested practices, not as the refinement and application of generally valid principles of instruction" (pp. 79-80).

The isolation of teachers is reinforced by the lack of staging in the teaching career. Although teacher pay goes up with seniority, few schools have distinctive ranks, such as "apprentice teacher" and "master teacher." Ranks in professions, like all prestige hierarchies, can be useful for a number of reasons. First, they potentially provide senior guidance for younger recruits. A teacher hierarchy may also stimulate ambitions for career advancement, leading practitioners to give more thought to their craft. In the current structure, by contrast, many of the more talented teachers simply leave for what they hope will be more lucrative pastures.

Behavioral Consequences of Ambiguity and Uncertainty. According to Lortie (1975), these four occupational characteristics encourage a common set of attitudes among teachers:

- *Defensiveness:* a desire to protect the sanctity of the classroom from any outside interruptions or any deviations from schedule

- *Conservatism:* a tendency to rely on trial and error rather than any more reliable guide to effective practice

- *Pragmatism:* an unwillingness to experiment and a hostility to the kind of idealism that asks teachers to do more than "get through the day without major catastrophes"

- *Elitism:* a tendency to favor the few students who provide teachers with the majority of their psychic rewards, rather than looking for across-the-board improvements in an impartial and clinical spirit

It is easy to see how these attitudes might develop. People who feel insecure tend to be defensive about what they can control and unwilling to try new ways that could lead to further insecurity. They may also be more likely to overvalue signs of acceptance, such as nods, smiles, and words of appreciation. These tendencies are reinforced by the recruitment of so many who are "people oriented," looking for emotional rather than clinical satisfactions from teaching. (Certainly, where success is always tenuous and failure is common, teachers cannot be blamed for looking for satisfaction from a few high-performing students, the unconscious elitism that Lortie notes.) Finally, people who lack the social support of collegial culture or supervision from more experienced and knowledgeable colleagues are unlikely to change their "tried and true" methods. The isolation from colleagues that American teachers experience is, fortunately, not universal. In many countries, teachers share experiences, exciting lesson plans, and other craft knowledge much more frequently with one another.

Studies of teaching in the United States since Lortie's (1975) classic study have found that the uncertainty of teaching remains as strong as ever and has, if anything, become more severe as more students have come to school poorly prepared for learning. The sense of isolation that Lortie emphasized has also remained strong (Hargreaves 1993). Indeed, political pressures to legislate what goes on in the classroom and cultural clashes between teachers of different backgrounds and philosophies have, if anything, reinforced teachers' already strong desires to build impregnable walls around their classrooms. Some recent writers have argued that teachers choose isolation because it allows them to conserve scarce time and energy to meet immediate instructional demands (Flinders 1988:25) and shields them from the "digressions and diversions involved in working with colleagues" (Hargreaves 1993:58).

Teachers' desires to seal off their classrooms are apparently so strong that experiments in restructuring teaching careers, through such means as creating master teacher categories, have generally proved only minimally successful. Master teachers, where they exist, are often greatly appreciated by novice teachers for the advice and reassurance they can provide. But they are frequently treated more as potential intruders than as potential guides to improved practice by rank-and-file teachers (Griffin 1985; Tauer 1996).

The Ecology and Culture of Classrooms

In biological and environmental science, ecology is the study of the environments in which species live and of the patterns of interspecies interaction. Ecological studies can include analysis of the size and type of terrain, the climate, the number of species and their population size, the patterns of their interaction, and the forces that change the balance of relationships.

Classrooms can be thought of as having an ecology, too. The environment and relationships in the classroom ecology vary along four dimensions: *resource* richness, *numbers* of students and aides, *time and duration* of lessons, and *grouping patterns*. Classrooms may be relatively rich in instructional resources (such as maps, textbooks, and posters) or relatively poor. They may include relatively many or relatively few students. They may or may not have the help of teacher's aides. Instructional periods may be long or short, punctuated by rest periods or not. The school day may be long or short, and similarly, the school year may vary greatly in length. Children may be grouped by ability or work in mixed-ability groups. They may work collectively in whole-class instruction most of the time, work individually, or work in small groups.

Instructional culture is another structural element in classroom organization. Instructional culture can be thought of as the accumulated understandings about teaching and learning that are dominant in a society. Comparative studies bring home the extent to which instructional cultures vary. In some instructional cultures, for example, errors are something to be ashamed of. In others, errors are honored as the only path to learning. In some instructional cultures, teachers tend to use many problems from everyday life, such as teaching geometry through carpet laying or measurement through marking the length of different vehicles. In others, problems are presented abstractly and are not directly connected in a hands-on way to problems of everyday life. Teachers may strive to maximize coverage or to concentrate on a smaller number of key problems, hoping for absolute understanding of truly strategic problems. Relatively difficult materials may be emphasized, or teachers may fear that difficult material will "turn off" students. In some instructional cultures, the emphasis is on memorizing names, dates, and facts. In others, the emphasis is on creative integration. Other instructional cultures emphasize a dialectic, or interaction, between "knowledge bits" and "integrative" projects.

The work of educational researchers Harold Stevenson and James Stigler (1992) provides a wonderful window into the "ecological" and cultural dimensions of classroom organization. Stevenson and Stigler made an intensive study of classroom activities in primary schools in two Japanese, two Chinese, and two American cities. They observed a number of variations in the three countries that exemplify differences in resource use, use of time, grouping practices, and instructional culture.

The most striking differences had to do with instructional culture. In Japan and China, differences in ability were downplayed and differences in effort placed in the foreground. Errors were not considered to reflect lack of ability, but rather lack of attention to the source of the error. Stevenson and Stigler (1992) describe one scene from a Japanese classroom that might never occur in the United States. A young Japanese student was having trouble drawing a three-dimensional cube. The teacher called the boy to the board and asked him to draw the cube. The boy failed repeatedly, but the teacher kept the boy at the board, providing help and asking the class whether the boy was improving. The boy showed no signs of embarrassment. Errors were not a cause for embarrassment in this classroom—or a threat to "self-esteem." They were treated as "an index of what still needs to be learned" and a necessary means to improvement. The boy remained at the board for nearly the full hour until he finally produced a passable three-dimensional cube.

This type of intensive focus on a particular problem or topic was also more characteristic of Asian classrooms than the race to cover many problems or topics, as is typical of U.S. teaching culture. Many more problems were also introduced in Asian classrooms with familiar, hands-on examples. Students in one classroom, for example, learned about measuring volume by first comparing the amount of liquid contained in bottles of various shapes and sizes.

Time use was also markedly different in the Asian and American class-rooms. Teachers were in the classroom fewer hours in China and Japan, but they were expected to work on lesson preparation after hours. They had much more organized and informal discussion with fellow teachers, which reduced the isolation characteristic of American classrooms. As Stevenson and Stigler (1992) point out, if teachers are overworked in the classroom, they cannot be expected to prepare interesting lessons after hours.

The organization of class time also differed. Students were taught to quickly perform classroom routines, such as sharpening pencils, so that teach-ers had more time to spend on lessons. Most important, Japanese and Chinese classrooms included many more recess breaks, once after every lesson and at least five a day. This schedule helped to refresh the children and made it easier for them to concentrate on the next lesson.

Almost as striking were the differences Stevenson and Stigler found in grouping patterns. Instead of dividing students by ability level, as is common in American classrooms, Japanese and Chinese teachers faced mixed-ability groups. In the Japanese *han* (or small group), faster learners were expected to help those who were having trouble, in effect becoming assistant teachers. Asian teachers spent more time in whole-class instruction than in individual or small-group instruction. Stevenson and Stigler speculated that children felt more involved in class activity if they were learning with their fellow class-mates rather than alone at their seats completing workbook assignments. American students, they observed, seemed lonelier than Asian students—more on their own and less supported by others. In another notable difference, Asian primary school students also helped with classroom discipline, acting as delegates of the teacher in quieting disruptive children.

Although American parents lament the size of classes, class size did not explain the differences Stevenson and Stigler (1992) found in the effectiveness of teaching practices. Japanese and Chinese classrooms actually include more students than American classrooms, averaging between 38 and 50 students. Nor do Asian schools have more teachers. By reducing the time spent on rou-tines and by relying more on whole-class instruction, Asian teachers can effec-tively teach groups as large as 45 to 50. Their fewer number of hours in the classroom allows them to remain relatively fresh for the high-energy perfor-mances of instruction.

Stevenson and Stigler point out that American stereotypes of Asian stu-dents as docile and deferential do not explain the differences they found. Indeed, the Asian students they studied were lively, engaged, and question-ing—not the passive vessels of some stereotypes. What differed was the social organization and culture of classroom life, not the personalities of the children.

CLASSROOM INTERACTION PATTERNS

Teachers and students enter an environment that has been largely created for them. They may have little control over the structural elements of this environment. For example, they cannot change the number of students in their classrooms or how frequently recesses occur. Once they enter the classroom, however, they also construct a world through their own actions and interactions. This last section of the chapter explores the process by which classroom reality is constructed through the interaction of teachers and students.

Importance of Classroom Order and Consensus

Classroom order is a precondition for teaching and learning. If students are whispering to each other, throwing objects at one other, running around the room, or openly ridiculing their teacher, the classroom is too chaotic for learning to occur. Not surprisingly, research shows a strong positive association between good order in the classroom, teacher confidence, and higher levels of learning (Coleman, Hoffer, and Kilgore 1982; Newman, Rutter, and Smith 1989). Moreover, principals who do not back up teachers efforts to maintain order are consistently cited as the single most important source of low teacher morale—more than low pay, job demands, or hard-to-reach children (Moeller 1964; Dworkin 1987).

Willard Waller (1932), the first important American sociologist of schooling, observed that a natural conflict exists between the teacher's need for order in the classroom and the spontaneity of children. He noted that teachers must simultaneously create a rapport with students and exercise enough authority to maintain classroom order. Waller emphasized that teachers of his day often worked to create this "mixed rapport" (i.e., rapport mixed with respect or fear) by evoking role types with high cultural prestige (such as "the officer and gentleman," "the patriarch," "the kindly adult," even "the love object"). This emphasis is no doubt dated.

However, teachers continue to face the problem of how to create a rapport mixed with respect for classroom order. Somehow teachers must walk the line between too much firmness, which makes some children afraid to try, and too much friendliness, which makes some children feel that "anything goes." Most teachers today depend on a clearly communicated and graduated set of responses to misbehavior. It begins with warnings ("I need your attention, Ben") that may be repeated at least once or twice. It escalates to threats of punishment ("If you can't be quiet, Ben, I'm going to have to put you in time out"). These threats give way to sanctions ("I'm sorry, Benjamin, but you are now in time out for the rest of this period"). Repeated violations of classroom order or more serious infractions (such as punching or stealing) may lead to a visit with the school's disciplinarian and an unwelcomed call home.

More than order is necessary, however. A minimal consensus on the value of learning is also necessary for classrooms to work well. This consensus is not as easy to establish as order. For many students, real agreement about the value of learning would require something like a conversion experience, a change of loyalties. Teachers, however, have three resources for gaining minimal consensus on the value of learning. The first resource—and historically the most important—is the students' acceptance of the legitimate authority represented by the institution and by the teacher as an agent of the institution. The second is the school's (usually) implicit offer of a valuable exchange—the exchange of valuable knowledge and credentials in return for cooperation and respect (Willis 1979). This has become a more common form of legitimation over time, but one that is problematic. Where knowledge and credentials are considered beyond reach or not worth having, the very basis of classroom cooperation is disrupted. Moreover, even where the exchange is accepted, the terms of the exchange may be subject to frequent renegotiation. Finally, some students—though mainly the better ones—are attracted by the substantive interest of the materials and activities of the classroom.

Understanding and Misunderstanding in Classroom Interaction

Chapter 1 observed that teachers and their students communicate through symbolic expressions, interpretations of those expressions, and responses in light of those interpretations. This fairly complex mental process occurs simultaneously on both sides of the interaction. One reason that clarity in teaching is of such central importance is that children are not experienced in filling in background information or unstated steps in an argument. Without great clarity and much repetition, shadows are likely to fall between the expressions of teachers and the interpretations of those expressions by students.

The complexity of classroom interaction also creates room for a rich variety of cultural misunderstandings and unconscious biases. Ethnographers have documented some of the cultural misunderstandings that arise from differences in symbolic gestures in the classroom. For example, Asian and Native American children are taught that it is rude or impertinent to look adults in the eye. White male teachers may interpret this aversion as a lack of confidence or forthrightness. Similarly, many working-class children in England have not learned that in the norms of middle-class society, if you don't understand something, you generally don't admit it and rather assume that you will eventually understand. Middle-class teachers may experience the "obvious" questions of working-class students as indications of "dullness," when other students may be equally perplexed but too savvy to admit it.

Status cues are among the most prevalent unconscious influences on teacher interpretations of their students' behaviors. A well-known study by the sociologist Ray Rist (1970) shows how important these status cues can be at an extreme. Rist found that teachers in kindergarten classes he studied in Washington, D.C. unconsciously connected indicators of social status with indicators of academic aptitude. Children who wore clean clothes, whose hair was nicely done, who addressed the teacher respectfully, and who spoke standard English were placed in the top reading group and received the most attention from the teacher. Children who were unkempt, unclean, ill mannered, or poor English speakers were relegated to the back of the class. By substituting status cues for more direct evidence of academic potential, teachers inadvertently undermined their expressed commitments to equality of opportunity. Other studies have confirmed the emphasis of the Rist study on the potentially powerful, but largely unconscious, influence of status cues (see, e.g., Bernstein 1975, chap. 6; Erickson 1975).

Characteristics of Effective Teachers

The Rist (1970) study (and those like it) are useful cautionary tales, but it would be wrong to assume that only people who are very much like one another in social background are capable of communicating effectively. Teachers need not come from the same background as their students or adhere to one set of "ideal teaching behaviors" to be effective in the classroom.[29] By the time most students reach second or third grade, they are relatively skilled at symbolic interaction. They are able to read, adapt to, and learn from different types of personalities. They learn to interpret a teacher's gestures in the context of his or her particular manner of communicating. Most teachers are practiced in drawing out different kinds of students. Moreover, norms of fairness place boundaries around teachers' social bias. Even studies that find aspects of social bias in evaluation usually find that objective student performance has a stronger influence (Erickson 1975; DiMaggio and Mohr 1985).

"Traditional" versus "Progressive" Pedagogy. At the same time, some teachers are demonstrably more effective than others in reaching their students. Students in their classes learn more and are more engaged while in class. What are the qualities and practices of effective teachers? In the United States, advocates of two very different answers to this question have pursued a debate for over a century.

Those who support *traditional pedagogical theory* believe that effective teaching consists of clarity in explanation, step-by-step mastery of subject matter, repetition, and continuous feedback on performance, culminating in letter grades "with real meaning." In the late nineteenth and early twentieth centuries, traditional educators were challenged by advocates of what came to be known as *progressive pedagogical theory* (Dewey [1916] 1966; Cremin 1961). Progressive pedagogy took a child-centered view of learning, arguing that stimulating a child's natural curiosity is the key to effective learning. Educational progressives argued that teachers should provide curricula of interest to children, rather than curricula that educators alone find enlightening or uplifting. They also felt that teachers should vary their methods, using field trips, hands-on projects, and student-centered discussions to complement lecturing, board work, and seat work. In general, the progressives believed in de-emphasizing evaluation and emphasizing getting to know children and allowing them to learn through doing.

Both schools of thought have something important to offer, and both, left to their own devices, can also go badly astray. Studies of teacher effectiveness in the United States have converged on the conclusion that both *task leadership* and *socioemotional leadership* are essential. (In this, they replicate the conclusions of leadership studies in other institutional settings; see Perrow 1986, chap. 2.) Task leadership, a strong point of traditionalists, involves such matters as efficiently organizing activities and schedules, providing clear instructions, monitoring performance, and providing feedback. Socioemotional leadership, a strong point of progressives, involves such matters as developing rapport in the group, creating a considerate and positive environment, contributing to the social pleasures of a work group's life, listening to concerns of members of the work group, and discussing thoroughly any issues that come up in accomplishing the work.

Table 8.1 summarizes the following discussion of effective teaching techniques from both perspectives.

One of the most consistent findings in the literature is that the sheer amount of time on task is related to the amount of learning (Edmonds 1979; Dreeben and Gamoran 1986). Thus, the more time spent on curricular materials and the less time spent on warming up, following classroom routines, housekeeping, and sharing nonschool experiences, the better for the learning climate. As seemingly trivial a matter as increasing the number of school days from 175 to 185 has been associated with increased achievement (Goodlad 1984:96), as have summer learning programs (Heyns 1978). Also supporting the traditionalists' view, researchers have found that effective teachers have high standards that they expect students to reach. To be precise: Expectations

TABLE 8.1

Characteristics Associated with Effective Teachers

From traditional pedagogy	From progressive pedagogy
Concentration on task-oriented activities	Varied daily routine
Emphasis on reading and writing	Use of many different kinds of learning materials
Clearly communicated expectations	Student participation
High (but not out of reach) expectations	Hands-on activities
Quick correction of errors	Responsiveness to individual student's experiences and needs
Diagnostic quizzes	Ample praise for students' contributions
Clarity and repetition in lectures	Positive emotional tone, rather than flat tone
Strong (but not exclusive) emphasis on meaningful grades	

should be high but not out of reach, and they should be very clearly communicated and consistently maintained.

One especially interesting study by Robert Dreeben and Adam Gamoran (1986) brings home the importance of high expectations. Dreeben and Gamoran examined 13 first-grade classrooms in three Chicago area school districts. When they compared children who had had similar levels of "reading readiness" at the beginning of the year, they found that scores on reading tests administered at the end of the year varied primarily by the sheer amount of time spent on reading and by the number of words covered over the school year. Neither students' race nor the family's socioeconomic status had an independently significant influence on reading achievement, although both were correlated with the amount and difficulty of instruction offered by the schools. Dreeben and Gamoran conclude that poor children are sometimes short-changed because their teachers fail to give them assignments challenging enough to stimulate their potential intellectual growth.

Continuous and serious monitoring of performance is another emphasis of traditional pedagogy that appears to be essentially on the mark. Prompt correction of errors is necessary so that students know what they need to work on. Frequent diagnostic quizzes can be a major help for this purpose. Indeed, good evidence exists that the learning climate of virtually every classroom would be improved if teachers gave short, three- or four-question diagnostic quizzes at the end of every class meeting to see whether students were paying attention and whether they learned the most important points of the day's lesson.

Although these elements of traditional pedagogy are well supported in the educational research, an overly rigid conception of the traditional approach can be counterproductive. Students need to feel that teachers are interested in them and have their interests in mind. Traditionalists often get better performance from the more motivated students but are more likely to turn off marginal students.

For reasons like these, the research evidence suggests that effective teachers also draw on practices associated with the progressive tradition. They draw on students' experience and natural interests in the world. For example, children can learn about quantities by repetitive practice of sums or, more effectively, by working in an imaginary store and making change for their "customers." Effective teachers also make their classrooms inviting places by hanging attractive posters on the walls and decorating in other ways. They vary the daily routine, using different kinds of learning materials—from instructional videos to small-group discussions to field trips. Most of all, they encourage students' active participation by frequently breaking lectures for discussions. They make students feel like an important part of the class. They seize on student participation—by accepting and clarifying student answers and by using their ideas where possible. They provide praise for good performance, although they do not praise so lavishly that praise itself becomes devalued. Finally, effective teachers convey a sense of deep interest and enthusiasm in their work. They vary voice pitch and gestures to maintain a vibrant emotional tone, rather than a flat monotone—just as anyone who was truly interested in a subject would. (See Boocock 1972:129-49; Goodlad 1984, chap. 4.)[30]

Some students are well prepared to focus on curricular materials for long concentrated stretches. But for younger and less prepared children, the classroom must sustain interest to transmit knowledge. Some teachers have the gift for organizing activities that build student commitment to the classroom and ultimately to its academic mission. As Michael Huberman (1993) writes: "Acting out legends, singing in class, conducting an apparently aimless physics experiment suggested by pupils, reading parts of a play . . . [many teachers] suspect, perhaps with good reason, that the reactions of amused curiosity or real engagement will pay off further down the line" (p. 43).

Effective teaching practices are less common in secondary schools than in primary schools because of differences in school and classroom organization.

Primary school teachers have the same children all day. They are able to get to know their 30 children better than a secondary school teacher can possibly get to know the 150-200 students he or she sees during the school day. Primary school teachers may, therefore, feel the need to make the children's "home base" an attractive place to be. They also have more flexibility in managing time; they are not chained to the 50-minute subject period, as secondary school teachers are.

These factors increase the incentive of secondary school teachers to communicate their curricular materials as efficiently as possible. Teacher-centered lecturing, combined perhaps with a small amount of discussion, is widely believed to be the most efficient (if not the most effective) method for communicating the relatively complex ideas of secondary school courses (see, e.g., Cuban 1993, chap. 8). Secondary school teachers could probably do better if they were to implement some of the findings from the research literature, but many are understandably more concerned about "getting through the day" in a challenging environment than they are in using research to change tried-and-true practices.

Teacher Expectations and Student Performance. The greatest teaching deficiency in the United States is that teachers do not expect enough of their students. Indeed, teachers often react to signs of student disengagement by trying to make school less taxing and more enjoyable. Because they fear losing students, they feel that light material will stimulate their students to try harder and to be more interested in school (Sizer 1984, chap. 5; Powell et al. 1985; Steinberg 1996:75-6). But most students, instead of trying harder when offered light material, respond by further disengaging from their studies (Sedlak et al. 1986; Metz 1993).

One extreme sign of reduced expectations is the phenomenon of "social promotion." Social promotion means passing children to the next grade even when they have failed to demonstrate minimal mastery over the materials covered in the current grade. One source of social promotion is the dubious theory that if students are required to stay back a grade, their self-esteem may be permanently harmed. In addition, school administrators often worry that their schools will look bad if too many children are held back. The phenomenon of social promotion is a good example of how democratic pressures and bureaucratic interests can undermine the cultural standards on which both the schooling system and a truly strong democracy depend.

High expectations are important, but they are not all-powerful. A famous study by Robert Rosenthal and Lenore Jacobsen, *Pygmalion in the Classroom* (1968), is often cited in support of the conclusion that teacher expectations are the single most important key to student performance, but this study has come under criticism for presenting an overly optimistic view of the power of teacher expectations. In the original study, the researchers chose 20 percent of students at random from each of six classes in a San Francisco school. They gave a test to all students in the study, a test they misrepresented as predicting "intellectual blooming." Rosenthal and Jacobsen then told the teachers of the six classes that the test indicated which students were destined to show large intellectual gains during the academic year (the experimental subjects, of course). Pre- and posttests showed that among first and second graders the experimental subjects did in fact show higher than average gains from the beginning to the end of the year. The obvious interpretation is that teachers had high expectations for the predicted "bloomers" and that these expectations made a difference in how the children performed. By "facial expression, posture, and perhaps by her touch, the teacher may have communicated to the children of the experimental group that she expected improved intellectual performance" (Rosenthal and Jacobsen 1968:180).

A closer look at Rosenthal and Jacobsen's study, however, raises doubts about just how powerful teacher expectations really are. Changes in line with the "self-fulfilling prophecy" did not occur in the higher grades, and in a few cases the change scores of the experimental subjects were actually lower than those of the control group, the group of students not predicted to "bloom" during the year. Subsequent replications of Rosenthal and Jacobsen's study have tended to confirm these qualifications to the original study. It may be that by grade 3 most children have acquired an academic self-conception that is difficult to revise very much in the course of a year. Some may not be capable of doing more challenging work. Many more may not think themselves able. Still others may not see enough relevance of schooling to their life goals to exchange respectful attention and hard work for the advantages of better understanding and higher grades. High standards are important, but they are not all-powerful.

Cultural Matches in Classroom Interaction

Teaching methods that mix traditional and progressive elements generally work well in the United States, but they would not necessarily work well elsewhere. A "caring" American style teacher might simply confuse Asian students, just as a cultivated European might seem insufferable to American students. Indeed, different societies provide rather different conceptions of what ideal teaching looks like. These divergent ideals suggest that effective teaching practices are not entirely universal. To be effective, teaching practices must align with the pedagogical ideals of the culture in which they exist and thereby fit the expectations of students who have become attuned to that culture. Where these alignments do not exist, students are likely to be confused or hostile and teachers less effective than they might otherwise be.

The Ideal Teacher in China and Japan. "In Asia, the ideal teacher is a skilled performer. As with the actor or musician, the substance of the curriculum becomes the script or the score; the goal is to perform the role or piece as effectively and creatively as possible" (Stevenson and Stigler 1992:166-7). The teacher's job is to lead students through coherent and engaging lesson plans that bring them eventually to new knowledge. Thus, Asian teachers are expected to be lively and responsive to students, and they do not feel much pressure to be sensitive and nurturing. Stevenson and Stigler (1992) found that the teachers they surveyed in Beijing, China chose clarity and enthusiasm as the most important attributes of good teachers, whereas teachers in Chicago chose sensitivity and patience far more frequently (pp. 166-7). To summarize, the cultural ideals of teaching in Asia can be described as skillful performance, clarity and coherence in lesson planning, and (as noted earlier) an appreciation for the role of effort and errors in the process of acquiring new knowledge.

Elite English and French Styles. At the upper reaches of English and French secondary and higher education, teachers embody an entirely different cultural style. The more admired teachers often have "a certain gracious demeanor and a talent for witty and pleasant conversation" (Rothblatt 1968:190). In this respect, the ideal teacher is the person of broad knowledge who is nevertheless at ease with the repartee of polite society. While some "humourless college authoritarians" have always been found in these settings, the most admired teachers worked hard to present the appearance of effortlessness. They displayed their learning through intriguing lecture themes and provocative questioning, and they encouraged bantering exchanges between themselves and their students. The English literary critic Cyril Connolly ([1938] 1973) provides a reminiscence of one such teacher at Eton College, the leading British preparatory school:

> Wells taught the classical specialists; he was a fine cricketer and a judge
> of claret, a man of taste with a humour of understatement in the Cambridge
> style. [He] was theatrical, he liked knotty points and great issues, puns and
> dramatic gestures. He was . . . fond of paradoxes and we learnt to turn out
> a bright essay on such a subject as "Nothing succeeds like failure" or "Noth-
> ing fails like success." (P. 220)

Corresponding to the values of their teachers, elite English and French students are expected to show signs of brilliance, not mere correctness or competence. In France, the cult of brilliance reaches its apex in the *grandes écoles* and in the schools preparing students for admissions to these highly selective institutions. The sociologist Pierre Bourdieu (1988) conducted a study of some 150 student records from one such preparatory school for girls. Bourdieu analyzed the remarks made by instructors supporting grades on each of five or six exercises submitted by the girls. He found that the descriptive adjectives "careful," "conscientious," and "thorough" were located closer to the pole indicating poor performance (marks supported by such adjectives as "simplistic," "vulgar," and "insipid") than to the pole indicating excellent performance (supported by such adjectives as "masterful," "cultivated," and "ingenious"). Nor were the adjectives "sensible" or "right" terms of praise in this hierarchy of professorial judgments (Bourdieu 1988:195-208). They, too, were slightly closer to the pole indicating poor performance.

The persistence of the cultural ideal of aristocratic brilliance is a tribute to the staying power of "court society," where serious matters of state mixed with the lightness and wit of high society. As the aristocracy receded in importance, new classes adapted the old cultural ideals to their particular situations. The gentry (men and women of property and established name in the countryside), urban professionals, and intellectuals—each in their own way—took up the old cultural ideals as a way of expressing a lifestyle and values markedly different from that of the more consistently sober-minded and profit-conscious business classes who gained power in the eighteenth and nineteenth centuries.

Today, the cult of aristocratic brilliance remains important primarily in those institutions and disciplines least influenced by the democratic and bureaucratic revolutions of the era of mass education—in self-consciously elite preparatory schools in England and France, in highly selective undergraduate colleges, and in departments of the humanities. Although democracy and science clearly favor the dedicated specialist over the brilliant and cultivated generalist,0 it is much too early to write an epitaph for the cultivated scholar as a cultural model. So long as there is something to preserve in humanistic wisdom and something to be gained in status from the expression of cultivation united with wit, the European literati will undoubtedly continue to live on as a cultural model.

●●●●●●●●●●●●●

HOMO ACADEMICUS

Throughout his career, the French sociologist Pierre Bourdieu has been sensitive to the relationship between language and social power. From his earliest studies of the French educational system (Bourdieu and

Passeron 1977), he has emphasized the connection between professorial evaluations and students' social class backgrounds. Few students, Bourdieu argues, have the kind of experiences that allow them to present themselves as highly cultivated. Few travel, listen to sophisticated discussions at the dinner table, or are encouraged to read serious literature. Professorial judgments, therefore, are in large part social class judgments.

Professorial affinities for cultivation and sophisticated wit are for Bourdieu a form of "symbolic violence" directed against the lower classes. Categorizations of one student as "brilliant" and another as "dull" are, he argues, reinforcements of the social hierarchy in linguistic terms that may seem to be unbiased assessments of underlying aptitudes. In one of his recent studies, *Homo Academicus*, Bourdieu has continued his critique of symbolic violence by correlating descriptive remarks on student exercises with the social class background of students. Although the correlations are not perfect, Bourdieu did find a relatively strong pattern. Those exercises characterized in the most positive terms tended to be written by children of professors, doctors, diplomats, and executives. Those characterized in the most negative terms tended to be written by children of tradesmen, clerks, and craftsmen (Bourdieu 1988:195-208).

Bourdieu's work is often seen as having far more relevance to French society than to societies like the United States, in which "high culture" elites play a significantly less influential role (see, e.g., Lamont 1992). Nevertheless, Bourdieu should be credited with pioneering efforts to unmask the unconscious social codes in some academic evaluative language—and the role these codes play in helping the "culturally affluent" to reproduce their relatively privileged positions in society. Even in the United States, high-culture experiences have been shown to influence girls' high school grades independent of their measured intelligence and the amount of time they spend studying (DiMaggio and Mohr 1985).

• •

Third World Teaching Styles. Cultural models in the Third World provide a contrast both to the skilled performers of Asia and the clever gentlemen-scholars who help to prepare elites in Britain and France. Teaching styles in most developing countries are teacher centered to an extreme. Students are expected to copy what is on the board and to memorize textbooks; they are not expected to engage with their textbooks or lessons in any more probing way. The more authoritarian methods typical of Third World classrooms are evident in a study reported by Pfau (1980), which compared classroom behaviors in several fifth-grade classes in the United States and Nepal. In Nepal, some 80 percent of class time was spent on lectures. In the United States, lecturing accounted for just 40 percent of class time. Pfau counted three times as much student speaking and teacher questioning of students in the United States as in Nepal. Group projects, student demonstrations, library research, and field trips were almost unknown in Nepal. In the United States, they accounted for small but measurable increments of activity, approximately one-fifth of class time overall. The findings are similar for other developing countries (see Lockheed, Fonancier, and Bianchi 1989; Lockheed 1993:31).

In the United States, teacher-centered classrooms typically include a strong emphasis on testing. In the developing world, however, teacher-centered methods go hand in hand with a decided lack of interest in evaluation. In the Philippines, less than one-third of fifth-grade science teachers, and those mainly in the cities, reported using tests frequently (Lockheed et al. 1989). In Nigeria, only 10 percent of primary school teachers said they relied on testing (Ali and Akubue 1988), and in Botswana, students were observed taking tests only 1 percent of the time (Fuller and Snyder 1989).

The sources of autocratic teaching in the Third World are similar to those that made autocratic teaching methods common in eighteenth- and nineteenth-century America. Teachers are poorly prepared and teach under difficult circumstances. Children do not reliably show up for class and are often not prepared even when they do attend. Resources are often extremely limited. Only the unusual teacher is willing to take risks by loosening the reins of authority in such circumstances. The pressures that teachers feel to focus attention on themselves are reinforced by traditional models of authority, which emphasize the decisive role of the leader and the unquestioning deference of followers.

We need, then, to take a complex view of cross-cultural differences. Specific kinds of societies give rise to specific teaching ideals, and these ideals shape the expectations of teachers and students alike. At the same time, some basic principles of effective teaching are apparently universal. In developing countries, for example, research shows that significant gains in student performance are associated with many of the same factors that also make a difference in the United States. These include better qualified and more knowledgeable teachers, larger amounts of time spent in class on academic studies rather than on ancillary activities, more opportunities for students to participate actively in class through questioning and discussion, and continuous evaluation of student progress through the use of tests and other feedback (Fuller and Clarke 1994).

CONCLUSION

Study of teaching and learning requires looking at the characteristics that teachers and students bring with them to the classroom, the social structure of classrooms, and the process of interaction itself.

Teachers and students meet in the classroom, but their capacities and interests are largely formed outside the classroom. Teachers are most likely to have high academic standards when they have done well themselves in school, have had a rigorous subject matter training, and are highly respected and well remunerated by society. Students are most likely to be engaged with classroom activity when their parents and their communities provide high levels of support for learning, when they have enough time to study, and when they see the relevance of schooling to their adult life plans. Some controversial learning theorists suggest that students differ also in the learning styles they bring to school and that schools need to provide opportunities keyed to these differences.

Most portraits of great teachers describe one-to-one relationships, because teaching ideally occurs between an individual teacher who knows how to bring out the best in an individual student. These portraits suggest that schooling ought ideally to be organized as a craft production industry, although it is actually organized as a bureaucratic production industry. Teachers in bureaucratic settings face a number of problems. They are subject to a great many rules and can be interrupted from teaching by a number of intruding events. They work with large numbers of diverse and unequally motivated students. They therefore cannot be certain of succeeding with many of their students. In addition, academic achievement is only one goal of schooling; thus, teachers must decide priorities in a climate of competing expectations. Under these uncertain circumstances, many teachers try to wall off their classrooms, thereby depriving themselves of collegial support. These occupational circumstances often create attitudes of defensiveness, conservatism, pragmatism, and unconscious elitism among teachers.

Teaching and learning are further conditioned by structural features of classroom life. These structural features include the number of students and aides in the classroom, how they are grouped for instruction, and how time is divided during the day. Smaller numbers of students and larger numbers of aides often help with instruction, as do frequent recess periods during the day. Instructional culture can also be considered part of the classroom structure. Instructional culture is another structural element. Instructional culture refers to the assumptions about teaching and learning that prevail among educators. The instructional culture in East Asia emphasizes in-depth coverage of a smaller number of topics than American teachers cover. It also encourages a more favorable attitude toward errors and a sense that effort, rather than ability, is the most important factor in learning. Other societies have developed different cultural understandings of teaching and learning.

Once teachers and students gather in classrooms, they also construct a world through their actions and interactions. Classroom order is a prerequisite to all other effective communication. Even in orderly classrooms, communication can break down due to misinterpretations of teacher or student behavior or because of poor instructional techniques. In the United States, a long-running debate has divided advocates of traditional and progressive techniques. The research evidence supports some aspects of traditional pedagogy (such as clarity and repetition, high expectations, quick feedback, and rigorous evaluation) and some aspects of progressive pedagogy (such as hands-on learning, use of frequent discussion, and use of varied media to convey lessons). Comparative studies indicate that a wide variety of effective pedagogical styles are possible, so long as specific cultural styles are widely accepted by both teachers and students.

CHAPTER 9

School Reform and the Possibilities of Schooling

Sociology can tell us a great many things about how schools operate as social institutions in different societies, but can it also help us to make improvements in schools? To some extent, the kinds of changes people want to see in schools reflect their values, and sociology cannot tell people what to value. But sociology can clarify the range of values that inspire reform movements, and it can show what kinds of reform programs are most likely to succeed.

School reform in most societies has been primarily a top-down affair. Political leaders have developed plans for reorganizing schools and then mobilized support for those plans. Top-down mobilization is also common in the United States, but it is accompanied by higher levels of popular involvement in school reform. Even today, at a time when the public has become indifferent or opposed to many government activities, public schools remain an object of intense public interest and concern in the United States (Elam, Rose, and Gallup 1993).

Because Americans expect much of their schools, and invest so much of their hopes as a society in schools, they are keenly disappointed when the schools seem not to be measuring up. It is not surprising that periods of dissatisfaction with the schools have been as common or nearly as common in the United States as periods of satisfaction.

This chapter discusses the range of reforms that have been proposed for American schools and why some reforms have succeeded and others have failed. It discusses why efforts to raise standards became so important in recent years and the various programs that were introduced for improving educational standards. It concentrates on efforts to improve schools in the inner cities, because urban schools face the most difficult circumstances and reformers have focused much of their attention on them. The chapter concludes by using the research on reform to discuss the ingredients that go into making good schools.

A TYPOLOGY OF SCHOOL REFORMS: THE FOUR *ES*

Four primary values have informed American school reform movements: desires to improve efficiency, raise standards, enhance children's full range of powers, and increase equity. It is, therefore, only a small stretch to say that the three *R*s of school curriculum are matched by the "four *E*s" of school reform: *efficiency, excellence, enhancement* (of children's development), and *equity*. At any rate, schools are subject to these four major reform impulses.

The first reform impulse, and the one with the most enduring appeal to school administrators, has to do with improving the efficiency of schooling. These reforms reflect a sensitivity to bureaucratic organizational principles and (often) to market principles of efficient allocation of students to job-relevant curricula. They involve the introduction of new forms of categorizing and controlling personnel and school practices and sometimes also the introduction of entirely new types of schools or school tracks (such as secondary school commercial and vocational tracks).

Two reform impulses have their roots mainly in the teaching staff, but administrators often find them appealing as well. These are reforms connected to excellence (or improved academic standards) and those connected to enhancement of children's full range of intellectual and emotional powers. Reform movements aimed at improving academic standards may encourage stiffer requirements, more time in the school day, new evaluation procedures, more "elevated" educational materials and the like. Reform efforts aimed at enhancing children's development may include such add-ons as music and art programs, extracurricular activities, and multipurpose rooms. They may also involve more child-centered activities, such as field trips, hands-on science projects, more arts projects, and more colorful and interesting classroom decor.

Finally, movements aimed at improving equity are usually the project of democratic reformers, who wish to use the schools to make society more just. These reforms involve educational programs aimed at providing additional or compensatory education for disadvantaged groups (such as Head Start), integrating socially subordinate groups (such as desegregation plans), or preventing self-destructive or otherwise dangerous behaviors on the part of socially alienated at-risk groups.

Table 9.1 lists some of the school reforms that fall into each category.

TABLE 9.1

Types of School Reforms: The Four Es

1. Efficiency reforms
   a. New types of schools (e.g., junior high schools, community colleges)
   b. New tracks within existing schools (e.g., vocational and commercial tracks in high schools)
   c. Introduction of standardized categories (e.g., course credit units, standard divisions in the school day, standardized educational requirements for teachers)
   d. New forms of district-level organization (standard-sized schools and classrooms, articulation arrangements between levels, etc.)
2. Excellence reforms
   a. New curricular subjects (e.g., science, computers)
   b. New instructional methods (e.g., "new math")
   c. Upgraded teacher training standards
   d. Upgraded graduation standards
   e. New forms of evaluation (e.g., national standardized tests)
   f. Tougher grading standards and/or higher expectations
   g. Longer school days or school years
3. Enhancement reforms
   a. New types of schools (e.g., kindergartens, alternative schools)
   b. Facility/activity "add-ons" (e.g., multipurpose rooms, extracurricular activities, computer labs)
   c. New curricular subjects (e.g., art, physical education)
   d. New instructional methods (e.g., "learning by doing," field trips, "open classrooms")
   e. New forms of evaluation (e.g., portfolios)
   f. Additional classroom amenities (e.g., posters, artwork, movable desks, activity centers)
4. Equity reforms
   a. New compensatory programs (e.g., Head Start, Title I, aid for students with disabilities)
   b. New integrative programs (e.g., busing for purposes of integration, bilingual education)
   c. New prevention programs (e.g., drug education, parent education, AIDS education)

Cyclical Theories of School Reform

A common image of school reform is that it occurs in cycles, with alternating periods of "liberal" and "conservative" reform. In these *cyclical theories*, liberal reforms are defined as those that make the schools more open to previously excluded groups, such as children from minority groups, or that take a more child-centered and creative approach to learning. Conservative reforms, by contrast, are defined as those that go "back to basics" and insist that students work harder to meet high academic standards.

In such theories, the 1830s and 1840s (the age of the common school movement), the 1920s and 1930s (the age of John Dewey's progressive education), and the 1960s and early 1970s (the Great Society and War on Poverty period) are seen as periods of liberal reform. The 1890s (the era of administrative reform and "the one best system"), the 1950s (the era of the Sputnik scare and "meritocracy"), and the 1980s (the era of public alarm about economic competitiveness) are seen as periods of conservative reform. In some cyclical theories, periods of liberal and conservative reform are thought to be systematically linked. The argument goes as follows: The more relaxed and inclusive standards brought on by liberal reforms feed into dissatisfaction among conservatives, and the rigidity of conservative approaches eventually fuels demands for more inclusive and child-centered schooling (Tyack and Cuban 1995:40-54).

Although cyclical theories contain kernels of truth, they present too many problems to be accepted as completely accurate descriptions of the main patterns of school reform activity in the United States. Some reform efforts do not easily fit the liberal and conservative typology, either because they do not have a clearly identifiable political character—what is the political character of the once-innovative junior high school, for example?—or because they do not fit the popular delineation of liberal and conservative periods. The 1980s, for example, were marked by movements both toward multicultural curricula, a liberal reform, and toward greater academic rigor, typically a conservative interest.

Perhaps most important, as the historians David Tyack and Larry Cuban (1995) have emphasized, cyclical theories tend to overemphasize policy statements and underemphasize what is going on in classrooms. Schools do change—by adding new forms of organization, new technologies, new kinds of students—but "institutional developments in education may have an internal dynamic of their own only loosely connected with the periods of widespread and intense attention to schooling that we call periods of educational reform" (Tyack and Cuban 1995:47).

Correlates of Successful Reforms

Not all reforms are readily adopted, and some fade quickly after a year or two of experimentation. The historical record suggests a great deal more immediate and enduring acceptance of reforms that do not radically alter the prevailing cultural understandings of what schools do and of those that contribute measurably to the interests of the major actors in schools. Reforms that make school life more interesting, such as extracurricular activities and field trips, are easy to assimilate. Reforms that compromise, or seem to compromise, the ability of teachers to discharge their duties are ignored, treated with foot-dragging reluctance, or adapted to fit the circumstances of teachers. This is why some instructional technologies, like film and television, have not made strong inroads into the classroom.

Some reforms try to change social relations through schooling. Examples include school desegregation and bilingual education. These social reforms are connected to the fourth *E* of school reform: equity. Some social reforms have succeeded in providing greater opportunity for all students. Head Start programs for preschool children, services for disabled students, and even bilingual programs have continued to be popular long after they were initiated. However, social reforms that are threatening to important constituencies or cost too much for the perceived good they deliver will always come under criticism. Even relatively effective and low-cost reforms may become unpopular when the balance of political power changes, as happened recently in the case of affirmative action programs.

Successful social reforms mobilize important constituencies that refuse to let the reforms die. Typically, they are also mandated into law in a way that allows compliance to be easily monitored. These factors help to explain the success, for example, of bilingual education programs, in spite of frequent pedagogical criticism of these programs (see, e.g., Porter 1990).

The historical evidence suggests that school reforms are more likely to be adopted when the reforms

- Create more efficient organization for administrators
- Permit teachers to use more involving instruction (provided that the reforms do not threaten to displace teachers or create burdensome time demands)
- Give students more incentives to attend school
- Do not threaten important political constituencies
- Are backed up by the mandate of law, particularly if compliance can be readily monitored (see also Tyack and Cuban 1995:57-8)

CONTEMPORARY SCHOOL REFORM

School reform efforts of today fit into this larger context. Although cyclical theories of reform are not wholly convincing, it is true that at various times public attention has focused on one or another of the four *E*s. Reformers at the end of the nineteenth century, impressed by the new world of business organization, wanted to make the schools into paragons of efficiency. In the 1910s and 1920s, progressive educators wanted to make schoolwork more creative and to encourage the expressive faculties of children as a way to engage their minds. This is the period in which movable furniture, eye-catching posters, hands-on experiments, and field trips were introduced into the schools. During the War on Poverty in the 1960s, equity issues were squarely at the center of reform efforts. To increase the opportunities of the disadvantaged, reformers developed a large number of programs—from preschool Head Start programs to Pell grants for low-income college students.

A Crisis of Declining Standards?

Since the 1980s, excellence has been the watchword of school reform. Educational standards became the dominant issue among school reformers for some good and some not very good reasons. The recent era of reform began in the late 1970s, when educators and the public became troubled by the perceived decline in American secondary schools. Some educators saw declining quality as an unintended consequence of the previous era's emphasis on equity (see, e.g., Ravitch 1983). Others pointed a finger at lowered expectations and watered-down curricula designed more for short-term relevance than for long-term educational value (see, e.g., Hirsch 1987, chap. 1).

Many indicators from the period do suggest growing problems in American schools. High levels of choice among electives tended to reinforce the generally anti-intellectual flavor of secondary school in the United States. The "general track" (which included such low-level courses as driver's education, typing, training for adulthood, and home economics) enrolled more than 40 percent of all students in the late 1970s, up from 12 percent in the previous decade (Adelman 1983). By the late 1970s, only the top 5 to 10 percent of students took languages for four years or advanced math or physics. Many schools, perhaps as many as two-thirds, dropped calculus and physics altogether (Holmes and MacLean 1989:34). Average SAT scores fell, verbal scores by more than 40 points. Reports of school violence were also rampant during the period. Each month, some 7 percent of high school students were assaulted by fellow students and as many as 10 percent were robbed (Toby 1980).

The alienated atmosphere in many high schools created foreboding and fear. Billyclub- and bullhorn-wielding principals like Joe Clark in Elizabeth City, New Jersey briefly became heroes for their no-nonsense approach to school thuggery. State legislatures hurried to pass minimal-competency exams for students and teachers. Portraits of "good schools" and high-achieving classes in troubled neighborhoods became a popular staple of educational sociology (see, e.g., Comer 1980; Lightfoot 1983; Ravitch 1985).

Researchers also propounded lists of the core elements of "effective schools" (Edmonds 1979; Rutter et al. 1979). Most of these lists played into the worries of the age about declining discipline and lowered expectations. According to the educational reformer Ron Edmonds (1979), even schools in the poorest communities could be effective provided that

- The academic mission of the school was pursued diligently by hard-driving principals
- A disciplined and orderly atmosphere was carefully guarded and enforced by principals and teachers
- Teachers were well trained and academically oriented
- Students spent their time in class on task
- Students had regular and demanding homework assignments
- Students received regular individualized attention

A widely publicized study of private and public high schools by James Coleman and colleagues (Coleman, Hoffer, and Kilgore 1982) bolstered Edmonds's conclusions. This study found that order and discipline were higher in private schools and that expectations were also higher. These academic climate characteristics, lacking in the public schools, had a salutary influence on learning. In the study, this influence was apparent even after student background characteristics and academic abilities were statistically controlled.

A number of important commission reports from the 1980s urged concerted national action to meet the crisis in American secondary schools. The most famous of the reports was *A Nation at Risk* (National Commission on Excellence in Education 1983), written by a presidential commission. Like the other reports, *A Nation at Risk* recited the dismal statistics of educational decline and public dissatisfaction, and it linked the fate of the American economy in a competitive world to the fate of America's schools. "History is not kind to idlers," the report warned. "We are now faced by determined, well-educated and strongly motivated competitors. There is a redistribution of trained capability throughout the globe. We have committed acts of unthinking, unilateral educational disarmament" (pp. 5-6).

Social movements need to mobilize resources and emotional support to succeed. The "excellence" movement of the 1980s certainly mobilized a tremendous amount of emotional support. As many as 20 prestigious commissions weighed in with complaints about the state of American schools, and the press was filled with reports of danger and reform.

To mobilize public support, the movement exaggerated the crisis facing American schools. American schools during this period were not guilty of "unilateral educational disarmament." In fact, some indicators suggest that the schools were performing better than they ever had before (Bracey 1991; Carson, Huelskamp, and Woodall 1992; Berliner and Biddle 1995). The declines in SAT scores partly reflected the increasing numbers of students who were taking the test during the period. Because of the way test scores are calculated, small decreases in the number of correct answers show up as large declines in average scores. At the top end of the scale, one error can drop scores by 50 points (Berliner and Biddle 1995:16). While providing more opportunities for minorities and women than in the past, the United States continued to produce more scientists and engineers than other industrial countries (Berliner and Biddle 1995:95-100).

As in previous efforts to raise standards, reformers of the 1980s relied on the specter of an external threat to help build support for change. In this case, the threat came from the economic success of the Japanese and other rising East Asian societies; in the past, it had come from the industrial success of the Germans (the 1890s) and the geopolitical competition of the Soviets (the 1950s). These threats, too, were overstated. Although many American businesses were experiencing competitive difficulties in the 1970s, worker productivity in the United States did not lag behind other countries in the world (Berliner and Biddle 1995:92-4).

The rhetoric of crisis precipitated a great outpouring of reform legislation and programmatic activity to improve schooling. A majority of states increased high school graduation and teacher training requirements. Many also raised teacher salaries (Johnson 1985). School leaders tried to implement Edmonds's (1979) and others' principles of effective schools.

These efforts produced a good record of improvement. School achievement among American secondary school students increased in the 1980s and 1990s, and American students began to look very good on most international assessments of educational achievement. Racial gaps in achievement remain sizable, but narrowed significantly in the 1980s and 1990s. Some analysts credit state-level reforms of graduation requirements and teacher training for these improvements (Ravitch 1995:70-85).

Programs to Improve Urban Schools

Educational improvement remained more elusive in the poor and racially isolated communities of urban America, where public schools face the toughest problems financially and socially. The tax base in the cities lags well behind that in suburban communities, and children come disproportionately from the lowest rungs of the socioeconomic ladder. Many of the urban poor grew up in a culture of alienation from majority institutions and values.

In this unpromising terrain, the reform spirit of the 1980s made heroes out of those educators, many of them university professors, who claimed to know how to turn around failing school systems. These reformers thought they could turn the schools around through new kinds of instructional work in the classroom, through new kinds of relationships in the community, or through new organizational designs.

Standards-Based Solutions. One set of solutions, following Edmonds's (1979) effective schools argument, emphasized greater intensity in academic work and higher standards. Among the best known of these standards-based solutions were the following.

- Success for All (Robert Slavin, Johns Hopkins University)

This program began in Slavin's home community of Baltimore in the early 1980s and spread to many other cities. It provided intensive instruction in reading for inner-city children in grades kindergarten through 3. Tutors were the most important feature of the program. They received special training and worked individually with children who were failing to keep up with their classmates in reading. Children were organized for the program by reading level rather than by age. Staff worked with parents to help them work with their children out of class. The children's progress was monitored on a regular eight-week cycle with feedback to parents (Slavin et al. 1990).

- Accelerated Schools (Henry Levin, Stanford University)

This program was based on the idea that all children should be treated as "gifted students" and given enriched educational materials rather than the "watered-down" curricula that had become commonplace. Special efforts were made to design curricular material that would be interesting to students but also challenging. The program emphasized thematic units that integrated a variety of subjects into the study of a single topic (Levin 1990).

- Coalition of Essential Schools (Theodore Sizer, Brown University)

This program formed a consortium of schools largely serving the urban poor. Participating schools committed themselves to maintaining essential intellectual goals for all students in a supportive environment emphasizing active learning (Sizer 1986).

Community involvement programs. Another set of solutions attempted to increase the community's involvement in the schools. Many of these efforts focused on parental involvement, but an even larger number emphasized the importance of business-education partnerships.

James Comer, a professor in the Yale School of Medicine, was perhaps the best-known advocate of community-based solutions. Comer's program, which began in New Haven schools in the mid-1970s, was based on the premise that parents are potentially schools' most important resource. Comer's program organized administrators, teachers, counselors, and parents into several interacting "teams." To facilitate parental involvement, Comer's management and governance teams designed and carried out a social activities calendar for the school year, with parents playing a primary role in implementing the activities. In addition, parents were encouraged to volunteer in the schools as teacher aides, librarians, study hall monitors, and the like. The Comer program also included a social skills curriculum to teach students how to make good decisions in their interactions with others and "mental health teams" to deal quickly and comprehensively with specific behavioral problems in the schools (Comer 1980).

Community outreach also occurred through efforts to involve the business world in the schools. By the mid-1980s, nearly every large city and nearly every large corporation had some type of *business-education partnership.* The New York businessman Eugene Lang stimulated these efforts when he offered to pay for college for every sixth-grade student at his Harlem alma mater who stayed in school and kept up good grades. (Ninety percent of the children took him up on the offer.) Following Lang's lead, hundreds of corporations (and many wealthy individuals) "adopted" schools in the 1980s. They sent equipment, money, and mentors to local schools to help with instruction and inspiration. Other programs, like the Boston Compact, were implemented by consortia area businesses and district school superintendents. Participating businesses guaranteed part-time and summer employment to students who stayed in school and kept up their grades (Deng 1991).

Structural Changes. A third set of solutions sought structural changes to overcome bureaucratic rigidities and political intrusions. Of these structural solutions, *school choice* programs gained the most attention. John Chubb of the Brookings Institution and Terry Moe of Stanford University became well known for advocating "choice" programs that encouraged schools to compete for student "consumers." Chubb and Moe (1989) foresaw a time when many specialized schools would spring up to attract children with special interests. Parents would be free to choose among a variety of schools in the public and private sector.

A variety of choice programs sprang up in this period, all based on a strong faith in the magic of the market. These included some within-school district plans involving only public schools, some interdistrict plans involving public schools (including, in Minnesota, a very large-scale statewide plan), and some usually small-scale and experimental public-private programs. In the public-private plans, parents were typically given a voucher to pay for their children's schooling if they chose a private school, or the schools themselves were reimbursed by the public school district.

Magnet schools were another popular structural solution. These schools allowed children with special interests in a particular subject (such as computers or the performing arts) to attend schools designed around those interests. Although magnets were originally associated with "gifted and talented" programs, these quickly became a minority of the magnet offerings. The vast majority of the programs (almost 90 percent) were based on a particular subject matter emphasis or instructional approach or some combination of specialized curriculum and method (Blank, Levine, and Steel 1996). Some other magnet programs specialized in particular instructional approaches, such as open classrooms, the Montessori method, or basic skills. By 1991, some 230 school districts, enrolling a quarter of all the country's schoolchildren, offered magnet school programs. The number of curricular emphases grew proportionately, to include everything from aerospace technology and biotechnology to "travel and tourism," ROTC, cosmetology, and animal care (Blank et al. 1996).

School-based management, another structural reform, advocated the reorganization of authority relations rather than enrollment patterns. Its champions argued that "empowering" principals and teachers by moving decision-making authority from the superintendents' office to the schools themselves would be enough to make a substantial difference in how well the schools operated (Clune and White 1988; Malen, Ogawa, and Kranz 1990).

Successes and Disappointments in Urban School Reform

Short-term improvements were reported for many of the school reform programs. However, sociologists have known for some time that bursts of energy often follow the initial introduction of a change, any change. This phenomenon even has a name: the *Hawthorne effect*, after the General Electric factory in Hawthorne, California where it was first observed. But the improvements that result from initial interventions are often short-lived. They fade as the novelty of the intervention wears off. Surprisingly few rigorous long-term evaluations of the school reform programs were conducted. In the absence of these kinds of evaluations, no one knows whether the programs were successful. In fact, we have reasons to be doubtful about many of them.

Problematic School Reform Programs. Some community participation-based programs showed good results over the short term, but the suspicion persists that these programs depend on the charisma of a singular leader and are difficult to institutionalize on a long-term basis in poor, unstable communities.

Both the sense of promise and the nagging doubts go back to the 1960s. At that time, principal Samuel Shepard of St. Louis, Missouri was the only urban school reformer who proved that he could bring children up to national grade-level performance. Shepard went house to house and had parents sign contracts to monitor their children's schoolwork and to set aside a clean, well-lit place for their children to do homework. He also brought parents into the school to participate and help out. When Shepard retired, the program faltered.

The Comer program in New Haven and elsewhere is based on similar principles, and it, too, showed good results in early evaluations (Comer 1980). But Comer and his associates have not demonstrated that the program can become successfully institutionalized over the long term in settings where Comer himself has not been continuously involved. Comer has observed that the program's success depends less on "mechanisms" than on the energy and commitment of participants.

Business-education partnerships have had a mixed record. The majority of businesses were involved with their schools at only a superficial level. These partnerships failed to make much of a difference, and the businesses involved usually quietly broke off ties after a year or two (Deng 1991).

School choice programs have proven to be extremely popular with parents and politicians (Elmore and Fuller 1996), but the results of experiments with choice are mixed as well. Without a doubt, some schools that grew up as "alternative schools" in early choice experiments, schools such as principal Deborah Meier's Central Park East schools in East Harlem, are beacons of light. The programs at Meier's four Central Park East schools were tailored to attract students' interests and housed in small communities of 250 students. The schools achieved strikingly strong results: 90 percent of Central Park East students went on to college from a school district in which drop-out rates of more than 50 percent were common (Meier 1995, chap. 2).

However, most choice programs have proven primarily to help the best informed and most highly motivated families. The evidence points to a "creaming off" phenomenon, in which bad schools do not improve to keep up, as the market model predicts they should, but rather stagnate or sink further as the more motivated families leave (Moore and Davenport 1990; Wells 1991; Radner 1991). These kinds of effects have been shown in several U.S. school districts (see, e.g., Lee, Croninger, and Smith 1996; Martinez, Godin, and Kenerer 1996; Wells 1996; Witte 1996) and also in the most comprehensive study of choice in Europe, a study of the Scottish experience (Willms and Echols 1993).

Policy analysts Richard Elmore and Bruce Fuller (1996) have concluded that in the absence of serious progress in improving classroom instruction in schools serving the urban poor, "it is unlikely that choice will do anything other than simply move high achievers around from one school to another, mistaking the effect of concentrating strong and motivated students for the effect of the choice system" (p. 200).

Magnet school programs have helped many cities with their desegregation efforts by bringing minority students into predominantly white schools, and white students into predominantly minority schools (Blank et al. 1996). They also tend to be very well liked by students and parents who are involved in them. However, they have some of the same problematic consequences for social stratification as other choice programs. They attract better educated and more highly motivated families and therefore encourage the concentration of less highly educated and less motivated families at the bottom of the system (Blank 1989). Definitive studies have not been conducted on the effects of magnet schools on student achievement. Logically, the 40 percent of magnet schools now geared to specialized subject matter (such as performing arts or animal care) seem unlikely to raise performance in subjects outside the school's major area of emphasis. On the other hand, those geared to distinctive instructional approaches may have positive effects on achievement; it will be interesting to see if they do.

The findings on choice programs and magnet schools encourage mixed feelings. Surely, we should not sacrifice motivated families to a failing system. But at the same time we might legitimately worry about the further isolation of schools at the bottom if they are deprived of precisely the kinds of parents who are their natural leaders.

Still more troubling is the finding that in some inner-city communities even the highly motivated families who take advantage of school choice opportunities do not gain very much from their participation. Studies of the Milwaukee public-private choice experiments suggest that turnover in school populations is so great in poor urban areas that the continuity needed to sustain a learning community may be difficult to achieve. The performance of choice students has varied from year to year, but they do not appear to show better achievement overall than similar low-income students who have remained in their neighborhood schools. After controlling for the expected effects of student background factors, choice students have, in general, shown higher reading scores than Milwaukee public school students, but they have also shown lower math scores (Witte 1996:130).

Schools in communities like inner-city Milwaukee need a strong academic ethos, orderly environments, consistently high levels of parental participation in the life of the school, and academically focused principals more than they need choice or other purely structural changes. Structural changes like choice do not automatically produce these qualities of good schools.

Promising School Reform Programs. The clearest example of a successful program is Robert Slavin's (Slavin et al. 1990) tutor-based and reading-intensive Success for All program (see boxed text). Slavin's program has been rigorously and repeatedly evaluated. The results show significantly enhanced language and reading skills in preschool and primary grades, reduced special education referrals, and reduced numbers of grade repeaters. These results are consistent with the work of researchers who argue that weak preparation in reading is the single most important culprit in the poor subsequent school performance of inner-city children (Slavin, Karweit, and Madden 1989; Farkas 1993). Once remediation is necessary, it is often too late.

• • • • • • • • • • • • •

SUCCESS FOR ALL

Is it possible to give all children a strong foundation in reading, even those who are at risk of early failure? Robert Slavin has shown that it can be done. Slavin and his associates (Slavin et al. 1990) believe that students must be prevented from needing remedial attention. Once students need remediation, the battle is often lost.

Here's how the program works: Tutors work directly with students who are having trouble keeping up with their reading groups. First graders have the highest priority. They take students out of their homerooms during periods other than reading and math. In general, they stress the same skills as the student is currently learning in reading, but they also attempt to identify learning deficits and to use different strategies to teach the same skills. Tutors and teachers meet regularly to coordinate their approaches to particular students. Once students begin to read primers, the program uses cooperative learning activities built around story structure, prediction of story lines, summarization, vocabulary building, decoding practice, writing, and direct instruction in reading comprehension skills. Student progress is assessed every eight weeks. Family support teams work to encourage parental involvement and to help students who are not receiving adequate sleep or nutrition, who need eyeglasses, who are not attending school regularly, and who are exhibiting serious behavior problems.

We can be confident that Success for All works because Slavin's group has been careful to evaluate the program rigorously—and usually using more than one measure of reading competence. Where possible, Success for All schools are matched with a control school similar in poverty level, historical achievement level, ethnicity of the student body, and other factors. The results of evaluations of 15 Success for All schools in seven states show that the program improves student performance in reading and that it usually has the largest effects with the bottom 25 percent of the class. In these evaluations, significant effects were not found on every measure at every grade level, but the program showed effects in a great majority of schools and grade levels, and measures of reading competence. In many cases, Success for All students read several months or even a grade level ahead of the students with whom they were matched. Indeed, the only school that failed to show positive effects of Success for All was a school in rural Caldwell, Idaho. This had less to do with a weakness in the Success for All program than with the unusual strength of the control school. The control school seems to have been an exceptionally effective school—a new facility with a highly motivated principal and teaching staff.

By the mid 1990s, Slavin's Success for All program was being implemented in 85 schools in 19 U.S. states. The findings' greatest importance, according to Slavin (Slavin et al. 1994), is "in demonstrating that substantially greater success for disadvantaged students can be routinely ensured in schools that are neither exceptional nor extraordinary—schools that were not producing great success before the program was introduced" (p. 647).

Success for All can be an expensive program if it requires that additional teaching staff be brought into the classroom. However, many schools have been able to use compensatory education funds from the federal government to implement the program (Slavin et al. 1994).

If well-focused instructional help in the classroom is one promising factor, strong incentives for achievement can be another. When Eugene Lang offered to partially finance the college tuition of every member of a Harlem sixth-grade class who made it to college, he found himself paying for more than 90 percent of the students—in a school where a 75 percent drop-out rate had been typical! (Lang also helped with counseling and motivational support for the families of his "adopted" students.) This is, needless to say, a fairly expensive offer.

Fortunately, it appears that business communities can also get together to stimulate better performance at a less daunting price. The Philadelphia High School Academies, for example, showed a good record by using the promise of full-time employment in supporting businesses as an incentive to improve attendance and school performance. The Boston business community promised to hire thousands of high school students in summer jobs and to give preference to graduates of the city schools for permanent entry-level employment, if the Boston school system improved the attendance and achievement of high school graduates and reduced the drop-out rate. The business community delivered on its promises, employing thousands of local high school students. However, attendance and achievement in the schools increased only modestly (and no more statistically than the improving national trends would have predicted). Dropouts actually increased as the schools raised academic standards to meet the Boston Compact's goals.

Thus, although the evidence is not entirely conclusive, two factors appear to be frequently associated with successful urban school reform programs:

- Enrichment of classroom life through well-focused and continuous instructional aid
- Encouragement of student aspirations through practical incentives for achievement in the form of jobs or help with college tuition

Another Model for Urban Schools. Are more effective schools really possible in the inner cities and the poorest rural areas, in the absence of funds to support programs like Slavin's Success for All program or Lang's tuition incentives?

The educational researchers Anthony Bryk, Valerie Lee, and Peter Holland (1993) have suggested that academic and communal characteristics of Catholic schools point in the right direction. Bryk et al. showed that Catholic schools achieve better results among the urban poor than public schools, even after the social and academic characteristics of students are statistically controlled. The better performance of Catholic schools, the researchers conclude, is the result of their ability to keep children focused on academic pursuits, in their ability to create a communal environment, and in their inspirational values.

Catholic schools have a more focused academic orientation than public schools and do not allow for as much individual choice in course-taking patterns. Teachers are not notably better in the classroom than their public school counterparts (and they may in fact be less good overall), but they make extra efforts to be engaged with their students and to involve parents. In return, they expect reciprocation on the part of students and parents. Many decisions are made after wide consultation and discussion rather than handed down from on high. Finally, an "inspirational ideology" is at the center of the community.

> Fundamental to Catholic schools are beliefs about the dignity of each person and a shared responsibility for advancing a just and caring society. . . . When such understandings meld to a coherent organizational structure with adequate resources, desirable academic and social consequences can result. (Bryk et al. 1993:312)

THE POSSIBILITIES OF SCHOOLING

Schools of the future may very well be different in some important respects from those we see today. For one thing, computers, with their interactive and multisensory potential, will become more central in the classroom. Although they are now still mainly used for drill work (Pelgrum and Plomp 1993), they may in the near future help to open up the world for children in ways that textbooks alone cannot do (see, e.g., Papert 1993). In addition, in spite of the misgivings of researchers, we may see many more specialized secondary schools in the future. Multicultural and global curricula, already a force, seem likely to become increasingly important as well.

• • • • • • • • • • • • • •

COMPUTERS IN THE CLASSROOM

Computers will almost certainly play an even more important role than they now do in classrooms of the future. This is a little surprising, considering that technology has usually been a bust in the classroom. Radio, television, and film have all failed to make large inroads in classroom life (Tyack and Cuban 1995). The difference between these earlier technologies and computers is that computers are interactive and offer a wide range of choice in learning experiences for teachers and students alike.

Computers began to enter classrooms some 20 years ago. Their entry into school life has not been without problems. Many schools remain "unwired," and the existence of computer resources has become one of the major stratifying resources in school systems. Just as computer use for analytical purposes has become more and more a marker of high-level jobs, so computer resources have become a marker of better schools. Many teachers continue to use computers for unimaginative drill work, whereas others substitute net searches for learning experiences. In the latter cases, "data smog"—or information overload—can be a problem.

Where they are used effectively, computers can be a tremendous learning resource. From the beginning, some teachers were able to take advantage of the interactive quality and versatility of computers. One school in rural Louisiana used computers to develop a folklife archive about their community. They interviewed friends and relatives for reminiscences, folktales, recipes, crafts, and celebrations. They transformed these interviews into files that combined text, graphics, animation, and sound, creating interactive documents with multiple layers of information. The archives fed into classroom activities. Native Americans came into class to help students build authentic Choctaw huts, famous cooks came in to instruct on local recipes, scuba divers came to talk about sea life in the Gulf. Photographs taken at these events were integrated with text in the archives (Gooden 1996, chap. 2).

At a school in south Philadelphia, science instructors used computers to aid in the building of a greenhouse and the study of plant life. Computers were used to record growth data, conduct plant growth simulations, and write reports on topics from photosynthesis to acid rain. Students got hands-on experience with plant life in the greenhouse and intellectual reflection on natural processes through the computing facilities. Students and teachers also began to use electronic bulletin boards and networks to do research and to establish links with other schools. They shared statistics on water and air quality and other data (Gooden 1996, chap. 3).

In addition to the information resources of the Internet, some teachers now have access to enormously sophisticated educational software. Children can simulate the growth and management of towns and cities, follow intergalactic space travelers to solve problems that help them save the universe, look at and listen to different countries of the world while learning history. Thanks to these creative programs, children who attend today's best schools will be learning how to do research and how to think in an integrated way at an earlier age than any previous generation.

• •

But these innovations alone cannot create the well-ordered, academically enriched learning communities most people want their schools to be. These are not the "magic bullets" that some of their advocates imagine. Other panaceas have been proposed in the past, and most have fallen short of the expectations of their promoters. There is a "sticky" quality to what can be done in bureaucratic, grouped-learning systems, especially those like public schools, which process such very unstandardized "raw material." Most reform is, therefore, slow, patient work.

In this book, I have intended to explain mass schooling as a social institution: where it came from, why different patterns of organization and practice exist, and what consequences these different patterns have for societies and their individual members. In these last few pages of the book, I would like to look at schooling in a more prescriptive way—that is, in terms of the ideals that schools can represent and how they might represent those ideals more effectively than they currently do.

Which Educational Values Should We Promote?

The first question for those who presume to prescribe is: What constitutes health? The first conclusion is that all the major values associated with school reform movements represent desirable goods:

- Efficiency is associated with the economical use and conservation of scarce resources.
- Excellence is associated with high cultural attainment.
- Enhancement is associated with the fostering possibilities for more complete development.
- Equity is associated with prevailing standards of justice and fairness.

And yet we often lack a metric for deciding whether one good is more important than another. To promote efficiency, we might give children with different aptitudes different kinds of schooling. But this efficiency may be purchased at the expense of equity among groups. Which value should take priority? In many instances, logical solutions cannot be defined; the values are incommensurable. Tradeoffs may be possible, but how these tradeoffs are made will depend on how the two goods are weighted and also the thresholds below which a tradeoff is unacceptable.

Much depends, therefore, on how we weigh various goods and what thresholds we consider acceptable. Having looked at schooling systems for some time, I believe that the best protection for a progressive, democratic society and the best hope for individuals occur when the state provides essentially the same education for all through secondary school and when educators do not trim their commitment to high standards of academic and personal excellence.

The political theorist Benjamin Barber titled his book about schooling *An Aristocracy of Everyone* (1992), and this title captures the spirit with which I look at the possibilities of schooling. As Barber observes, the great dream of the Enlightenment was that ordinary people could gain the cultural knowledge and refined understandings that were once reserved for inherited wealth. Most liberals of the seventeenth and eighteenth centuries believed that a market society required the widespread diffusion of knowledge and good standards of social behavior. Certainly, this was the view of John Locke, the most important advocate of a social order based on the maximization of individual freedoms (Gray 1989). Democratic and republican forms of government required self-limiting virtues and just discriminations, and these could be produced only through schooling that aimed to produce excellence in all citizens.

In contemporary work on schooling, however, the idea of excellence has become tied more or less exclusively to a narrow, test-based version of academic merit. But tests alone do not measure merit. Beautifully written and vigorously argued essays, well-crafted research projects, provocative questions—these too are marks of inquiring and able minds. Worse yet, the reasons political leaders put forward to justify pursuing academic excellence are exclusively tied to prospects for economic advancement, either at the individual or societal level. The economic rewards of academic excellence are obviously important, but they are not the only important rewards: People who think well will also have the opportunity to experience a richer appreciation of the world they inhabit and a greater self-awareness. Schools can also foster excellence in character, in the conduct of social relations, and in community life.

Today, a narrowly economic outlook threatens to override the ideals of high-quality education for all that animated the American common school movement and its Enlightenment precursors. Although we retain faith in the power of the schools to provide training that helps in the labor market, we have already, to some degree, lost our faith in the power of the schools to lift our minds and spirits and to build the foundations of a democratic community.

Educators themselves are partly to blame. When educational leaders accepted differentiated secondary school curricula in the early twentieth century in the name of "social efficiency" and "student interest," they helped to reduce the democratic faith in the possibilities of schooling. The work of political theorists like Benjamin Barber, of empirical social scientists like Anthony Bryk, and of school reformers like Deborah Meier remind us that we do not have to settle for a diminished version of what schools can be.

Which School Qualities Should We Prefer?

Thanks to these and other writers, we have good evidence about the school characteristics that can enhance the possibilities for children: the possibilities that they will become self-disciplined and considerate in their conduct and accomplished in their thought processes. Like Ron Edmonds's (1979) principles of effective schools, this list emphasizes the importance of good order and high standards, but it also includes some other qualities. Good schools, regardless of location, have the following qualities:

- They have adequate resources.
- They are of a relatively small size.
- They express high academic expectations and are organized in ways that reflect those expectations.
- They are staffed by well-trained and highly motivated teachers.
- They include strong elements of communal organization.
- They mobilize the voluntary involvement of students, parents, and others in the learning and social activities of the school.

The first point is the most basic, and it is often taken for granted: Good schools require adequate resources. An appropriate physical plant is critical for high-quality learning. Well-maintained schools signal to children and their families that education is important and may help to inspire children to make the commitment to learning. By contrast, dilapidated and overcrowded buildings signal that education is not a high priority. Maintaining an appropriate physical plant, especially in older cities, can be an expensive proposition. In 1993, the school board in the city of New York proposed a $28.1 *billion* program to rebuild existing schools, construct new schools, and support educational add-ons such as computer technology (Citizen's Budget Commission 1996:2).

The need for adequate resources seems like a truism (and may even seem like an invitation to waste, as it has been at times in New York and other cities), but it means that taxpayers will need to continue their historically strong commitment to schooling. The market is an alternative to public support, but it is not as equitable an alternative.

Second, good schools are relatively small. As the school reformer Deborah Meier (1995) wrote, "Large schools neither nourish the spirit nor educate the mind . . . what big schools do is remind most of us that we don't count for a lot" (p. 107). Being known (and therefore at least potentially appreciated) is among the strongest benefits of small schools. As Meier notes, students at large high schools often find that no teacher knows them well enough to write a college reference letter that sounds authentic. But at her small secondary school in East Harlem, "the shyest and least engaged student would not have suffered the fate that the average big school student takes for granted" (ibid., p. 112). The empirical evidence indicates that small schools pull more students into active participation in the life of the school community and thereby create a stronger sense of satisfaction and engagement (Lindsay 1982).

Small schools also foster the natural interpenetration of adult and student cultures, rather than a strict separation between the two. Interacting on a regular basis with adults outside the classroom is important for the kinds of conversions that schools hope to make:

> In part, after all, we teachers are trying to convert our children to a set of adult intellectual standards and appreciations—our love affair with literature and history, science and math, logic and reason, accuracy and precision. . . . This in turn requires joint membership in an attractive community representing such values as well as a myriad of interactions across generations. . . . [Small schools] offer a chance, not a guarantee, that children will glimpse possibilities that make them want to be grown-ups. (Meier 1995:113)

Schools in poor neighborhoods are now playing roles that are more than simply educational. They provide parental counseling, baby-sitting services, an oasis out of harm's way, in some places a one-stop social services agency (Graham 1993). The difficult circumstances of these communities have led some reformers to believe that schools need, above all, to offer encouragement and support rather than challenging academic standards. This is a prescription for decline. Schools have the opportunity to help children to develop their minds and their spirits, to transmit socially useful skills and personally useful habits of behavior. But schools can do this only if they create commitments to the learning community rather than only to the "support system" of the school.

Good schools keep their priorities straight by expressing high expectations and a real passion about learning. Good academic standards in turn cannot be built on weak foundations. Children cannot learn unless their basic language skills are adequate. When school districts have extra resources, the research suggests these should go into providing classroom aides in the early primary grades to make sure that all children are at or above grade level in reading. Effective schools are, moreover, usually intellectually challenging places. The academic focus of the school is communicated through the structure of expectations and the consistency with which these expectations are enforced. Teachers spend their time in class on task and assign regular homework. Basic rules of conduct are consistently enforced.

These good standards do not mean that teachers spend less time thinking about how to make their lessons engaging. Good teaching is a creative joining of opposites: passion and rationality, evocation and instrumentality, objectivity and compassion. Children learn by separating things into analytical bits and joining things together into integrative wholes, by thinking and speaking, by memorization and play. Teaching is an art of activating interest and preserving important tensions, as much as it is a science of conveying information and understandings. Because good teaching is difficult work, good schools provide ways for teachers to talk to one another about their craft, but they allow effective independent-minded teachers to go their own way.

Some of the most important qualities of good schools cannot be mandated; they have to grow. Communal organization is one of the most important of these. Communal organization means high levels of interaction guided by common values and many opportunities to share in governance. Communal organization cannot be achieved without either highly involved families (the typical case in affluent suburbs) or leadership that builds consensus and trust and actively reaches out to families (the more common case in poor urban settings).

In many schools, communal organization also requires consistent representation of an inspirational ideology that gives meaning to the life of the school community. Bryk and his colleagues (Bryk et al. 1993) have provided a vivid depiction of how important such an inspirational ideology is in the life of urban Catholic schools. Other integrative ideologies can more appropriately reflect the values of other communities, but all integrative ideologies find a way to celebrate the importance of each individual life and to link these individual lives to a meaningful, larger purpose.

Good schools find ways, finally, to mobilize commitments. For this purpose, perhaps the most important quality of all is simply the well-focused effort of those who care about learning to act on their commitments. Not long ago, the educational historian Patricia Graham wrote a book about school reform titled *S.O.S.* (1992). The familiar abbreviation stood for a less familiar idea: sustain our schools. In Graham's view, communities—families, government, higher education, and business—do not need to *save* the public schools so much as to *sustain* them: "Most of all, the schools need people who will . . . be knowledgeable about their fields, skilled in their pedagogy, passionate in their concern for their students, and committed to educating all our children well" (Graham 1992:170).

Teachers and principals search for the right metaphors to convey these understandings. One teacher likens the process of sustaining learning to planting seeds. "Some [seeds] fall on inhospitable ground and don't grow, some of them aren't going to be watered or taken care of, but some of them grow and produce other seeds and pretty soon you have a forest." Another suggests that the reason for her school's success is that the principal is "out there in his hip boots helping with the cement work" (Gooden 1996:74, 79).

In life, there are virtuous as well as vicious cycles. Wise and persistent involvement in the life of schools by parents, volunteers, and other community members can stimulate virtuous cycles. Even a little effort can be reciprocated, and even a little reciprocated effort is an important base on which to build.

NOTES

CHAPTER 1

1. Among the last generation of critics of schooling, see, for example, Goodman (1960), Neill (1960), Holt (1964), and Kozol (1968). This is a criticism that resonates with the larger social critique of European Romanticism and originates particularly in the writings of the French political philosopher Jean-Jacques Rousseau ([1762] 1911).

2. In the discussion that follows, students who have studied sociology before will see the influence of some important sociologists of the past. The discussion of the macrohistorical level of analysis is inspired by the work of the great German sociologist Max Weber ([1921] 1978). The discussion of the institutional level has its roots in the work of two midcentury American sociologists, Robert K. Merton ([1949] 1968, chaps. 2, 10-11) and Philip Selznick (1949, 1957) and one contemporary sociologist, John Meyer (Meyer and Rowan 1978). The discussion of the microinteraction level is influenced by the "structured interactionism" of sociologists Willard Waller (1932) and Erving Goffman (1959, 1974) and the "dramatism" of literary theorist and social critic Kenneth Burke (1969).

CHAPTER 2

3. The poorer countries of Europe resemble other European systems in structure but not in the outcomes they produce. Portugal, Ireland, Greece, Poland, and at least the southern region of Italy and nonmetropolitan Spain have lagged in school development throughout the modern period despite strong rhetorical commitments to mass schooling. Modernizing leaders in these states were not able to decisively gain the upper hand over the landed nobility, the traditional Church, and communal resistance (Soysal and Strong 1989). Compulsory schooling laws were passed, but enrollments remained low. Even today, educational attainments remain much lower in these countries than elsewhere in Europe (Organization for Economic Cooperation and Development [OECD] 1996:33). Compulsory schooling tends to end earlier than elsewhere in

schooling are high (ibid., p. 124), and government expenditures on schooling comparatively low (p. 65). The problems of Italian schooling were for many years compounded by a higher education system poorly adjusted to labor market conditions (Barbagli 1982).

4. The right of school districts in the same state to spend very different amounts on children was affirmed by American courts beginning with *Serrano v. Priest* (1971).

5. At the elementary school level, industrial societies also differ in one other important way: by how much of education is under public as opposed to private control. In the Netherlands, for instance, private schooling has developed in defense of linguistic and religious differences. In countries such as Spain and France, where the Roman Catholic Church once controlled education, Catholic private education very frequently remains a popular alternative to public schooling. In Japan, private schools mainly provide opportunities for students who are struggling in the public sector. Only in England and parts of the United States are parts of the private sector primarily associated with the desire of professional and managerial elites to avoid the public sector. The private sector rarely counts for more than 10 percent of total primary or secondary enrollments. (See Table 1.2 in Chapter 1.)

6. Other efforts to construct typologies of educational systems include, notably, Hopper (1968), Kerr (1979), and Allmendinger (1989).

7. The number of universities in the two countries is more similar than these figures suggest. Of the 325 institutions of higher education in Germany, 112 are universities. Of the approximately 2,250 four-year colleges and universities in the United States, just 238 are universities. The great majority of U.S. colleges are smaller "comprehensive colleges," liberal arts colleges, or specialized institutions, such as theological seminaries or art institutes.

8. As compared to Sweden and France, some countries (such as Denmark) have somewhat smaller vocational enrollments in upper secondary school. Others (such as Belgium and Switzerland) have higher vocational enrollments. The latter lean in the direction of German style limits on academic schooling, and they frequently provide a considerable amount of apprenticeship training, again following the German model. The contrast between Social Democratic egalitarianism and German style "hierarchization" and skill building helps to explain these divergent tendencies.

Chapter 4

9. In 1893, a famous statement by the National Education Association's "Committee of Ten" called for a common secondary school curriculum for all students regardless of their origins or likely destinations. This resistance melted away by 1910, as secondary school attendance continued to double each decade and new, less literate populations of students began to enter secondary schools. In 1906, the Douglas Commission helped to legitimate public vocational

education by arguing that children who leave school at the completion of seventh grade "would find further training of a practical character attractive ... if it prepared them for industries" (p. 73). In 1918, a statement of "Cardinal Principles" by the National Education Association called for increased choice in curricular offerings so that each individual could "find his [proper] place."

10. The Stanford team collected this information by examining a wide range of official policy statements, collected by United Nations agencies among others, and also more specific historical studies. The data have to be approached with some caution. Not all continents are proportionately represented in each time period. Several countries in which mass education is poorly institutionalized are missing altogether. Most important, official proclamations about what is supposed to happen in school and actual practices in school may differ substantially in many countries (Meyer, Kamens, and Benavot 1992, chap. 3). This slippage no doubt reduces the accuracy of the findings. It is well known, as we saw in Chapter 3, that rural schools in poor countries do not strictly follow government-sanctioned plans. Lessons may make up but a small part of the school day, in the midst of taking care of the classroom and the school grounds, playing, and getting settled for work (Hornberger 1987). Official policies affect the actual practices of schooling, only where a relatively high level of consensus or tight administrative controls exist (Stevenson and Baker 1991).

11. Some people like to look back on "golden ages" in which the great majority of people showed an active interest in the life of the mind. It may be that some of these golden ages resemble the stories told about them. People in colonial America, for example, apparently followed legal developments with real avidity and liked to dispute ideas about religion and politics. For the most part, however, golden ages turn out on closer inspection to be rather disappointing. If we look at the education of the entire population in the 1950s, for example, the results are depressing. Minorities, in particular, suffered extremely poor educational circumstances (see, e.g., Bracey 1991).

CHAPTER 5

12. As compared to such moral staples of the classroom as honesty, patriotism, and industry, the more strictly intellectual ethos of contemplation, reflection, judgment, and aesthetic appreciation was usually very limited in its penetration. To the extent that it was important, it developed mainly among upper-class groups in upper secondary and higher education. The acceptance and especially the persistence of this more intellectualist ethos depended, of course, on previous socialization and on continuing reinforcement (Feldman and Newcomb 1969).

13. Indeed, one of the important categorical understandings students learn in school translates quite directly into adult life: the status categories of schooling itself. Children learn that dropouts, high school graduates, community college graduates, and college graduates have distinct statuses in society (Kamens 1981).

14. Perhaps to balance the unfair criticisms of adolescent culture, sociologists have often gone out of their way to note beneficial effects. In a line of argument that built on Cold War sentiments, some sociologists commended the pluralism of the American high school as complementing the pluralism of American life and explicitly contrasted this pluralism with the potential authoritarianism of a single-status hierarchy based on academics. This argument suggested that the more ways to succeed in school, the more likely a majority of students would end up as confident and well-adjusted adults. Sometimes the images of youth culture were more positive still. During the later 1950s and 1960s, some sociologists provided admiring portraits of the independent, "life-embracing," and uncompromising spirit of youth culture. These sociologists interpreted youth culture as a source of socially revitalizing opposition to the life-denying pieties of adult authorities (see, e.g., Freidenberg 1959; Goodman 1960; Flacks 1971).

CHAPTER 6

15. The coming of the credential society was foreseen in the early part of this century by the great German sociologist Max Weber ([1921] 1946): "When we hear from all sides the demand for an introduction of regular curricula and special examinations, the reason behind it is, of course, not a suddenly awakened 'thirst for education' but the desire for . . . [the] monopolization of [positions] by the owners of educational certificates" (p. 241). For significant recent analyses of social stratification and credentialism, see Collins (1979) and Brown (1995).

16. Fischer and his colleagues (Fischer et al. 1996) specified that John, Jr. have a father with a blue-collar occupation. The man they selected from the "class structure and income determination" data set of Erik Olin Wright had the median income for blue-collar men of the World War I generation.

17. Educational expansion itself may trigger at least some of this occupational upgrading. When the supply of future professionals is growing and the cost of professional labor is therefore comparatively low, employers may respond by producing goods and services that disproportionately require the labor of professionals. In all likelihood, this "supply side" influence on occupational upgrading is relatively weak compared to the influence of technological change, productivity increases in agriculture and manufacturing, and consumer demand for professional services.

18. I am grateful to Michael Hout for sending me the General Social Survey tables used in this paragraph. The IQ measure here is based on word recognition. There may be an effect of college graduation itself on word recognition, leading to greater similarity among college graduates of different backgrounds than would be true if the ability measure preceded rather than followed college attendance.

19. In status attainment studies, statistical controls are used to "hold constant" all differences among variables in the model (i.e., all measured differences among people) except the one under consideration. In thinking about these models

people sometimes wonder, what kind of person comes from a high-status family and has high cognitive ability, good grades in school, but low aspirations? Indeed, we would have to be doubtful about conclusions based on such unusual and nonconforming people. However, this objection is not persuasive. The net effects of variables in status attainment models are influenced by incremental differences that show up frequently in the population, and they are pieced together from many cases without necessarily relying on extreme comparisons. This does not mean that the assumptions and procedures used in this research are completely defensible. A serious problem does exist with the assumption that the variables included in a model are uncorrelated with variables omitted. In fact, such correlations are undoubtedly common. It is implausible, therefore, to think of statistical controls as equivalent to mock experiments in which random assignment prevails after all controls in the model are applied.

20. Other countries, such as Germany and Hungary, may also show decreasing class inequalities in higher-level educational transitions. Studies are at this point inconclusive. See Erikson and Jonsson (1996:4-5).

21. Because people often exaggerate the connection between educational expansion and social opportunity, some sociologists argue that one of the primary functions of schooling may be to provide *legitimation* for the system of social stratification (Bowles and Gintis 1976)—that is, to make it seem fair, even as it works disproportionately to the advantage of the already privileged.

Chapter 7

22. As specialists in the constitutive influence of social relations, sociologists tend to be skeptical of explanations that focus too much on genetic endowments. But in reality, genetic advantages and disadvantages do figure into the likelihood that people will succeed or fail in school. If we focus only on families in which children's emerging interests are actively supported, we can clearly see that some children have aptitudes for art and computers, others for languages and word play. Children know what gives them pleasure, and, by comparing themselves to other children and by hearing the feedback of adults, they soon learn to invest energy and passion in the activities for which they have an aptitude. Researchers continue to disagree about how much intelligence is genetically determined and how much is socially conditioned, or how much is based on interactions between the two. New studies of twins raised separately have led to a greater emphasis on genetic factors (Bouchard et al. 1990).

23. Are some societies more prone to racial and ethnic bias than others? Historical circumstances seem to matter more than any sociological or political variables. Certainly, both democracies and socialist states have been marked by harsh treatment of minorities—even by instances of ethnicide. The exceedingly brutal treatment of Native Americans by the European settlers in the United States is well known. Socialist regimes sometimes encouraged ethnic hostilities by recruiting elites from one or two dominant ethnic groups, such as the Montenegrans and Croats in the former Yugoslavia and the Russians and Geor-

gians in the former Soviet Union (Echols 1981). Nor does the argument that European societies are particularly biased against "dark-skinned peoples" hold much water, because extreme forms of ethnic hatred are common among Africans and Asians. One difference is that Europeans have had the technological and political capacity for effective genocide. However, it seems likely that hatred of outgroups is part of the human condition. It can be stimulated by pride, fear, greed, unusually large numbers of culturally different newcomers, and politicians seeking to exploit resentments for personal or partisan gain.

24. Later selection is not, however, invariably connected to greater chances for lower-status children. Halsey, Heath, and Ridge (1980) showed that the abolition of the "11-plus" examination and the trend toward later selection in Great Britain had little impact on the relative educational chances of working-class youths. Instead, class differences in educational attainment remained "remarkably stable" across men born before and after the major changes in the British system. Those working-class children who entered schooling after the abolition of 11-plus examination and the tripartite system of secondary education fared no better than those who entered before the 11-plus examination and the tripartite system was abolished. The unusually strong class divisions in English society, discussed in Chapter 2, may be largely responsible for this result. These divisions have created a strong tendency for working-class children to flee schooling as soon as they reach the minimal school-leaving age.

25. Tracks need not be distinguished in all three ways (i.e., by motivational climate, institutional linkage, and prestige) to show significant net effects. One or two of these distinctions will do. In the industrialized world, the *grandes écoles* in France and the top public universities in Japan have among the strongest direct links to high-status occupations. These are well known as the "elite tracks." Nevertheless, the motivational press is intense only in the French case (Suleiman 1978). In Japan, virtually all students treat college as a time for enjoying friends and social life between the competitive wars of secondary school and corporate careers. However, the tight and densely networked links between these prestigious institutions and elite jobs give a large net boost to students, even in the absence of a supportive motivational climate (Cummings 1985).

26. When credentials are very highly valued on the market, (e.g., in the case of medical degrees today), competition for them is also intense. The competition raises the expected standards of performance, in most cases, and may further increase the economic value associated with those who ultimately succeed in gaining the credential. This mechanism is one reason why college majors have such different value in the labor market.

CHAPTER 8

27. On the basis of these passages from the irascible Twain (see Chapter 1), the contemplative Rodriguez, and vibrant Alcott, one suspects that the characters who leave strong marks on young minds are tuned to a similar enough emo-

tional key to break through the reserves of pride and uncertainty that are such great staffs of life and such great barriers to learning.

28. Asa Hilliard (1976) discusses how a person with an exclusively analytical style would function on a task more suited to a "relational" style: If asked to learn a dance, the analytical learner is "very likely to draw feet on the floor and to break the dance down into steps . . . to learn the dance 'piecemeal.' " For the relational learner, on the other hand, "details are likely to be blurred, standards faintly adhered to or the dance itself may be modified with no real concern for right or wrong so much as 'fit' or 'harmony' " (p. 42).

29. Some early studies of teacher effectiveness attempted to correlate student achievement with particular teacher behaviors: how often teachers smiled or snapped their fingers or stomped their feet. Not surprisingly, these studies were completely unsuccessful (see Boocock 1972:129-30).

30. These conclusions tell us what kinds of teacher traits will work best with average students in mixed-ability classrooms. To some degree, different kinds of teaching techniques may work best with some kinds of personalities than others. For example, more aloof and autocratic teachers do well with students who are responsive to authority, but they do very poorly with rebellious students. (For a discussion of some of these complexities, see Boocock 1972:129-49.)

REFERENCES

Abbott, Andrew. 1988. *The System of Professions: An Essay on the Division of Expert Labor.* Chicago: University of Chicago Press.

Adelman, Clifford. 1983. "Devaluation, Diffusion and the College Connection: A Study of High School Transcripts, 1964-1981." Paper prepared for the National Commission on Excellence in Education, U.S. Department of Education.

Alexander, Karl L., Aaron M. Pallas, and Scott Holupka. 1987. "Consistency and Change in Educational Stratification: Recent Trends Regarding Social Background and College Access." *Research in Social Stratification and Mobility* 6:161-85.

Ali, Anthony and Augustine Akubue. 1988. "Nigerian Primary Schools and Compliance with Nigerian National Policy on Education: An Evaluation of Continuous Assessment Practices." *Education Review* 12:625-37.

Allmendinger, Jutta. 1989. "Educational Systems and Labor Market Outcomes." *European Sociological Review* 5:231-50.

Alrabaa, Sami. 1985. "The Sex Division of Labor in Syrian School Textbooks." *International Review of Education* 31:335-48.

Amsden, Alice H. 1989. *Asia's Next Giant: South Korea and Late Industrialization.* New York: Oxford University Press.

Anderson, C. Arnold and Mary Jean Bowman, eds. 1965. *Education and Economic Development.* Chicago: Aldine.

Anderson, J. E. 1975. "The Organization of Support and the Management of Self-Help Schools: A Case Study of Kenya." Pp. 363-89 in *Conflict and Harmony in Education in Tropical Africa,* edited by Godfrey N. Brown and Mervyn Hiskett. London: Allen and Unwin.

Andersson, Bengt-Erik. 1969. *Studies in Adolescent Behavior: Project YG—Youth in Goteberg.* Stockholm: Almqvist and Wiksell.

Angus, David and Jeffrey Mirel. 1995. "Rhetoric and Reality: The American High School Curriculum, 1945-1990." Pp. 295-328 in *Learning from the Past: What History Teaches about School Reform,* edited by Diane Ravitch and Maris A. Vinovskis. Baltimore: Johns Hopkins University Press.

Anyon, Jean. 1979. "Ideology and United States History Textbooks." *Harvard Educational Review* 41:361-86.

———. 1980. "Social Class and the Hidden Curriculum of Work." *Journal of Education* 162:67-92.

Archer, Margaret. 1979. *The Social Origins of Educational Systems.* London and Beverly Hills, CA: Sage.

Arnold, Matthew. [1869] 1949. "Culture and Anarchy." In *The Portable Matthew Arnold,* edited by Lionel Trilling. New York: Viking.

Arnove, Robert. 1986. *Education and Revolution in Nicaragua.* New York: Praeger.

Arum, Richard and Yossi Shavit. 1995. "Secondary Vocational Education and the Transition from School to Work." *Sociology of Education* 68:187-204.

Asante, Molefi. 1987. *The Afrocentric Idea.* Philadelphia: Temple University Press.

Assal, Adel, and Edwin Farrell. 1992. "Attempts to Make Meaning of Terror: Family, Play and School in Time of Civil War." *Anthropology and Education Quarterly* 23:275-90.

Bailes, Kendall. 1979. *Technology and Society under Lenin and Stalin.* Princeton, NJ: Princeton University Press.

Bailey, Linda. 1995. "Time Use among Teachers: Context Paper for Germany." Unpublished paper, University of Michigan, Center for Human Growth and Development, Ann Arbor, MI.

Bailey, Thomas and Roger Waldinger. 1991. "Primary, Secondary, and Enclave Labor Markets: A Training Systems Approach." *American Sociological Review* 56:432-45.

Baker, John R. 1974. *Race.* Oxford: Oxford University Press.

Baker, Therese and William Velez. 1996. "Access to and Opportunity in Postsecondary Education in the United States: A Review." *Sociology of Education* 69 (extra issue): 82-101.

Barbagli, Marzio. 1982. *Educating for Unemployment: Politics, Labor Markets, and the School System—Italy, 1857-1973.* New York: Columbia University Press.

Barber, Benjamin R. 1992. *An Aristocracy of Everyone: The Politics of Education and the Future of America.* New York: Ballantine.

Benavot, Adam and David Kamens. 1989. "The Curricular Content of Primary Education in Developing Countries." PPR Working Paper No. 237, World Bank, Washington, DC.

Benavot, Adam and Phyllis Riddle. 1988. "National Estimates of the Expansion of Mass Education, 1870-1940." *Sociology of Education* 61:191-210.

Bendix, Reinhard. 1968. "The Extension of Citizenship to the Lower Classes." Pp. 233-56 in *State and Society: A Reader in Comparative Political Sociology,* edited by Reinhard Bendix et al. Boston: Little, Brown.

Bennett, William J. 1993. *The Book of Virtues.* New York: Simon & Schuster.

Berg, Ivar. 1970. *Education and Jobs: The Great Training Robbery.* New York: Praeger.

Bergentoft, Rune. 1994. "Foreign Language Instruction: A Comparative Perspective." *Annals of the American Academy of Political and Social Science* 532 (March): 8-34.

Berliner, David C. and Bruce J. Biddle. 1995. *The Manufactured Crisis: Myth, Fraud, and the Attack on America's Public Schools.* Reading, MA: Addison-Wesley.

Bernal, Martin. 1987. *Black Athena: The Afroasiatic Roots of Classical Civilization.* New Brunswick, NJ: Rutgers University Press.

Bernstein, Basil. 1961. "Social Class and Linguistic Development: A Theory of Social Learning." Pp. 288-314 in *Education, Economy, and Society,* edited by A. H. Halsey, Jean Floud, and C. Arnold Anderson. New York: Free Press.

———. 1971. "On the Classification and Framing of Educational Knowledge." Pp. 47-69 in *Knowledge and Control: New Directions for the Sociology of Education,* edited by M. F. D. Young. London: Collier-Macmillan.

———. 1975. *Class, Codes, and Control.* Vol. 3. London: Routledge and Kegan Paul.

Bernstein, Richard. 1994. *Dictatorship of Virtue: Multiculturalism and the Battle for America's Future.* New York: Knopf.

Berthoft, Rowland T. 1971. *An Unsettled People.* New York: Harper and Row.

"The Best Schools in the World." 1991. *Newsweek* 118 (December 2): 50-4.

Bidwell, Charles and Robert Dreeben. 1992. "School Organization and Curriculum." Pp. 345-62 in *Handbook of Research on Curriculum,* edited by Philip W. Jackson. New York: Macmillan.

Blackburn, Robin M. and Michael Mann. 1979. *The Working Class in the Labour Market.* London: Macmillan.

Blank, Rolf. 1989. *Educational Effects of Magnet High Schools.* Madison, WI: National Center on Effective Secondary Schools.

Blank, Rolf K., Roger E. Levine, and Lauri Steel. 1996. "After 15 years: Magnet Schools in Urban Education." Pp. 154-72 in *Who Chooses? Who Loses?* edited by Bruce Fuller and Richard F. Elmore. New York: Teachers College Press.

Blaug, Mark. 1987. *The Economics of Education and the Education of an Economist.* New York: New York University Press.

Bloch, Marc. 1961. *Feudal Society.* Vol. 1. Chicago: University of Chicago Press.

Block, N. J. and Gerald Dworkin. 1976. "IQ, Heritability, and Inequality." Pp. 410-540 in *The IQ Controversy,* edited by N. J. Block and Gerald Dworkin. New York: Random House.

Blossfeld, Hans-Peter. 1992. "Is the German Dual System a Model for a Modern Vocational Training System?" *International Journal of Comparative Sociology* 3:168-81.

Blossfeld, Hans-Peter and Yossi Shavit. 1993. "Persisting Barriers: Changes in Educational Opportunities in Thirteen Countries." Pp. 1-24 in *Persistent Inequality,* edited by Yossi Shavit and Hans-Peter Blossfeld. Boulder, CO: Westview.

Blumberg, Rae Lesser. 1984. "A General Theory of Gender Stratification." In *Sociological Theory, 1984,* edited by Randall Collins. San Francisco: Jossey-Bass.

Boocock, Sarane S. 1972. *An Introduction to the Sociology of Learning.* New York: Houghton-Mifflin.

Bouchard, Thomas J. et al. 1990. "Sources of Human Psychological Differences: The Minnesota Study of Twins Reared Apart." *Science* 250, 4978 (October 12): 223-9.

Boudon, Raymond. 1974. *Education, Opportunity, and Social Inequality.* New York: John Wiley.

———. 1979. "The 1970s in France: A Period of Student Retreat." *Higher Education* 8:669-81.

Bourdieu, Pierre. 1973. "Cultural Reproduction and Social Reproduction." Pp. 71-112 in *Knowledge, Education and Cultural Change,* edited by Richard Brown. London: Tavistock.

———. 1979. *Outline of a Theory of Practice.* Cambridge, UK: Cambridge University Press.

———. 1984. *Distinction.* Cambridge, MA: Harvard University Press.

———. 1988. *Homo Academicus.* London: Polity.

Bourdieu, Pierre and Jean-Claude Passeron. 1977. *Reproduction.* Beverly Hills, CA: Sage.

Bowles, Samuel and Herbert Gintis. 1976. *Schooling in Capitalist America.* New York: Basic Books.

Bracey, Gerald W. 1991. "Why Can't They Be Like We Were?" *Phi Delta Kappan* 73:104-17.

Brint, Steven. 1994. *In an Age of Experts: The Changing Role of Professionals in Politics and Public Life.* Princeton, NJ: Princeton University Press.

Brint, Steven and Jerome Karabel. 1989. *The Diverted Dream: Community Colleges and the Promise of Educational Opportunity in America, 1900-1980.* New York: Oxford University Press.

———. 1991. "Institutional Origins and Transformations: The Case of American Community Colleges." Pp. 337-60 in *The New Institutionalism in Organizational Studies,* edited by Paul J. DiMaggio and Walter W. Powell. Chicago: University of Chicago Press.

Bronfenbrenner, Urie. 1970. *Two Worlds of Childhood: U.S. and U.S.S.R.* New York: Russell Sage.

Brown, David K. 1995. *Degrees of Control: A Sociology of Educational Expansion and Occupational Credentialism.* New York: Teachers College Press.

Bryk, Anthony S., Valerie E. Lee, and Peter B. Holland. 1993. *Catholic Schools and the Common Good.* Cambridge, MA: Harvard University Press.

Bryk, Anthony S. and Stephen W. Raudenbush. 1988. "Toward a More Appropriate Conceptualization of Research on School Effects: A Three-Level Hierarchical Linear Model." *American Journal of Education* 97:65-108.

Burke, Kenneth. 1969. *A Grammar of Motives.* Berkeley: University of California Press.

Byrne, Eileen M. 1978. *Women and Education.* London: Tavistock.

Campbell, Richard T. 1983. "Status Attainment Research: The End of the Beginning or the Beginning of the End?" *Sociology of Education* 58:47-62.

Capelli, Peter. 1992. "College Students and the Workplace: Assessing Performance to Improve the Fit." *Change* 24, 6 (November/December): 55-61.

Carceles, Gabriel. 1979. "Development of Education in the World: A Summary Statistical Review." *International Review of Education* 25:147-66.

Carnegie, Andrew. 1889. "Wealth." *North American Review* 148:653-64.

Carnoy, Matin and Joel Samoff. 1990. *Education and Social Transformation in the Third World.* Princeton, NJ: Princeton University Press.

Carson, C. C., R. M. Huelskamp, and T. D. Woodall. 1992. "Perspectives on Education in America." *Journal of Educational Research* 86:259-310.

Cha, Yun-Kyung. 1992. "The Origins and Expansion of Primary School Curricula, 1800-1920." Pp. 63-73 in *School Knowledge for the Masses,* edited by John W. Meyer, David H. Kamens, and Aaron Benavot. London: Falmer.

Chubb, John E. and Terry M. Moe. 1989. *Politics, Markets, and America's Schools.* Washington, DC: Brookings Institution.

Citizen's Budget Commission. 1996. *School Buildings for the Next Century.* New York: Citizen's Budget Commission.

Clark, Burton R. 1961. "The 'Cooling Out' Function in Higher Education." Pp. 513-21 in *Education, Economy, and Society,* edited by A. H. Halsey et al. New York: Free Press.

———. 1985. "Conclusions." Pp. 290-325 in *The School and the University,* edited by Burton R. Clark. Berkeley: University of California Press.

Clark, Reginald. 1983. *Family Life and School Achievement.* Chicago: University of Chicago Press.

Clark, Roger. 1992. "Multinational Corporate Investment and Women's Participation in Higher Education in Noncore Nations." *Sociology of Education* 65:37-47.

Clasen, Donna R. and B. Bradford Brown. 1986. "The Relationship between Adolescent Peer Groups and School Performance." Unpublished paper presented at the annual meeting of the American Educational Research Association, San Francisco.

Clune, William and Paula White. 1988. *School-Based Management: Institutional Variation, Implementation and Issues for Further Research.* New Brunswick, NJ: Center for Policy Research in Education.

Cohen, David K. 1985. "Origins." In *The Shopping Mall High School: Winners and Losers in the Educational Marketplace,* by Arthur G. Powell, Eleanor Farrar, and David K. Cohen. Boston: Houghton-Mifflin.

Cohen, Elizabeth G. 1984. "Talking and Working Together: Status, Interaction and Learning." Pp. 171-87 in *Instructional Groups in the Classroom: Organization and Processes,* edited by P. Peterson and L. Wilkinson. New York: Academic Press.

Cohen, Phyllis C. 1982. *A Calculating People: The Spread of Numeracy in Early America.* Chicago: University of Chicago Press.

Cohen, Rosalie. 1969. "Conceptual Styles, Culture Conflict, and Nonverbal Tests of Intelligence." *American Anthropologist* 71:828-56.

Coleman, James S. 1961. *The Adolescent Society.* New York: Free Press.

Coleman, James S. et al. 1966. *Equality of Educational Opportunity.* Washington, DC: Government Printing Office.

Coleman, James and Thomas Hoffer. 1987. *Public and Private High Schools: The Impact of Communities.* New York: Basic Books.

Coleman, James S., Thomas Hoffer, and Sally Kilgore. 1982. *High School Achievement: Public, Catholic and Private Schools Compared.* New York: Basic Books.

Collins, Randall. 1977. "Some Comparative Principles of Educational Stratification." *Harvard Educational Review* 47:1-27.

———. 1979. *The Credential Society.* New York: Academic Press.

———. 1988. *Theoretical Sociology.* San Diego: Harcourt Brace Jovanovich.

Comer, James P. 1980. *School Power: Implications of an Intervention Project.* New York: Free Press.

Conant, James Bryant. 1938. "The Future of Our Higher Education." *Harper's Magazine* 176 (May): 561-70.

———. 1940. "Education for a Classless Society: The Jeffersonian Tradition." *The Atlantic* 165 (May): 593-602.

Congressional Budget Office. 1992. "The Use of Grants and Loans to Help Finance Undergraduate Education." Washington, DC: Congressional Budget Office. CBO Staff Memorandum. Mimeo.

Connolly, Cyril. [1938] 1973. *Enemies of Promise.* London: Andre Deutsch.

Connor, Walter B. 1979. *Socialism, Politics and Equality.* New York: Columbia University Press.

Cookson, Peter W., Jr. and Caroline H. Persell. 1985. *Preparing for Power: America's Elite Boarding Schools.* New York: Basic Books.

Cooperative Institutional Research Program (CIRP). 1987. *The American Freshman: Twenty Year Trends, 1966-1985.* Los Angeles: Higher Education Research Institute, Graduate School of Education, University of California, Los Angeles.

Craig, John E. 1981. "The Expansion of Education." *Review of Research in Education* 9:151-213.

Crain, Robert L. 1984. "The Quality of American High School Graduates: What Personnel Officers Say and Do About It." Baltimore: Center for the Social Organization of Schools, Johns Hopkins University. Report No. 354.

Cremin, Lawrence A., ed. 1957. *The Republic and the School: Horace Mann on the Education of Free Men.* New York: Teachers College Press.

———. 1961. *The Transformation of the School.* New York: Vintage.

Cuban, Larry. 1993. *How Teachers Taught: Constancy and Change in American Classrooms, 1880-1990.* 2d ed. New York: Teachers College Press.

Cubberly, Ellwood P. 1922. *A Brief History of Education.* Boston: Houghton-Mifflin.

Cummings, William K. 1985. "Japan" Pp. 131-59 in *The School and the University,* edited by Burton R. Clark. Berkeley: University of California Press.

Davies, Scott and Neil Guppy. 1996. "Fields of Study, College Selectivity, and Student Inequalities in Higher Education." Unpublished paper, Department of Sociology, McMaster University.

Davis, James A. 1965. *Undergraduate Career Decisions.* Chicago: Aldine.

de Crèvecoeur, Michel-Guillaume-Jean. [J. Hector St. John, pseud.]. [1783] 1912. *Letters of an American Farmer.* New York: E. F. Dutton.

Delbanco, Andrew. 1996. "Scholarships for the Rich." *New York Times Magazine* (Sept. 1):36:9.

Deng, Louise. 1991. "Towards the Collaborative Community: The Transformations and Changing Potentials of Business-School Partnerships for Educational Reform." Unpublished paper, Department of American Studies, Yale University.

Denison, Edward F. 1962. "Education, Economic Growth and Gaps in Information." *Journal of Political Economy* (suppl.) 70: 124-8.

Desai, Uday. 1991. "Determinants of Educational Performance in India: The Role of Home and Family." *International Review of Education* 37:245-65.

Dewey, John. [1916] 1966. *Democracy and Education.* New York: Free Press.

Diamond, Larry, Juan J. Linz, and Seymour Martin Lipset, eds. 1986. *Democracy in Developing Countries.* Boulder, CO: L. Rienner; London: Adamantine.

DiMaggio, Paul J. and John Mohr. 1985. "Cultural Capital, Educational Attainment and Marital Selection." *American Journal of Sociology* 90:1231-61.

DiPrete, Thomas A. and David B. Grusky. 1990. "Structure and Trend in the Process of Social Stratification." *American Journal of Sociology* 96:107-44.

Dobson, Richard B. 1977. "Social Status and Inequality of Access to Higher Education in the USSR." Pp. 254-74 in *Power and Inequality in Education,* edited by Jerome Karabel and A. H. Halsey. New York: Oxford University Press.

Dore, Ronald P. 1975. *The Diploma Disease: Education, Qualification, and Development.* Berkeley: University of California Press.

Dougherty, Kevin J. 1987. "The Effects of Community Colleges: Aid or Hindrance to Socioeconomic Attainment?" *Sociology of Education* 60:86-103.

———. 1994. *The Contradictory College: The Conflicting Origins, Impacts and Future of the Community College.* Albany: State University of New York Press.

Douglas Commission. 1906. *Report of the Massachusetts Commission on Industrial and Technical Education.* Boston: Commonwealth of Massachusetts.

Downey, Douglas. 1995. "When Bigger Is Not Better: Family Size, Parental Resources and Children's Educational Performance." *American Sociological Review* 60:746-61.

Dreeben, Robert. 1968. *On What Is Learned in School.* Reading, MA: Addison-Wesley.

Dreeben, Robert and Adam Gamoran. 1986. "Race, Instruction, and Learning." *American Sociological Review* 51:660-9.

Dreze, Jean and Amartya Sen. 1995. *India: Economic Development and Social Opportunities.* Delhi: Oxford University Press.

Durkheim, Émile. [1938] 1977. *The Evolution of Educational Thought.* London: Routledge and Kegan Paul.

Dworkin, Anthony G. 1987. *Teacher Burnout in the Public Schools.* Albany: State University of New York Press.

Dye, David A. and Martin Reck. 1989. "College Grade Point Average as a Predictor of Adult Success." *Public Personnel Management* 18:235-41.

Echols, John M. 1981. "Racial and Ethnic Inequality: The Comparative Impact of Socialism." *Comparative Political Studies* 13:403-44.

Eckstein, Max A. and Harold J. Noah. 1993. *Secondary School Examinations: International Perspectives on Policies and Practice.* New Haven, CT: Yale University Press.

Eckstrom, Ruth B., Margaret E. Goertz, Judith M. Pollack, and Donald A. Rock. 1987. "Who Drops Out of High School and Why? Findings from a National Study." Pp. 52-69 in *School Dropouts: Patterns and Policies,* edited by Gary Natriello. New York: Teachers College Press.

Edmonds, Ronald. 1979. "Effective Schools for the Urban Poor." *Educational Leadership* 38:15-24.

Edwards, Newton and Herman G. Richey. 1963. *The School and the American Social Order.* 2d ed. Boston: Houghton-Mifflin.

Elam, Stanley H., Lowell C. Rose, and Alec M. Gallup. 1993. "The 25th Annual Phi Delta Kappan Gallup Poll of the Public's Attitude toward the Public Schools." *Phi Delta Kappan* 75:137-53.

Elmore, Richard F. and Bruce Fuller. 1996. "Conclusion: Empirical Research on Educational Choice." Pp. 187-200 in *Who Chooses? Who Loses?* edited by Bruce Fuller and Richard F. Elmore. New York: Teachers College Press.

Elson, Ruth. 1964. *Guardians of Tradition: American Schoolbooks of the Nineteenth Century.* Lincoln: University of Nebraska Press.

Erickson, Frederick. 1975. "Gatekeeping and the Melting Pot." *Harvard Educational Review* 45:44-70.

Erikson, Robert and John H. Goldthorpe. 1992. *The Constant Flux: A Study of Class Mobility in Industrial Society.* Oxford: Clarendon.

Erikson, Robert and Jan O. Jonsson. 1996. "Explaining Class Inequality in Education: The Swedish Test Case." Pp. 1-65 in *Can Education Be Equalized?* edited by Robert Erikson and Jan O. Jonsson. Boulder, CO: Westview.

Eshiwani, G. S. 1985. "Kenya: System of Education." Pp. 2803-10 in *International Encyclopedia of Education,* edited by T. Neville Postlethwaite and Torsten Husen. New York: Elsevier.

Etzioni, Amitai. 1968. *The Active Society.* New York: Free Press.

Fagen, Richard. 1969. *The Transformation of Political Culture in Cuba.* Stanford, CA: Stanford University Press.

Farkas, George. 1993. "Structured Tutoring for At-Risk Children in the Early Years." *Applied Behavioral Science Review* 1:69-92.

Farkas, Steve and Jean Johnson. 1996. *Given the Circumstances: Teachers Talk about Public Education Today.* New York: Public Agenda.

Featherman, David L., Lancaster Jones, and Robert M. Hauser. 1975. "Assumptions of Mobility Research in the United States: The Case of Occupational Status." *Social Science Research* 4:329-60.

Featherman, David L. and Robert M. Hauser. 1978. *Opportunity and Change.* New York: Academic Press.

Feldman, Kenneth and Theodore M. Newcomb. 1969. *The Impact of College on Students.* San Francisco: Jossey-Bass.

Finkelstein, Martin J., Robert K. Seal, and Jack H. Schuster. 1995. "The American Faculty in Transition: A First Look at the New Academic Generation." Unpublished manuscript prepared for the National Center for Education Statistics.

Fischer, Claude S., Michael Hout, Martin Sanchez Jankowski, Samuel R. Lucas, Ann Swidler, and Kim Voss. 1996. *Inequality by Design.* Princeton, NJ: Princeton University Press.

Fitzgerald, Frances. 1979. *America Revised: History Schoolbooks in the 20th Century.* Boston: Little, Brown.

Fitzpatrick, Sheila. 1979. *Education and Social Mobility in the Soviet Union, 1921-1934.* Cambridge, UK: Cambridge University Press.

Flacks, Richard. 1971. *Youth and Social Change.* Chicago: Markham.

Flinders, David J. 1988. "Teacher Isolation and the New Reform." *Journal of Curriculum Studies* 4:17-29.

Foster, Philip. 1965. "The Vocational School Fallacy in Development Planning." Pp. 142-66 in *Education and Economic Development*, edited by C. Arnold Anderson and Mary Jean Bowman. Chicago: Aldine.

———. 1985. "Africa." Pp. 217-38 in *The School and the University*, edited by Burton R. Clark. Berkeley: University of California Press.

Frank, David F., Evan Schofer, and John Charles Torres. 1994. "Rethinking History: Change in the University Curriculum, 1910-90." *Sociology of Education* 67:231-42.

Freidenberg, Edgar Z. 1959. *The Vanishing Adolescent.* Boston: Beacon.

Friedan, Betty. 1963. *The Feminine Mystique.* New York: Dell.

Fujita, Hidenori. 1986. "A Crisis of Legitimacy in Japanese Education—Meritocracy and Cohesion." *Bulletin of the Faculty of Education, Nagoya University* 32:117-23.

Fuller, Bruce and Conrad W. Snyder, Jr. 1989. "Vocal Teachers, Silent Pupils? Life in Botswana Classrooms." Paper presented at the annual meeting of the Comparative and International Education Society, Boston.

Fuller, Bruce and Richard Rubinson, 1992. "Does the State Expand Schooling?" Pp. 1-30 in *The Political Construction of Education*, edited by Bruce Fuller and Richard Rubinson. New York: Praeger.

Fuller, Bruce and Prema Clarke. 1994. "Raising School Effects While Ignoring Culture: Local Conditions and the Influence of Classroom Tools, Rules and Pedagogy." *Review of Educational Research* 64:119-57.

Gamoran, Adam. 1992. "The Variable Effects of High School Tracking." *American Sociological Review* 57:812-28.

———. 1996. "Curriculum Standardization and Equality of Opportunity in Scottish Education: 1984-90." *Sociology of Education* 69:1-21.

Gamoran, Adam and Robert D. Mare. 1989. "Secondary School Tracking and Educational Inequality: Compensation, Reinforcement or Neutrality?" *American Journal of Sociology* 94:1146-83.

Gannicott, Kenneth G. and C. David Throsby. 1992. "Educational Quality in Economic Development: Ten Propositions and an Application to the South Pacific." *International Education Review* 38:223-39.

Garms, Walter L., Jr. 1968. "The Correlates of Educational Effort." *Comparative Education Review* 12:281-99.

Garnier, Maurice and Michael Hout. 1976. "Inequality of Educational Opportunity in France and the United States." *Social Science Research* 5:225-46.

Gates, Henry Louis, Jr. 1992. *Loose Canons: Notes of the Culture Wars.* New York: Oxford University Press.

Geertz, Clifford. 1973. *The Interpretation of Cultures.* New York: Basic Books.

Geiger, H. Kent. 1968. *The Family in Soviet Russia.* Cambridge, MA: Harvard University Press.

General Accounting Office (GAO). 1995. *Restructuring Student Aid Could Reduce Low-Income Dropout Rate.* Washington, DC: General Accounting Office. GAO/HEHS Report 95-48.

Gerson, Kathleen. 1985. *Hard Choices.* Berkeley: University of California Press.

Gibson, Margaret A. 1991. "Ethnicity, Gender and Social Class: The School Adaptation Patterns of West Indian Youth." Pp. 169-203 in *Minority Status and Schooling: A Comparative Study of Immigration and Involuntary Minorities,* edited by Margaret A. Gibson and John U. Ogbu. New York and London: Garland.

Glazer, Nathan. 1997. *We Are All Multiculturalists Now.* Cambridge, MA: Harvard University Press.

Goffman, Erving. 1959. *The Presentation of Self in Everyday Life.* Garden City, NY: Doubleday.

———. 1974. *Frame Analysis: An Essay on the Organization of Experience.* Cambridge, MA: Harvard University Press.

Goldin, Claudia. 1992. "The Meaning of College in the Lives of American Women: The Past 100 Years." Working Paper No. 4099, National Bureau of Economic Research, Cambridge, MA.

Goldthorpe, John H. 1996. "Problems of Meritocracy." Pp. 255-88 in *Can Education Be Equalized?* edited by Robert Erikson and Jan O. Jonsson. Boulder, CO: Westview.

Good, Thomas and Jere Brophy. 1987. *Looking in Classrooms.* 4th ed. New York: Harper and Row.

Gooden, Andrea R. 1996. *Computers in the Classroom: How Teachers and Students Are Using Technology to Transform Learning.* San Francisco: Jossey-Bass.

Goodlad, John I. 1984. *A Place Called School: Prospects for the Future.* New York: McGraw-Hill.

Goodman, Paul. 1960. *Growing Up Absurd: Problems of Youth in the Organized System.* New York: Random House.

Goodson, Ivor. 1988. *The Making of Curriculum: Collected Essays.* London: Falmer.

Graff, Gerald. 1987. *Professing Literature: An Institutional History.* Chicago: University of Chicago Press.

Graham, Patricia Aljberg. 1992. *S.O.S.: Sustain Our Schools.* New York: Hill and Wang.

———. 1993. "What America Has Expected of Its Schools over the Past Century." *American Journal of Education* 101:83-98.

Grasso, John and John Shea. 1979. *Vocational Education and Training: Impact on Youth.* Berkeley, CA: Carnegie Foundation for the Advancement of Teaching.

Gray, John. 1989. *Liberalisms: Essays in Political Philosophy.* London: Routledge.

Green, Sharon Weiner. 1988. *Barron's How to Prepare for the CBEST.* Hauppuage, NY: Barron's Education Series.

Griffin, Gary A. 1985. "The School as a Workplace and the Master Teacher Concept." *Elementary School Journal* 86:1-16.

Grubb, W. Norton and Marvin Lazerson. 1975. "Rally Round the Workplace: Continuities and Fallacies in Career Education." *Harvard Educational Review* 54:429-51.

Grusky, David B. and Robert M. Hauser. 1984. "Comparative Social Mobility Revisited: Models of Divergence and Convergence in 16 Countries." *American Sociological Review* 49:19-38.

Hacker, Andrew. 1990. "Transnational America." *New York Times Book Review,* November 22, pp. 19-24.

Hale-Benson, Janice. 1982. *Black Children: Their Roots, Culture, and Learning Styles.* Provo, UT: Brigham Young University Press.

Hall, Roberta M. 1983. "The College Classroom: A Chilly Climate for Women?" Washington, DC: American Association of University Women. Mimeo.

Halsey, A. H., Anthony Heath, and J. M. Ridge. 1980. *Origins and Destinations.* Oxford: Clarendon.

Hamilton, David and Associates. 1980. "Notes on the Origin of the Educational Terms Class and Curriculum." Paper presented at the annual meeting of the American Educational Research Association, Boston.

Hamilton, Stephen F. 1990. *Apprenticeship for Adulthood: Preparing Youth for the Future.* New York: Free Press.

Hanson, E. Mark. 1996. "Educational Change under Autocratic and Democratic Governments: The Case of Argentina." *Comparative Education* 32:303-17.

Harbison, Frederick and Charles A. Myers. 1964. *Education, Manpower, and Economic Growth.* New York: McGraw-Hill.

Hargreaves, Andy. 1993. "Individualism and Individuality: Reinterpreting the Teacher Culture." Pp. 51-76 in *Teachers' Work: Individuals, Colleagues, and Contexts,* edited by Judith W. Little and Milbrey W. McLaughlin. New York: Teachers College Press.

Hauser, Robert M. 1992. "The Decline in the College Entry of African-Americans: Findings in Search of an Explanation." Pp. 271-306 in *Prejudice, Politics, and Race in America Today,* edited by Paul Sniderman et al. Stanford, CA: Stanford University Press.

Hauser, Robert M., John Robert Warren, Min-Hsiung Huang, and Wendy Y. Carter. 1996. "Occupational Status, Education and Social Mobility in the Meritocracy." CDE Working Paper No. 96-18, Center for Demography and Ecology, University of Wisconsin, Madison, WI.

Haveman, Heather A. and Lisa E. Cohen. 1994. "The Ecological Dynamics of Careers: The Impact of Organizational Founding, Dissolution, and Merger on Job Mobility." *American Journal of Sociology* 100:104-52.

Heidenheimer, Arnold J. 1973. "The Politics of Public Education, Health and Welfare in the U.S.A. and Western Europe: How Growth and Reform Potential Have Differed." *British Journal of Political Science* 3:315-40.

Heidenheimer, Arnold J., Hugh Heclo, and Carolyn T. Adams. 1983. "Education Policy." Pp. 21-51 in *Comparative Public Policy,* edited by Arnold J. Heidenheimer, Hugh Heclo, and Carolyn T. Adams. New York: St. Martin's.

Herrnstein, Richard and Charles Murray. 1994. *The Bell Curve.* New York: Free Press.

Heyneman, Stephen and William A. Loxley. 1983. "The Effect of Primary-School Quality on Academic Achievement across Twenty-Nine High- and Low-Income Countries." *American Journal of Sociology* 88:1162-94.

Heyneman, Stephen P. 1993. "Educational Quality and the Crisis of Educational Research." *International Review of Education* 39:511-7.

Heyns, Barbara. 1974. "Social Selection and Stratification within Schools." *American Journal of Sociology* 79:1434-51.

Heyns, Barbara. 1978. *Summer Learning and the Effects of Schooling.* New York: Academic Press.

Higher Education Research Institute. 1996. *The American Freshman: National Norms for 1995.* Los Angeles: Higher Education Research Institute, Graduate School of Education, University of Los Angeles.

Hilliard, Asa G. 1976. "Alternatives to IQ Testing: An Approach to the Identification of Gifted Minority Students." Final report to the California State Department of Education. Sacramento: California State Department of Education.

Hirsch, E. D., Jr. 1987. *Cultural Literacy.* New York: Viking.

Hogan, Daniel B. 1979. *The Regulation of Psychotherapists.* Vol. 1. Cambridge, MA: Ballinger.

Hoggart, Richard. 1957. *The Uses of Literacy.* New York: Chatto and Windus.

Holmes, Brian and Martin MacLean. 1989. *The Curriculum: A Comparative Perspective.* London: Unwin Hyman.

Holt, John. 1964. *How Children Fail.* New York: Pittman.

Hopper, Earl I. 1968. "A Typology for the Classification of Educational Systems." *Sociology* 2:29-46.

Hornberger, Nancy H. 1987. "Schooltime, Classtime, and Academic Learning Time in Rural Highland Puno, Peru." *Anthropology and Education Quarterly* 18:207-21.

Hout, Michael. 1988. "Expanding Universalism, Less Structural Mobility: The American Occupational Structure in the 1980s." *American Journal of Sociology* 93:1358-400.

Hout, Michael, Adrian E. Raftery, and Eleanor O. Bell. 1993. "Making the Grade: Educational Stratification in the United States, 1925-1989." Pp. 25-49 in *Persistent Inequality: Changing Inequality in 13 Countries,* edited by Yossi Shavit and Hans-Peter Blossfeld. Boulder, CO: Westview.

Hout, Michael and Daniel P. Dohan. 1996. "Two Paths to Educational Opportunity: Class and Educational Selection in Sweden and the United States." Pp. 207-32 in *Can Education Be Equalized?* edited by Robert Erikson and Jan O. Jonsson. Boulder, CO: Westview.

Howard, Ann. 1986. "College Experience and Managerial Performance." *Journal of Applied Psychology* 71:530-52.

Howard, Suzanne. 1970. "A Comparative Study of Urban and Rural Teacher Roles in a Changing Society, Lebanon." Unpublished doctoral dissertation, University of Michigan, School of Education.

Huber, Joan and Glenna Spitze. 1983. *Sex Stratification: Children, Housework and Jobs.* New York: Academic Press.

Huberman, Michael. 1993. "The Model of the Independent Artisan in Teachers' Professional Relations." Pp. 11-50 in *Teachers' Work: Individuals, Colleagues, and Contexts,* edited by Judith W. Little and Milbrey W. McLaughlin. New York: Teachers College Press.

———. 1971. "Does Broader Educational Opportunity Mean Lower Standards?" *International Review of Education* 17:77-89.

———. 1979. "IEA in Retrospect." *Comparative Educational Review* 23:371-85.

Husen, Torsten, Albert Tuijnman, and W. D. Halls, eds. 1992. *Schooling in Modern European Society: A Report of the Academia Europeaea.* Oxford: Pergamon.

Inkeles, Alex. 1979. "National Differences in Scholastic Performance." *Comparative Educational Review* 23:386-407.

Inkeles, Alex and Larry J. Sirowy. 1983. "Convergent and Divergent Trends in National Educational Systems." *Social Forces* 62:303-33.

Ishida, Hiroshi, Walter Muller, and John M. Ridge. 1995. "Class Origin, Class Destination, and Education: A Cross-National Study of Ten Industrial Societies." *American Journal of Sociology* 101:145-93.

Jackson, Philip W. 1968. *Life in Classrooms.* Troy, MO; Holt, Rinehart & Winston.

Jackson, Philip W., Robert E. Boostrom, and David T. Hansen. 1993. *The Moral Life of Schools.* San Francisco: Jossey-Bass.

Jacobs, Jerry A. 1995. "Gender and Academic Specialties: Trends among College Degree Recipients during the 1980s." *Sociology of Education* 68:81-98.

———. 1996. "Gender Inequality and Higher Education." *Annual Review of Sociology* 22:153-85.

Jencks, Christopher et al. 1972. *Inequality.* New York: Harper and Row.

Jencks, Christopher et al. 1979. *Who Gets Ahead?* New York: Basic Books.

Jencks, Christopher, James Crouse, and Peter Mueser. 1983. "The Wisconsin Model of Status Attainment: A National Replication with Improved Measures of Ability and Aspiration." *Sociology of Education* 56:3-19.

Jessor, Richard and Shirley L. Jessor. 1977. *Problem Behavior and Psychosocial Development: A Longitudinal Study of Youth.* New York: Academic Press.

Johnson, Sharon. 1985. "The Fourth 'R' Is for Reform." *New York Times Education Survey* (spring): 17-8.

Jonsson, Jan O. 1993. "Persisting Inequalities in Sweden." Pp. 101-32 in *Persistent Inequality,* edited by Yossi Shavit and Hans-Peter Blossfeld. Boulder, CO: Westview.

Kamens, David. 1981. "Organizational and Institutional Socialization in Education." *Research in the Sociology of Education and Socialization* 2:111-26.

———. 1992. "Variant Forms: Cases of Countries with Distinct Curricula." Pp. 74-83 in *School Knowledge for the Masses,* edited by John W. Meyer, David H. Kamens, and Aaron Benavot. London: Falmer.

Kamens, David and Aaron Benavot. 1992. "A Comparative and Historical Analysis of Mathematics and Science Curricula, 1800-1986." Pp. 101-23 in *School Knowledge for the Masses,* edited by John W. Meyer, David H. Kamens, and Aaron Benavot. London: Falmer.

Kamens, David H., John W. Meyer, and Aaron Benavot. 1996. "Worldwide Patterns in Academic Secondary Education Curricula." *Comparative Education Review* 40:116-38.

Kanaga, T. 1994. "Japan: System of Education." Pp 3078-86 in *International Encyclopedia of Education,* edited by Torsten Husen and T. Neville Postlethwaite. New York: Elsevier.

Karen, David. 1991. "The Politics of Class, Race and Gender: Access to Higher Education in the United States, 1960-1986." *American Journal of Education* 99:208-37.

Katz, Lawrence and Kevin M. Murphy. 1992. "Changes in Relative Wages, 1963-1987: Supply and Demand Factors." *Quarterly Journal of Economics* 107:35-78.

Kazin, Alfred. 1951. *A Walker in the City.* New York: Grove.

Keddie, Nell. 1971. "Classroom Knowledge." Pp. 133-60 in *Knowledge and Control: New Directions for the Sociology of Knowledge,* edited by Michael F. D. Young. London: Collier-Macmillan.

Keeves, John P. 1986. "Science Education: The Contribution of IEA Research to a World Perspective." Pp. 19-44 in *International Educational Research: Essays in Honor of Torsten Husen,* edited by T. Neville Postlethwaite. Oxford: Pergamon.

Kelley, Jonathan. 1978. "Wealth and Family Background in the Occupational Career: Theory and Cross-Cultural Data." *British Journal of Sociology* 29:94-109.

Kennedy, Paul. 1996. "The Ends of the Earth: A Journey at the Dawn of the 21st Century." *New York Review of Books* 43 (September): 20-2.

Kerblay, Basile H. 1983. *Modern Soviet Society.* New York: Pantheon.

Kerkhoff, Alan C. 1974. "Stratification Processes and Outcomes in England and the United States." *American Sociological Review* 39:789-801.

Kerkhoff, Alan C., Richard T. Campbell, and Idee Wingfield-Laird. 1985. "Social Mobility in Great Britain and the United States." *American Journal of Sociology* 91: 281-308.

Kerr, Clark. 1979. "Five Strategies for Education and Their Major Variants." *Comparative Education Review* 23:171-82.

Kevles, Daniel J. 1995. "E Pluribus Unabomber." *New Yorker* 71 (August 14): 2-4.

Kimball, Bruce. 1986. *Orators and Philosophers: A History of the Idea of Liberal Education.* New York: Teachers College Press.

Kingdom of Cambodia. 1994. *Rebuilding Quality Education and Training in Cambodia.* Phnom Penh: Ministry of Education, Youth and Sport.

Kingston, Paul W. and John C. Smart. 1990. "The Economic Payoff to Prestigious Colleges" Pp. 147-74 in *The High-Status Track: Studies in Elite Schools and Stratification,* edited by Paul W. Kingston and Lionel S. Lewis. Albany: State University of New York Press.

Kliebard, Herbert M. 1986. *The Struggle for the American Curriculum.* London: Routledge and Kegan Paul.

———. 1992. "Constructing a History of the American Curriculum." Pp. 157-85 in *Handbook of Research on Curriculum,* edited by Philip W. Jackson. New York: Macmillan.

Klitgaard, Robert E. 1985. *Choosing Elites.* New York: Basic Books.

Kohn, Melvin L. 1972. *Class and Conformity.* Homewood, IL: Dorsey.

Kottcamp, Robert B., Eugene F. Provenzo, Jr., and Marilyn M. Cohn. 1986. "Stability and Change in a Profession: Two Decades of Teacher Attitudes, 1964-84." *Phi Delta Kappan* 67:559-67.

Kozol, Jonathan. 1968. *Death at an Early Age: The Destruction of the Hearts and Minds of Negro Children in the Boston Schools.* New York: Bantam.

———. 1987. *Savage Inequalities: Children in America's Schools.* New York: HarperCollins.

Kramer, Rita. 1991. *Ed School Follies: The Miseducation of America's Teachers.* New York: Free Press.

Labaree, David F. 1988. *The Making of an American High School: The Credentials Market and the Central High School of Philadelphia, 1838-1939.* New Haven, CT: Yale University Press.

Lamont, Michele. 1992. *Men, Money, and Morals.* Chicago: University of Chicago Press.

Lareau, Annette. 1987. "Social Class Differences in Family-School Relationships: The Importance of Cultural Capital." *Sociology of Education* 60:73-85.

Lasch, Christopher. 1995. *The Revolt of the Elites and the Betrayal of Democracy.* New York: Norton.

Lave, Jean. 1988. *Cognition in Practice: Mind, Mathematics and Culture in Everyday Life.* Cambridge, UK: Cambridge University Press.

Lee, Valerie E., Robert G. Croninger, and Julia B. Smith. 1996. "Equity and Choice in Detroit." Pp. 70-91 in *Who Chooses? Who Loses?* edited by Bruce Fuller and Richard F. Elmore. New York: Teachers College Press.

Lee, Yongsook. 1991. "Koreans in Japan and the United States." Pp. 139-65 in *Minority Status and Schooling: A Comparative Study of Immigrants and Involuntary Minorities,* edited by Margaret A. Gibson and John U. Ogbu. New York: Garland.

Leftwich, Adrian, 1995. "Bringing Politics Back In: Towards a Model of the Development State." *Journal of Development Studies* 31:400-27.

Lehmann, R. H. 1994. "Germany: System of Education." Pp. 2470-80 in *International Encyclopedia of Education,* edited by Torsten Husen and T. Neville Postlethwaite. New York: Elsevier.

Lerner, Daniel. 1958. *The Passing of Traditional Society: Modernizing the Middle East.* Glencoe, IL: Free Press.

Levin, Henry M. 1990. "Building School Capacity for Effective Teacher Empowerment: Applications to Elementary Schools with At-Risk Students." Paper prepared for the Project on Teacher Empowerment in the Center for Policy Research in Education, Stanford University, Stanford, CA.

Levine, Arthur and Jeanette Cureton. 1992. "The Quiet Revolution: Eleven Facts about Multiculturalism and the Curriculum." *Change* 24 (January/February): 24-9.

Levy, Daniel C. 1986. *Higher Education and the State in Latin America.* Chicago: University of Chicago Press.

Lewis, Catherine C. 1995. *Educating Hearts and Minds: Reflections on Japanese Preschool and Elementary Education.* Cambridge, UK: Cambridge University Press.

Liaison Committee of the Regents of the University of California and the California State Board of Education. 1955. *A Restudy of the Needs of California in Higher Education.* Sacramento: California State Department of Education.

Liebenow, J. Gus. 1987. "The Military Factor in African Politics: A Twenty-Five Year Perspective." Pp. 126-59 in *African Independence: The First 25 Years,* edited by Gwendolen M. Carter and Patrick O'Meara. Bloomington: Indiana University Press.

Lieberman, Ann and Lynne Miller. 1987. "The Social Realities of Teaching." Pp. 1-15 in *Teachers, Their World, and Their Work,* by Ann Lieberman and Lynne Miller. Washington, DC: Association for Supervision and Curriculum Development.

Lieberson, Stanley. 1961. "A Societal Theory of Ethnic Relations." *American Sociological Review* 26:902-10.

———. 1980. *A Piece of the Pie: Black and White Immigrants since 1880.* Berkeley: University of California Press.

Lightfoot, Sarah Lawrence. 1983. *The Good High School: Portraits in Character and Culture.* New York: Basic Books.

Lincoln, Abraham. [1859] 1953. "Address to the Wisconsin State Agricultural Society." Pp. 471-82 in *The Collected Works of Abraham Lincoln,* vol. 3, edited by Roy P. Basler and Christian O. Basler. New Brunswick, NJ: Rutgers University Press.

Lindsay, Paul. 1982. "The Effect of High School Size on Student Participation, Satisfaction and Attendance." *Educational Evaluation and Policy Analysis* 4 (spring): 57-65.

Lipset, Seymour Martin and Hans Zetterberg. 1956. "A Theory of Social Mobility." *Transactions of the Third World Congress of Sociology* 2:155-77.

Lockheed, Marlaine E. 1993. "The Condition of Primary Education in Developing Countries." Pp. 20-40 in *Effective Schools in Developing Countries,* edited by Henry M. Levin and Marlaine E. Lockheed. London: Falmer.

Lockheed, Marlaine E., Josefina Fonancier, and Leonard J. Bianchi. 1989. "Effective Primary Level Science Teaching in the Philippines." PPR Working Paper No. WPS 208, World Bank, Washington, DC.

Lockheed, Marlaine E., Adrian Verspoor, and Associates. 1990. *Improving Primary Education in Developing Countries: A Review of Policy Options.* Washington, DC: World Bank.

London, Howard. 1979. *The Culture of a Community College.* New York: Praeger.

Lortie, Dan C. 1975. *Schoolteacher.* Chicago: University of Chicago Press.

Lowenthal, Leo. 1957. *Literature and the Image of Man.* Boston: Beacon.

Lucas, Samuel R. 1996. "Selective Attrition in a Newly Hostile Regime: The Case of 1980 Sophomores." *Social Forces* 75:999-1019.

MacLeod, Jay. 1987. *Ain't No Makin' It: Leveled Aspirations in a Low-Income Neighborhood.* Boulder, CO: Westview.

Malen, Betty, Rodney T. Ogawa, and Jennifer Kranz. 1990. "What Do We Know about School Based Management? A Case Study of the Literature—A Call for Research." Pp. 289-342 in *Choice and Control in American Education,* vol. 2, edited by William Clune and John F. Witte. London: Falmer.

Mann, Dale. 1986. "Can We Help Dropouts? Thinking about the Undoable." Pp. 3-19 in *School Dropouts: Patterns and Policies*, edited by Gary Natriello. New York: Teachers College Press.

Mare, Robert. 1980. "Social Background and School Continuation Decisions." *Journal of the American Statistical Association* 75:295-305.

Marklund, Sixten. 1994. "Sweden: System of Education." Pp. 5866-73 in *International Encyclopedia of Education*, edited by Torsten Husen and T. Neville Postlethwaite. New York: Elsevier.

Marrou, Henri. [1948] 1982. *A History of Education in Antiquity*. Translated by George Lamb. Madison: University of Wisconsin Press.

Martinez, Valerie, Kenneth Godin, and Frank R. Kenerer. 1996. "Public School Choice in San Antonio: Who Chooses and With What Effects?" Pp. 50-69 in *Who Chooses? Who Loses?* edited by Bruce Fuller and Richard F. Elmore. New York: Teachers College Press.

Mateju, Petr. 1993. "Who Won and Who Lost in a Socialist Redistribution in Czechoslovakia?" Pp. 251-72 in *Persisting Inequalities*, edited by Yossi Shavit and Hans-Peter Blossfeld. Boulder, CO: Westview.

Maurice, Marc, Francois Sellier, and Jean-Jacques Silvestre. 1986. *The Social Foundations of Industrial Power*. Cambridge, MA: MIT Press.

McConnell, James. 1985. *English Public Schools*. London: Herbert.

McDill, Edward L., Edmund D. Meyer, Jr., and Leo C. Rigby. 1967. "Institutional Effects on the Academic Behavior of High School Students." *Sociology of Education* 40:181-99.

McKernan, John R., Jr. 1994. *Making the Grade: How a New Youth Apprenticeship System Can Change Our Schools and Save American Jobs*. Boston: Little, Brown.

McPherson, Andrew and J. Douglas Willms. 1987. "Equalisation and Improvement: Some Effects of Comprehensive Reorganisation in Scotland." *Sociology* 21:509-39.

McPherson, Michael S. and Morton Owen Schapiro. 1995. "Future Needs for Postsecondary Education." *Change* (July/August): 26-32.

Mehan, Hugh. 1993. "Beneath the Skin and between the Ears: A Case Study of the Politics of Representation." Pp. 241-68 in *Understanding Practice: Perspectives on Activity and Context*, edited by Seth Chaiklin and Jean Lave. Cambridge, UK: Cambridge University Press.

Meier, Deborah. 1995. *The Power of Their Ideas: Lessons for America from a Small School in Harlem*. Boston: Beacon.

Merton, Robert K. [1949] 1968. *Social Theory and Social Structure*. New York: Free Press.

Metz, Mary Haywood. 1993. "Teachers' Ultimate Dependence on Their Students." Pp. 104-36 in *Teachers' Work: Individuals, Colleagues, and Contexts*, edited by Judith W. Little and Milbrey W. McLaughlin. New York: Teachers College Press.

Meyer, John W., David H. Kamens, and Aaron Benavot. 1992. *School Knowledge for the Masses*. London: Falmer.

Meyer, John W., Joane Nagel, and Conrad W. Snyder, Jr. 1993. "The Expansion of Mass Education in Botswana: Local and World Society Perspectives." *Comparative Education Review* 37:454-75.

Meyer, John W., Francisco O. Ramirez, Richard Rubinson, and John Boli-Bennett. 1979. "The World Education Revolution, 1950-1970." Pp. 37-55 in *National Development and the World System*, edited by John W. Meyer and Michael T. Hannan. Chicago: University of Chicago Press.

Meyer, John W. and Brian Rowan. 1978. "The Structure of Educational Organizations." Pp. 78-109 in *Environments and Organizations*, edited by Marshall Meyer et al. San Francisco: Jossey-Bass.

Meyer, John W., Francisco Ramirez, and Yasmin N. Soysal. 1992. "World Expansion of Mass Education, 1870-1980." *Sociology of Education* 65:128-49.

Meyer, John W., David B. Tyack, Joane Nagel, and Audri Gordon. 1979. "Public Education as Nation-Building in America, 1870-1930." *American Journal of Sociology* 85:591-613.

Miller, L. Scott. 1995. *An American Imperative*. New Haven, CT: Yale University Press.

Mincer, Jacob and S. Polachek. 1974. "Family Investment in Human Capital: Earnings of Women." *Journal of Political Economy* 82:S76-S111.

Moeller, Gerald H. 1964. "Bureaucracy and Teachers' Sense of Power." *School Review* 72:137-57.

Moll, Terence. 1992. "Mickey Mouse Numbers and Inequality Research in Developing Countries." *Journal of Development Studies* 28:689-704.

Monchalban, A. 1994. "France: System of Education." Pp. 3377-85 in *International Encyclopedia of Education*, edited by Torsten Husen and T. Neville Postlethwaite. New York: Elsevier.

Monk-Turner, Elizabeth. 1990. "The Occupational Achievements of Community and Four-Year College Entrants." *American Sociological Review* 55:719-25.

Moore, Donald R. and Suzanne Davenport. 1990. "School Choice: The New and Improved Sorting Machine." Pp. 187-223 in *Choice in Education: Potential and Problems*, edited by William L. Boyd and Herbert J. Walberg. Berkeley, CA: McCutcheon.

Mortenson, Thomas. 1995. "Savage . . . Inequalities: Educational Attainment by Family Income, 1970 to 1994." *Postsecondary Education Opportunity: The Mortenson Research Letter*. Mimeo.

Muller, Walter. 1996. "Class Inequalities in Educational Outcomes: Sweden in Comparative Perspective." Pp. 145-82 in *Can Education Be Equalized?* edited by Robert Erikson and Jan O. Jonsson. Boulder, CO: Westview.

Murnane, Richard, John Willett, and Frank Levy. 1995. "The Growing Importance of Cognitive Skills in Wage Determination." *Review of Economics and Statistics* 77:251-66.

National Center for Educational Statistics (NCES). 1985. *High School and Beyond: An Analysis of Course Taking Patterns in Secondary Schools as Related to School Characteristics.* Washington, DC: Government Printing Office.

———. 1994. *Digest of Education Statistics, 1994.* Washington, DC: Government Printing Office.

———. 1996. *Pursuing Excellence: A Study of U.S. Eighth-Grade Mathematics and Science Teaching, Learning, Curriculum, and Achievement in International Context.* Washington, DC: Government Printing Office.

National Commission on Excellence in Education. 1983. *A Nation at Risk.* Washington, DC: Government Printing Office.

Neave, Guy R. 1985. "France." Pp. 10-44 in *The School and the University,* edited by Burton R. Clark. Berkeley: University of California Press.

Neill, A. S. 1960. *Summerhill: A Radical Approach to Child-Rearing.* New York: Hart.

Newman, Fred M., Robert A. Rutter, and Marshall S. Smith. 1989. "Organizational Factors That Affect Teachers' Sense of Efficacy, Community and Expectations." *Sociology of Education* 62:221-38.

Noah, Harold J. 1987. "Reflections." *Comparative Education Review* 31:137-49.

Oak Glen School (Oak Glen, California). 1873. "Rules for Teachers." Mimeo.

Oakes, Jeannie. 1985. *Keeping Track: How Schools Structure Inequality.* New Haven, CT: Yale University Press.

———. 1994. "More Than Misapplied Technology: A Normative and Political Response to Hallinan on Tracking." *Sociology of Education* 67:84-9.

Oakes, Jeannie, Adam Gamoran, and Reba N. Page. 1992. "Curriculum and Differentiation: Opportunities, Outcomes and Meanings." Pp. 570-608 in *Handbook of Research on Curriculum,* edited by Philip W. Jackson. Washington, DC: American Educational Research Association.

Odeotola, Theophilus O. 1982. *Military Regimes and Development: A Comparative Analysis of African States.* London: Allen and Unwin.

Ogbu, John U. 1978. *Minority Education and Caste: The American System in Cross-Cultural Perspective.* New York: Academic Press.

Organization for Economic Cooperation and Development (OECD). 1994. *Education at a Glance: OECD Indicators.* Paris: OECD.

———. 1995. *Education at a Glance: OECD Indicators.* Paris: OECD.

———. 1996. *Education at a Glance: OECD Indicators.* Paris: OECD.

Orwell, George. [1952] 1968. "Such, Such Were the Joys." Pp. 330-69 in *In Front of Your Nose 1945-1950: Collected Essays, Journalism and Letters of George Orwell,* edited by Sonia Orwell and Ian Angus. New York: Harcourt, Brace and World.

Osberg, Lars. 1984. *Economic Inequality in the United States.* Armonk, NY: M. E. Sharpe.

Papert, Seymour. 1993. *The Children's Machine: Rethinking School in the Age of the Computer.* New York: Basic Books.

Park, Robert E. and Ernest W. Burgess. 1921. *Introduction to the Science of Sociology.* Chicago: University of Chicago Press.

Parsons, Talcott. 1959. "The School Class as a Social System: Some of Its Functions in American Society." *Harvard Educational Review* 29:297-318.

Pelgrum, Willem J. and Tjeerd Plomp. 1993. *The IEA Study of Computers in Education: Implementation of an Innovation in 21 Education Systems.* Oxford: Pergamon.

Peng, Samuel S. 1977. "Trends in the Entry to Higher Education, 1961-1972." *Educational Researcher* 6, 1: 15-9.

Perrow, Charles. 1986. *Complex Organizations: A Critical Essay.* New York: Random House.

Pfau, Richard F. 1980. "The Comparative Study of Classroom Behaviors." *Comparative Education Review* 24:400-14.

Pfeffer, Jeffrey and Gerald M. Salancik. 1978. *The External Control of Organizations.* New York: Harper and Row.

Pomponio, Alice and David F. Lancy. 1986. "A Pen or a Bushknife? School, Work, and 'Personal Investment' in Papua, New Guinea." *Anthropology and Education Quarterly* 17:40-61.

Porter, Rosalie P. 1990. *Forked Tongue: The Politics of Bilingual Education.* New York: Basic Books.

Powell, Arthur G., Eleanor Farrar, and David K. Cohen. 1985. *The Shopping Mall High School: Winners and Losers in the Educational Marketplace.* Boston: Houghton-Mifflin.

Presseisen, Barbara Z., Robert J. Sternberg, Kurt W. Fischer, Catharine C. Knight, and Reuven Feurerstein. 1990. *Learning and Thinking Styles: Classroom Interaction.* Washington, DC: National Education Association.

Psacharopoulos, George. 1986. "The Planning of Education: Where Do We Stand?" *Comparative Education Review* 30:560-73.

———. 1987. "To Vocationalize or Not to Vocationalize? That Is the Curriculur Question." *International Review of Education* 33:187-211.

Psacharopoulos, George and Zafiris Tzannatos. 1992. *Women's Pay in Latin America: Overview and Methodology.* Washington, DC: World Bank.

Public Agenda. 1997. "Getting By: What American Teenagers Really Think about Their Schools." Washington, DC: Public Agenda. Mimeo.

Radner, Ephraim. 1991. "Research on Choice in Urban Education." Unpublished manuscript, Department of Sociology, Project on Urban School Reform, Yale University.

Rashdall, Hastings. [1895] 1936. *The Universities of Europe in the Middle Ages,* vol. 1, edited by F. M. Powicke and A. B. Emden. Oxford: Oxford University Press.

Ravitch, Diane. 1983. *The Troubled Crusade: American Education, 1945-1980.* New York: Basic Books.

———. 1985. "A Good School." Pp. 275-94 in *The Schools We Deserve,* by Diane Ravitch. New York: Basic Books.

———. 1995. *National Standards in American Education.* Washington, DC: Brookings Institution.

Ravitch, Diane and Chester Finn, Jr. 1987. *What America's Seventeen Year Olds Know.* New York: Harper and Row.

Reskin, Barbara. 1993. "Sex Segregation in the Workplace." *Annual Review of Sociology* 19:241-70.

Rice, Joseph M. 1893. *The Public School System of the United States.* New York: Century.

Riche, Martha Farnsworth. 1991. "We're All Minorities Now." *American Demographics* 13, 10 (October): 26-34.

Riesman, David and Ruell Denney. 1951. "Football in America: A Study in Culture Diffusion." *American Quarterly* 3:309-25.

Ringer, Fritz K. 1969. *The Decline of the German Mandarins: The German Academic Community, 1890-1933.* Cambridge, MA: Harvard University Press.

———. 1979. *Education and Society in Modern Europe.* Bloomington: Indiana University Press.

———. 1992. *Fields of Knowledge: French Academic Culture in Comparative Perspective.* Cambridge, UK: Cambridge University Press.

Rist, Ray C. 1970. "Student Social Class and Teachers' Expectations: The Self-Fulfilling Prophecy in Ghetto Education." *Harvard Educational Review* 40:411-50.

Robertson, Claire. 1985. "A Growing Dilemma: Women and Change in African Primary Education, 1950-1980." Pp. 17-35 in *Women and Development in Africa,* edited by Gideon Were. Nairobi: Gideon S. Were.

Robinson, Robert V. 1984. "Reproducing Class Relations in Industrial Capitalism." *American Sociological Review* 49:182-96.

Robinson, Robert V. and Maurice Garnier. 1985. "Class Reproduction among Men and Women in France: Reproduction Theory on Its Home Ground." *American Journal of Sociology* 91:250-80.

Rodriguez, Richard. 1982. *Hunger of Memory.* Boston: David R. Godine.

Rohlen, Thomas P. 1983. *Japan's High Schools.* Berkeley: University of California Press.

Rosenbaum, James E. and Takehiko Kariya. 1989. "From High School to Work: Market and Institutional Mechanisms in Japan." *American Journal of Sociology* 94:1334-65.

Rosenfelt, Deborah S. 1994. "Definitive ???: Women's Studies, Multicultural Education and Curriculum Transformation in Policy and Practice in the United States." *Women's Studies Quarterly* 22:26-41.

Rosenthal, Robert and Lenore Jacobsen. 1968. *Pygmalion in the Classroom.* New York: Holt, Rinehart and Winston.

Rothblatt, Sheldon. 1968. *The Revolution of the Dons: Cambridge and Society in Victorian England.* New York: Basic Books.

Rousseau, Jean-Jacques. [1762] 1911. *Emile, or Education.* New York: J. M. Dent.

———. [1754] 1964. "Discourse on the Origins and Foundations of Inequality among Men." Pp. 78-228 in *The First and Second Discourses,* edited by Roger D. Masters. New York: St. Martin's.

Rutter, Michael et al. 1979. *Fifteen Thousand Hours: Secondary Schools and Their Effects on Children.* Cambridge, MA: Harvard University Press.

Sadker, Myra and David Sadker. 1994. *Failing at Fairness: How America's Schools Cheat Girls.* New York: Scribner.

Schiefelbein, Ernesto. 1985. "Latin America." Pp. 195-216 in *The School and the University,* edited by Burton R. Clark. Berkeley: University of California Press.

Schmitter, Philippe C. 1971. "Military Intervention, Political Competitiveness and Public Policy in Latin America, 1950-1967." Pp. 425-506 in *On Military Intervention,* edited by Morris Janowitz and Jacques van Doorn. Rotterdam: Rotterdam University Press.

Schultz, Theodore W. 1961. "Investment in Human Capital." *American Economic Review* 51:1-17.

Sedlak, Michael W., Christopher W. Wheeler, Diane C. Pullin, and Philip A. Cusick. 1986. *Selling Students Short: Classroom Bargains and Academic Reform in the American High School.* New York: Teachers College Press.

Sellar, Walter C. and Robert J. Yeatman. 1931. *1066 and All That: A Memorable History of England.* New York: Dutton.

Selznick, Philip. 1949. *The TVA and the Grass Roots: A Study in the Sociology of Formal Organization.* Berkeley: University of California Press.

———. 1957. *Leadership in Administration: A Sociological Interpretation.* Evanston, IL: Row, Peterson.

Serrano v. Priest, 96 Cal. Rptr. 601 (Sept. 20, 1971).

Sewell, William H., Archibald O. Haller, and Alejandro Portes. 1969. "The Educational and Early Occupational Attainment Process." *American Sociological Review* 34:82-92.

Sewell, William H. and Robert M. Hauser. 1975. *Occupation and Earnings: Achievement in the Early Career.* New York: Academic Press.

Sewell, William H. and Vimal P. Shah. 1967. "Socioeconomic Status, Intelligence, and Attainment of Higher Education." *Sociology of Education* 40:1-23.

Shah, Saed and Jefferson Eastmond. 1977. *Primary Education in the Rural Villages of Pakistan, 1976-77.* Islamabad: Ministry of Education.

Sharp, Patricia T. and Randy M. Wood. 1992. "Moral Values: A Study of Selected Third- and Fifth-Grade Reading and Social Studies Textbooks." *Religion and Public Education* 19:143-53.

Shields, James J. 1992. "Japan." Pp. 321-43 in *International Handbook of Educational Reform,* edited by Peter W. Cookson, Alan R. Sadovnik, and Susan F. Semel. New York: Greenwood.

Shils, Edward A. [1962] 1975. "The Military in the Political Development of the New States." Pp. 483-516 in *Center and Periphery: Essays in Macro-Sociology.* Chicago: University of Chicago Press.

Sizer, Theodore R. 1984. *Horace's Compromise: The Dilemma of the American High School.* Boston: Houghton Mifflin.

———. 1986. "Rebuilding: First Steps by the Coalition of Essential Schools." *Phi Delta Kappan* 68, 9: 37-42.

Skidmore, Thomas E. and Peter H. Smith. 1989. *Modern Latin America.* New York: Oxford University Press.

Slavin, Robert E. 1980. "Cooperative Learning." *Review of Educational Research* 50:315-42.

———. 1994. *Cooperative Learning: Theory, Research and Practice.* 2d ed. Boston: Allyn and Bacon.

Slavin, Robert E., Nancy L. Karweit, and Nancy A. Madden. 1989. *Effective Programs for Students at Risk.* Boston: Allyn and Bacon.

Slavin, Robert E., Nancy A. Madden, Lawrence J. Dolan, Barbara A. Wasik, Steven M. Ross, and Lana J. Smith. 1994. " 'Whenever and Wherever We Choose': The Replication of 'Success for All.' " *Phi Delta Kappan* 75:639-47.

Slavin, Robert E., Nancy A. Madden, Nancy L. Karweit, Barbara J. Livermon, and Lawrence Dolan. 1990. "Success for All: First-Year Outcomes of a Comprehensive Plan for Reforming Urban Education." *American Educational Research Journal* 27:255-78.

Slavin, Robert E. and Eileen Oickle. 1981. "Effects of Cooperative Learning Teams on Student Achievement and Race Relations." *Sociology of Education* 54:174-80.

Soares, Joseph. 1997. "Embattled Academic Traditions." Unpublished manuscript, Department of Sociology, Yale University.

Sowell, Thomas. 1981. *Ethnic America: A History.* New York: Basic Books.

———. 1992. *Inside American Education: The Decline, the Deception, the Dogmas.* New York: Free Press.

Soysal, Yasmin N. and David Strong. 1989. "Construction of the First Mass Education Systems in Western Europe." *Sociology of Education* 62:277-88.

Spence, Michael. 1974. *Market Signalling: Informational Transfer in Hiring and Related Screening.* Cambridge, MA: Harvard University Press.

Squires, Gregory. 1979. *Education and Jobs: The Imbalancing of the Social Machinery.* New Brunswick, NJ: Transaction Books.

Stallmann, H. 1990. "Lehrer und Lehrerbildung in der Bundesrepublik Deutschland und in der Deutschen Demokratischen Republik. In *Pädagogische Berufe in der Bundesrepublik Deutschland und in der Deutschen Demokratischen Republik,* edited by S. Baske. Berlin: Duncker & Humblot.

Steinberg, Laurence with Bradford Brown and Sanford M. Dornbusch. 1996. *Beyond the Classroom: Why School Reform Has Failed and What Parents Need to Do.* New York: Simon & Schuster.

Steinberg, Stephen. 1981. *The Ethnic Myth.* New York: Atheneum.

Steinmetz, George and Erik Olin Wright. 1989. "The Fall and Rise of the Petty Bourgeoisie: Changing Patterns of Self-Employment in the Postwar United States." *American Journal of Sociology* 94:973-1018.

Stepan, Alfred. 1978. *The State and Society: Peru in Comparative Perspective.* Princeton, NJ: Princeton University Press.

Sternberg, Robert J. 1988. *The Triarchic Mind: A New Theory of Human Intelligence.* New York: Viking.

Stevenson, David Lee and David P. Baker. 1991. "State Control of the Curriculum and Classroom Instruction." *Sociology of Education* 64:1-11.

Stevenson, Harold W. and James W. Stigler. 1992. *The Learning Gap: Why Our Schools Are Failing and What We Can Learn from Japanese and Chinese Education.* New York: Summit.

Stinchcombe, Arthur L. 1959. "Bureaucratic and Craft Administration." *Administrative Sciences Quarterly* 4:168-87.

———. 1964. *Rebellion in a High School.* Chicago: Quadrangle.

Strauss, Anselm. 1959. *Masks and Mirrors: The Transformation of Identity.* Glencoe, IL: Free Press.

Stromquist, Nelly P. 1989. "Determinants of Educational Participation and Achievement of Women in the Third World: A Review of the Evidence and a Theoretical Critique." *Review of Educational Research* 59:143-83.

———. 1993. "Sex Equity Legislation in Education: The State as Promoter of Women's Rights." *Review of Educational Research* 63:379-407.

Suleiman, Ezra N. 1978. *Elites in French Society.* Princeton, NJ: Princeton University Press.

Swedish Institute. 1995. "Upper Secondary and Adult Education in Sweden." Stockholm: Swedish Institute. Mimeo.

———. 1996. "Compulsory Education in Sweden." Stockholm: Swedish Institute. Mimeo.

Szelenyi, Sonja and Karen Aschaffenburg. 1993. "Inequalities of Opportunity in Hungary." Pp. 273-302 in *Persisting Inequalities,* edited by Yossi Shavit and Hans-Peter Blossfeld. Boulder, CO: Westview.

Tauer, Susan M. 1996. "The Mentor-Protege Relationship and Its Effects on Experienced Teachers." ERIC Document No. ED 397 004.

Teichler, Ulrich. 1985. "The Federal Republic of Germany." Pp. 45-76 in *The School and the University,* edited by Burton R. Clark. Berkeley: University of California Press.

Thorne, Barrie. 1995. *Gender Play: Girls and Boys in School.* New Brunswick, NJ: Rutgers University Press.

Thurow, Lester. 1973. "Education and Economic Equality." *The Public Interest* 28:66-81.

Toby, Jackson. 1980. "Crime in American Schools." *The Public Interest* 58:18-42.

Tocqueville, Alexis de. [1835/1840] 1981. *Democracy in America.* New York: Modern Library College Editions.

Touré, Sekou. 1965. "Education and Social Progress." Pp. 125-40 in *Education and Nation-Building in Africa*, edited by L. Gray Cowan, James O'Connell, and David G. Scanlon. New York: Praeger.

Treiman, Donald J. and Harry B. G. Ganzeboom. 1990. "Cross-National Comparative Status Attainment Research." *Research in Social Stratification and Mobility* 9:105-27.

Treiman, Donald J. and Patricia A. Roos. 1983. "Sex and Earnings in Industrial Society: A Nine-Nation Comparison." *American Journal of Sociology* 89:612-50.

Treiman, Donald J. and Kin-Bor Yip. 1988. "Educational and Occupational Attainments in 21 Countries." Pp. 373-94 in *Cross-National Research in Sociology*, edited by Melvin L. Kohn. Newbury Park, CA: Sage.

Trow, Martin. 1961. "The Second Transformation of American Secondary Education." *International Journal of Comparative Sociology* 2:144-66.

Turner, Ralph H. 1960. "Sponsored and Contest Mobility and the School System." *American Sociological Review* 25:855-67.

Twain, Mark. [1896] 1972. *Life on the Mississippi*. New York: Harper and Row.

Tyack, David B. 1996. "Preserving the Republic by Educating Republicans." Unpublished paper presented at the Conference on Common Values and Social Diversity, Center for Advanced Study in the Behavioral Sciences, Stanford University, Stanford, CA.

Tyack, David B. and Larry Cuban. 1995. *Tinkering toward Utopia: A Century of Public School Reform*. Cambridge, MA: Harvard University Press.

Tyack, David B. and Elisabeth Hansot. 1982. *Managers of Virtue: Public School Leadership in America, 1820-1980*. New York: Basic Books.

Tye, Kenneth A. 1985. *The Junior High School: School in Search of a Mission*. Lanham, MD: University Press of America.

United Nations Development Project (UNDP). 1994. *Human Development Report 1994*. Delhi: Oxford University Press.

United Nations Education, Scientific, and Cultural Organization (UNESCO). 1991. *Development of Education in Africa: Statistical Review*. Paris: UNESCO.

———. 1993. *Development of Education in the Arab States: A Statistical Review and Projections*. Paris: UNESCO.

———. 1994. *UNESCO Statistical Yearbook, 1994*. Paris: UNESCO.

United Nations International Conference on Population and Development. 1995. *Population and Development*. New York: United Nations.

U.S. Bureau of the Census. 1975. *Historical Statistics of the United States, Colonial Times to 1970, Part 1*. Washington, DC: Government Printing Office.

———. 1994a. "More Education Means Higher Career Earnings." Statistical Brief, August.

———. 1994b. *Statistical Abstract of the United States, 1994*. 114th ed. Washington, DC: Government Printing Office.

U.S. Department of Education. 1995. *Digest of Education Statistics*. Washington, DC: Government Printing Office.

U.S. Office of Education. 1944. *Biennial Survey of Education*, vol. 2, *Statistics of Higher Education, 1939-40 and 1941-42*. Washington, DC: Department of Health, Education, and Welfare.

Useem, Michael. 1989. *Liberal Education and the Corporation*. New York: Aldine de Gruyter.

Useem, Michael and Jerome Karabel. 1986. "Pathways to Top Corporate Management." *American Sociological Review* 51:184-200.

van den Berghe, Pierre L. 1970. *Race and Racism: A Comparative Perspective*. New York: John Wiley.

von der Mehden, Fred R. 1969. *Politics of Developing Nations*. 2d ed. Englewood Cliffs, NJ: Prentice Hall.

Waller, Willard. 1932. *The Sociology of Teaching*. New York: John Wiley.

Wallerstein, Immanuel. 1974. *Capitalist Agriculture and the Origins of the European World Economy in the 16th Century*. New York: Academic Press.

Warner, W. Lloyd with Marcia Meeker and Enneth Eells. 1949. *Social Class in America*. Chicago: Science Research Associates.

Weakliem, David, Julia McQuillan, and Tracy Schauer. 1995. "Toward Meritocracy? Changing Social-Class Differences in Intellectual Ability." *Sociology of Education* 68:271-86.

Weber, Max. [1921] 1946. "Bureaucracy." Pp. 196-244 in *From Max Weber*, edited by Hans Gerth and C. Wright Mills. New York: Oxford University Press.

———. [1921] 1978. *Economy and Society*. Berkeley: University of California Press.

Wells, Amy Stuart. 1991. "Choice in Education: Examining the Evidence on Equity." *Teachers College Record* 93:156-73.

———. 1996. "African-American Students' Views of School Choice." Pp. 25-49 in *Who Chooses? Who Loses?* edited by Bruce Fuller and Richard F. Elmore. New York: Teachers College Press.

Welter, Rush. 1962. *Popular Education and Democratic Thought in America*. New York: Columbia University Press.

White, Merry I. 1987. *Japan's Educational Challenge*. New York: Free Press.

———. 1993. *The Material Child: Coming of Age in Japan and America*. New York: Free Press.

Widner, Jennifer A. 1992. *The Rise of a Party-State in Kenya: From "Harambee!" to "Nyayo!"* Berkeley: University of California Press.

Wilkinson, Louise C. and Cora B. Marrett. 1985. *Gender Influence in Classroom Interaction*. Orlando, FL: Academic Press.

Williams, Raymond. 1961. *The Long Revolution*. London: Chatto and Windus.

Willingham, Warren W. 1985. "Success in College: The Role of Personal Qualities and Academic Ability." New York: College Entrance Examination Board.

Willis, Paul. 1979. *Learning to Labour: How Working Class Kids Get Working Class Jobs.* Westmead, UK: Saxon House.

Willms, J. Douglas and Frank Echols. 1993. "The Scottish Experience of Parental Choice in Schools." Pp. 49-68 in *School Choice: Examining the Evidence,* edited by Edith Rasell and Richard Rothstein. Washington, DC: Economic Policy Institute.

Wilson, William Julius. 1987. *The Truly Disadvantaged: The Inner City, the Underclass, and Public Policy.* Chicago: University of Chicago Press.

Winkler, Donald R. 1990. *Higher Education in Latin America: Issues of Efficiency and Equity.* Discussion Paper 77. Washington, DC: World Bank.

Withey, Stephen. 1971. *A Degree and What Else? Correlates and Consequences of College Education.* New York: McGraw-Hill.

Witte, John F. 1996. "Who Benefits from the Milwaukee Choice Program?" Pp. 118-37 in *Who Chooses? Who Loses?* edited by Bruce Fuller and Richard F. Elmore. New York: Teachers College Press.

Witte, John F., Andrea B. Bailey, and Christopher A. Thorn. 1993. "Third-Year Report: Milwaukee Parental Choice Program." Unpublished manuscript, Department of Political Science, University of Wisconsin–Madison.

Wong, Sandra. 1991. "Evaluating the Context of Textbooks: Public Interest and Professional Authority." *Sociology of Education* 64:11-8.

World Bank. 1988. *Education in Sub-Saharan Africa: Policies for Adjustment, Revitalization and Expansion.* Washington, DC: World Bank.

———. 1993. *The East Asian Miracle: Economic Growth and Public Policy.* Washington, DC: World Bank.

———. 1995. *Priorities and Strategies for Education: A World Bank Review.* Washington, DC: World Bank.

Wuthnow, Robert. 1996. *Poor Richard's Principle.* Princeton, NJ: Princeton University Press.

Wylie, Laurence. 1974. *Village in the Vaucluse.* 3d ed. Cambridge, MA: Harvard University Press.

Wyllie, Irvin G. 1954. *The Self-Made Man in America: The Myth of Rags to Riches.* New Brunswick, NJ: Rutgers University Press.

Young, Michael. 1958. *The Rise of the Meritocracy.* London: Thames and Hudson.

Zeng, K. M. 1996. "Prayer, Luck and Spiritual Strength—The Desecularization of Entrance Examination Systems in East Asia." *Comparative Education Review* 40:264-79.

INDEX

Knight, C. C., 248
Knowledge. *See* School knowledge
Kohn, M. L., 141
Korea, primary schools in, 196
Korean schooling system:
    and Japanese schooling system, 47
Korean universal primary schooling, 96
Kottcamp, R. B., 240, 241
Kozol, J., 9, 40, 298
Kramer, R., 241
Kranz, J., 284
Kuwait, higher education in, 86

L

Labaree, D. F., 20, 36, 111, 145, 234, 235
Lamont, M., 128, 270
Lancaster, Joseph, 144
Lancasterian schools, 144-145
Lancy, D. F., 247
Lang, Eugene, 283, 289
Lareau, A., 141, 183, 210
Lasch, C., 173
Lave, J., 129
Lawrenceville (prep school), 212
Lazerson, M., 168
Learning styles, 248-250
    analytical, 249, 250
    cultural differences theories, 249, 272
    relational, 249-250
Lebanese schooling system, 71
Lee, V. E., 286, 289, 290, 296
Lee, Y., 216
Leftwich, A., 92, 97
Lehmann, R. H., 41, 42
Lerner, D., 67
Levin, H., 282
Levine, A., 122, 123
Levine, R. E., 284, 286
Levy, D. C., 79
Levy, F., 172
Lewis, C. C., 157

Liaison Committee of the Regents of
    the University of California and the
    California State Board of Education,
    198
Liberal education, 104-106
Liebenow, J. G., 79
Lieberman, A., 15
Lieberson, S., 214, 215, 218, 219
Lightfoot, S. L., 280
Lincoln, A., 173
Lindsay, P., 295
Linz, J. J., 82
Lipset, S. M., 82, 184, 185, 186
Literacy campaigns, 77-78, 99
Livermon, B. J., 282, 287
Locke, John, 293
Lockheed, M. E., 71, 73, 84, 129, 246,
    271
London, H., 183, 211
Lortie, D. C., 240, 254, 255, 256, 257
Lowenthal, L., 148
Low-income countries, deterioration
    of schooling in, 87, 90
Loxley, W. A., 224
Lucas, S. R., 176, 177, 178, 191, 198, 209,
    216, 301

M

MacLeod, J., 166, 167, 168, 211
Macro-historical analysis, 18-21
Madden, N. A., 282, 287, 288, 289
Magnet schools, 284, 286
Malawi, actual school time in, 87
Malaysia, equality of opportunity in,
    196-197
Malen, B., 284
Mali, school enrollment in, 86
Mann, D., 227
Mann, Horace, 35, 136
Mann, M., 180
Mare, R., 193, 231
Marklund, S., 50
Marrett, C. B., 222